FUNDAMENTALS OF POLARIMETRIC REMOTE SENSING

Also Available from SPIE Press Exclusively Published by New Age International Pvt. Ltd.

Fourier-Transform Spectroscopy Instrumentation Engineering
Vidi Saptari
ISBN: 978-81-224-2823-0, Original Edition Price: $ 48.00, Indian Edition Price: Rs. 395.00

Tissue Optics : Light Scattering Methods and *Instruments for Medical Diagnosis,* 2nd Ed.
Valery Tuchin
ISBN: 978-81-224-2829-2, Original Edition Price: $ 99.00, Indian Edition Price: Rs. 995.00

Local Approximation Techniques in Signal and Image Processing
Vladimir Katkovnik, Karen Egiazarian, Jaakko Astola
ISBN: 978-81-224-2830-8, Original Edition Price: $ 99.00, Indian Edition Price: Rs. 695.00

Logic-based Nonlinear Image Processing
Stephen Marshall
ISBN: 978-81-224-2825-4, Original Edition Price: $ 51.00, Indian Edition Price: Rs. 395.00

Introduction to the Optical Transfer Function
Charles S. Williams, Orville A. Becklund
ISBN: 978-81-224-2831-5, Original Edition Price: $ 78.00, Indian Edition Price: Rs. 695.00

Digital and Analog Fiber Optic Communications for CATV and FTTx Applications
Avigdor Brillant
ISBN: 978-81-224-2832-2, Original Edition Price: $ 115.00, Indian Edition Price: Rs. 999.00

Infrared Fibers and Their Applications
James A. Harrington
ISBN: 978-81-224-2827-8, Original Edition Price: $ 78.00, Indian Edition Price: Rs. 495.00

Optoelectronics of Solar Cells
Greg P. Smestad
ISBN: 978-81-224-2826-1, Original Edition Price: $ 46.00, Indian Edition Price: Rs. 395.00

MOEMS: Micro-Opto-Electro-Mechanical Systems
Manouchehr E. Motamedi
ISBN: 978-81-224-2833-9, Original Edition Price: $ 113.00, Indian Edition Price: Rs. 795.00

Introduction to Image Stabilization
Scott W. Teare, Sergio R. Restaino
ISBN: 978-81-224-2822-3, Original Edition Price: $ 51.00, Indian Edition Price: Rs. 395.00

Fundamentals of Polarimetric Remote Sensing
John R. Schott
ISBN: 978-81-224-2834-6, Original Edition Price: $ 68.00, Indian Edition Price: Rs. 395.00

Fundamentals of Infrared Detector Materials
Michael A. Kinch
ISBN: 978-81-224-2824-7, Original Edition Price: $ 61.00, Indian Edition Price: Rs. 395.00

FUNDAMENTALS OF POLARIMETRIC REMOTE SENSING

JOHN R. SCHOTT

Tutorial Texts in Optical Engineering
Volume TT81

SPIE
PRESS
Bellingham, Washington USA

NEW AGE

First Indian Sub-Continent Edition : 2010
by New Age International (P) Ltd., Publishers

Branches:

- 36, Malikarjuna Temple Street, Opp. ICWA, Basavanagudi, **Bangalore**-560 004. Tel.: (080) 26677815, Telefax: 26615247, E-mail: bangalore@newagepublishers.com
- 26, Damodaran Street, T. Nagar, **Chennai**-600 017. Tel.: (044) 24353401, Telefax: 24351463, E-mail: chennai@newagepublishers.com
- CC-39/1016, Carrier Station Road, Ernakulam South, **Cochin**-682 016. Tel.: (0484) 2377004, Telefax: 4051303, E-mail: cochin@newagepublishers.com
- Hemsen Complex, Mohd. Shah Road, Paltan Bazar, Near Starline Hotel, **Guwahati**-781 008. Tel.: (0361) 2513881, Telefax: 2543669, E-mail: guwahati@newagepublishers.com
- No. 105, 1st Floor, Madhiray Kaveri Tower, 3-2-19, Azam Jahi Road, Nimboliadda, **Hyderabad**-500 027. Tel.: (040) 24652456, Telefax: 24652457, E-mail: hyderabad@newagepublishers.com
- RDB Chambers (Formerly Lotus Cinema)106A, 1st Floor, S.N. Banerjee Road, **Kolkata**-700 014. Tel.: (033) 22273773, Telefax: 22275247, E-mail: kolkata@newagepublishers.com
- 16-A, Jopling Road, **Lucknow**-226 001. Tel.: (0522) 2209578, 4045297, Telefax: 2204098, E-mail: lucknow@newagepublishers.com
- 142C, Victor House, Ground Floor, N.M. Joshi Marg, Lower Parel, **Mumbai**-400 013. Tel.: (022) 24927869, Telefax: 24915415, E-mail: mumbai@newagepublishers.com
- 22, Golden House, Daryaganj, **New Delhi**-110 002. Tel.: (011) 23262370, 23262368, Telefax: 43551305, E-mail: sales@newagepublishers.com

---

Printed in India at V. K. Printers, Delhi.
C-09-11-4195

ISBN: 978-81-224-2834-6
Original Edition Price: $ 68.00
Indian Edition Price: Rs. 395.00

PUBLISHING FOR ONE WORLD
NEW AGE INTERNATIONAL (P) LIMITED, PUBLISHERS
4835/24, Ansari Road, Daryaganj, New Delhi-110002
Visit us at **www.newagepublishers.com**

Introduction to the Series

Since its inception in 1989, the Tutorial Texts (TT) series has grown to more than 80 titles covering many diverse fields of science and engineering. The initial idea for the series was to make material presented in SPIE short courses available to those who could not attend and to provide a reference text for those who could. Thus, many of the texts in this series are generated by augmenting course notes with descriptive text that further illuminates the subject. In this way, the TT becomes an excellent stand-alone reference that finds a much wider audience than only short course attendees.

Tutorial Texts have grown in popularity and in the scope of material covered since 1989. They no longer necessarily stem from short courses; rather, they are often generated by experts in the field. They are popular because they provide a ready reference to those wishing to learn about emerging technologies or the latest information within their field. The topics within the series have grown from the initial areas of geometrical optics, optical detectors, and image processing to include the emerging fields of nanotechnology, biomedical optics, fiber optics, and laser technologies. Authors contributing to the TT series are instructed to provide introductory material so that those new to the field may use the book as a starting point to get a basic grasp of the material. It is hoped that some readers may develop sufficient interest to take a short course by the author or pursue further research in more advanced books to delve deeper into the subject.

The books in this series are distinguished from other technical monographs and textbooks in the way in which the material is presented. In keeping with the tutorial nature of the series, there is an emphasis on the use of graphical and illustrative material to better elucidate basic and advanced concepts. There is also heavy use of tabular reference data and numerous examples to further explain the concepts presented. The publishing time for the books is kept to a minimum so that the books will be as timely and up-to-date as possible. Furthermore, these introductory books are competitively priced compared to more traditional books on the same subject.

When a proposal for a text is received, each proposal is evaluated to determine the relevance of the proposed topic. This initial reviewing process has been very helpful to authors in identifying, early in the writing process, the need for additional material or other changes in approach that would serve to strengthen the text. Once a manuscript is completed, it is peer reviewed to ensure that chapters communicate accurately the essential ingredients of the science and technologies under discussion.

It is my goal to maintain the style and quality of books in the series and to further expand the topic areas to include new emerging fields as they become of interest to our reading audience.

James A. Harrington
Rutgers University

Dedicated to the undergraduates who have forced me to look at old problems in new ways, the practicing scientists and engineers who have kept me grounded, and the graduate students who have opened new doors for me. You have enriched my life. I hope I have, in some small way, returned the favor.

Contents

Preface

This book was motivated by a short course on polarimetric remote sensing that I taught for industry about a year ago. I had supervised three doctoral students on thesis topics involving this subject and when I was asked to teach the course I thought it would be relatively easy to pull the course material together. In the months leading up to the course I discovered two things. First, as is so often the case, in preparing to teach the topic I found I knew far less than I thought I knew and dramatically less than I needed to know to teach a course. Second, I found that while there is a good treatment of polarization principles in the electro-optics literature, the treatment from the remote sensing perspective was quite scarce. In particular, while there were many journal and conference papers on specific topics, there was nowhere to send a student to get a good start on the fundamentals that they would need to prepare to delve into the more specific topics in the journals. So, to make a long story short, with considerable effort, I pulled together a variety of material and taught the course.

Afterwards, I realized I had the foundation for an introductory book that might save others getting started in this field from a similar effort. As a result, I spent the last year fleshing out the initial material, with a good deal of help from dedicated colleagues. The final book focuses on passive electro-optical polarimetric remote sensing in the visible through the thermal infrared (0.4–14 μm).

Polarimetric remote sensing is a relatively new field. It has champions who tout that polarimetric measurements are uncorrelated with traditional measurements of the magnitude and spectral content of the electromagnetic signal and should therefore add significant information. Likewise, it has detractors who point out that often the sought for contrasts between targets and backgrounds or between phenomena are not observed or are not as dramatic as they might be using some other sensing approach. I believe the jury is still out regarding how much utility we will eventually find in passive polarimetric remote sensing and what its role should be relative to other sensing approaches (e.g., multispectral). One of the main reasons for this is that polarimetric signatures are a rather involved function of source, target, and sensor geometry. Potential users must develop a more thorough knowledge of the relevant source-target-propagation-sensor physics to determine the true utility of this modality for their application. Once we understand and apply the relevant physics, we can develop tools to make it easier for other users to guide collection, processing, and analysis to improve signature contrast and determine the true utility of polarimetric remote sensing. It is for these students of the relevant physics (myself included) that I have written this book. I hope you find it a useful starting point for exploring this largely unexplored field.

As I listen today to the waves crashing on the beach, drowned out periodically by the thunder rumbling across the sky and watch the bay lit up by lightning, I can't help but be reminded how rich and complex nature is and how rewarding its study can be.

John R. Schott, Ph.D.
Wyldewood Beach
Port Colborne, Ontario
February 2009

Acknowledgments

Let me begin by introducing and thanking the coauthors. They are nearly all current or former students and several are colleagues at the Digital Imaging and Remote Sensing (DIRS) Laboratory at RIT. Lieutenant Colonel James R. Shell II, Ph.D. (Chapters 6, 7, and 10) and Dr. Michael G. Gartley (Chapters 10, 11, and 12) did their Ph.D. work on polarimetric scene simulation in the reflective and thermal infrared regions, respectively. I drew on their work and expertise not only in the chapters cited but throughout the text. Chabitha Devaraj is a current student and David Pogorzala, Dr. David Messinger, and Dr. Adam Goodenough are members of my research staff. They helped in particular with some of the scene simulations in Chapter 7. Finally, Scott D. Brown (Chapters 7 and 10) has been the engine behind the DIRSIG software for many years, as well as friend and colleague. He contributed to essentially all the DIRSIG results.

I also want to thank my graphics and administrative team who made this book a reality in a short time. Sharah Blankenship provided artistic guidance, graphics, and layout for the entire text, as well as the visuals for the various courses I've taught based on these materials. Cindy Schultz provided typing, editing coordination, and overall administrative support to all of us, as well as to our reviewers.

In an effort to avoid propagating blunders in this field that we are all studying, I asked a number of colleagues to review chapters, or in a few cases, the entire book, to catch errors and recommend improvements. Many thanks to Dr. Emmett Ientilucci and Dr. David Messinger of DIRS, Christopher Tome at ITT, Dr. Scott Tyo at the University of Arizona, Dr. Bradley Henderson at Los Alamos National Laboratory, and Dr. Thomas Caudill and Matthew Fetrow at AFRL. I am also grateful for editorial help from Dara Burrows at SPIE.

Finally, I'd like to thank the Faculty and Staff of the Digital Imaging and Remote Sensing (DIRS) Laboratory at the Rochester Institute of Technology who have supported me so effectively and who generously allowed me to pursue my writing muse.

List of Contributors

Scott D. Brown
Rochester Institute of Technology, USA

Chabitha Devaraj
Rochester Institute of Technology, USA

Adam Goodenough
Rochester Institute of Technology, USA

Michael G. Gartley
Rochester Institute of Technology, USA

David W. Messinger
Rochester Institute of Technology, USA

David Pogorzala
Rochester Institute of Technology, USA

James R. Shell II
US Air Force, USA

John R. Schott

Chapter 1 Introduction

1.1 Scope

Polarimetric Remote Sensing is a relatively new and largely undeveloped field. If we begin with a simple definition of remote sensing as the science or process associated with learning about the world without coming into physical contact with it, then, in its broadest definition, polarimetric remote sensing is just the subset of remote sensing that uses the polarized nature of electromagnetic (EM) energy to learn about the world. In order to keep this to a brief introductory text, we need to restrict our interest to a small subset of the much broader field that might be encompassed by this general definition. This section will describe the aspects of polarimetric remote sensing that we will consider here.

To begin, we will emphasize remote sensing of the earth. Many of the techniques we will present are applicable to planetary astronomy; however, we will not pursue these applications. Furthermore, we will focus on sensing the earth at geospatial scales where human activities are dominant. By this we mean that we are interested in spatial scales where objects such as agricultural fields and roads or smaller objects such as buildings and vehicles are sampled (i.e., tens of meters to fractions of meters). As we will see, human activities often change the polarization state of the EM energy reflected or emitted from the surface of the earth, so, looking at spatial scales where we can see human influence is one of the most interesting areas of potential utility for polarimetric sensing. To further limit our scope, we will focus on passive remote sensing in the visible through thermal infrared regions of the spectrum (0.4–14 μm). Polarimetric sensing using radar systems has been shown to have significant value for various applications [Elachi (1987) and Henderson and Lewis (1998)]. However, the relevant source-target-sensor physics and phenomenology are different enough from the electro-optical phenomenology that they will not be covered here. On the other hand, much of the material presented here is relevant to active sensing in the electro-optical region using polarimetric *LIDAR*. We choose not to include treatment of this topic only to maintain a focus on somewhat more widely accessible data.

While much of the laboratory work on polarimetric sensing has used radiometers (polarimeters), we will emphasize imaging systems. *Polarimetric Imaging*

(PI) has come into widespread use in both the laboratory and the field with the ready availability of two-dimensional digital focal plane arrays and the associated processing electronics. Since much of our interest is in looking for information associated with spatial variation in polarimetric signatures, we will focus on PI systems for data acquisition. Finally, while the PI systems can be used at distances of mm to 1000s of km from the subject (which we will generically refer to as the target), we will emphasize relatively high standoff systems. Thus we are talking about the conventional use of the term remote sensing to imply aerial or satellite sensing; however, we will also include sensing from a distant vantage point (e.g., neighboring hill).

This book is targeted at remote sensing scientists and engineers and assumes a modest knowledge of quantitative remote sensing at a level covered in introductory courses [Schowengerdt (2006), Richards, (1999), or Schott (2007)]. Because the general physics and phenomenology of polarized radiation and the sensing of polarized radiation are well covered in the literature [Collett (1993), Shurcliff (1962), Kliger et al. (1990), and Goldstein (2003)] we cover only those aspects essential to an introductory level knowledge of the remote sensing issues. Thus we assume a general knowledge of physics that any student of physical science or engineering would receive and build on that.

Our treatment emphasizes coverage of the end-to-end process of polarimetric remote sensing. This includes the nature of polarized radiation, its propagation, the phenomenology associated with energy-matter interactions, polarimetric sensing, and data visualization and processing. Our goal is to provide an introductory treatment for remote sensing scientists working at any point along the polarimetric imaging chain. By emphasizing the fundamental phenomenology, we intend to provide the user with a set of tools that will allow them to apply these principles to understand and apply polarimetric concepts to a variety of applications. Because application to a particular discipline generally requires significant knowledge of the subject area, we have chosen to restrict our scope to the underlying phenomenology. This is in part to control the size of this treatment but also because, due to the relatively recent development of polarimetric sensing, its potential utility to many applications has not been explored.

1.2 Perspective on the Field

The polarized behavior of light was first reported in 1669 by Erasmus Bartholinus who observed the double refraction of light in *calcite* crystals (aka calspar or Iceland spar) [Collett (1993)]. Since then, the field of optics has been rich with literature on the nature and application of polarized radiation [Shurcliff (1962)]. Over the years, applications have been developed in most areas of optics ranging from microscopic to astronomical observation. However, as Tyo et al. (2006) point out, it was more than 300 years later in the mid 1970s that the use of polarized sensing first appeared in the remote sensing literature. While the topic crops up in the literature through the early 1990s, most of the earth remote sensing work was restricted to polarized photography from space. The poor spatial resolution of this imagery restricted its application somewhat, but led to efforts using polarization to study the atmosphere and oceans. Indeed, in 1996 the first POLDER instrument was launched into space and led to a number of studies using polarized radiation to study the atmosphere [Deschamps et al. (1994)]. Regrettably, POLDER's 6 km pixel size prevented it from sampling the human scale targets that are our focus.

Over the last ten to twenty years, much more literature on polarimetric phenomenology related to remote sensing of manmade and natural materials has begun to appear. This work spans the reflective through the thermal region of the spectrum (0.4–14 μm). Advances in the sensor field have also made operational remote sensing more possible. It is this increase in the scientific literature that makes this book possible; many of these contributions will be cited in the appropriate chapters.

We should point out that the value of PI remote sensing has not been well established for many applications. Indeed, the question of the utility of PI for many applications is likely to remain in doubt for some time due to the lack of operational PI data at appropriate scales. Essentially all of the studies we report here were conducted as part of research programs run in laboratories, from towers, or as part of very limited flight programs. This lack of data continues to prevent many application scientists from evaluating the value of PI remote sensing. The problem is compounded by the relatively complex geometry associated with polarimetric signatures. As emphasized throughout this text, the PI signature is very much a function of source-target-sensor geometry and environment. As a result, unless acquired as part of a well-designed experiment, a small number of PI images may not effectively address the potential utility of PI for a particular application. In fact, results from such limited studies may be unrealistically optimistic or pessimistic. Indeed, it is the need for better understanding by the potential user community of the subtleties of PI that prompted the development and structuring of this text.

For example, most remote sensing data is acquired from near-vertical viewing sensors with high solar elevation angles. This is due to a combination of factors: convenience in mounting the instrument, maximizing resolution and signal-to-noise levels, minimizing atmospheric effects, and reducing geometric distortion. It turns out that vertical viewing minimizes PI signatures for most applications. Thus, a simple test study conducted with a PI sensor in a conventional orientation may inappropriately suggest limited utility. Regrettably, this does not mean that well-designed studies will always show significant utility for PI remote sensing. Rather, to properly assess the value of PI, we need to understand the relevant aspects of polarimetric phenomenology as they impact the end-to-end process of image formation and analysis. Based on this understanding, we can use a combination of analysis and properly designed experiments to assess utility and, where there is value, to design effective operational collection programs. Thus, throughout the text we heavily emphasize understanding of phenomenology and modeling of the PI source-target-sensor and environment so that the user can apply the tools described here to their scenarios and applications.

To motivate the potential of PI, let us examine the fundamental characteristics of EM radiation. EM radiation can be characterized by *amplitude*, *frequency* (*wavelength*), *polarization*, and *coherence*. The earliest remote sensing focused almost entirely on the amplitude of EM radiation in the visible spectral region. By sampling how the amplitude varied with location (spatial frequencies), we formed and then analyzed images. Most of the advances focused on reducing sample sizes (higher spatial resolution). We also sampled the amplitude in time, leading to change detection at low temporal frequencies and dynamic imaging (or persistent surveillance) at higher temporal frequencies. As we began to push the limits of amplitude-driven signatures, the remote sensing community turned to the spectral nature of EM radiation to try to find more diverse and therefore, more informative signatures. Over the years this has led to broadband sampling from the visible through the longwave infrared, then to multispectral sampling in several broadbands, and now to imaging *spectroscopy* where we sample hundreds of narrow spectral bands. Because the variation in amplitude is often decorrelated spatially and spectrally, the data is of higher dimension and carries more information. Thus, the spectral dimension has enabled the development of more diverse and subtler signatures, allowing us to effectively apply remote sensing to a wide range of applications [Rencz (1998) and Ustin (2004)]. The polarization of EM radiation is, in general, decorrelated with amplitude and frequency, offering the potential to increase the dimension and therefore, the information available. The spectral dimensions are most often governed by the molecular makeup of the target, while the polarimetric dimensions are governed by target geometry and surface properties. However, unlike spatial and spectral signatures, which are reasonably stable with viewing geometry, polarimetric signatures can vary substantially with viewing geometry. Thus, while polarimetric signatures offer an interesting possibility for increasing the dimension of remotely sensed data, they also present new collection, modeling, and analysis challenges. For passive remote sensing (i.e., sensing without an active radiation source (e.g., laser)) the polarimetric character of EM radiation represents a largely untapped dimension that can be analyzed to see if it leads to new or improved signatures for a specific application. For the applications we will consider here, the EM field can be considered to be spatially incoherent, so coherence issues will not be addressed. However, for certain polarimetric LIDAR applications, the interplay of spatial coherence and polarization state should be considered [Wolf (2003)].

1.3 Structure of the Book

The first nine chapters of this text attempt to provide a basic understanding of the end-to-end remote sensing polarimetric imaging process. Chapter 2 reviews the fundamentals of radiometry that are necessary for propagating EM radiation and developing the governing equations needed to describe polarimetric signals.

Chapter 3 reviews the wave nature of EM radiation and introduces the polarimetric characteristics of EM radiation. Chapter 4 introduces the *Stokes* parameters, a practical way to represent the polarimetric nature of a beam. Chapter 5 introduces the Mueller matrix as a way to characterize polarimetric energy matter interactions. In particular, the means to represent reflection and transmission of beams characterized by Stokes vectors are introduced. Chapter 6 introduces the *polarimetric bidirectional reflectance distribution function* (pBRDF), which is the fundamental tool used to describe the polarimetric behavior of real-world (i.e., nonoptical) materials. The pBRDF is the fundamental building block for understanding polarimetric remote sensing. It also represents a fundamental difference between the standard optical treatment of polarization and polarization for remote sensing (or for that matter, polarimetric sensing of any irregular surface). The remaining chapters all use the pBRDF concept to describe the various stages of the end-to-end PI process. Chapter 7 introduces a governing equation for polarimetric remote sensing and incorporates the polarimetric behavior of the atmosphere into the equation. We also begin in Chapter 7 to introduce simulation and modeling tools to visualize the polarimetric behavior of the atmosphere. Having developed a means to describe the polarimetric radiance reaching a sensor in Chapter 7, Chapter 8 addresses polarimetric sensors. This is a very rich and rapidly evolving field which we treat at a relatively high level. We introduce the basic principles behind the most common designs and their limitations but avoid the esoteric details of specific designs. We close the general treatment with Chapter 9 where PI data visualization and some basic processing techniques are introduced.

Because the pBRDF of materials is so critical to PI signatures, we describe a simple field method to measure it in Chapter 10 and then provide examples of ways to use synthetic image generation tools to model polarization signatures based on the pBRDF. In Chapters 11 and 12 we change wavelength regimes to go from the reflective region of the spectrum (0.4−2.5 μm) to the thermal emissive region (3−14 μm). Chapter 11 discusses the pBRDF in the emissive region and develops an appropriate governing equation. Finally, Chapter 12 parallels Chapter 10 by introducing a simple field method to measure the polarimetric emissive behavior of materials and then uses synthetic image generation tools to visualize PI behavior in the thermal infrared.

References

Collett, E. (1993). *Polarized Light: Fundamentals and Applications*. Marcel Dekker, New York.

Deschamps, P.Y., Bréon, F.c.-M., Leroy, M., Podair, A., Bricaud, A., Buriez, J.C., & Sèze, G.e. (1994). "The POLDER mission: Instrument characteristics and scientific objectives." *IEEE Transactions on Geoscience and Remote Sensing*, Vol. 32, No. 3, pp. 598–615.

Elachi, C. (1987). *Introduction to the Physics and Techniques of Remote Sensing*. Wiley, New York.

Estes, J.E., & Thorley, G.A., eds. (1983). "Interpretation and Applications." *Manual of Remote Sensing*, Vol. 2, R.N. Colwell, ed. American Society of Photogrammetry, Falls Church.

Goldstein, D.H. (2003). *Polarized Light*. 2nd edition, Marcel Dekker Inc., New York.

Henderson, F.M., & Lewis, A.J., eds. (1998). *Manual of Remote Sensing: Vol. 2, Principles and Applications of Imaging Radar*. 3rd Ed. Wiley, New York.

Kliger, D.S., Lewis, J.W., & Randall, C.E. (1990). *Polarized Light in Optics and Spectroscopy*. Academic Press, San Diego.

Richards, J.A. (1999). *Remote Sensing Digital Image Analysis: An Introduction*. 3rd Ed., Springer, New York.

Schott, J.R. (2007). *Remote Sensing: The Image Chain Approach*, 2nd Ed., Oxford University Press, New York.

Schowengerdt, R.A. (2006). *Remote Sensing. Models and methods for image processing*. Elsevier Science & Technology Books.

Shurcliff, W.A. (1962). *Polarized Light: Production and Use*. Harvard University Press, Cambridge.

Tyo, J.S., Goldstein, D.L., Chenault, D.B., & Shaw, J.A. (2006). "Review of passive imaging polarimetry for remote sensing applications." *Applied Optics*, Vol. 45, No. 22, pp. 5453–5469.

Rencz, A., ed. (1998). *Manual of Remote Sensing Vol. 3, Remote Sensing for the Earth Sciences*. 3rd Ed., Wiley, New York.

Ustin, S., ed. (2004). "Remote Sensing for Natural Resource Management and Environmental Monitoring," *Manual of Remote Sensing*, 3rd Ed., Vol. 4, Wiley, New York.

Wolf, E. (2003). "Unified theory of coherence and polarization of random electromagnetic beams." *Physics Letters A*, Vol. 312, pp. 263–267.

John R. Schott

Chapter 2
Review of Radiometry

This chapter is excerpted from Schott (2007). It contains a review of radiometric principles that are used extensively in later chapters as we develop governing equations that describe the reflective and emissive behavior of polarized signals reaching remote platforms.

2.1 Radiometric Terms

Radiometry is formally defined as the science of characterizing or measuring how much EM energy is present at, or associated with, some location or direction in space. It has evolved separately in the fields of physics, illumination or vision, and engineering, and as a result, a host of terms are used to describe various radiometric concepts. Often one concept has several different names; it is also common for the same term (e.g., intensity) to mean different things to different authors. To provide a common framework, we will briefly review the definitions of the relevant physical parameters and radiometric terms. An emphasis will be placed on the units of measure in this section and throughout the book to ensure a clearer understanding—units are usually designated with square brackets ([ ]) for clarity, and, where relevant, a unit's cancellation analysis may be performed within square brackets. In reading other authors, particularly older works or work drawn from other disciplines, the reader should carefully evaluate the author's definitions and units of measure to determine what term is being applied to each radiometric concept. The definitions used throughout this volume are consistent with those established by the *Commission Internationale de l'Eclairage* (CIE) and adopted by most international societies [see CIE (1970)]. In addition, to the extent practical, the parameters, nomenclature, and symbology are consistent with the relevant reference material [see Grum and Becherer (1979) and Nicodemus (1976)].

2.1.1 Definition of terms

For most radiometric considerations, we can use the ray/particle simplification of optics. This approach is based on geometric optics and assumes that light travels in straight lines and transfers energy in discrete packets or *quanta*. The physical optics effects of diffraction and interference associated with the wave nature of EM energy can be largely ignored in simple radiometric calculations in the visible and thermal infrared. The wave nature of EM energy is important in image formation; understanding the polarimetric behavior and will be treated in Chapter 3.

Recall that wavelength (λ [μm]), frequency (ν [sec^{-1}]), and the *speed of light* (c [m/sec]) are related as:

$$c = \lambda \nu, \tag{2.1}$$

where wavelength is the distance between two similar consecutive elements (same phase) in a wave representation (e.g., peak-to-peak or trough-to-trough). It is commonly referred to in units of micrometers [μm = 10^{-6} m] or nanometers [nm = 10^{-9} m]. Frequency is the number of waves (cycles) that would travel past a fixed point in 1 second and has units of hertz, cycles per unit time [Hz], or [sec^{-1}]. The speed of light clearly has units of distance per second and in vacuum has a constant value of $2.9979 \cdot 10^8$ m/sec. Spectral references will generally be given with respect to wavelength. However, some computations are more readily represented by the *wave number* ν' [cm^{-1}], which is simply the number of waves that would fit in a 1-cm length, i.e.,

$$\nu' = \frac{1}{\lambda}[\mathrm{cm}^{-1}] = \frac{\nu}{c}. \tag{2.2}$$

The common spectral regions and the nomenclature used in this volume are delineated in Fig. 2.1. In radiometric calculations, it is generally easier to think of energy as being transferred in terms of energy packets or quanta in accordance with quantum theory. The particle or energy carrier is called a *photon*, and each photon carries *energy*

$$q = h\nu = hc / \lambda [\mathrm{joules}]. \tag{2.3}$$

where $h = 6.6256 \cdot 10^{-34}$ [joules·sec] is *Planck's constant*, and energy is expressed as joules [J]. Thus, we see that shorter wavelength photons carry more energy than longer wavelength photons. This becomes very important when we begin to look at the spectral response of detectors in Chapter 7. The total energy (Q) in a beam or ray is a function of the number and spectral makeup of the photons according to

$$Q = \sum q_i = \sum_{i=1} n_i h \nu_i, \tag{2.4}$$

where the sum is over all frequencies present and n_i is the number of photons at each frequency.

It is usually more convenient to think of a beam or bundle of rays not in terms of the total energy but rather in terms of the rate at which the energy is passing or propagating (cf. Fig. 2.2(a)). This rate of flow of energy is called the *radiant flux*, or *power* (Φ), and is defined as the first derivative of the radiant energy with respect to time (t), i.e.,

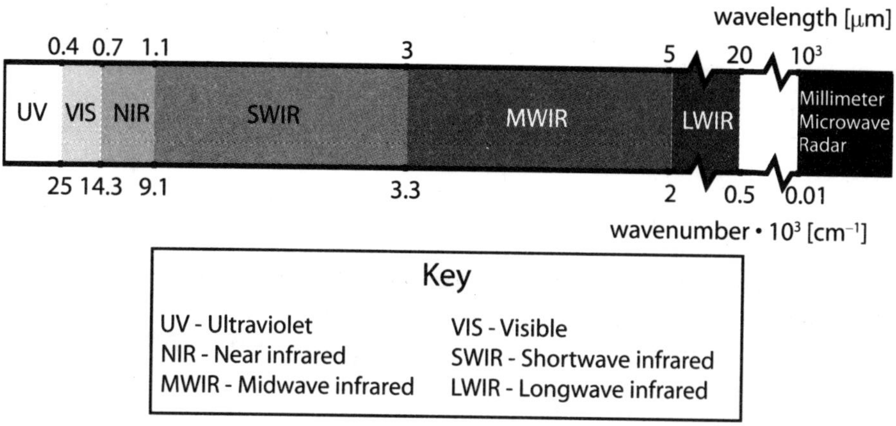

Figure 2.1 Nomenclature for various regions of the electromagnetic spectrum.

$$\Phi = \frac{dQ}{dt}[\text{W}]. \tag{2.5}$$

Often we are interested in the rate at which the radiant flux is delivered to a surface (e.g., the responsive surface of a detector). This concept is given the term *irradiance* (E) and is defined as

$$E = E(x, y) = \frac{d\Phi}{dA}[\text{Wm}^{-2}], \tag{2.6}$$

where dA [m^2] is an area element on the surface of interest, and (x,y) are generic spatial location parameters that, for convenience, will generally not be explicitly expressed. Equation (2.6) is characteristic of a shorthand we will use to indicate a simplification of notation where E and $E(x,y)$ are identical, but the dependence on x and y will be explicitly stated only where it is required for clarity. Irradiance, as illustrated in Fig. 2.2(b), is the flux per unit area *onto* a surface. It is very similar to *radiant exitance*, which is defined as

$$M = M(x, y) = \frac{d\Phi}{dA}[\text{Wm}^{-2}] \tag{2.7}$$

and describes the flux per unit area *away from* a surface (cf. Fig. 2.2(c)). This term describes the power per unit area radiated by a source or reflected from a surface.

Both the irradiance and the exitance provide spatial information about the flux, but provide no angular or directional information. The simplest term used to describe directional or dispersive information about the flux is the *radiant intensity* (I), defined as

$$I = I(\theta, \phi) = \frac{d\Phi}{d\Omega}[\text{Wsr}^{-1}], \tag{2.8}$$

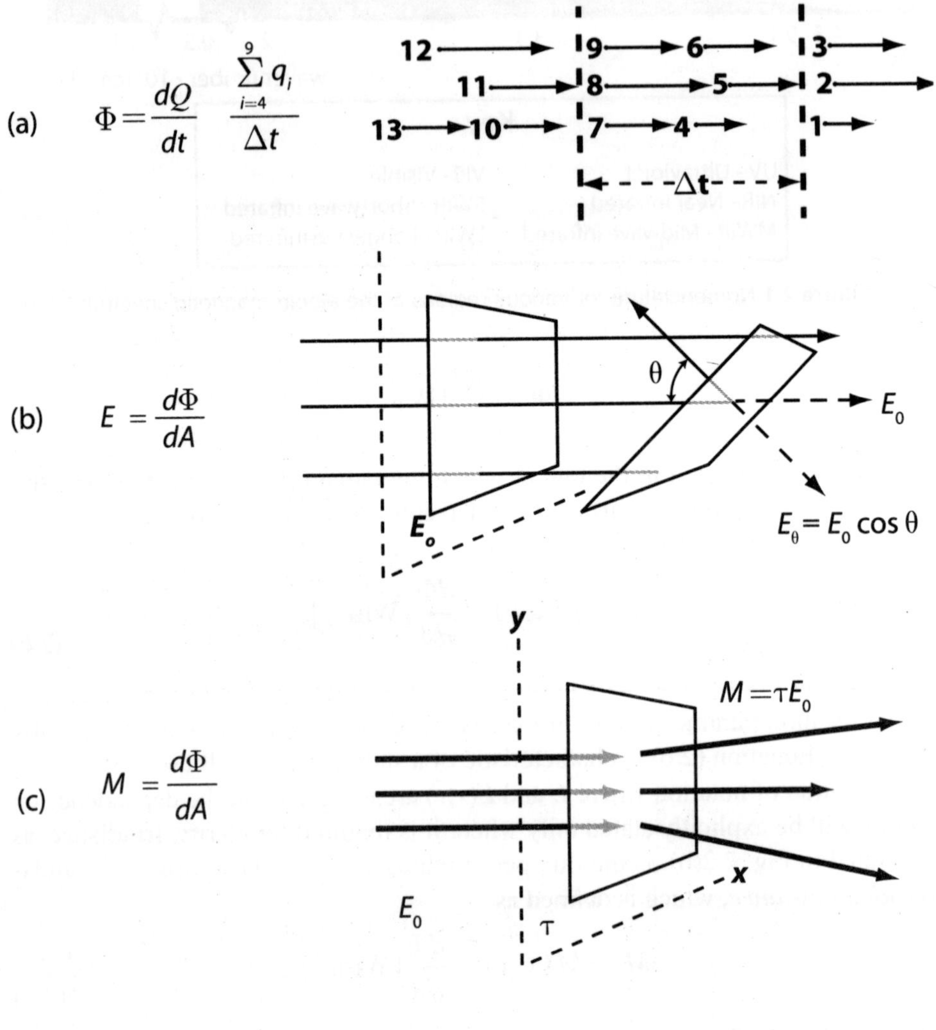

Figure 2.2(a–c) Illustration of radiometry definitions. (a) Radiant flux: time rate of energy delivery, production, or propagation. (b) Irradiance: flux per unit area onto a surface. (The first surface is perpendicular to the incident flux and has irradiance E_0. The second is rotated through the angle θ and has a flux E_θ.) (c) Radiant emittance or radiant exitance: flux per unit area away from the surface. (A surface with E_0 irradiance from the left and transmission τ would have exitance M away from the right side.)

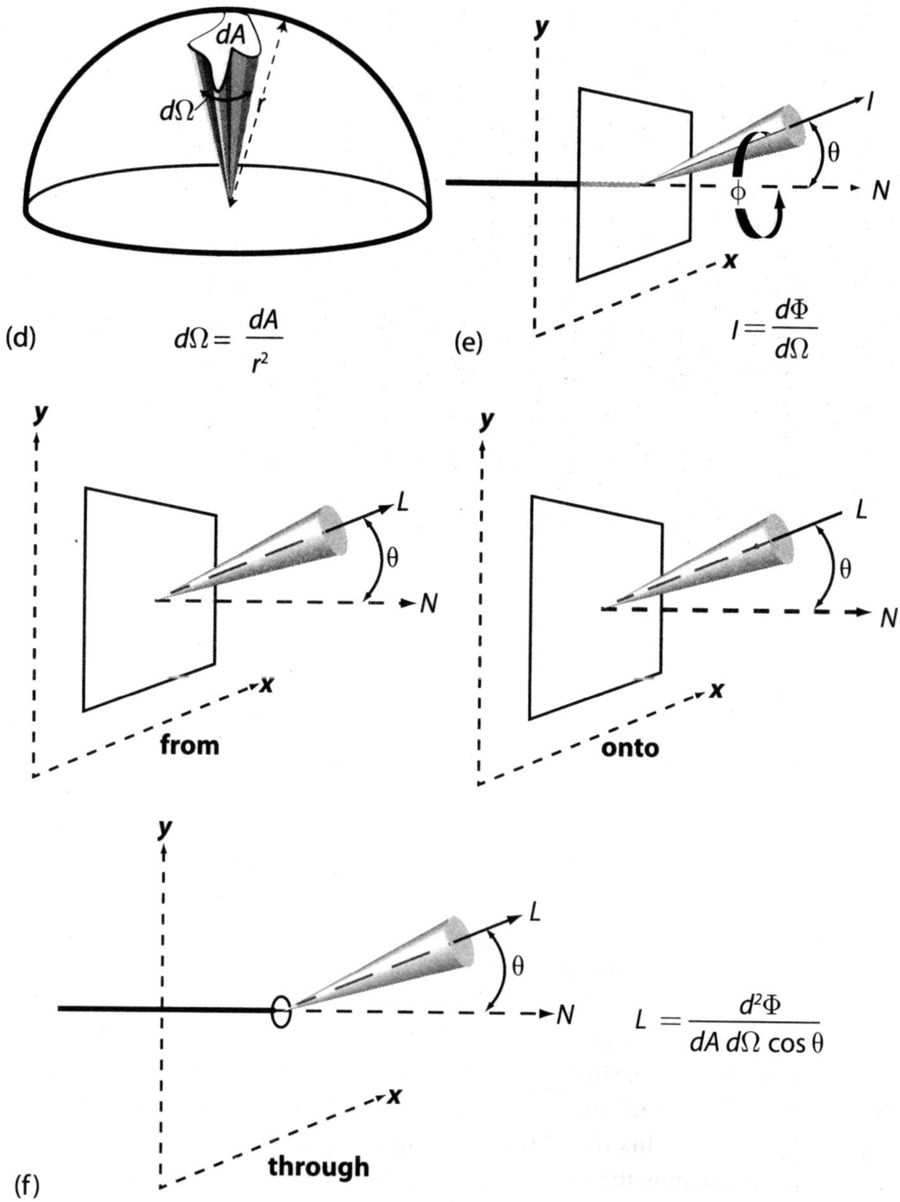

Figure 2.2(d–f) Illustration of radiometry definitions. (d) Element of solid angle [steradian]. (e) Radiant intensity: flux per unit solid angle into the direction defined by θ and ϕ, where θ is the angle from the normal to a reference surface, and ϕ is an azimuthal angle. (f) Radiance: flux per unit projected area per unit solid angle from, onto, or through the plane. N is the normal to the plane.

where $d\Omega = dA/r^2$[*steradian*, sr] is the element of solid angle. The element of solid angle is defined as the conic angle encompassing the area element dA on the surface of a sphere of radius (r) (cf. Fig. 2.2(d)), and θ and ϕ are generic orientation angles (as illustrated in Fig. 2.2(e)) that will not be explicitly expressed unless required.

The radiant intensity describes the flux per unit solid angle from a point source into a particular direction. While the intensity provides directional information, it does not provide any spatial information. The use of the *radiance* term (L [$Wm^{-2}sr^{-1}$]) to characterize the flux overcomes this limitation. It is the most complex of the radiometric terms we will consider, but also the most useful and ubiquitous. It is defined as

$$L = L(x, y, \theta, \phi) = \frac{d^2\Phi}{dA\cos\theta d\Omega} = \frac{dE}{d\Omega\cos\theta} = \frac{dI}{dA\cos\theta} = \frac{dM}{d\Omega\cos\theta}, \quad (2.9)$$

where x and y define a location in the plane of interest, and θ and ϕ are angles that define the direction of interest relative to the normal to the plane. The radiance is the flux per unit projected area (at the specified location in the plane of interest) per unit solid angle (in the direction specified relative to the reference plane). Note that while radiant exitance and intensity are generally source terms and irradiance is generally associated with receivers or detectors, radiance can be used to characterize the flux from or onto a surface, as well as the flux through any arbitrary surface in space [cf. Fig. 2.2(f)]. In addition, it has some very useful properties of constancy of propagation that make it an attractive parameter to use in most treatments of radiation propagation. Nicodemus (1976) demonstrates the important concept of the constancy of radiance through an isotropic lossless media (i.e., no transmission losses and unit index of refraction). Referring to Fig. 2.3, we assume a beam of energy with constant radiance across the profile of the beam. We select two arbitrary points along the beam and two surfaces with arbitrary orientation containing those points. It may be convenient to conceptualize the first surface as a source (i.e., the earth's surface) and the second as a sensor. If we consider the flux associated with a bundle of rays at surface 1 contained in a surface element dA_1 (which are also contained in dA_2 on surface 2) we see that in a lossless medium, the flux $d\Phi_1$ through dA_1 must equal the flux $d\Phi_2$ through dA_2. We want to evaluate how the radiance at surface 1 (L_1) is related to the radiance at surface 2 (L_2). We see that the radiance L_1 along the primary ray at p_1 toward the surface element dA_2 is, by definition

$$L_1 = \frac{d^2\Phi_1}{dA_1\cos\theta_1 d\Omega_{12}} \quad (2.10)$$

and the radiance at p_2 is

$$L_2 = \frac{d^2\Phi_2}{dA_2\cos\theta_2 d\Omega_{21}}, \quad (2.11)$$

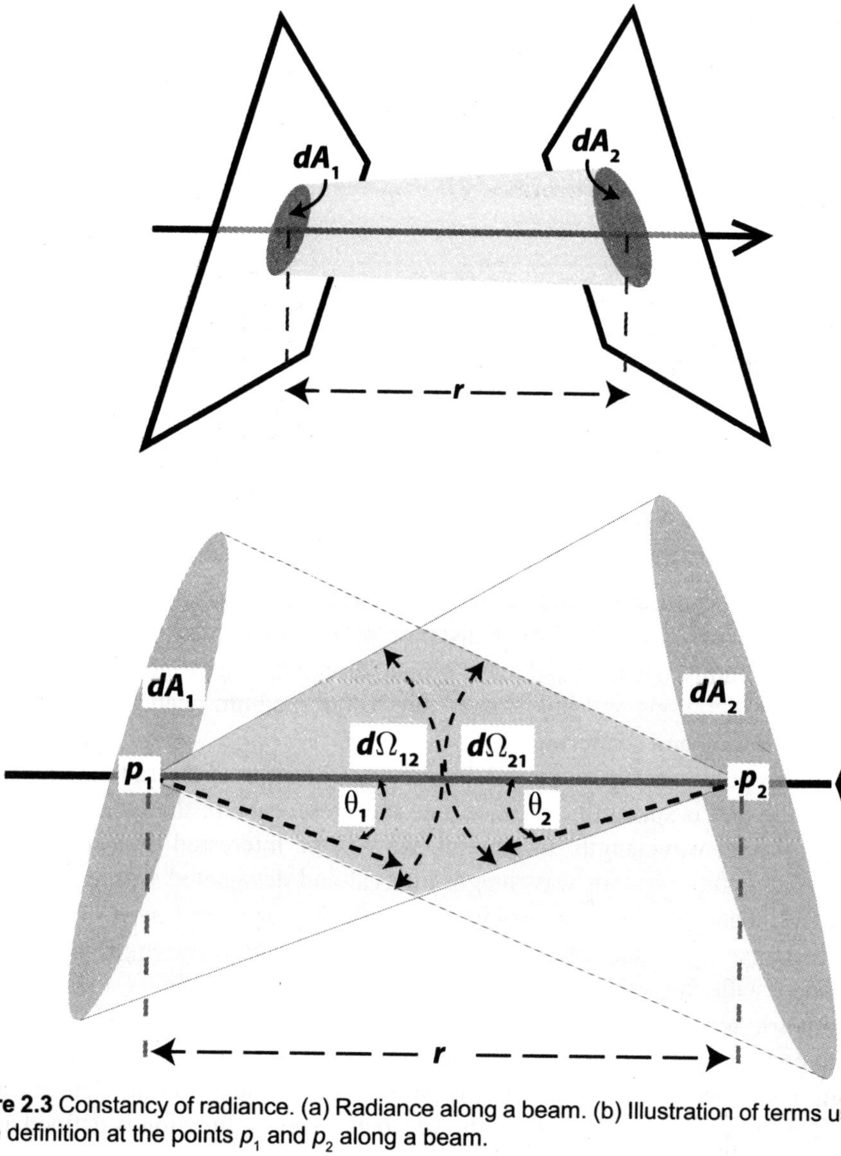

(a)

(b)

Figure 2.3 Constancy of radiance. (a) Radiance along a beam. (b) Illustration of terms used in the definition at the points p_1 and p_2 along a beam.

where θ_1 and θ_2 are the angles from the ray normal to the surface to the primary ray, and $d\Omega_{12}$ is the element of solid angle encompassed by the area element dA_2 at p_1, and similarly, $d\Omega_{21}$ is the element of solid angle encompassed by the area element dA_1 at p_2. If we let r represent the arbitrary distance between p_1 and p_2, we see that the *throughput* ($\mathcal{T}$) can be expressed as

$$\mathcal{T}_1 = dA_1 \cos\theta_1 d\Omega_{12} = dA_1 \cos\theta_1 \frac{dA_2 \cos\theta_2}{r^2} \tag{2.12a}$$

$$\mathcal{T}_2 = dA_2 \cos\theta_2 d\Omega_{21} = dA_2 \cos\theta_2 \frac{dA_1 \cos\theta_1}{r^2} \tag{2.12b}$$

and that $\mathcal{T}_1 = \mathcal{T}_2 = \mathcal{T}$. Expressing the radiance as

$$L_1 = \frac{d^2\Phi_1}{\mathcal{T}_1} \tag{2.13}$$

and

$$L_2 = \frac{d^2\Phi_2}{\mathcal{T}_2} \tag{2.14}$$

and recalling that $d\Phi_1 = d\Phi_2 = d\Phi$, we have

$$L_1 = L_2 = \frac{d^2\Phi r^2}{dA_1 \cos\theta_1 dA_2 \cos\theta_2} = \frac{d^2\Phi}{\mathcal{T}}. \tag{2.15}$$

Since all the terms in this analysis were completely arbitrary, we see that the radiance along a ray is constant over distance in a lossless medium. Thus, it is the term most readily used for radiation propagation, since it is independent of geometric considerations and only losses due to the medium need to be considered (e.g., absorption and scattering).

To this point, we have ignored the spectral character of the radiometric terms. In fact, the flux is spectrally variable, and therefore, each of the radiometric terms will vary with wavelength. In general, we will be interested in *spectral density* expressed as flux per unit wavelength interval and designated with a wavelength subscript. Thus, the spectral irradiance would be expressed as $E_\lambda[\mathrm{Wm^{-2}\mu m^{-1}}]$. The responsivity of the detectors is also a function of wavelength and must be cascaded with the spectral flux to generate effective bandpass values for the radiometric terms (i.e., What is the effective magnitude of the radiometric term relative to the spectral response of the detector?). The *responsivity* at each wavelength is defined as the signal out (S) per unit flux incident on the detector at the wavelength of interest. Therefore, the *spectral response* function is defined as

$$R(\lambda) = \frac{dS}{d\Phi(\lambda)}, \tag{2.16}$$

with units of [amps $\mathrm{W^{-1}}$] or [volts $\mathrm{W^{-1}}$], depending on the signal out of the detector. The unitless peak normalized spectral response function is

$$R'(\lambda) = \frac{R(\lambda)}{R(\lambda)_{\max}}, \tag{2.17}$$

where $R(\lambda)_{\max}$ is the maximum value of the $R(\lambda)$ function. Thus, $R'(\lambda)$ is normalized to a maximum value of unity. The peak normalized *effective value* of a radiometric term over the detector bandpass is then obtained by weighting the radiometric term by this normalized response value (cf. Fig. 2.4). For example,

$$L = L_{\text{eff}} = \int_0^\infty L_\lambda R'(\lambda)d\lambda \ [\text{Wm}^{-2}\text{sr}^{-1}], \tag{2.18}$$

where the subscript (eff) is usually implied, rather than explicitly indicated, and a numerical approximation to the integral is used in practice. The signal output from a sensor can be computed by integrating the spectral flux weighted by the spectral response function according to

$$S = \int_0^\infty \Phi_\lambda R(\lambda)d\lambda, \tag{2.19}$$

where the output signal (S) has units of amps or volts depending on the type of detector, and the integral or its numerical approximation needs to be performed only over the nonzero spectral response range. It is convenient to define the effective bandpass responsivity (R) such that the product of the effective responsivity and the total flux yields the observed signal, i.e.,

$$R\Phi_{\text{tot}} - R\Phi - S - \int_0^\infty \Phi_\lambda R(\lambda)d\lambda. \tag{2.20}$$

Substituting the integral form of Φ_{tot} and rearranging yields an expression for the *effective responsivity* of

$$R = \frac{\int_0^\infty \Phi_\lambda R(\lambda)d\lambda}{\int_0^\infty \Phi_\lambda d\lambda}. \tag{2.21}$$

It is important to recognize that when the bandpass value for responsivity is used, it is calculated for a specific source spectral distribution. The same detector will exhibit different bandpass responsivity values when irradiated by sources with differing spectral distributions.

In dealing with imaging spectroscopy, it is often useful to use effective spectral radiometric terms. This is the constant value the radiometric term would need over the sensor bandpass to generate the observed signal. For *effective spectral radiance*, this would require the following expression to be true:

$$S = \int L_\lambda R(\lambda) A\Omega \cos\theta d\lambda = L_{\lambda\text{eff}} \int R(\lambda) A\Omega \cos\theta d\lambda, \tag{2.22}$$

yielding an expression for the effective spectral radiance of

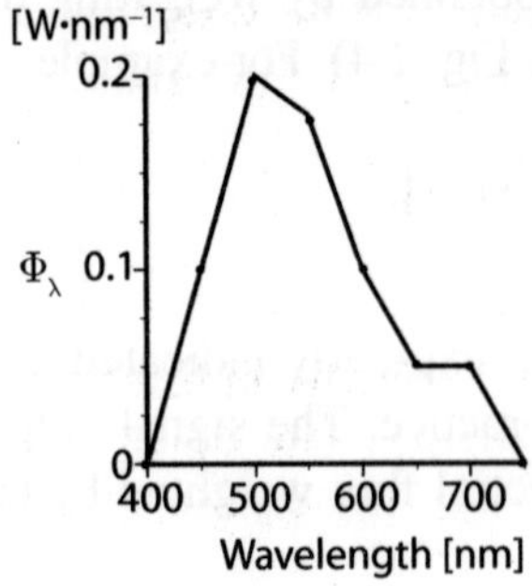

Given			Calculated	
λ [nm]	Φ_l [Wnm^{-1}]	$R(\lambda)$[V/W]	$R'(\lambda)$	$\Phi_\lambda/\int\Phi_\lambda d\lambda$
400	0	0	0	0
450	0.1	0	0	2.94×10^{-3}
500	0.2	1	0.25	5.88×10^{-3}
550	0.18	2	0.5	5.29×10^{-3}
600	0.1	3	0.75	2.94×10^{-3}
650	0.05	4	1	1.47×10^{-3}
700	0.05	2	0.5	1.47×10^{-3}
750	0	0	0	0

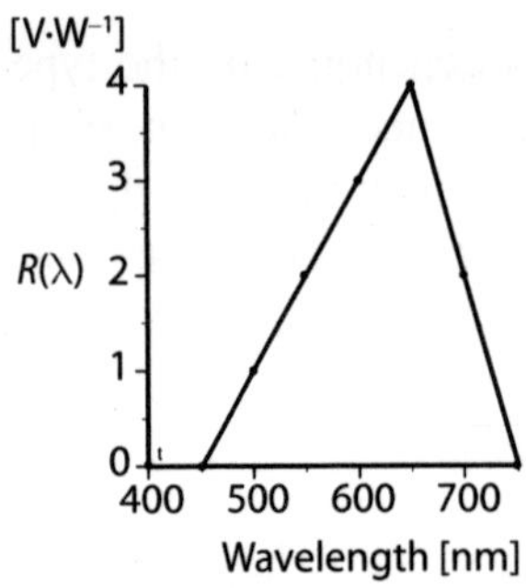

$$= \int\Phi_\lambda d\lambda = \Sigma\Phi_\lambda\Delta\lambda = 34 \text{ [W]}$$

$$\Phi_{eff} = \int\Phi_\lambda R'(\lambda)d\lambda = \Sigma\Phi_\lambda R'(\lambda)\Delta\lambda = 14.5 \text{ [W]}$$

$$R = \int R(\lambda)\frac{\Phi_\lambda}{\int\Phi_\lambda d\lambda}\, d\lambda = \Sigma R(\lambda)\frac{\Phi_\lambda}{\Sigma\Phi_\lambda d\lambda}\,\Delta\lambda = 1.7 \text{ [V/W]}$$

$$S = \int\Phi_\lambda R(\lambda)d\lambda = 58 \text{ [V]}$$

$$S = R\Phi \cong 58 \text{ [V]}$$

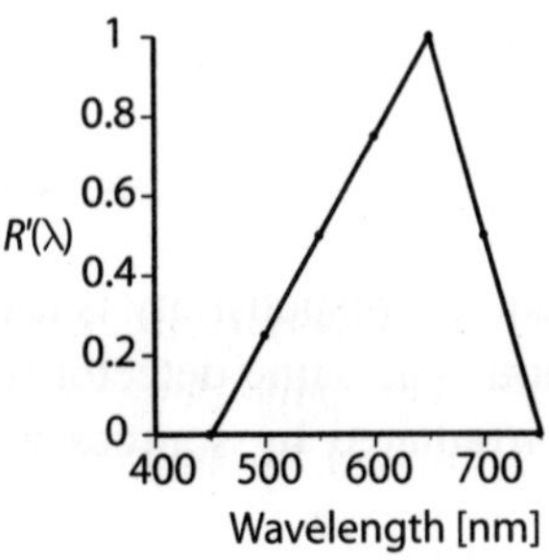

$$\Phi_{\lambda eff} = \int\Phi_\lambda R(\lambda)d\lambda/\int R(\lambda)d\lambda = 58\text{[v]}/600 \text{ [VW}^{-1}\text{nm]}$$
$$= 0.097 \text{ [Wnm}^{-1}]$$

Figure 2.4 Effective flux and responsivity sample calculations.

$$L_{\lambda\text{eff}} = \frac{\int L_\lambda R(\lambda)d\lambda}{\int R(\lambda)d\lambda} = \frac{\int L_\lambda R'(\lambda)d\lambda}{\int R'(\lambda)d\lambda} = \frac{L_{\text{eff}}}{\Delta\lambda_{\text{eff}}}[\text{Wm}^{-2}sr^{-1}\mu m^{-1}], \tag{2.23}$$

where $\Delta\lambda_{\text{eff}}$ is sometimes referred to as the effective *spectral bandwidth*. Similar expressions can be derived for all the radiometric terms. In general, for narrow spectral bands and spectrally smooth equations, the effective spectral values are good estimates of the actual spectral values.

2.1.2 Blackbody radiators

One of the cornerstones of modern physics and a critical element of quantitative radiometric remote sensing is the formula for spectral exitance from a blackbody radiator. A *blackbody* is an idealized surface or cavity that has the property that all incident electromagnetic flux is perfectly absorbed and then reradiated (i.e., the reflectivity is zero and absorptivity is one). Planck (1901) derived an expression for the spectral radiant exitance from a blackbody based on statistical calculation of the vibrational energy states between the atoms and the assumption that the vibrational resonation between the atoms could only emit or absorb energy in discrete levels proportional to the frequency of the oscillation state. Thus, all of the energy states are defined by $Q = mh\nu$, where m can take on only integer values, h was an empirically derived value that we now refer to as *Planck's constant*, and ν is the frequency of oscillation. Einstein's later work on the quantum theory of light and the concept of the photon provided the theoretical foundation for Planck's results [cf. Einstein (1905)]. The Planck or *blackbody radiation equation* for the spectral radiant exitance from a surface is

$$M_\lambda = 2\pi hc^2\lambda^{-5}(e^{\frac{hc}{\lambda kT}} - 1)^{-1}[Wm^{-2}\mu m^{-1}], \tag{2.24}$$

where T is the temperature in degrees Kelvin, k is the *Boltzmann gas constant* ($1.38\cdot10^{-23}$ JK^{-1}), and h and c are the Planck constant and the speed of light as previously defined. Examination of the Planck equation shows that radiant exitance is a function of both temperature and wavelength. By holding temperature fixed at selected values, a family of blackbody curves can be generated (as shown in Fig. 2.5) relating spectral exitance to wavelength. These curves show how the exitance increases with temperature and that it is a well-behaved function whose peak value shifts to shorter wavelengths as the temperature increases. In practice, the ideal blackbody can be approximated only by imperfect absorbers. To describe this phenomenon, we introduce the concept of *emissivity* ($\varepsilon(\lambda)$) defined as the ratio of the spectral exitance ($M_\lambda(T)$) from an object at temperature (T) to the exitance from a blackbody at that same temperature ($M_{\lambda BB}(T)$):

$$\varepsilon(\lambda) = \frac{M_\lambda(T)}{M_{\lambda BB}(T)}. \tag{2.25}$$

The emissivity describes how well an object radiates energy compared to the perfect blackbody radiator and is a unitless value with a range from 0 to 1. Objects whose emissivity is approximately constant with wavelength are referred to as *gray bodies*, while objects with spectrally varying emissivities are called *selective radiators*. Objects that approximate *gray-body* radiators over all or in part of the spectrum are often described or approximated by a blackbody that would

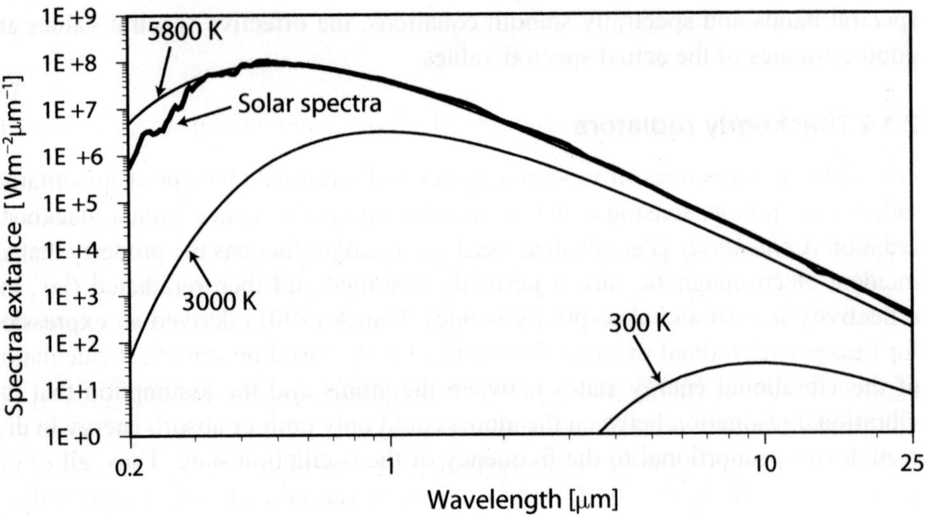

Figure 2.5 Blackbody curves and solar exitance spectra.

produce the equivalent exitance. The exitance from the sun can be approximated by a blackbody at approximately 5800 K (cf. Fig. 2.5).

It is important to recognize that emissivity is a fundamental property of matter, as are absorptivity, reflectivity, and transmissivity. In the formalism we have introduced, the *transmissivity* is the ability of the material to allow the flux to propagate through it. The *transmittance* or *transmission* (τ) can be expressed as the unitless ratio of the exitance from the back of a sample (M_τ) to the irradiance on the front of the sample (E_i):

$$\tau = \frac{M_\tau}{E_i}. \tag{2.26}$$

Clearly, the spectral transmittance ($\tau(\lambda)$) is simply the ratio of the spectral exitance to the spectral irradiance. Similarly, the *reflectivity* is the ability of the material to turn incident flux back into the hemisphere above the material, and the *reflectance* (r) can be expressed as the ratio of the exitance from the front of a sample (M_r) to the irradiance onto the front of the sample:

$$r = \frac{M_r}{E_i}. \tag{2.27}$$

Finally, the *absorptivity* is the ability of the material to remove electromagnetic flux from the system by converting incident flux to another form of energy (e.g., thermal energy). The *absorptance* (α) can be expressed as the ratio of the flux per unit area incident on the surface that is converted to another form of energy (M_α) to the irradiance onto the surface:

$$\alpha = \frac{M_\alpha}{E_i}. \tag{2.28}$$

Since conservation of energy requires all of the incident flux to be absorbed, transmitted, or reflected, we have

$$\alpha + \tau + r = 1, \tag{2.29}$$

or in the case of an opaque material, where τ is zero, we have

$$\alpha + r = 1. \tag{2.30}$$

Furthermore, according to Grum and Becherer (1979), *Kirchoff's law* states that the emissivity must be numerically equal to the absorptance for surfaces in thermodynamic equilibrium (i.e., good absorbers are good emitters). Therefore, we can also express the conservation of energy relationship as

$$\varepsilon + \tau + r = 1, \tag{2.31}$$

or for opaque objects, as

$$\varepsilon + r = 1. \tag{2.32}$$

We can compute the total exitance from a blackbody by integrating the Planck equation over all wavelengths. This yields the familiar *Stefan-Boltzmann* equation

$$\begin{aligned} M &= \int_0^\infty M_\lambda d\lambda = \int 2\pi hc^2\lambda^{-5}\left(e^{\frac{hc}{\lambda kT}} - 1\right)^{-1} d\lambda \\ &= \frac{2\pi^5 k^4 T^4}{15c^2h^3} = \sigma T^4, \end{aligned} \tag{2.33}$$

where σ ($5.67 \cdot 10^{-8}\mathrm{Wm^{-2}K^{-4}}$) is the Stefan-Boltzmann constant. It is important to recognize that this fourth-power relationship holds only for the integral over all wavelengths and is primarily useful for energy exchange calculations in thermodynamics. The exitance within a bandpass can be expressed as

$$M = \int_{\lambda_1}^{\lambda_2} M_\lambda d\lambda \tag{2.34}$$

and must be solved in numerical form since no closed form solution exists. Another fundamental natural law can be derived from the Planck equation by taking the first derivative with respect to wavelength and setting it equal to zero:

$$\frac{dM_\lambda}{d\lambda} = 0. \tag{2.35}$$

Since we have already seen that the Planck equation is well behaved with a single maximum, the zero point in the first derivative will yield the wavelength of maximum exitance. Solving Eq. (2.35) and rearranging produces the *Wien displacement law*

$$\lambda_{max} = \frac{A}{T}, \tag{2.36}$$

where A (2898 μm·K) is the Wien displacement constant. This expression predicts that the peak radiance from the sun at approximately 6000 K will occur in the visible portion of the spectrum at approximately 0.5 μm and that the peak flux for an object near the earth's ambient temperature of 300 K will occur at approximately 10 μm (cf. Fig. 2.5). This is conveniently in the center of an atmospheric transmission window, which is extensively used for studying the thermal characteristics of the earth (see chapters 11 and 12).

The radiometric concepts introduced in this chapter will be used extensively in Chapters 6 through 12 as we develop and utilize the governing radiometric equations for polarimetric imaging.

References

CIE (1970). "International lighting vocabulary." *CIE Publication*, No. 17 (E-1.1), International Commission on Illumination (CIE), Paris.

Einstein, A. (1905). "On a heuristic viewpoint concerning the production and transformation of light." *Annalen der Physik,* Vol. 17. [cf. English translation by Arons, A.B. & Peppard, M.B. (1968). *American Journal of Physics*, Vol. 33, No. 5, pp. 367–374].

Grum, F., & Becherer, R.J. (1979). *Optical Radiation Measurements (Vol.1 Radiometry)*, Academic Press, New York.

Nicodemus, F.E. (1976). "Self-study manual on optical radiation measurements: Part 1–Concepts," Chaps. 1 to 3. *NBS Technical Note 910–1*, U.S. Dept. of Commerce, National Bureau of Standards, Washington, DC.

Planck, M. (1901). *Annalen der Physik,* Vol. 4, No. 3, p. 553.

Schott, J.R. (2007). *Remote Sensing: The Image Chain Approach.* 2nd Ed., Oxford University Press, New York.

John R. Schott

Chapter 3
The Wave Nature of EM Energy and an Introduction of the Polarization Ellipse

This chapter continues our review of basic physics by reminding the reader of ways to describe the wave nature of EM energy and introducing ways to describe the polarimetric properties of a beam of energy. These topics are covered in greater detail in Collett (1993) and Goldstein (2003).

3.1 Wave Nature of EM Energy

The polarimetric properties of light are most easily introduced using the wave nature of EM energy. So we begin with a brief review from freshman physics applicable to fully polarized radiation.

Recall that the *electric field* associated with a beam of EM energy traveling in the z direction can be described in terms of the vector sum of the electric fields of two transverse component waves oscillating at right angles to each other and to the direction of propagation. The *field strength* at any location (z) and time (t) can be expressed as

$$\mathcal{E}_{\mathrm{x}} = \mathcal{E}_{0\mathrm{x}} \sin(\omega t - kz) = \mathcal{E}_{0\mathrm{x}} \sin\left(\omega t - 2\pi \frac{z}{\lambda}\right) \tag{3.1}$$

$$\mathcal{E}_{\mathrm{y}} = \mathcal{E}_{0\mathrm{y}} \sin(\omega t - kz) = \mathcal{E}_{0\mathrm{y}} \sin\left(\omega t - 2\pi \frac{z}{\lambda}\right), \tag{3.2}$$

where $\mathcal{E}_{\mathrm{x}}$ and $\mathcal{E}_{\mathrm{y}}$ are the instantaneous *amplitudes* of the x and y components, $\mathcal{E}_{0\mathrm{x}}$ and $\mathcal{E}_{0\mathrm{y}}$ are the maximum amplitudes, t is time, $\omega = 2\pi v$ is the *angular frequency*, v is the frequency [cycles/sec], $k = \omega/c$, c is the velocity of the wave in the medium, z is the location along the direction of the propagation, and λ is the wavelength. Note that at any fixed location z_1 along the beam, these equations indicate that the beam will oscillate at rates of the order of 10^{15} cycles per second (visible light in

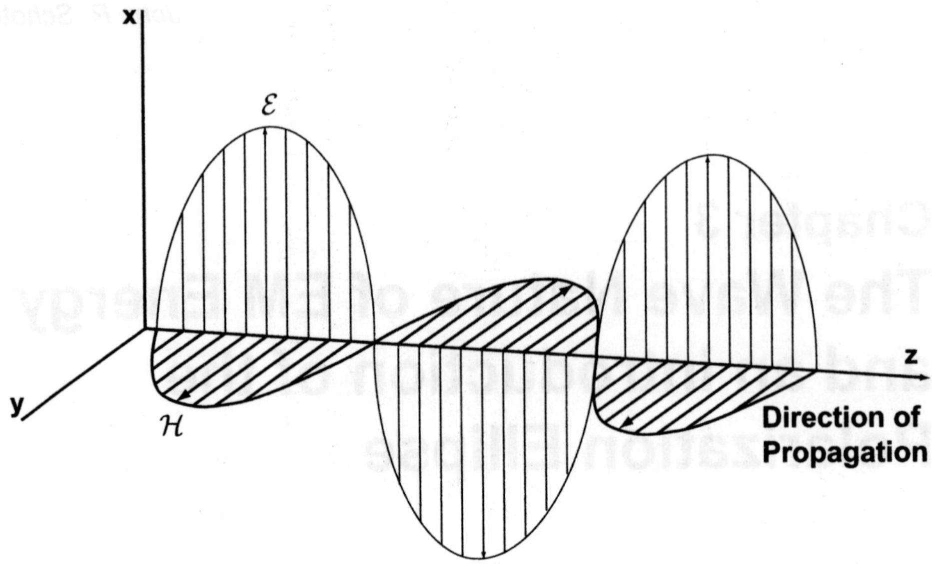

Figure 3.1 Fluctuations in the electric ($\mathcal{E}$) and magnetic ($\mathcal{H}$) fields giving rise to propagation of electromagnetic radiation in the *z* direction.

air) and/or that at any fixed point in time the field will oscillate along the beam in a sinusoidal fashion (Fig. 3.1). This expression can be written to include a shift in phase as

$$\mathcal{E}_x = \mathcal{E}_{0x} \sin(\omega t - kz + \phi_x) \tag{3.3}$$

$$\mathcal{E}_y = \mathcal{E}_{0y} \sin(\omega t - kz + \phi_y), \tag{3.4}$$

where ϕ_x and ϕ_y are the *phase* shift (Fig. 3.2). Also note that

$$\sin\left(\theta + \frac{\pi}{2}\right) = \cos\theta, \tag{3.5}$$

i.e., the sine and cosine expression for the equation of a wave are equivalent with an appropriate phase shift. Furthermore, since the initial phase is often irrelevant (i.e., arbitrary) and only the phase difference is meaningful, the sine or cosine representations are both commonly used; we will use both to familiarize the user with both conventions.

To reinforce our understanding of the observable properties of EM energy, we will follow Collett's (1993) lead and briefly review the interference experiment conducted by Thomas Young around the year 1800. In this experiment Young took a monochromatic source of light and illuminated two equidistant pinholes. The light from the pinholes was allowed to combine and was observed on a screen parallel to the plane of the pinholes and at a distance from the pinholes (Fig. 3.3). The resulting beam was not uniform but showed distinct bright and dark bands. We wish to see if these patterns are predicted by the wave expression for EM

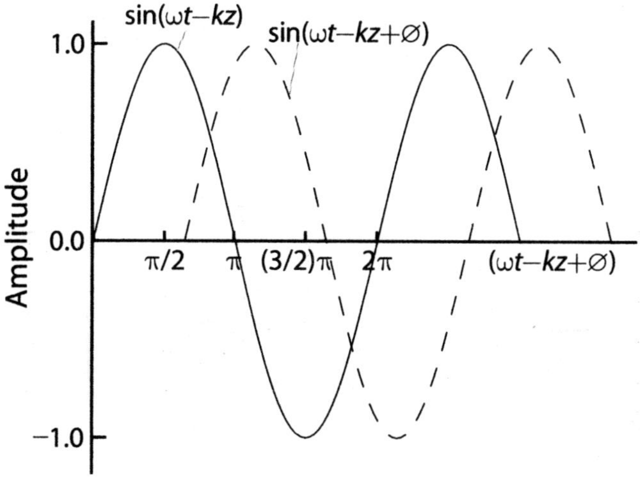

Figure 3.2 Illustration of phase shift in a sine wave.

radiation. Based on Huygens' principle, we can assume that each pinhole acts as a secondary source from which waves emanate.

The equations for the amplitude of the waves from the two sources at a point $p(x,y)$ located a distance ℓ_1 from source 1 and ℓ_2 from source 2 can be expressed as:

$$\mathcal{E}_1 = \mathcal{E}_{01} \sin(\omega t - k\ell_1) \tag{3.6}$$

$$\mathcal{E}_2 = \mathcal{E}_{02} \sin(\omega t - k\ell_2), \tag{3.7}$$

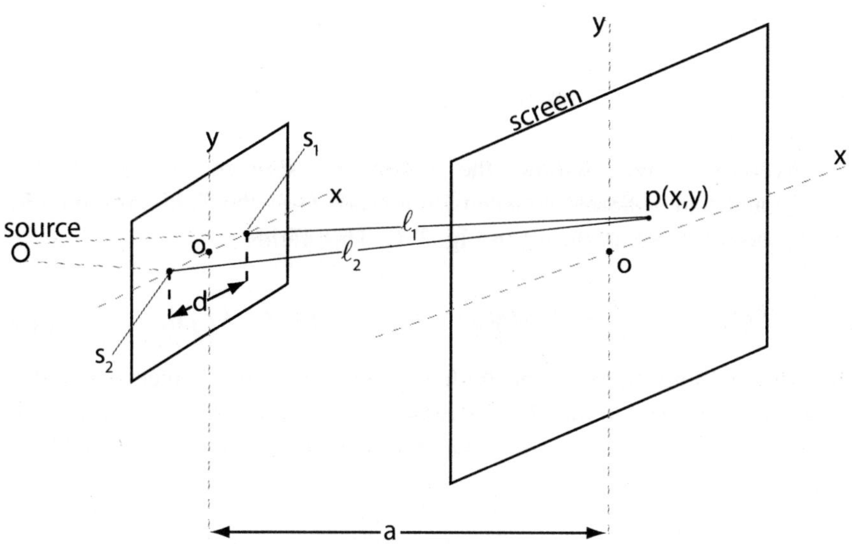

Figure 3.3 Illustration of Young's interference experiment.

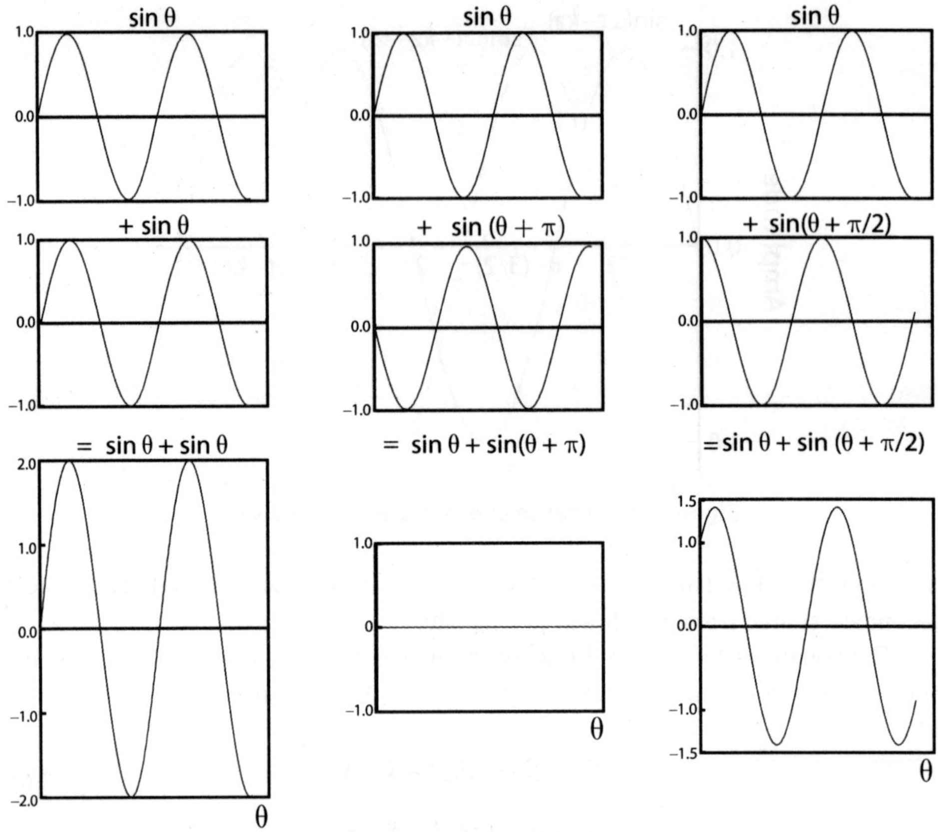

Figure 3.4 Coherent superposition concept: wave amplitude of the combined wave will be enhanced or suppressed based on the relative phase.

where $\mathcal{E}_{01}$ and $\mathcal{E}_{02}$ are the maximum amplitudes for the field from each source and we are not differentiating between the *x* and *y* component of the transverse field (this is common practice for a randomly polarized beam, i.e., $\mathcal{E}_{01x} = \mathcal{E}_{01y}$ and the phases are random).

For convenience, we assume the secondary sources are equal (i.e., $\mathcal{E}_{01} = \mathcal{E}_{02} = \mathcal{E}_0$) and that coherent *superposition* holds (i.e., the field strength adds coherently based on phase as shown in Fig. 3.4). This yields

$$\mathcal{E}(t) = \mathcal{E}_1 + \mathcal{E}_2 = \mathcal{E}_0[\sin(\omega t - k\ell_1) + \sin(\omega t - k\ell_2)]. \tag{3.8}$$

Since we observe (both visually and with all relevant sensors) over a period of time that is long compared to the 10^{-15} temporal period of the wave, we must take a time average of Eq. (3.8) to represent the observed field strength. This yields

$$\langle \mathcal{E}(t) \rangle = \lim_{T\to\infty} \frac{\int_0^T \mathcal{E}(t)dt}{\int_0^T dt} = \lim_{T\to\infty} \frac{1}{T}\int_0^T \mathcal{E}(t)dt$$
$$= \lim_{T\to\infty} \frac{\mathcal{E}_0}{T}\int [\sin(\omega t - k\ell_1) + \sin(\omega t - k\ell_2)]dt. \tag{3.9}$$

Using the trigonometric identity that

$$\sin(\omega t - k\ell) = \sin(\omega t)\cos(k\ell) - \cos(\omega t)\sin(k\ell), \tag{3.10}$$

we see that on substituting this expression into Eq. (3.9), every term will have a $\sin(\omega t)$ or $\cos(\omega t)$ term plus time independent multipliers. The time average of sine waves (or cosine waves) is zero yielding:

$$\langle \mathcal{E}(t) \rangle = 0. \tag{3.11}$$

But as we pointed out, Young observed a clear signal that varied spatially (though not temporally). Thus, he and (we) must not be observing the field strength as expressed by the wave equation. Rather, we observe the amplitude squared, which also exhibits coherent superposition. It is referred to in optics as the *intensity* ($\mathcal{I}$) and is proportional to the energy term (Q) used in radiometry. Note that this is not the same as the radiant intensity [W/sr] used in radiometry, though it is proportional to it.

The time average squared amplitude of an arbitrary beam (Fig. 3.5) can be expressed, in general, as

$$\mathcal{I} = \langle \mathcal{E}^2(t) \rangle = \lim_{T\to\infty} \frac{1}{T}\int_0^T \mathcal{E}^2(t)dt$$
$$= \lim_{T\to\infty} \frac{1}{T}\int_0^T \mathcal{E}_0^2 \sin^2(\omega t - k\ell)dt = \frac{\mathcal{E}_0^2}{2}\mathcal{I}_0. \tag{3.12}$$

For our case from Eq. (3.8) we have

$$\mathcal{E}^2(t) = \mathcal{E}_0^2[\sin^2(\omega t - k\ell_1) + \sin^2(\omega t - k\ell_2) + 2\sin(\omega t - k\ell_1)\sin(\omega t - k\ell_2)]. \tag{3.13}$$

With a little trigonometry and substitution, Eq. (3.12) yields

$$\mathcal{I} = \langle \mathcal{E}^2(t) \rangle = 2\mathcal{I}_0[1 + \cos k(\ell_2 - \ell_1)] = 4\mathcal{I}_0 \cos^2\left[\frac{k(\ell_2 - \ell_1)}{2}\right], \tag{3.14}$$

where $\mathcal{I}$ will vary from zero to $4\mathcal{I}_0$, yielding four times the maximum energy from a single source (not two times as we might expect for incoherent combination) as the path length difference ($\Delta\ell = \ell_1 - \ell_2$) changes. For our experiment as described in Fig. 3.3,

$$\ell_1^2 = a^2 + y^2 + \left(x - \frac{d}{2}\right)^2 = a^2 + y^2 + x^2 - xd + \frac{d^2}{4} \tag{3.15a}$$

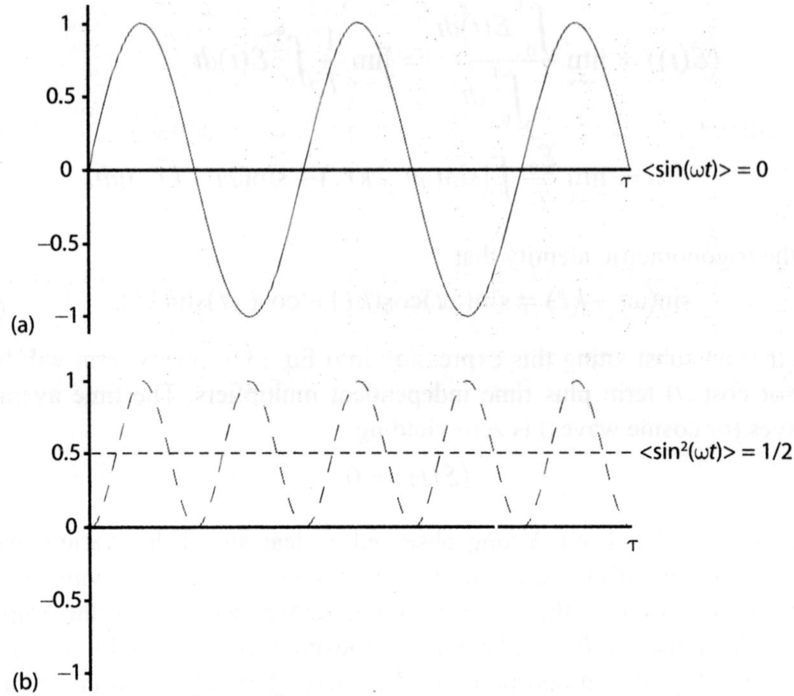

Figure 3.5 Time averaging over $\sin(\omega t)$ and over $\sin^2(\omega t)$. (a) The time average of $\sin(\omega t)$ over a cycle is zero and therefore over many cycles is zero. (b) The time average of $\sin^2(\omega t)$ over a cycle is ½ and therefore over many cycles $<\mathcal{E}_0^2 \sin^2(\omega t)> = ½\mathcal{E}_0^2$.

$$\ell_2^2 = a^2 + y^2 + \left(x + \frac{d}{2}\right)^2 = a^2 + y^2 + x^2 + xd + \frac{d^2}{4} \tag{3.15b}$$

or

$$\ell_2^2 - \ell_1^2 = 2xd. \tag{3.16}$$

This can be re-expressed as

$$(\ell_2 - \ell_1)(\ell_2 + \ell_1) = 2xd. \tag{3.17}$$

If x and y are small compared to a, then

$$\ell_2 + \ell_1 \approx 2a, \tag{3.18}$$

yielding

$$\Delta\ell = \ell_2 - \ell_1 = \frac{xd}{a}. \tag{3.19}$$

Substituting Eq. (3.14) yields

$$\mathcal{I} = 4\mathcal{I}_0 \cos^2\left(\frac{kxd}{2a}\right). \tag{3.20}$$

Recalling that $k = \omega/c = 2\pi/\lambda$, we see that Eq. (3.20) will yield maxima when

$$\frac{kxd}{2a} = \frac{2\pi xd}{2\lambda a} \tag{3.21}$$

is an integer multiple of π and nulls or becomes zero when it equals an integer multiple of $\pi+(1/2)\pi$, producing maxima at

$$x = \frac{a\lambda n}{d} \text{ for } n = 0, \pm 1, \pm 2... \tag{3.22}$$

and minima at

$$x = \frac{a\lambda}{d}\left(n + \frac{1}{2}\right) \text{ for } n = 0, \pm 1, \pm 2.... \tag{3.23}$$

Therefore, if we let $\lambda = 0.59$ μm, $d = 0.001$ m, and $a = 2$ m, then the distance to the first bright region from the central bright spot should be

$$x = \frac{2 \cdot 0.59 \cdot 10^{-6}}{0.001} = 0.0012\,\text{m} = 1.2\,\text{mm}. \tag{3.24}$$

This example reminds us that while most physics and optics texts describe EM radiation in terms of the amplitude of the electric field, the observable for all of the relevant calculations and for all of the polarimetric terms we will consider is the squared amplitude of the wave equations (i.e., the intensity ($\mathcal{I}$) or from radiometry, the energy (Q)). Because all of the basic physical concepts are built on the field equations, we will continue to use them for the fundamentals with a goal of moving into measurable radiometric expressions.

3.2 The Polarization Ellipse

Based on the fundamental concepts from the previous section, we can now formally introduce the polarized nature of EM energy. To begin, we once again express the transverse components of an optical field propagating in the z direction as

$$\mathcal{E}_x(z,t) = \mathcal{E}_{0x} \cos(\tau + \phi_x) \tag{3.25}$$

and

$$\mathcal{E}_y(z,t) = \mathcal{E}_{0y} \cos(\tau + \phi_y), \tag{3.26}$$

where $\tau = \omega t - kz$ is referred to as the *propagator* and ϕ_x and ϕ_y are the phases. $\mathcal{E}_x(z,t)$ and $\mathcal{E}_y(z,t)$ describe the component of a vector at any time (t) and over time,

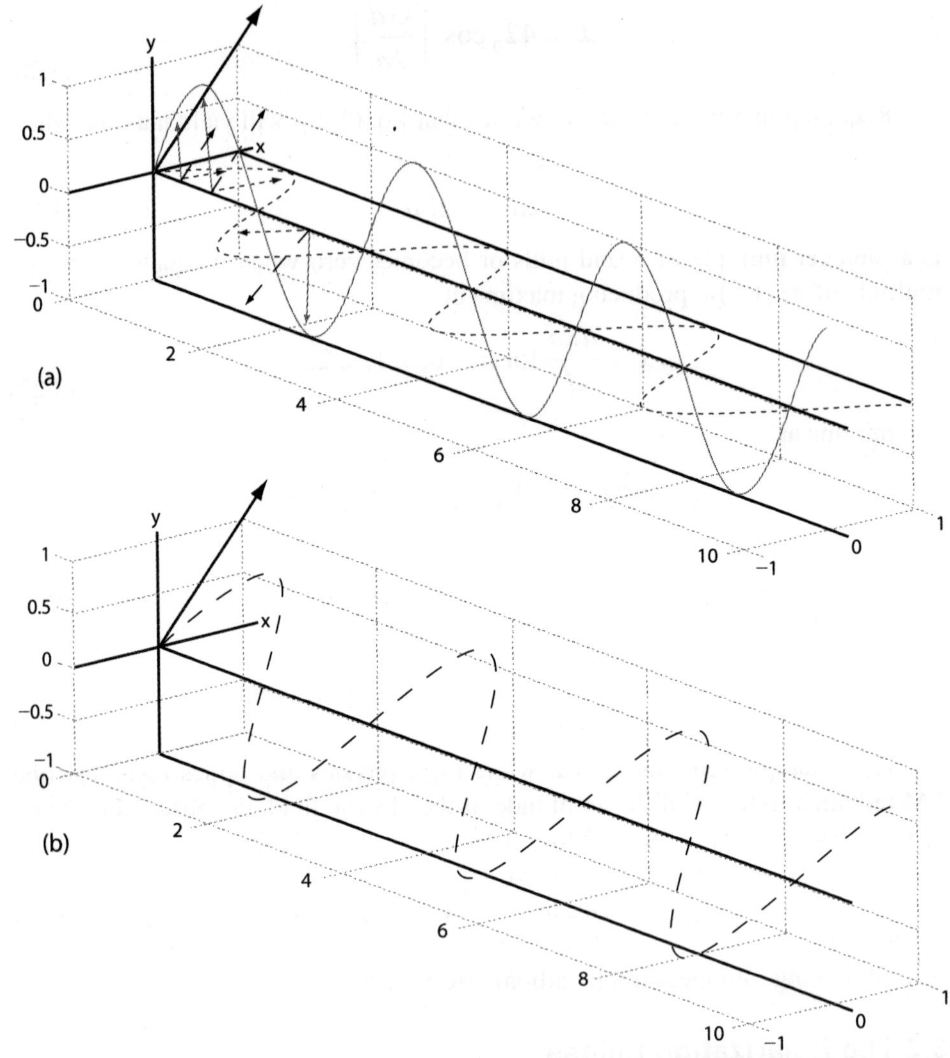

Figure 3.6 Fluctuations in the horizontal ($\mathcal{E}_x$) and vertical ($\mathcal{E}_y$) fields give rise to a vector sum that varies in direction and magnitude. (a) Case of $\mathcal{E}_x$ and $\mathcal{E}_y$ in phase, i.e., $\phi_x = \phi_y$. (b) The vector sum is a curve that, in this case, is in the plane at 45 deg to the x, y axis.

the vector sum describes a locus of points that can be represented by a curve (Fig. 3.6).

Equations (3.25) and (3.26) can be combined and manipulated to yield

$$\frac{\mathcal{E}_x^2}{\mathcal{E}_{0x}^2}+\frac{\mathcal{E}_y^2}{\mathcal{E}_{0y}^2}+\frac{-2\mathcal{E}_x\mathcal{E}_y}{\mathcal{E}_{0x}\mathcal{E}_{0y}}\cos\phi=\sin^2\phi, \tag{3.27}$$

where

$$\phi=\phi_y-\phi_x \tag{3.28}$$

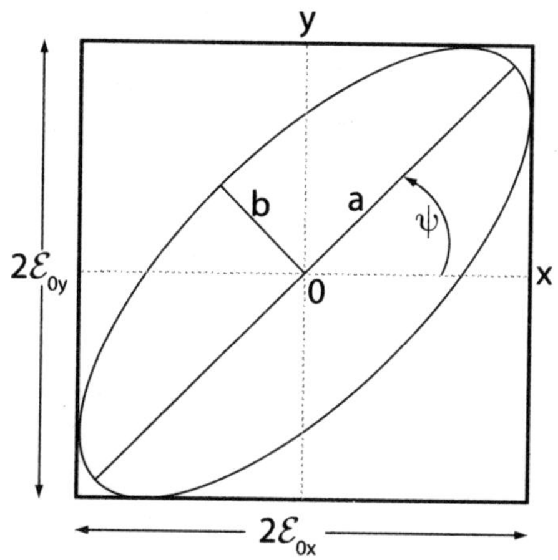

Figure 3.7 Illustration of the polarization ellipse and the polarization angle (ψ).

is the phase difference between the two components.

Equation (3.27) describes an ellipse rotated through an angle ψ (Fig. 3.7) where

$$\tan 2\psi = \frac{2\mathcal{E}_{0x}\mathcal{E}_{0y}\cos\phi}{\mathcal{E}_{0x}^2 - \mathcal{E}_{0y}^2} \tag{3.29}$$

and represents the pattern traced by the EM vector in time at a fixed plane ($z = z_0$).

Recall that electromagnetic energy can be represented as two mutually perpendicular electric ($\mathcal{E}$) and magnetic ($\mathcal{H}$) waves traveling in a direction (z) perpendicular to the direction of oscillation of both waves (cf. Fig. 3.1). Randomly polarized EM energy is composed of many superimposed waves whose electric fields vary in orientation so that no preferential orientation can be discerned (see Hecht (1990) for a more complete treatment of polarization principles.) In contrast, for a plane-polarized wave, also called linear polarization, the electric (and therefore also the magnetic) field varies only in a single plane. More generally, due to phase differences in the constituent waves, the orientation of the *polarization ellipse* may rotate over time and the amplitude may vary. This results in the general case of *elliptically polarized radiation* as described by Eq. (3.27). The amplitude of the electric field vector appears to trace an ellipse when viewed backward along the direction of propagation (cf. Fig. 3.8).

However, the ellipse does not capture the left- or right-hand rotation of the vector as it propagates. We capture this rotation by a convention that is based on observing the vector as it moves toward us along the positive z axis. If the rotation of the tip of the field vector is clockwise, the polarization is said to be *right-handed*; the polarization is *left-handed* if the field vector rotates in a counterclockwise fashion (Fig. 3.8). Note that this convention is commonly used in

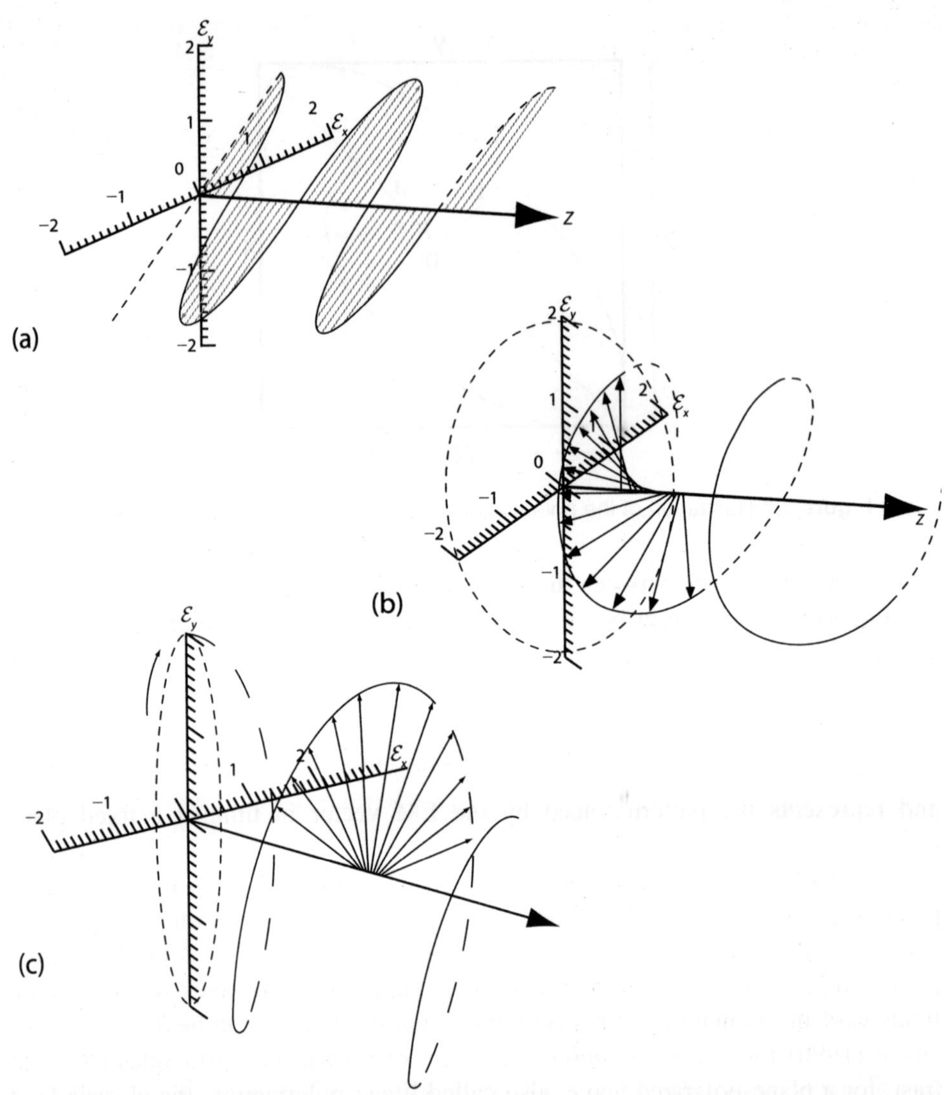

Figure 3.8 Polarization concepts. (a) In linear polarization, the electric field vector varies in a fixed plane that would form a line if projected onto the *x*,*y* plane. (b) For circular polarization, the electric field magnitude vector rotates such that it would trace a circle (counterclockwise in this case) when projected onto the *x*,*y* plane as a function of time. (c) In the general case of elliptically polarized radiation, the electric field vector rotates and changes in magnitude such that its tip would trace an ellipse (clockwise in this case) when projected onto the *x*,*y* plane.

physics and optics, while the opposite convention is common in some other fields. Since many fields contribute to remote sensing, the reader is likely to encounter both conventions in the literature and should carefully verify which convention is in use. Circular and plane polarization can be thought of as special cases of elliptical polarization. For *circular polarization*, the amplitude remains constant while the orientation angle of the vector sum changes, and for *linear polarization*, the magnitude varies while the orientation angle remains fixed.

3.3 Special (Degenerate) Forms of the Polarization Ellipse

The general polarization ellipse described by Eq. (3.27) can take on many specialized forms, which we will introduce in this section.

3.3.1 Linear polarization

Linear polarization occurs when the aggregate electric field vector forms a locus of points that oscillates only in a single plane. For the case of horizontal linear polarization, this can be expressed as

$$\mathcal{E}_x(z,t) = \mathcal{E}_{0x}\cos(\tau + \phi_x) \tag{3.30a}$$

and

$$\mathcal{E}_y(z,t) = 0. \tag{3.30b}$$

For the case of vertical linear polarization,

$$\mathcal{E}_x(z,t) = 0 \tag{3.31a}$$

and

$$\mathcal{E}_y(z,t) = \mathcal{E}_{0y}\cos(\tau + \phi_y), \tag{3.31b}$$

where $\tau = \omega t - kz$.

More generally, if $\phi = 0$ or π, Eq. (3.27) reduces to

$$\mathcal{E}_y = \pm\frac{\mathcal{E}_{0y}}{\mathcal{E}_{0x}}\mathcal{E}_x, \tag{3.32}$$

which we recognize as a straight line with zero intercept and slope $\pm(\mathcal{E}_{0y}/\mathcal{E}_{0x})$ ($\phi = 0$ yields positive slopes and $\phi = \pi$ yields negative slopes), representing linearly polarized radiation at orientations defined by the slope.

When $\mathcal{E}_{0y} = \mathcal{E}_{0x}$, the slope is 1, representing linear polarization oriented along the ±45-deg axis, ($\phi = 0$ is +45 deg and $\phi = \pi$ is −45 deg). Linearly polarized radiation is the form most commonly found in remote sensing of the earth and will receive most of our attention in later chapters.

3.3.2 Unrotated ellipse

Another special case of the polarization ellipse occurs if $\phi = \pi/2$ or $\phi = (3/2)\pi$, causing Eq. (3.27) to reduce to

$$\frac{\mathcal{E}_x^2}{\mathcal{E}_{0x}^2} + \frac{\mathcal{E}_y^2}{\mathcal{E}_{0y}^2} = 1, \tag{3.33}$$

which is the standard (i.e., unrotated) version of an ellipse.

If in addition to $\phi = \pi/2$ or $(3/2)\pi$, $\mathcal{E}_{0x} = \mathcal{E}_{0y} = \mathcal{E}_0$, then Eq. (3.33) becomes

$$\frac{\mathcal{E}_x^2}{\mathcal{E}_0^2} + \frac{\mathcal{E}_y^2}{\mathcal{E}_0^2} = 1, \tag{3.34}$$

which is the equation of a circle yielding circular polarization (right handed if $\phi = \pi/2$ or left handed if $\phi = (3/2)\pi$).

Goldstein (2003) points out that the polarization ellipse, while providing some insight into the nature of polarized radiation, has serious practical limitations. First, the description as we have presented it here is only applicable to fully polarized radiation which is very uncommon in nature. Furthermore, because it describes the EM field, we can't observe it directly. This leads us in the next chapter to the work of Sir George Gabriel Stokes, who developed a way to describe polarized radiation in terms of observable parameters.

References

Collett, E. (1993). *Polarized Light: Fundamentals and Applications*. Marcel Dekker, Inc. New York.

Goldstein, D.H. (2003). *Polarized Light*. 2nd Ed., Marcel Dekker Inc., New York.

Hecht, E. (1990). *Optics*. 2nd Ed., Addison-Wesley, Reading, MA.

John R. Schott

Chapter 4
Representation of the Polarimetric State of a Beam

In this chapter we introduce the Stokes parameters and the Stokes vector representation of a polarized beam. This representation is particularly important to us because it can be easily measured and is the most common way to represent a beam's propagation along a complex path such as we encounter in remote sensing. The Stokes representation is also important because it allows us to represent both fully and partially polarized beams. Our discussion in Chapter 3 presented ways to describe a beam in which all of the EM energy was polarized. For an unpolarized or randomly polarized beam, no preferred orientation or rotational behavior is associated with the electrical field. Most EM radiation is partially polarized and can be thought of as being composed of both an unpolarized component and a polarized component.

4.1 The Stokes Parameters

Recall from Eq. (3.27) that for a fully polarized beam, we can express the polarization ellipse as

$$\frac{\mathcal{E}_x^2(t)}{\mathcal{E}_{0x}^2}+\frac{\mathcal{E}_y^2(t)}{\mathcal{E}_{0y}^2}-\frac{2\mathcal{E}_x(t)\mathcal{E}_y(t)}{\mathcal{E}_{0x}\mathcal{E}_{0y}}\cos\phi=\sin^2\phi. \tag{4.1}$$

Stokes (1852) showed, with some algebraic manipulation including taking the time averages, that this leads to an expression of the form

$$(\mathcal{E}_{0x}^2+\mathcal{E}_{0y}^2)^2=(\mathcal{E}_{0x}^2-\mathcal{E}_{0y}^2)^2+(2\mathcal{E}_{0x}\mathcal{E}_{0y}\cos\phi)^2+(2\mathcal{E}_{0x}\mathcal{E}_{0y}\sin\phi)^2. \tag{4.2}$$

We can then define each of the four terms in the following manner:

$$S_0=\mathcal{E}_{0x}^2+\mathcal{E}_{0y}^2 \tag{4.3}$$

$$S_1=\mathcal{E}_{0x}^2-\mathcal{E}_{0y}^2 \tag{4.4}$$

$$S_2 = 2\mathcal{E}_{0x}\mathcal{E}_{0y}\cos\phi \tag{4.5}$$

$$S_3 = 2\mathcal{E}_{0x}\mathcal{E}_{0y}\sin\phi, \tag{4.6}$$

where S_0, S_1, S_2, and S_3 are referred to as the *Stokes parameters* for a plane wave. Note that the Stokes parameters are also commonly denoted by $S_0 = I$, $S_1 = Q$, $S_2 = U$, and $S_3 = V$ in the literature.

Substituting Eqs. (4.3)–(4.6) into Eq. (4.2) yields

$$S_0^2 = S_1^2 + S_2^2 + S_3^2. \tag{4.7}$$

The Stokes parameters are real observable quantities expressed in terms of optical intensities or radiometric energies. The S_0 term describes the total energy in a beam. The S_1 term describes the amount of linear horizontal or vertical polarization. The S_2 term describes the amount of linear ±45-deg polarization and the S_3 term describes the amount of right- or left-handed circular polarization. For partially polarized EM radiation sampled over a finite time, we find that $S_0^2 \geq S_1^2 + S_2^2 + S_3^2$. We also can express the *polarization angle*, introduced in Eq. (3.29), in terms of the Stokes parameters, since

$$\tan 2\psi = \frac{2\mathcal{E}_{0x}\mathcal{E}_{0y}\cos\phi}{\mathcal{E}_{0x}^2 - \mathcal{E}_{0y}^2} = \frac{S_2}{S_1}, \tag{4.8}$$

yielding

$$\psi = \frac{1}{2}\tan^{-1}\left(\frac{S_2}{S_1}\right). \tag{4.9}$$

The special (degenerate) cases discussed in Sec. 3.3 can be expressed in terms of the Stokes parameters. The expressions below show the Stokes parameter representations for fully polarized radiation.

Linear horizontal polarization (LHP): $\mathcal{E}_{0y} = 0$

$$\begin{aligned} S_0 &= \mathcal{E}_{0x}^2 \\ S_1 &= \mathcal{E}_{0x}^2 \\ S_2 &= 0 \\ S_3 &= 0 \end{aligned} \tag{4.10}$$

Linear vertical polarization (LVP): $\mathcal{E}_{0x} = 0$

$$\begin{aligned} S_0 &= \mathcal{E}_{0y}^2 \\ S_1 &= -\mathcal{E}_{0y}^2 \\ S_2 &= 0 \\ S_3 &= 0 \end{aligned} \tag{4.11}$$

Linear +45-deg polarization (L+45): $\phi = 0$, $\mathcal{E}_{0x} = \mathcal{E}_{0y} = \mathcal{E}_0$

$$\begin{aligned} S_0 &= 2\mathcal{E}_0^2 \\ S_1 &= 0 \\ S_2 &= 2\mathcal{E}_0^2 \\ S_3 &= 0 \end{aligned} \tag{4.12}$$

Linear −45-deg polarization (L−45): $\phi = \pi$, $\mathcal{E}_{0x} = \mathcal{E}_{0y} = \mathcal{E}_0$

$$\begin{aligned} S_0 &= 2\mathcal{E}_0^2 \\ S_1 &= 0 \\ S_2 &= -2\mathcal{E}_0^2 \\ S_3 &= 0 \end{aligned} \tag{4.13}$$

Right circular polarization (RCP): $\phi = (\pi/2)$, $\mathcal{E}_{0x} = \mathcal{E}_{0y} = \mathcal{E}_0$

$$\begin{aligned} S_0 &= 2\mathcal{E}_0^2 \\ S_1 &= 0 \\ S_2 &- 0 \\ S_3 &= 2\mathcal{E}_0^2 \end{aligned} \tag{4.14}$$

Left circular polarization (LCP): $\phi = (3/2)\pi$, $\mathcal{E}_{0x} = \mathcal{E}_{0y} = \mathcal{E}_0$

$$\begin{aligned} S_0 &= 2\mathcal{E}_0^2 \\ S_1 &= 0 \\ S_2 &= 0 \\ S_3 &= -2\mathcal{E}_0^2 \end{aligned} \tag{4.15}$$

Note that the L±45, RCP, and LCP beams as defined above have twice the total energy as the LHP and LVP beams. If $\mathcal{E}_{0x} = \mathcal{E}_{0y} = 1/\sqrt{2}\,\mathcal{E}_0$ in the L±45, RCP, and LCP beams, then $S_0 = \mathcal{E}_0^2$ in all cases (i.e., we would have the same energy in all the beams).

4.2 Stokes Vector Representation

The Stokes parameters are often arranged into a column vector for convenience of representation (i.e., they have no directional character). This yields

$$\mathbf{S} = \begin{bmatrix} S_0 \\ S_1 \\ S_2 \\ S_3 \end{bmatrix} = \begin{bmatrix} \mathcal{E}_{0x}^2 + \mathcal{E}_{0y}^2 \\ \mathcal{E}_{0x}^2 - \mathcal{E}_{0y}^2 \\ 2\mathcal{E}_{0x}\mathcal{E}_{0y}\cos\phi \\ 2\mathcal{E}_{0x}\mathcal{E}_{0y}\sin\phi \end{bmatrix}. \tag{4.16}$$

Note that we have introduced a notational convention which uses **bold** parameters to represent vectors and matrices. We will also use an arrow over a parameter at times to indicate a vector quantity when the directional character of the vector is important. The *Stokes vector* can be expressed in terms of the S_0 component (i.e., optical intensity or radiometric energy) times a normalized vector that yields

$$\mathbf{S} = S_0 \begin{bmatrix} \frac{S_0}{S_0} \\ \frac{S_1}{S_0} \\ \frac{S_2}{S_0} \\ \frac{S_3}{S_0} \end{bmatrix}. \tag{4.17}$$

For the special cases introduced above, this would yield

$$\mathbf{S}_{\mathrm{LHP}} = \mathcal{E}_0^2 \begin{bmatrix} 1 \\ 1 \\ 0 \\ 0 \end{bmatrix} \tag{4.18}$$

for linear horizontal polarization,

$$\mathbf{S}_{\mathrm{LVP}} = \mathcal{E}_0^2 \begin{bmatrix} 1 \\ -1 \\ 0 \\ 0 \end{bmatrix} \tag{4.19}$$

for linear vertical polarization,

$$\mathbf{S}_{L+45} = 2\mathcal{E}_0^2 \begin{bmatrix} 1 \\ 0 \\ 1 \\ 0 \end{bmatrix} \tag{4.20}$$

for linear +45-deg polarization,

$$\mathbf{S}_{L-45} = 2\mathcal{E}_0^2 \begin{bmatrix} 1 \\ 0 \\ -1 \\ 0 \end{bmatrix} \tag{4.21}$$

for linear –45-deg polarization,

$$\mathbf{S}_{RCP} = 2\mathcal{E}_0^2 \begin{bmatrix} 1 \\ 0 \\ 0 \\ 1 \end{bmatrix} \tag{4.22}$$

for right circular polarization, and

$$\mathbf{S}_{LCP} = 2\mathcal{E}_0^2 \begin{bmatrix} 1 \\ 0 \\ 0 \\ -1 \end{bmatrix} \tag{4.23}$$

for left circular polarization.

It is also common to refer to the normalized vector as the Stokes vector. This is convenient because the magnitude term is proportional to radiometric energy and can be replaced with any radiometric value to represent how much of the term is observable at each polarization.

Thus, an alternative representation is

$$\begin{bmatrix} E \\ E_H \\ E_{45} \\ E_C \end{bmatrix} = E\mathbf{S}, \tag{4.24}$$

where E is the scalar irradiance [W/m²], E_H is the horizontally polarized component of E, E_{45} is the +45 polarized component of E, E_C is the right circularly polarized component (note that negative values indicate vertical, −45-deg or left circular polarizations, respectively), and **S** is the S_0 normalized Stokes vector, i.e.,

$$\mathbf{S} = \begin{bmatrix} 1 \\ \frac{S_1}{S_0} \\ \frac{S_2}{S_0} \\ \frac{S_3}{S_0} \end{bmatrix}. \tag{4.25}$$

4.3 Methods to Characterize and Interpret Stokes Vectors

In most cases, EM radiation can be thought of as a combination of randomly polarized radiation and polarized radiation. If our sensor is insensitive to polarization (responds to all polarizations equally), then we need only address the aggregate average flux. On the other hand, if our sensor, either by design or by happenstance, is polarization sensitive, then we need to focus on the relative response of the sensor to different states of polarization. To address these cases, we will use the Stokes vector terminology, as it characterizes the time-averaged polarization state most directly applicable to operational sensing. The Stokes vector associated with a beam can be directly related to a simple set of measurements of the irradiance transmitted through a conceptual set of filters, as illustrated in Fig. 4.1 [see Stokes (1852)]. The filters are four linear polarizers oriented as shown and a right- and left-hand circular polarizer. All have nominal transmittance values of 50% to randomly polarized radiation (in practice, corrections must be made for actual transmittance values). The unnormalized Stokes parameters ($\hat{S}$) can then be calculated as

$$\hat{S}_0 = E_H + E_V\,, \tag{4.26}$$

$$\hat{S}_1 = E_H - E_V\,, \tag{4.27}$$

$$\hat{S}_2 = E_{+45} - E_{-45}\,, \tag{4.28}$$

and

$$\hat{S}_3 = E_R - E_L\,, \tag{4.29}$$

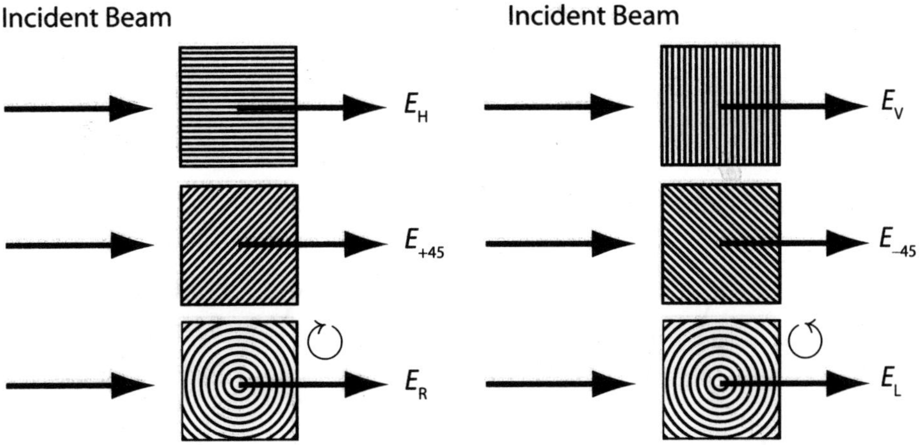

Figure 4.1 Polarization filters used to characterize the Stokes vector.

where $\hat{S}_0$ is the incident irradiance, and $\hat{S}_1$ is related to horizontal polarization (assuming the E_H polarizer is oriented to transmit horizontally polarized radiation) and will be positive when horizontal radiation dominates vertical and vice versa. $\hat{S}_2$ is related to polarization at 45-deg to the horizontal and will be positive when +45-deg polarization dominates 45 deg and vice versa. $\hat{S}_3$ is related to circular polarization and will be positive when right-hand polarization dominates left and vice versa. E_H through E_L are the measured irradiance values as illustrated in Fig. 4.1. In practice, we will see that the Stokes vector can be calculated from a simpler set of measurements. However, Fig. 4.1 helps to reinforce the meaning of the Stokes parameters.

As described in Eq. (4.25), the Stokes parameters are often normalized through division by the $\hat{S}_0$ value and collected into a vector that carries the polarization characteristics of the ray:

$$\mathbf{S} = \begin{bmatrix} \hat{S}_0 / \hat{S}_0 \\ \hat{S}_1 / \hat{S}_0 \\ \hat{S}_2 / \hat{S}_0 \\ \hat{S}_3 / \hat{S}_0 \end{bmatrix} = \begin{bmatrix} S_0 \\ S_1 \\ S_2 \\ S_3 \end{bmatrix} = \begin{bmatrix} 1 \\ S_1 \\ S_2 \\ S_3 \end{bmatrix}. \tag{4.30}$$

There are several potential methods to filter incoming radiation for measuring the linear Stokes parameters as shown in Fig. 4.2. Note that for passive remote sensing purposes, the degree of circular polarization is usually so small that we often only attempt to characterize the linear polarization state of a beam. A wide range of methods for sensing polarized radiation have been developed and will be discussed in more detail in Chapter 8. Table 4.1 and Fig. 4.3 aid in the intuitive analysis of some of the Stokes vectors.

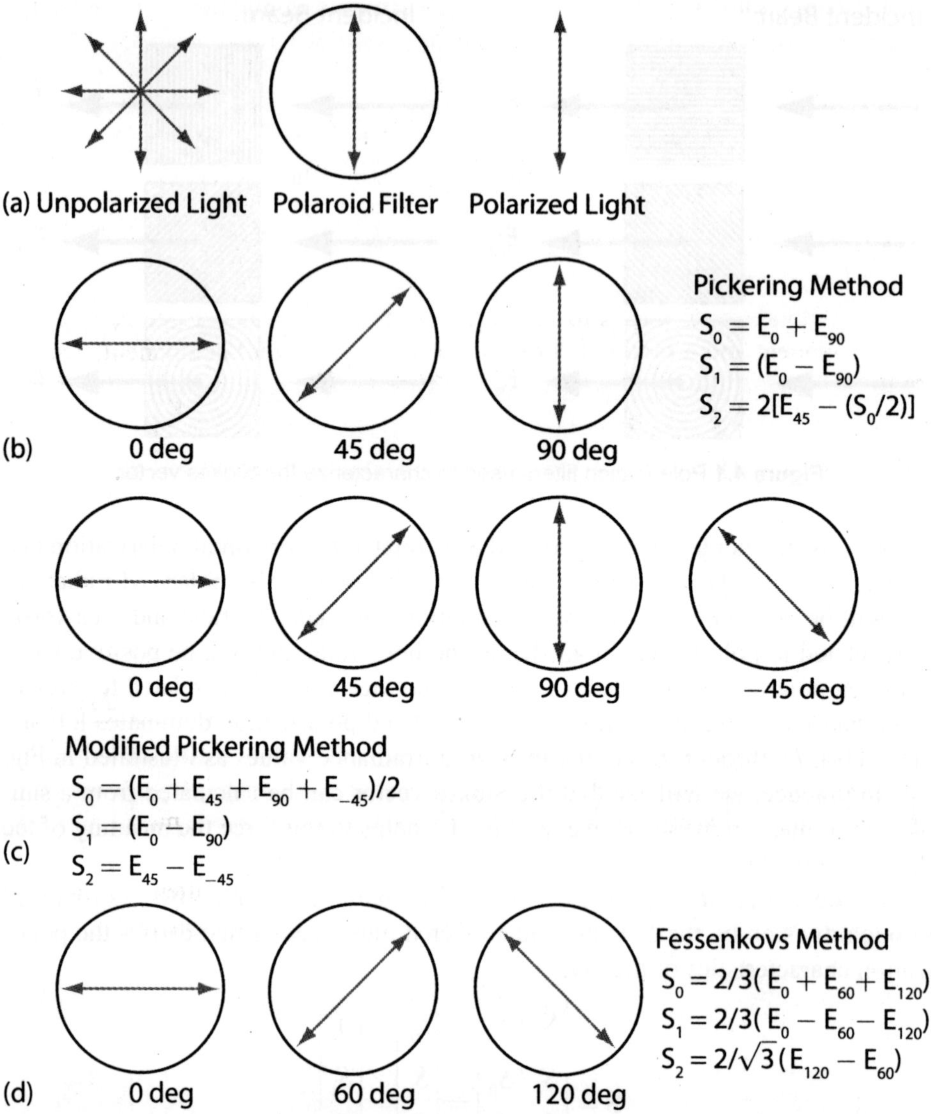

Figure 4.2 Methods to characterize Stokes vectors. Note that $E_{\varnothing}$ is the irradiance measured with the linear polarizer oriented to transmit at an angle $\varnothing$ measured from the horizontal. (See Chapter 8 for a more complete treatment.)

Table 4.1 Characterization of the polarization state based on the signs of the Stokes parameters.

Parameter	Positive	Negative
S_1	Horizontal dominates	Vertical dominates
S_2	+45 dominates	–45 dominates
S_3	Right-hand circular dominates	Left-hand circular dominates

It is important to recognize that the polarimetric components of the Stokes vectors are additive (i.e., they obey linear superposition), thus

$$\mathbf{S}_C = \mathbf{S}_A + \mathbf{S}_B = \begin{bmatrix} S_{A0} \\ S_{A1} \\ S_{A2} \\ S_{A3} \end{bmatrix} + \begin{bmatrix} S_{B0} \\ S_{B1} \\ S_{B2} \\ S_{B3} \end{bmatrix} = \begin{bmatrix} S_{A0} + S_{B0} \\ S_{A1} + S_{B1} \\ S_{A2} + S_{B2} \\ S_{A3} + S_{B3} \end{bmatrix} = \begin{bmatrix} S_{C0} \\ S_{C1} \\ S_{C2} \\ S_{C3} \end{bmatrix}. \tag{4.31}$$

This leads to a simple means to describe a beam in terms of a completely polarized component and a randomly polarized (i.e., unpolarized) component, according to

$$\mathbf{S}_{TOT} = \begin{bmatrix} \mathrm{DoP} \cdot S_0 \\ S_1 \\ S_2 \\ S_3 \end{bmatrix} + (1 - \mathrm{DoP}) \begin{bmatrix} S_0 \\ 0 \\ 0 \\ 0 \end{bmatrix}, \tag{4.32}$$

Polarization State	Symbol	Stokes Vector	Polarization State	Symbol	Stokes Vector
Horizontal	↔ ⊥ S	$\begin{pmatrix}1\\1\\0\\0\end{pmatrix}$	Vertical	↕ ∥ P	$\begin{pmatrix}1\\-1\\0\\0\end{pmatrix}$
Linear +45 deg	⤢	$\begin{pmatrix}1\\0\\1\\0\end{pmatrix}$	Linear −45 deg	⤡	$\begin{pmatrix}1\\0\\-1\\0\end{pmatrix}$
Right-Hand Circular	↻	$\begin{pmatrix}1\\0\\0\\1\end{pmatrix}$	Left-Hand Circular	↺	$\begin{pmatrix}1\\0\\0\\-1\end{pmatrix}$
Random	*	$\begin{pmatrix}1\\0\\0\\0\end{pmatrix}$			

Figure 4.3 Stokes vectors.

where we define the *degree of polarization* (DoP) using the Stokes parameters for the total beam as

$$\text{DoP} = \frac{\sqrt{S_1^2 + S_2^2 + S_3^2}}{S_0} \tag{4.33}$$

and the *degree of linear polarization* (DoLP) as

$$\text{DoLP} = \frac{\sqrt{S_1^2 + S_2^2}}{S_0}, \tag{4.34}$$

which, if $S_3 \simeq 0$, as is often the case for passive sensing, yields

$$\text{DoP} \approx \text{DoLP} = \frac{\sqrt{S_1^2 + S_2^2}}{S_0}. \tag{4.35}$$

Finally, in closing this section, it is important to recognize that the reference frame in which we define the polarization orientation for Stokes vector characterization may change several times during the analysis of a problem. For example, our initial Stokes vectors may be defined relative to the solar illumination plane, (i.e., z is along the beam, y is in the illumination plane, and x is perpendicular to the plane). From a target material standpoint, the incident and reflected Stokes vector will typically be defined in a *target-referenced coordinate space* (i.e., relative to the target normal). Finally, the Stokes vector setup for analysis by the sensor will typically be in a reference frame defined by the target-sensor plane, (i.e., z along the beam, y in the target-sensor plane and x perpendicular to the target-sensor plane (Fig. 4.4)). Figure 4.5 shows a simple rotation of the horizontal reference axis through an angle θ_R. The Stokes vector associated with this new reference axis can be defined by

$$\mathbf{S}_\theta = \mathbf{R}(\theta)\mathbf{S}$$

$$\begin{bmatrix} S_0 \\ S_1 \\ S_2 \\ S_3 \end{bmatrix}_\theta = \begin{bmatrix} 1 & 0 & 0 & 0 \\ 0 & \cos 2\theta_R & \sin 2\theta_R & 0 \\ 0 & -\sin 2\theta_R & \cos 2\theta_R & 0 \\ 0 & 0 & 0 & 1 \end{bmatrix} \begin{bmatrix} S_0 \\ S_1 \\ S_2 \\ S_3 \end{bmatrix}, \tag{4.36}$$

where $\mathbf{S}_\theta$ is the Stokes vector in the rotational frame, $\mathbf{S}$ is the original Stokes vector, and $\mathbf{R}(\theta)$ is the *rotation matrix* associated with a rotation of the horizontal axis through an angle θ_R. Note that rotation has no impact on S_0 or S_3, since the magnitude of the radiometric term is unchanged and rotation about the z axis will not change the amount of circular polarization. Rotation also has no effect on the overall DoP; it only changes the relative amounts of the S_1 and S_2 components. It is also important to note that rotation through θ_R about the axis of propagation

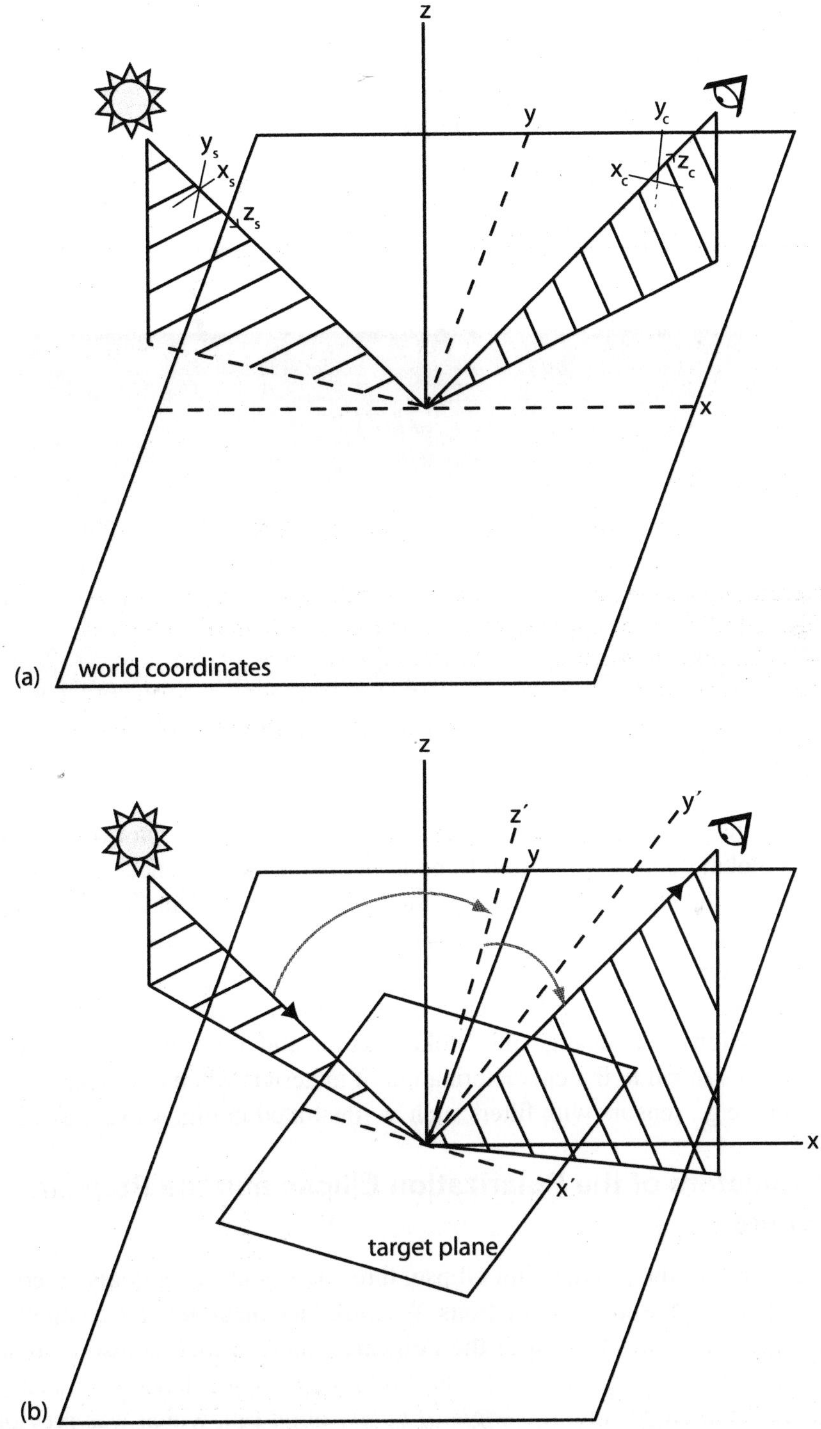

Figure 4.4 Polarimetric reference frames: (a) Illustration of polarization reference frames for the solar illumination plane(s) and camera view plane. (b) Illumination and view planes defined relative to the tilted target (x′,y′) plane and the target normal (z′).

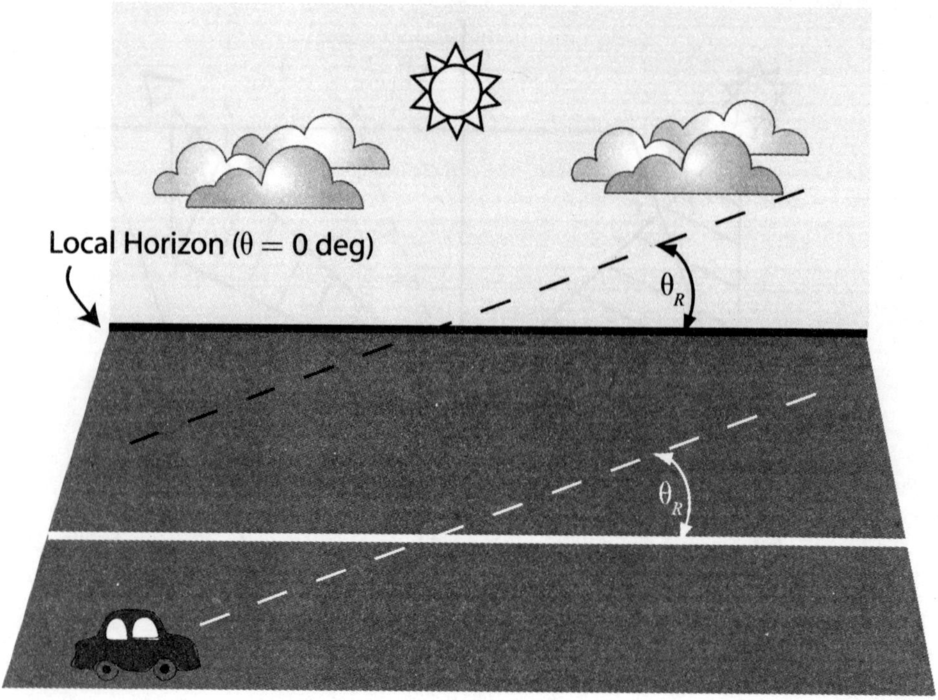

Figure 4.5 Geometry of imaging system alignment or the rotation of a given Stokes vector about the sensor line of sight.

also rotates the y axis. Thus, if we want to redefine a Stokes vector originally defined in a global coordinate system to be in the plane of incidence, it is sufficient to account for the change in rotation of the normal vector about the z axis (and to ascertain the zenith and azimuthal angles). We will return to this concept in more detail in Chapter 7.

We will see in Chapter 5 how each energy-matter interaction (e.g., reflection and transmission) will change the Stokes vector and how in certain cases the Stokes vector can aid in the characterization of materials when polarization-sensitive sensors (e.g., sensors with filters such as illustrated in Fig. 4.1) are available.

4.4 Parameters of the Polarization Ellipse and the Poincaré Sphere

When referring to the polarization ellipse, three angles are commonly referred to in the literature and used in calculations. We introduce them here for completeness and to support the introduction of the Poincaré sphere, which is also commonly used to characterize the polarization state and polarization behavior of materials.

The relevant angles are: the *angle of polarization* (ψ), which was previously introduced (Fig. 4.6) as

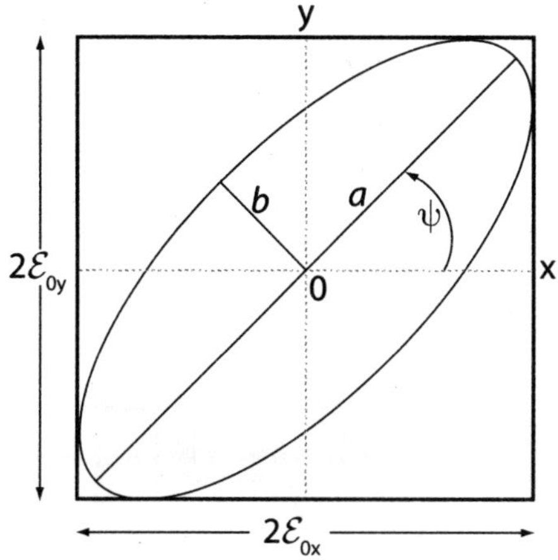

Figure 4.6 Illustration of the polarization ellipse and the polarization angle y (as previously seen in Chapter 3).

$$\tan 2\psi = \frac{2\mathcal{E}_{0x}\mathcal{E}_{0y}}{\mathcal{E}_{0x}^2 - \mathcal{E}_{0y}^2}\cos\phi = \frac{S_2}{S_1} \tag{4.37}$$

and the *auxiliary angle* (α), which is simply

$$\tan\alpha = \frac{\mathcal{E}_{0y}}{\mathcal{E}_{0x}}, \tag{4.38}$$

i.e., it describes the relative magnitude of the maximum amplitudes of the x and y fields.

The *ellipticity angle* (χ), which is defined in terms of the ratio of the minor axis (b) to the major axis (a) of the polarization ellipse as

$$\tan(\chi) = \frac{\pm b}{a}, \tag{4.39}$$

can also be expressed as

$$\sin 2\chi = (\sin 2\alpha)\sin\phi = \frac{2\mathcal{E}_{0x}\mathcal{E}_{0y}\sin\phi}{\mathcal{E}_{0x}^2 + \mathcal{E}_{0y}^2} = \frac{S_3}{S_0}. \tag{4.40}$$

If $\chi = \pm\pi/4$, we have circular polarization and if $\chi = 0$, we have linear polarization (i.e., $b = 0$).

Goldstein (2003) shows that we can express the normalized Stokes vector in terms of the polarization and ellipticity angles as

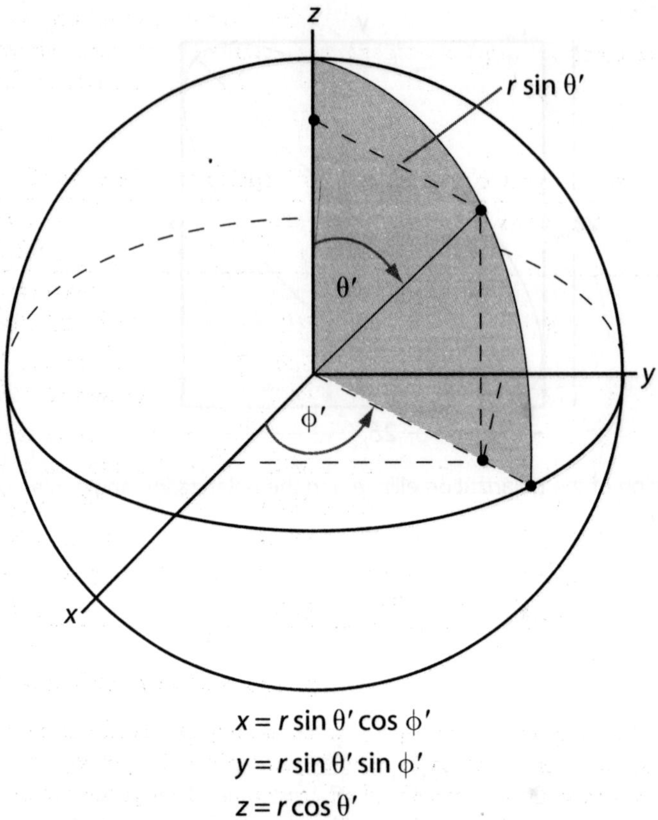

Figure 4.7 Relation between polar and Cartesian coordinates.

$$S = \begin{bmatrix} 1 \\ \cos 2\chi \cos 2\psi \\ \cos 2\chi \sin 2\psi \\ \sin 2\chi \end{bmatrix}. \tag{4.41}$$

He further demonstrates (Fig. 4.7) that the equations relating the polarization angles to the Stokes parameters resemble the equations relating spherical coordinates (r, θ',ϕ') to Cartesian coordinates (x, y, z):

$$x = r \sin\theta' \cos\phi', \tag{4.42a}$$

$$y = r \sin\theta' \sin\phi', \tag{4.42b}$$

$$z = r \cos\theta'. \tag{4.42c}$$

Indeed, if we let $\theta' = (\pi/2) - 2\chi$ and $\phi' = 2\psi$, the equations are identical. This leads to the use of spherical geometry to describe the polarization state of a beam

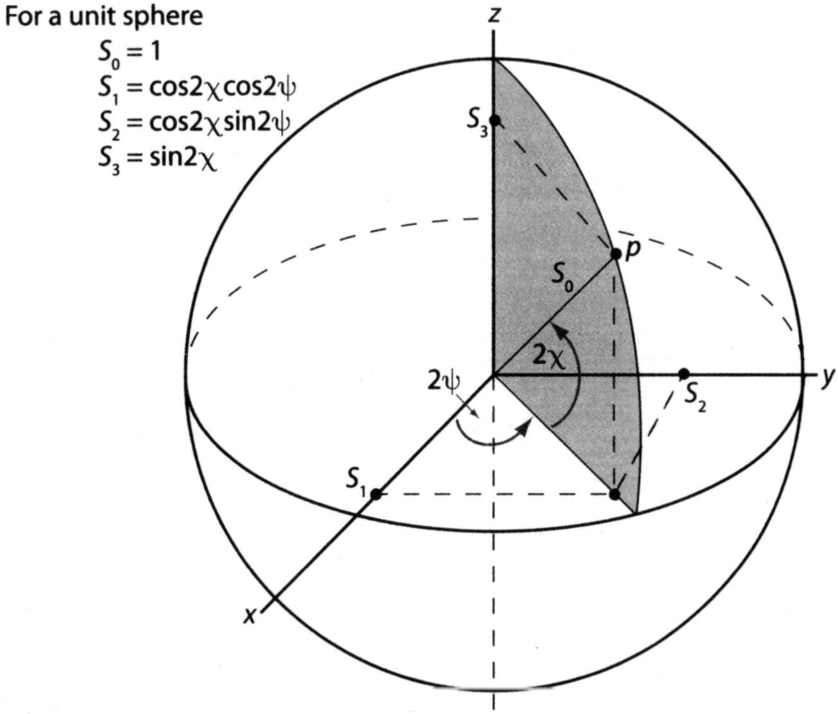

Figure 4.8 The Poincaré sphere used to represent the polarization state of a beam.

in terms of the ellipticity and polarization angles. Figure 4.8 uses a units radius sphere to show the relationship between the normalized Stokes parameters and the polarization and ellipticity angles, which can be expressed as

$$S_0 = 1, \tag{4.43}$$

$$S_1 = \cos 2\chi \cos 2\psi, \tag{4.44}$$

$$S_2 = \cos 2\chi \sin 2\psi, \tag{4.45}$$

and

$$S_3 = \sin 2\chi. \tag{4.46}$$

This use of a spherical projection to describe the polarization state of a beam was derived by Poincaré in 1892 (i.e., prior to the use of Stokes vectors) using a different approach but arriving at the same representation. The *Poincaré sphere*, as it is called, is still often used to represent the polarization state of the beam. Figure 4.9 illustrates the form of the polarization ellipse associated with various polarization and ellipticity angles to aid in developing a more intuitive sense of these parameters. Note that points near the "equator" of the sphere are linearly polarized, while points near the "poles" are circularly polarized.

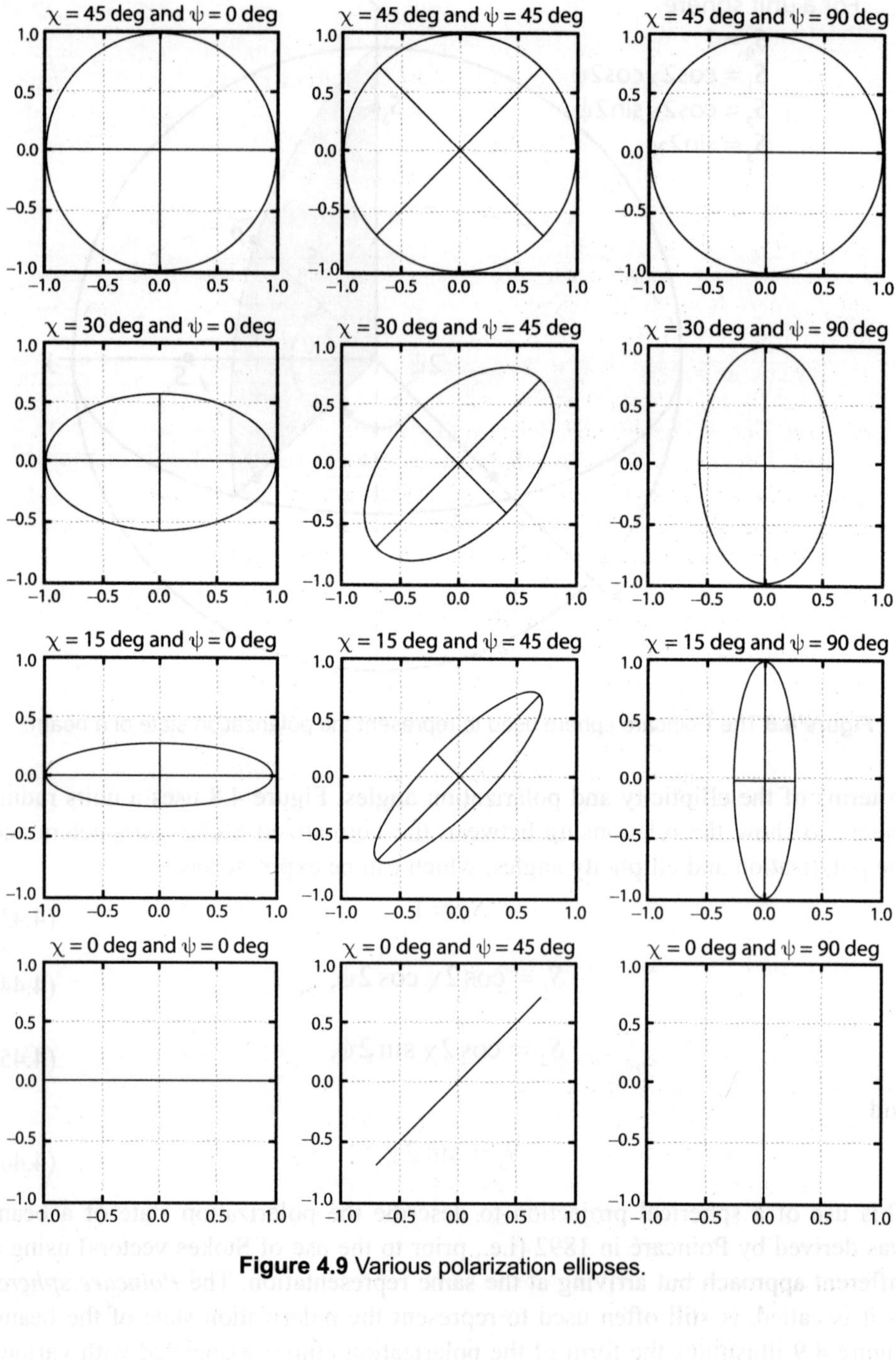

Figure 4.9 Various polarization ellipses.

References

Goldstein, D. (2003). *Polarized Light.* 2nd Ed., Marcel Dekker Inc., New York.

Poincaré, H. (1892). *Theorie Mathematique de la Lumiere II.* Carré, G., ed. (Gauthier-Villars, Paris, 1892), pp. 275–306.

Prosch, T., Hennings, D., & Raschke, E. (1983). "Video polarimetry: a new imaging technique in atmospheric science." *Applied Optics,* Vol. 22, No. 9, pp. 1360–1363.

Solomon, J.E. (1981). "Polarization imaging." *Applied Optics,* Vol. 20, No. 9, pp. 1537–1544.

Stokes, G.G. (1852). "On the composition and resolution of streams of polarized light from different sources." *Transactions of the Cambridge Philosophical Society,* Vol. 9, pp. 399–416. (reprinted in *Mathematical and Physical Papers*, Vol. III, Cambridge University Press, Cambridge, 1901).

Walraven, R. (1981). "Polarization imagery." *Optical Engineering,* Vol. 20, pp. 14–18.

John R. Schott

Chapter 5
Polarimetric Interactions: Reflection and Transmission

This chapter introduces the formalism we need to describe the interaction of a polarized beam with a reflective or transmissive medium. To simplify the discussion, we begin in this chapter with simple optically flat surfaces and move, in Chapter 6, to consideration of the more complex surfaces that represent the surfaces we wish to remotely sense. This chapter draws on classic texts on optics and polarization [e.g., Hecht (1990) and Goldstein (2003)], to which the reader is referred for a more thorough treatment.

5.1 Fresnel Specular Reflection

In Chapter 2 we introduced the concept of total reflection as the ratio of the exittance from a surface to the irradiance onto a surface and a similar term for the transmission. Fresnel (1866) showed that for radiation normally incident onto a planar dielectric surface (i.e., an optically flat surface), the reflectivity is a function only of the *index of refraction* of the two media and can be expressed as

$$r = \left(\frac{n_2 - n_1}{n_2 + n_1}\right)^2, \tag{5.1}$$

where n_1 is the index of refraction in the medium in which the wave is propagating (often air) and n_2 is the index of refraction of the second medium (i.e., the reflecting surface). If the medium is opaque, then the remainder of the energy is absorbed (i.e., $1-r$). If the medium is transmissive, the transmission through the interface is simply $\tau = 1-r$. For the more general case of radiation incident from an arbitrary angle, we must take into account the polarized nature of radiation.

Referring to Fig. 5.1 for reflection of radiation that is not incident normal to a surface, the *Fresnel surface reflection* can be expressed for radiation polarized perpendicular to the plane of incident flux as

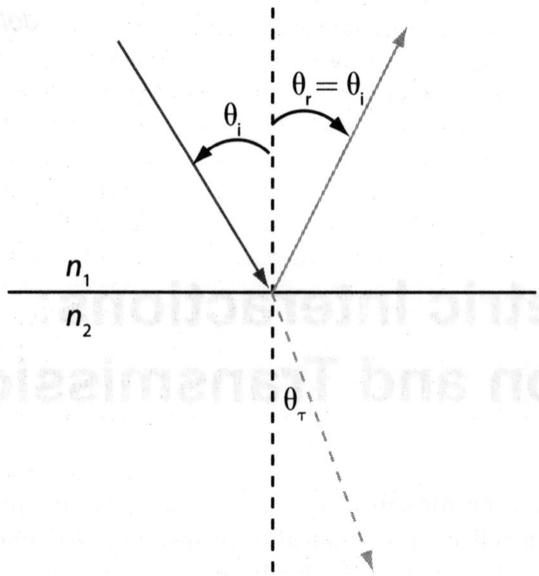

Figure 5.1 Illustration of parameters used in Fresnel surface reflectance and transmittance calculations.

$$r_\perp(\theta_i) = \left[\frac{(n^2 - \sin^2\theta_i)^{\frac{1}{2}} - \cos\theta_i}{(n^2 - \sin^2\theta_i)^{\frac{1}{2}} + \cos\theta_i}\right]^2 = [R_\perp]^2, \tag{5.2}$$

where $n = n_2/n_1$ is the relative index of refraction and $R_\perp$ is the *Fresnel reflectance coefficient* for the EM field. The *beam transmission* at the interface can be expressed as

$$\tau_{E\perp}(\theta_T) = [1 - r_\perp(\theta_i)]. \tag{5.3}$$

This would be the transmission associated with a collimated beam or the irradiance transmission. The *radiance transmission* (see Fig. 5.2), most commonly used, can be expressed as

$$\tau_{L\perp}(\theta_T) = [1 - r_\perp(\theta_i)]n^2, \tag{5.4}$$

due to the fact that the beam will be narrower in the denser medium. Also recognize that due to *Snell's law*, θ_i and θ_T are related as:

$$n_1 \sin\theta_i = n_2 \sin\theta_T. \tag{5.5}$$

Similarly, for flux polarized in the plane of incidence, the Fresnel surface reflectance can be expressed as:

$$r_\parallel = \left[\frac{n^2\cos\theta_i - (n^2 - \sin^2\theta_i)^{\frac{1}{2}}}{n^2\cos\theta_i + (n^2 - \sin^2\theta_i)^{\frac{1}{2}}}\right]^2 = [R_\parallel]^2, \tag{5.6}$$

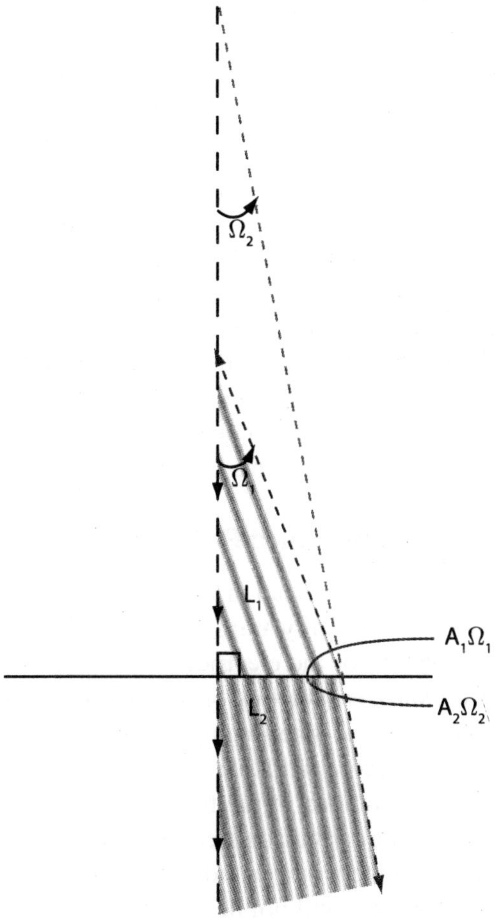

Figure 5.2 Illustration of the concept of radiance transmission where the beam is more dense (i.e., the solid angle is reduced) in the denser medium due to Snell's law increasing the effective transmission (i.e., the radiance transmission τ_L is greater than the beam transmission if $n_2 > n_1$).

where $R_{||}$ is the Fresnel reflectance coefficient for the EM field. The beam transmission can be expressed as

$$\tau_{E||}(\theta_\tau) = (1 - r_{||}), \tag{5.7}$$

and the radiance transmission as:

$$\tau_{L||}(\theta_\tau) = (1 - r_{||})n^2, \tag{5.8}$$

where we have dropped the dependency of r on θ_i for compactness.

For randomly polarized incident flux, the reflection can be computed as the average of the polarized components according to

$$r = \frac{r_{\parallel} + r_{\perp}}{2}. \tag{5.9}$$

Similarly,

$$\tau = \frac{\tau_{\parallel} + \tau_{\perp}}{2}. \tag{5.10}$$

These terms are valid only for optically smooth surfaces or specular reflection (i.e., for optically smooth surfaces, θ_r is equal and opposite to θ_i). More empirical expressions must be used for the irregular surfaces commonly encountered in remote sensing of the earth. For essentially all surfaces of interest for earth remote sensing, we have to treat the surfaces as rough or irregular, so the Fresnel equations are not directly applicable. To deal with these surfaces, Chapter 6 will introduce more involved reflectance terms that build on the Fresnel equations.

5.2 Polarized Transmission and Polarizing Materials

In order to study or sense the polarization state of a beam, we need to have materials (filters) that will differentially transmit or reflect the wave based on the orientation or state of rotation of the electrical field. One common method to do this is with a *wire grid polarizer* (see Fig. 5.3). These devices are made such that the spacing between the wires is small compared to the wavelength. The vector component of the incident electric field that is aligned parallel to the wires will be reflected or will induce oscillations in the filter material electrons that will convert the associated energy into heat dissipated in the wires. Conversely, the vector component perpendicular to the wires cannot induce an appreciable oscillation in the free electrons and therefore, will not be absorbed or reflected. Thus, the ideal wire grid polarizer would pass *all* of the electric field perpendicular to the grid and *none* of the field parallel to the grid. Historically, it was hard to make wire grids at visible wavelengths; however, improvements in microlithography are making it possible to work at shorter wavelengths. Wire grid polarizers are commonly used in the midwave and longwave infrared.

Conveniently, there are both naturally occurring and manmade materials whose structures induce the same effects on the electric field as the wire grid polarizer. The alignment of the crystalline structure can then allow incident flux to induce oscillation in the filter material electrons in one dimension and not the other, and the spacing in the crystalline structure is such that visible light is absorbed. Synthetic materials based on this principle are commercially available. Goldstein and Jones (2006) provide a characterization of these *sheet-polarizer* materials.

Note that these linear polarizers will transmit the vector component of the electric field parallel to the transmission axis of the polarizer (see Fig. 5.4). Thus, if we have a linearly polarized beam whose electric field was oriented at an angle θ from the transmissive axis of the polarizer, we should observe an amplitude of

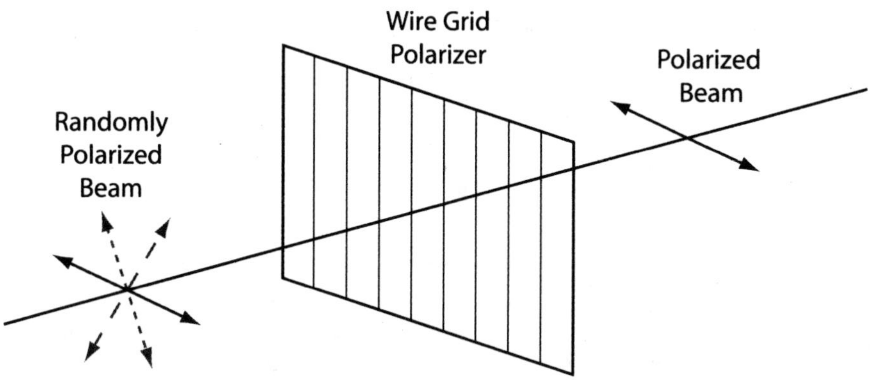

Figure 5.3 Wire grid polarizer. Note that the transmitted field is polarized perpendicularly to the orientation of the wires.

$$\mathcal{E}_{\tau 0} = \mathcal{E}_0 \cos\theta, \tag{5.11}$$

assuming unit transmission along the primary axis and zero transmission at right angles to the primary axis.

Thus, the irradiance in the beam, which is proportional to the square of the field amplitude, would be

$$E_{\tau 0} = E_0 \cos^2\theta \propto \mathcal{E}_0^2 \cos^2\theta, \tag{5.12}$$

where E_0 is the irradiance in the beam before the polarizer.

Note that if we oriented the same polarizing filter at 90 deg (see Fig. 5.4b), we would pass the sine component of θ, resulting in

$$\mathcal{E}_{\tau 90} = \mathcal{E}_0 \sin\theta, \tag{5.13}$$

and giving

$$E_{\tau 90} = E_0 \sin^2\theta \propto \mathcal{E}_0^2 \sin^2\theta \tag{5.14}$$

and

$$E_{\tau 0} + E_{\tau 90} = E_0 \cos^2\theta + E_0 \sin^2\theta = E_0. \tag{5.15}$$

These linear polarizers are often referred to as *analyzers* because they allow us to analyze the polarization state of a beam.

In order to analyze circularly polarized light, we need to introduce the optical elements known as *retarders* or *phase retarders*. These are made of materials in which one of the polarization states (x or y) lags in phase relative to the other as it propagates. Thus, on exiting the material, the relative phase and thus, the state of polarization will be shifted. Of particular interest is the *quarter wave plate*, which has the property of shifting the phase by $\pi/2$. Thus, a right circularly polarized beam that enters with a relative phase angle of $\phi = \pi/2$ emerges with a phase angle of $\phi = 0$ or π (i.e., it is diagonally polarized). If we placed a linear polarizer oriented to pass the diagonally polarized beam, we can use the retarder and the

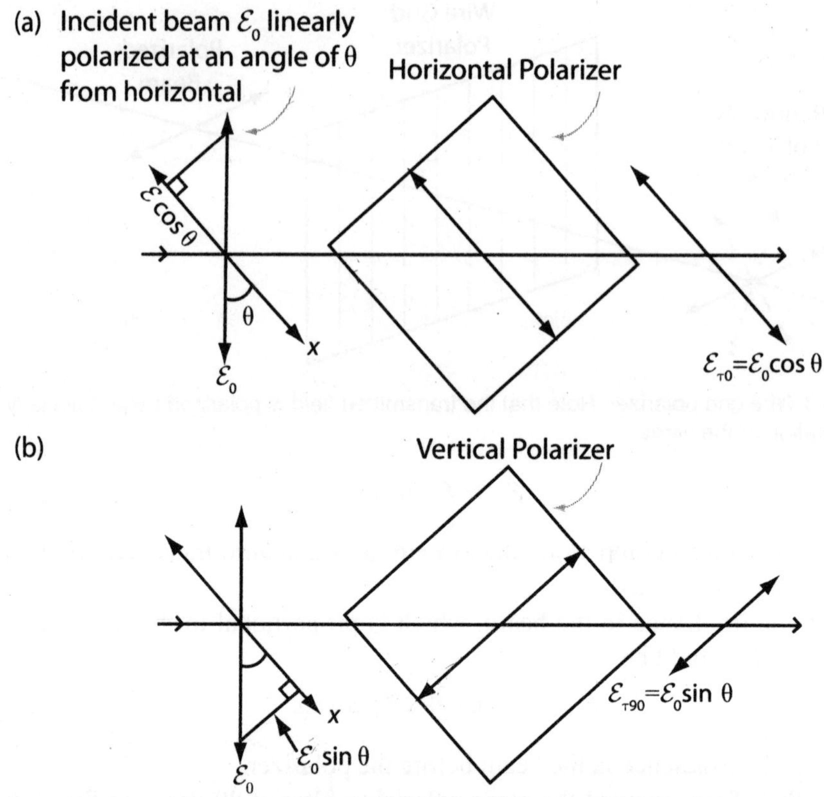

Figure 5.4 Illustration of how linear polarization filters pass the vector component of the electric field amplitude aligned with the polarizer's principal axis.

linear polarizer to form a *circular polarization filter* (see Fig. 5.5). A perfect version of such a filter would have unit transmission for the retarder, and one-half of the flux in a randomly polarized beam would pass through the retarder-analyzer combination. On the other hand, in the ideal case, all of the flux in a completely circularly polarized beam would pass through the retarder-analyzer combination.

Essentially all of the polarization-sensitive instruments we will discuss in Chapter 8 employ to their advantage some form of polarization filter to isolate the polarization of a beam. Regrettably, as we have seen from this discussion, most optical elements can introduce some polarization sensitivity to a beam (i.e., they may polarize to some extent a randomly polarized beam or they may differentially pass a polarized beam). This latter effect is of greatest concern because it will result in different signals out (digital count values) for the same incident radiance level, depending on the polarization state of the beam. This results in instruments calibrated with randomly polarized flux being miscalibrated for polarized flux. Therefore, we need to design nonpolarimetric instruments that are insensitive to

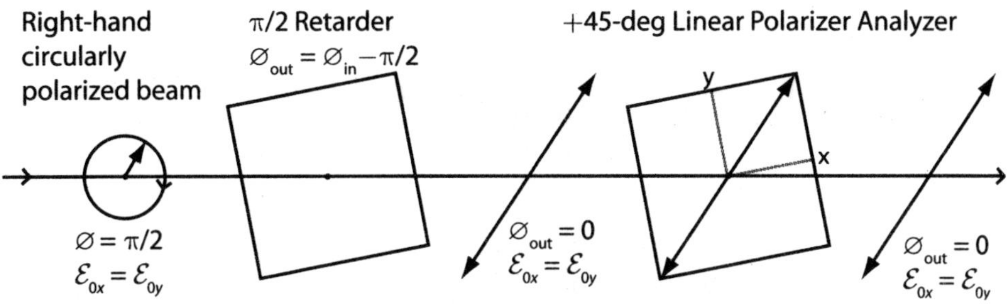

Figure 5.5 Use of a quarter wave plate (π/2 retarder) and a +45-deg linear polarizer to form a circular polarization filter. Note that left circular polarization would be completely blocked and a randomly polarized beam would be 50% transmitted for the ideal case.

polarization orientation and to carefully characterize the polarization sensitivity of all instruments.

5.3 The Mueller Matrix: Polarimetric Energy-Matter Interactions

Having developed a method to characterize the polarization behavior of a beam using the Stokes vector representation, we would like to have a means of describing the interaction of a beam with a transmitting or reflecting element. The *Mueller matrix* representation of an optical interaction provides the answer by relating the Stokes vector incident on the element ($\mathbf{S}_{in}$) to the Stokes vector, leaving the element ($\mathbf{S}_{out}$), according to

$$\mathbf{S}_{out} = \mathbf{M}\,\mathbf{S}_{in} \tag{5.16a}$$

$$\begin{bmatrix} S_0 \\ S_1 \\ S_2 \\ S_3 \end{bmatrix}_{out} = \begin{bmatrix} m_{00} & m_{01} & m_{02} & m_{03} \\ m_{10} & m_{11} & m_{12} & m_{13} \\ m_{20} & m_{21} & m_{22} & m_{23} \\ m_{30} & m_{31} & m_{32} & m_{33} \end{bmatrix} \begin{bmatrix} S_0 \\ S_1 \\ S_2 \\ S_3 \end{bmatrix}_{in}, \tag{5.16b}$$

where **M** is the Mueller matrix representing the energy exchange at the optical element [Mueller (1943)].

Several transmissive Mueller matrices are listed here as examples:

$$\mathbf{T}_{\ominus} = \frac{1}{2}\begin{bmatrix} 1 & 1 & 0 & 0 \\ 1 & 1 & 0 & 0 \\ 0 & 0 & 0 & 0 \\ 0 & 0 & 0 & 0 \end{bmatrix}, \text{ ideal horizontal polarizer,} \tag{5.17}$$

$$\mathbf{T}_{\Phi} = \frac{1}{2}\begin{bmatrix} 1 & -1 & 0 & 0 \\ -1 & 1 & 0 & 0 \\ 0 & 0 & 0 & 0 \\ 0 & 0 & 0 & 0 \end{bmatrix}, \text{ideal vertical polarizer,} \tag{5.18}$$

$$\mathbf{T}_{\oslash} = \frac{1}{2}\begin{bmatrix} 1 & 0 & 1 & 0 \\ 0 & 0 & 0 & 0 \\ 1 & 0 & 1 & 0 \\ 0 & 0 & 0 & 0 \end{bmatrix}, \text{ideal 45-deg linear polarizer,} \tag{5.19}$$

and

$$\mathbf{T}_{\otimes} = \frac{1}{2}\begin{bmatrix} 1 & 0 & -1 & 0 \\ 0 & 0 & 0 & 0 \\ -1 & 0 & 1 & 0 \\ 0 & 0 & 0 & 0 \end{bmatrix}, \text{ideal } -45\text{-deg linear polarizer,} \tag{5.20}$$

$$\mathbf{T}_{\mathrm{ND}} = \tau_{\mathrm{ND}}\begin{bmatrix} 1 & 0 & 0 & 0 \\ 0 & 1 & 0 & 0 \\ 0 & 0 & 1 & 0 \\ 0 & 0 & 0 & 1 \end{bmatrix}, \text{neutral density filter,} \tag{5.21}$$

with a *neutral density* value of (ND), i.e., this filter will have no effect except to reduce the amount of energy by ND (i.e., $\tau_{\mathrm{ND}} = 10^{-\mathrm{ND}}$) and finally,

$$\mathbf{T}_{\mathrm{dep}} = \begin{bmatrix} 1 & 0 & 0 & 0 \\ 0 & 0 & 0 & 0 \\ 0 & 0 & 0 & 0 \\ 0 & 0 & 0 & 0 \end{bmatrix}, \text{ideal depolarizing filter.} \tag{5.22}$$

It is important to note that the net effect of multiple filters is simply the ordered product of the Mueller matrices of the individual filters. Consider the following examples.

$$\mathbf{S}_{\mathrm{out}} = \mathbf{T}_{\ominus}\begin{bmatrix} 1 \\ 1 \\ 0 \\ 0 \end{bmatrix} = \frac{1}{2}\begin{bmatrix} 1 & 1 & 0 & 0 \\ 1 & 1 & 0 & 0 \\ 0 & 0 & 0 & 0 \\ 0 & 0 & 0 & 0 \end{bmatrix}\begin{bmatrix} 1 \\ 1 \\ 0 \\ 0 \end{bmatrix} = \frac{1}{2}\begin{bmatrix} 2 \\ 2 \\ 0 \\ 0 \end{bmatrix} = \begin{bmatrix} 1 \\ 1 \\ 0 \\ 0 \end{bmatrix}, \tag{5.23}$$

i.e., horizontally polarized radiation will pass unobstructed through an ideal horizontal polarizer.

$$\mathbf{S}_{out} = \mathbf{T}_{\oslash}\begin{bmatrix}1\\1\\0\\0\end{bmatrix} = \frac{1}{2}\begin{bmatrix}1 & 0 & 1 & 0\\0 & 0 & 0 & 0\\1 & 0 & 1 & 0\\0 & 0 & 0 & 0\end{bmatrix}\begin{bmatrix}1\\1\\0\\0\end{bmatrix} = \frac{1}{2}\begin{bmatrix}1\\0\\1\\0\end{bmatrix} = \begin{bmatrix}\frac{1}{2}\\0\\\frac{1}{2}\\0\end{bmatrix}, \tag{5.24}$$

i.e., horizontally polarized light will pass through an ideal 45-deg linear polarizer with 50% attenuation.

Consider the following somewhat counterintuitive example of a +45-deg linear polarizer followed by a vertical polarizing filter operating on a horizontally polarized beam:

$$\mathbf{S}_{out} = \mathbf{T}_{\Phi}\mathbf{T}_{\oslash}\begin{bmatrix}1\\1\\0\\0\end{bmatrix}. \tag{5.25}$$

Taking advantage of Eq. (5.24), this can be expressed as

$$\mathbf{S}_{out} = \mathbf{T}_{\Phi}\begin{bmatrix}\frac{1}{2}\\0\\\frac{1}{2}\\0\end{bmatrix} = \frac{1}{2}\begin{bmatrix}1 & -1 & 0 & 0\\-1 & 1 & 0 & 0\\0 & 0 & 0 & 0\\0 & 0 & 0 & 0\end{bmatrix}\begin{bmatrix}\frac{1}{2}\\0\\\frac{1}{2}\\0\end{bmatrix} = \frac{1}{2}\begin{bmatrix}\frac{1}{2}\\-\frac{1}{2}\\0\\0\end{bmatrix} = \begin{bmatrix}\frac{1}{4}\\-\frac{1}{4}\\0\\0\end{bmatrix}, \tag{5.26}$$

yielding a vertically polarized beam with one-fourth the energy.

The Mueller matrix for a *retarder* can be expressed as

$$\boldsymbol{M}_{\phi} = \begin{bmatrix}1 & 0 & 0 & 0\\0 & 1 & 0 & 0\\0 & 0 & \cos\phi & \sin\phi\\0 & 0 & -\sin\phi & \cos\phi\end{bmatrix}, \tag{5.27}$$

where ϕ is the phase shift of the retarder.

Recall that for a quarter wave plate, $\phi = \pi/2$, resulting in

$$\mathbf{M}_{\varnothing=90} = \begin{bmatrix}1 & 0 & 0 & 0\\0 & 1 & 0 & 0\\0 & 0 & 0 & 1\\0 & 0 & -1 & 0\end{bmatrix}. \tag{5.28}$$

Thus, a quarter wave plate (90-deg retarder) followed by a +45-deg linear polarizer operating on a right circularly polarized beam yields

$$\mathbf{S}_{\mathbf{out}} = \mathbf{T}_{\varnothing}\mathbf{M}_{\varnothing=90}\begin{bmatrix}1\\0\\0\\1\end{bmatrix} \tag{5.29a}$$

$$= \mathbf{T}_{\varnothing}\begin{bmatrix}1 & 0 & 0 & 0\\0 & 1 & 0 & 0\\0 & 0 & 0 & 1\\0 & 0 & -1 & 0\end{bmatrix}\begin{bmatrix}1\\0\\0\\1\end{bmatrix} = \mathbf{T}_{\varnothing}\begin{bmatrix}1\\0\\1\\0\end{bmatrix} \tag{5.29b}$$

$$= \frac{1}{2}\begin{bmatrix}1 & 0 & 1 & 0\\0 & 0 & 0 & 0\\1 & 0 & 1 & 0\\0 & 0 & 0 & 0\end{bmatrix}\begin{bmatrix}1\\0\\1\\0\end{bmatrix} = \frac{1}{2}\begin{bmatrix}2\\0\\2\\0\end{bmatrix} = \begin{bmatrix}1\\0\\1\\0\end{bmatrix}, \tag{5.29c}$$

i.e., the quarter wave retarder transforms the right circularly polarized energy to +45-deg linearly polarized energy (with no loss in energy), which then passes unobstructed through the +45-deg linear polarizer. Note that left circularly polarized light will be completely blocked by the second filter, having been converted to −45-deg linear by the retarder. Randomly polarized flux will be reduced in amplitude by 50% by the retarder-polarizer combination (i.e., the right circular polarization filter). We casually introduced the right circular polarization filter

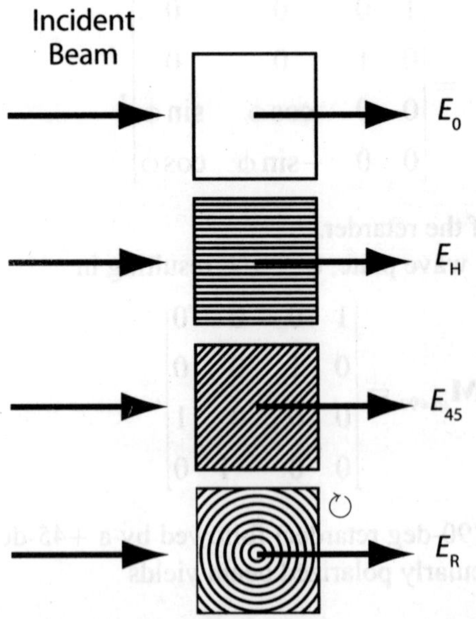

Figure 5.6 Polarization filters used to characterize the Stokes vector.

when we needed a filter set to define the Stokes parameters (see Fig. 5.6). We can now more formally express this filter as the retarder-linear polarizer combination described by Eq. (5.29).

Chang et al. (2002) show that the Mueller matrix representation for polarimetric *Fresnel reflection* of an incident beam expressed as a Stokes vector can be expressed as:

$$\mathbf{S}_R = \begin{bmatrix} S_0 \\ S_1 \\ S_2 \\ S_3 \end{bmatrix}_R = \frac{1}{2}\begin{bmatrix} r_\perp + r_\parallel & r_\perp - r_\parallel & 0 & 0 \\ r_\perp - r_\parallel & r_\perp + r_\parallel & 0 & 0 \\ 0 & 0 & 2\operatorname{Re}(R_\perp R_\parallel^*) & 2\operatorname{Im}(R_\perp R_\parallel^*) \\ 0 & 0 & -2\operatorname{Im}(R_\perp R_\parallel^*) & 2\operatorname{Re}(R_\perp R_\parallel^*) \end{bmatrix}\begin{bmatrix} S_0 \\ S_1 \\ S_2 \\ S_3 \end{bmatrix}, \quad (5.30)$$

where $r_\perp$ and $r_\parallel$ are defined in Eqs. (5.2) and (5.6), respectively, Re and Im represent the real and imagery parts, and the asterisk (*) represents the complex conjugate. This expression is valid only for optically smooth surfaces; as a result, we will need to develop more involved expressions to support the more irregular surfaces of interest for earth observation.

The Mueller matrix, as a way to characterize energy-matter interactions and particularly remotely sensed reflection, will be a cornerstone of the remainder of our discussions.

References

Chang, P.C.Y., Flitton, J.C., Hopcraft, K.I., Jakeman, E., Jordan, D., & Walker, J.G. (2002). "Importance of shadowing and multiple reflections in emission polarization." *Waves in Random Media*, Institute of Physics Publishing, Vol. 12, pp. 1–19.

Fresnel, A. (1866). "Memoire sur la loi des modifications que la reflection imprime a la lumiere polarisee." *Oeuvres Completes de Fresnel*, Vol. 1, H. de Senarmont, E. Verdet, and L. Fresnel.

Hecht, E. (1990). *Optics*. 2nd Ed., Addison-Wesley, Reading, MA.

Goldstein, D.H. (2003). *Polarized Light*. 2nd Ed., Marcel Dekker Inc., New York.

Goldstein, D.H., & Jones, D.G. (2006). "Characterization of commercial sheet polarizer material." *Proceedings of SPIE*, Vol. 6240, 62400J.

Mueller, H. (1943). "Memorandum on the polarization optics of the photo-elastic shutter." Report Number 2 of the OSRD project OEMSr 576.

James R. Shell II
John R. Schott

Chapter 6
Polarimetric Bidirectional Reflectance Distribution Functions (pBRDF)

In this chapter, we begin by introducing the scalar bidirectional reflectance distribution function (BRDF) used to describe directional reflectance. This treatment draws extensively from Schott (2007). We then proceed to describe a polar form of the BRDF or pBRDF and ways to measure and model the pBRDFs of materials. This treatment draws heavily from Shell (2005).

6.1 Bidirectional Reflectance Distribution Functions

In Chapter 2, we introduced the concept of radiance and the constancy of radiance during propagation in a lossless medium. This ease of propagation of radiance makes it the most convenient term to study for most remote sensing applications. However, what we often know is the irradiance onto a target we wish to observe. In order to convert the irradiance onto the target into radiance toward the detector, we need to consider the reflectance properties of materials. In general the reflectance properties are a function of wavelength, illumination angle, viewing angle and the polarization state of the incident flux. We need to develop a means to express the full impact of these dependencies on the reflected radiance and to develop a simpler expression for cases when full angular reflectance data are not available.

6.1.1 Ways to characterize reflectance

In Chapter 2, we introduced what we will now define to be the *total spectral reflectance* as:

$$r(\lambda) = \frac{M_\lambda}{E_\lambda}. \tag{6.1}$$

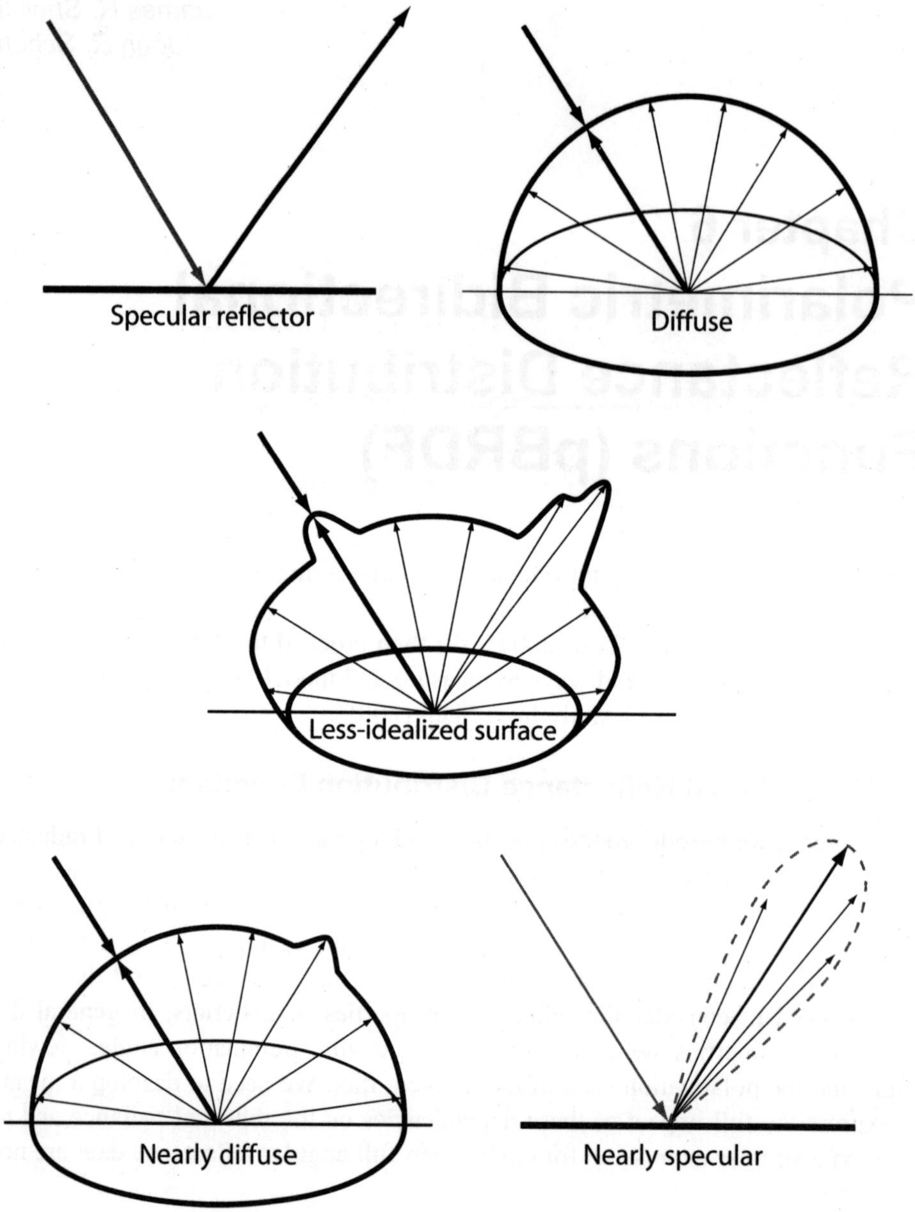

Figure 6.1 Reflectance characteristics of idealized surfaces.

This expression for reflectance, while perfectly valid, fails to provide us with any information about the directional distribution of the reflected flux. Our experience tells us that the directional characteristics of reflectance vary considerably from mirror-like surfaces (*specular*) (discussed in Chapter 5 and behaving according to Fresnel reflection theory) to surfaces that appear to have little or no directional character to their reflectance (*Lambertian* or *diffuse*). In Fig. 6.1, we

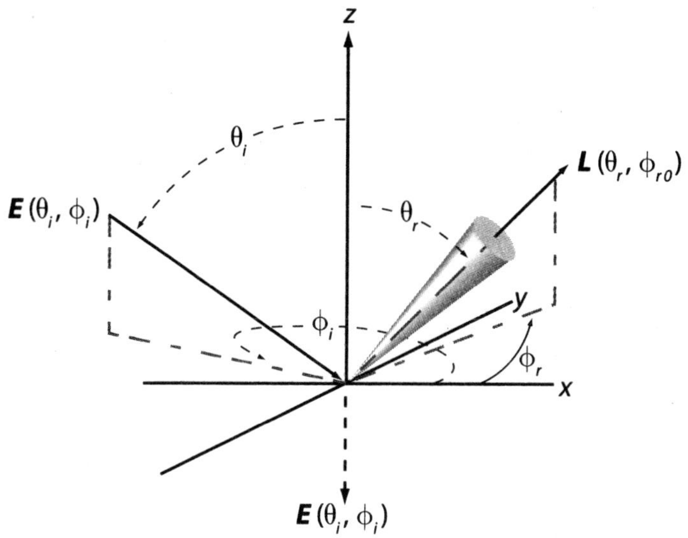

Figure 6.2 Bidirectional reflectance concept.

depict the angular reflectance characteristics of several idealized surfaces, as well as a more complex object. A perfectly specular object behaves like a mirror with flux reflected only into the direction exactly opposite to the incident ray. A nearly specular object will appear to have most of the reflected energy concentrated in a cone about the specular ray.

A perfectly diffuse surface appears to have the same amount of reflectance in all directions, while a nearly diffuse object will generally appear brighter in the specular direction. A less-idealized surface may appear brighter in the specular and backscatter directions and darker when viewed at grazing angles. Rough surfaces, such as tree canopies, will typically have a strong return from the backscatter direction, which is referred to as the "*hot spot.*" Recall that visual brightness or apparent reflectance is directly proportional to radiance, so that the vectors in Fig. 6.1 can be treated as the magnitude of the radiance in each direction. The surface that encloses the vectors can be thought of as a probability distribution function for the radiance in any direction. More formally (cf. Fig. 6.2) we can define the *bidirectional reflectance* to be the ratio of the radiance scattered into the direction described by the orientation angles θ_r and ϕ_r to the irradiance onto the surface from the θ_i, ϕ_i direction, i.e.,

$$f_{\text{BRDF}} = \frac{L(\theta_r, \phi_r)}{E(\theta_i, \phi_i)} [sr^{-1}]. \tag{6.2}$$

The *bidirectional reflectance distribution function* (BRDF) describes these bidirectional reflectance values for all combinations of input-output angles. The BRDF values will also change as a function of wavelength, so a complete characterization would include the wavelength-dependent BRDF, using the spectral values for irradiance and radiance in Eq. (6.2). The BRDF is actually a *scattering function* analogous to the *angular scattering coefficient* ($\beta_{sca}(\lambda,\theta)$) used to describe atmospheric scattering in Chapter 7.

It is often more convenient to describe directional reflectance in a unitless form. This is accomplished by introducing the *bidirectional reflectance factor* (r_{rF}). This is the ratio of the radiance reflected into a particular direction to the radiance that would be reflected into the same direction by a perfect *Lambertian radiator* illuminated in an identical fashion. The perfect Lambertian radiator is defined to have a total reflectivity of unity, and because it is Lambertian, will have the same radiance in all directions. Nicodemus et al. (1977) show how the reflectance factor (r_{rF}) is related to the bidirectional reflectance (r_{BRDF}) through a simple factor of π steradians, i.e.,

$$r_{\mathrm{BRDF}}[\mathrm{sr}^{-1}] = \frac{r_{rF}}{\pi[\mathrm{sr}]}. \tag{6.3}$$

In general, we will omit the *rF* subscript and use reflectance factors for the remainder of our discussion. Either the BRDF or the reflectance factor can be used to relate the incident irradiance from the θ_i, ϕ_i direction to the radiance into the θ_r, ϕ_r, direction according to

$$L(\theta_r,\phi_r) = E(\theta_i,\phi_i)\cos(\theta_i) f(\theta_i,\phi_i,\theta_r,\phi_r) = E(\theta_i,\phi_i)\cos(\theta_i)\frac{r_{rF}}{\pi}\left[\mathrm{W/m^2sr}\right]. \tag{6.4}$$

In addition to the bidirectional reflectance terms, two other terms describing reflectivity are commonly used. The first is the *directional-hemispheric reflectance*. This is the ratio of the exitance from a target to the irradiance onto the target from a particular direction. Conversely, according to reciprocity, it is the ratio of the radiance into a particular direction to the radiance (uniform from all angles) irradiating a target. The final reflectance term of interest is the *diffuse reflectance*. This is best described in reference to the instrumentation commonly used to measure it (cf. Fig. 6.3). The instrument is set up so that all of the flux from the sample is collected by an integrating sphere, with the exception of the flux into a narrow cone about the specular direction. This is compared to a reading from a "perfect" Lambertian reflector measured in the same manner. The diffuse reflectance can then be defined as the hemispheric reflectance with the specular component removed. If the light trap is not used, we measure the total hemispheric reflectance. The ratio of the diffuse reflectance (r_d) to the total reflectance (r_{tot}) provides a measure of the *diffuseness* (d) of the sample, i.e.,

$$d = \frac{r_d}{r_{tot}}. \tag{6.5}$$

A Lambertian reflector would be perfectly diffuse with a diffuseness of one. The more specular (less diffuse) a sample becomes, the lower its diffuseness, with a mirror having a value of zero. The specularity is often defined as one minus the diffuseness. Recognize that whether a surface can be treated as specular (with the

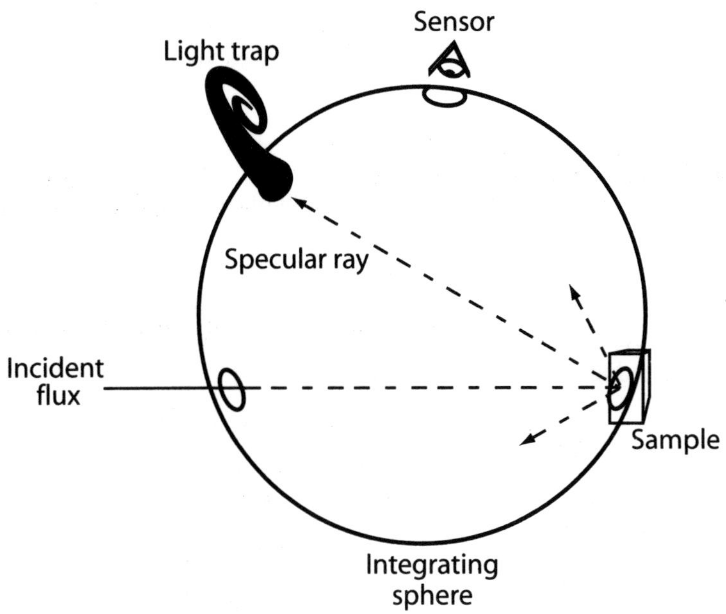

Figure 6.3 Schematic concept for measuring total and diffuse reflectance.

Fresnel equations used to good approximation) or rough (such that BRDF values or Lambertian assumptions are used) is a function of wavelength. A surface that appears smooth to flux at 10 mm may appear quite rough to flux at 0.5 μm.

6.2 Polarimetric Bidirectional Reflectance Distribution Functions (pBRDF)

6.2.1 Specular reflectors

In this section, we want to combine the Mueller matrix formalism introduced in Chapter 5 for describing polarimetric interactions with materials, with the BRDF concepts introduced in the previous section. From a remote sensing phenomenology standpoint, we will need to understand the reflective behavior of a polarized beam that can be captured by reflective Mueller matrices or collectively by the Mueller matrix representations of the polarimetric bidirectional reflectance distribution function (pBRDF).

We introduced the BRDF function and reflectance factors in Sec. 6.1. Using the Mueller matrix and Stokes vector representation, Flynn and Alexander (1995) show that the unpolarized BRDF expression has a polarized equivalent. Accordingly, the scalar expression

$$L = f\,E \tag{6.6a}$$

becomes

$$\mathbf{L} = f\,\mathbf{E}, \tag{6.6b}$$

where L[W/m²sr] is the observed radiance, E[W/m²] is the irradiance incident on the surface, f is the BRDF value [sr^{-1}], **L** is the Stokes vector representation of the radiance, i.e.,

$$\mathbf{L} = L\,\mathbf{S}_{\text{out}}, \tag{6.7}$$

E is the Stokes vector representation of the incident irradiance, i.e.,

$$\mathbf{E} = E\,\mathbf{S}_{\text{in}}, \tag{6.8}$$

f is the Mueller matrix representation of the polarimetric BRDF, and $\mathbf{S}_{\text{out}}$ and $\mathbf{S}_{\text{in}}$ are the normalized Stokes vectors associated with the radiance and irradiance beam. Thus, the radiance can be expressed as

$$\mathbf{L} = \mathrm{L}\begin{bmatrix} S_0 \\ S_1 \\ S_2 \\ S_3 \end{bmatrix}_{\text{out}} = \begin{bmatrix} f_{00} & f_{01} & f_{02} & f_{03} \\ f_{10} & f_{11} & f_{12} & f_{13} \\ f_{20} & f_{21} & f_{22} & f_{23} \\ f_{30} & f_{31} & f_{32} & f_{33} \end{bmatrix} \mathrm{E} \begin{bmatrix} S_0 \\ S_1 \\ S_2 \\ S_3 \end{bmatrix}_{\text{in}}, \tag{6.9}$$

which leads to

$$L_0 = E\,f_{00}\,\mathrm{S}_{0_{\text{in}}} + E\left(f_{01}\,S_{1_{\text{in}}} + f_{02}\,S_{2_{\text{in}}} + f_{03}\,S_{3_{\text{in}}}\right) \tag{6.10}$$

for the first term in the output radiance, which will yield Eq. (6.6a) only if all the terms in parentheses are zero.

Recall from Chapter 5 that we can write expressions for the parallel and perpendicular (Fresnel) reflectance from a planar surface based on the angle of illumination (θ_i) and the index of refraction

$$\hat{n} = n + ik, \tag{6.11}$$

where $\hat{n}$ is the complex index of refraction, n is the real part, k is the imaginary part, and $i = \sqrt{-1}$.

In Eq. (5.30), we introduced the Mueller matrix representation of the Fresnel equations. Goldstein (2003) shows that the *Fresnel reflectance*-based Mueller matrix for reflection from a dielectric plane can also be expressed as (Eq. 8-34 in Goldstein)

$$\mathrm{S_R} = \begin{bmatrix} \mathrm{S_0} \\ \mathrm{S_1} \\ \mathrm{S_2} \\ \mathrm{S_3} \end{bmatrix}_{\mathrm{R}} =$$

$$= \frac{1}{2}\left[\frac{\tan\theta_-}{\sin\theta_+}\right]^2 \begin{bmatrix} \cos^2\theta_- + \cos^2\theta_+ & \cos^2\theta_- - \cos^2\theta_+ & 0 & 0 \\ \cos^2\theta_- - \cos^2\theta_+ & \cos^2\theta_- + \cos^2\theta_+ & 0 & 0 \\ 0 & 0 & -2\cos\theta_+\cos\theta_- & 0 \\ 0 & 0 & 0 & -2\cos\theta_+\cos\theta_- \end{bmatrix} \begin{bmatrix} \mathrm{S_0} \\ \mathrm{S_1} \\ \mathrm{S_2} \\ \mathrm{S_3} \end{bmatrix}_{\text{in}}, \tag{6.12}$$

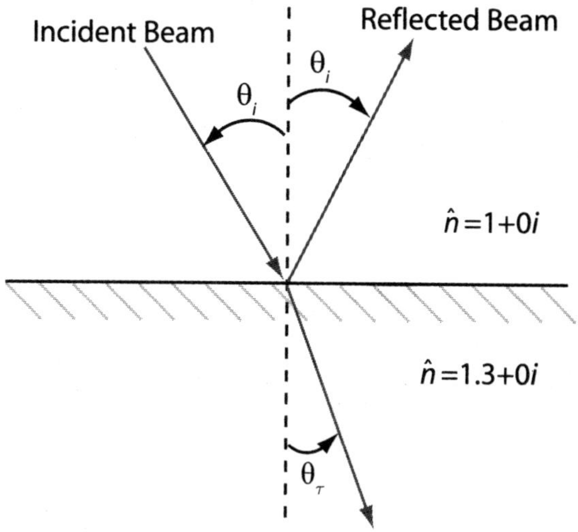

Figure 6.4 Illustration of terms used in the Mueller matrix representation of reflection from a dielectric plane.

where $\theta_+ = \theta_i + \theta_T, \theta_- = \theta_i - \theta_T, \theta_i$ is the illumination zenith angle, θ_T is the refracted angle, n is the index of refraction of the dielectric medium (incident beam assumed to be in air), and from Snell's law (see Fig. 6.4),

$$\theta_T = \sin^{-1}\left[\frac{1}{n}\sin\theta_i\right]. \tag{6.13}$$

This expression is valid only for direct specular reflection from perfectly flat surfaces and so will be of limited direct value. However, it is introduced here as it forms the basis for many models of the BRDF behavior of materials assumed to consist of many small planar facets. The Fresnel reflectance equations from Chapter 5 can be expressed more specifically in terms of only the angle of incidence and the complex index of refraction ($\hat{n} = n+ik$) as

$$r_\perp = \frac{(A-\cos\theta_i)^2 + B^2}{(A+\cos\theta_i)^2 + B^2} \tag{6.14}$$

$$r_\parallel = r_\perp\left[\frac{A-\sin\theta_i + \tan\theta_i + B^2}{A+\sin\theta_i + \tan\theta_i + B^2}\right], \tag{6.15}$$

where

$$A = \sqrt{\frac{\sqrt{C}+D}{2}}, \tag{6.16}$$

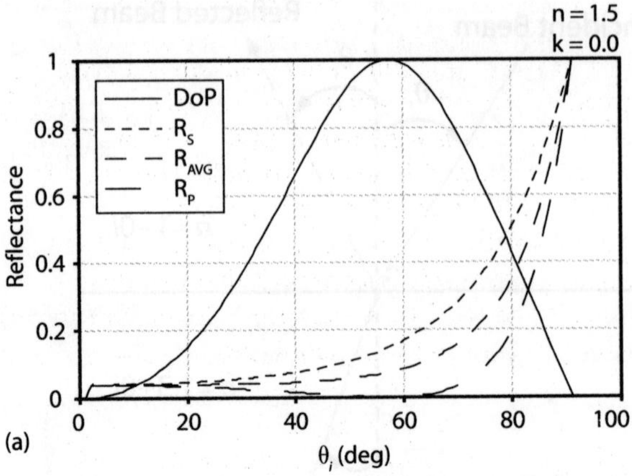

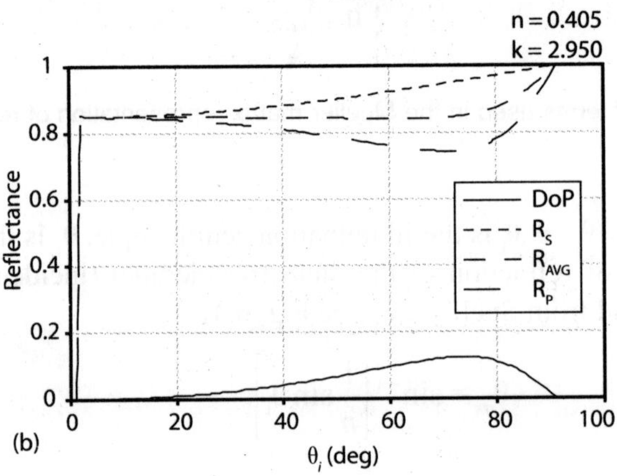

Figure 6.5 Polarized reflectance from (a) glass ($\tilde{n}_t = 1.5 + i0$) and (b) copper ($\tilde{n}_t = 0.405 + i2.95$) as a function of θ_i. The incident light is in air. Note that $R_S = R_\perp$ and $R_P = R_\parallel$.

$$B = \sqrt{\frac{\sqrt{C} - D}{2}}, \tag{6.17}$$

$$C = 4n^2k^2 + D^2, \tag{6.18}$$

and

$$D = n^2 - k^2 - \sin^2 \theta_i. \tag{6.19}$$

Examples of typical materials are shown in Fig. 6.5.

Note that randomly polarized radiation has one-half its electric field vector magnitude in the plane of incidence and one-half perpendicular to the plane of incidence. For normally incident and reflected light from both the dielectric and metal surface, equal amounts of energy will be reflected, resulting in no net polarization. In contrast, as the incidence (and therefore also the reflected energy) deviates from normal, more energy is reflected perpendicular (*S polarization* in

Fig. 6.5) to the plane of incidence (reflectance) than is reflected parallel (*P polarization* in Fig. 6.5) to the plane of incidence. This results in varying amounts of polarization as the angle changes. Note that at the *Brewster angle* for the dielectric, where all the *P*-polarized energy is absorbed, the degree of polarization goes to 1. It is also important to note that in the case of the metal, even though there is high reflectivity in both *S* and *P* polarizations, the amount of reflected energy is roughly equal, so the degree of polarization remains relatively small over all angles. It is also important to note that Figs. 6.4 and 6.5 show values for a particular wavelength. Changing the wavelength will result in different *n* and *k* values, which will produce both different reflectance values and different degrees of polarization.

6.2.2 Optical scatter from surfaces

Quantitative remote sensing in the visible and near infrared (VNIR) is based on measurements of reflected solar energy from the earth. It is from these measurements and estimates of the surface "reflectance" that algorithms and quantitative techniques may be applied to derive information from remotely sensed energy. Therefore, optical scatter or reflection phenomenology must be thoroughly understood, as this is the mechanism by which information unique to a specific material is translated into the reflected electromagnetic wave. This would seem to have been accomplished in Chapter 5 with the derivation of the Fresnel equations; however, real materials are significantly more complicated. This section examines optical scattering from surface reflections. Atmospheric optical scattering is also an important consideration but will not be addressed until Chapter 7.

In the preceding example of Fresnel reflectance, the reflectance magnitude was determined based entirely on the optical properties of the materials and the angle of incidence. In addition, the reflected energy is only directed in the plane of incidence at the reflected angle θ_r, where $\theta_r = \theta_i$, per the law of reflection. However, this is true only for perfectly planar or "smooth" surfaces that also have no internal scatter.

A quick look around is all it takes to realize that most surfaces are not perfect "mirror" surfaces (An interesting thought experiment is to consider a world in which all surfaces were perfect mirror surfaces. In this world, only sources of illumination would be visible and no objects could be discerned!), and even mirror surfaces are not perfect.

Two effects are responsible for energy reflected (or, more generally, energy scattered) outside the $\theta_r = \theta_i$ reflectance angle. First, all materials have some level of surface roughness. This results in a distribution of localized surface normals that are oriented in multiple directions, similar to individual sequins on a dress. Therefore, the Fresnel reflectance is actually distributed around a reflection angle according to the "roughness" of the material. The second and usually more significant phenomena directing energy out of the $\theta_r = \theta_i$ scattering angle is internal or volumetric scatter. Once light has entered a material, multiple internal scattering

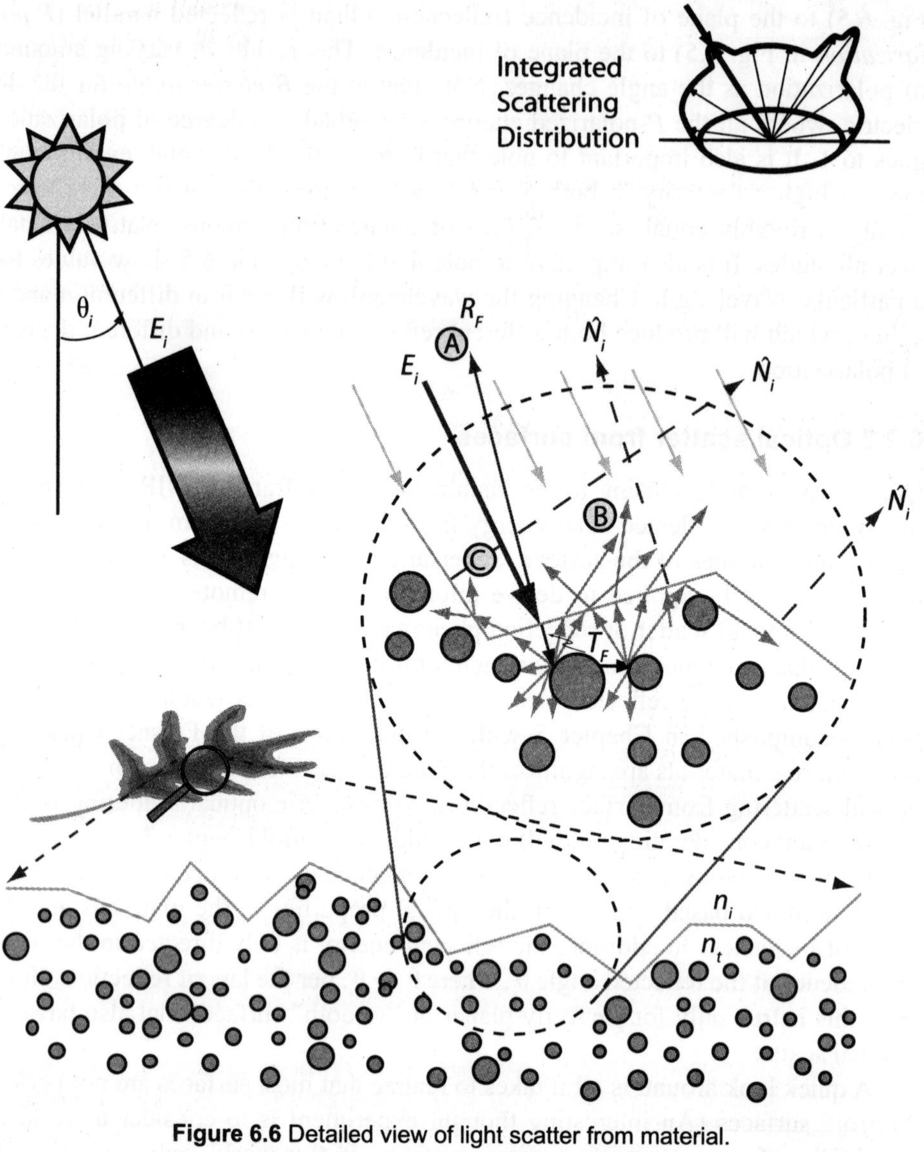

Figure 6.6 Detailed view of light scatter from material.

results in distributing the energy around the hemisphere. The internal scattering sources are also responsible for color by selective spectral absorption. Figure 6.6 illustrates this complex interaction.

In Fig. 6.6, several possible ray paths are noted. Incident irradiance ($\overrightarrow{E_i}$) may be reflected off the front surface of the material according to the local surface normal ($\hat{N}_i$) per the Fresnel reflection equation, giving R_F (type-A photons). Transmitted Fresnel irradiance (T_F) may then interact with a myriad of particles and molecules having selective absorption. After these single and multiple interactions, the energy may re-emerge from the surface, again according to the Fresnel equations (type-B photons). In most cases, the incident medium is air, which results in the real part of the refractive index of the transmitted medium being greater than the incident medium or $n_t > n_i$. This in turn results in total internal reflection for upward scattered radiance exceeding the critical angle relative to the local surface normal (as most have experienced, only a small area of the sky is visible when looking up while swimming underwater). Of course, after re-emerging from the surface, additional interactions with adjacent facets may also occur (type-C photons). Type-C photons may also originate from secondary surface reflections, or from two type-A interactions. Therefore, the integration of the type A, B and C photons over a solid receiving angle and material surface area A determines the magnitude and polarization of the reflectance in a given direction.

A few important conclusions may be made. The multiple, random scattering centers within a material have the net effect of depolarizing the fraction of T_F. This results in the diffuse component of scatter being highly randomly polarized. Also, the scattered radiance from dark materials, or those that highly absorb T_F, have a higher relative Fresnel reflection component (R_F) (which is polarized), since the magnitude of re-emerging scattered energy is low. This results in the DoP being inversely proportional to a material's reflectance and has been termed the *Umov effect* [Umov (1905)]—a phenomenon that will be further investigated.

A means for characterizing this directional scatter is the BRDF, which may be thought of as quantitatively defining the qualitative property of "shininess." A material may be described as being diffuse or specular; for example, a mirror is highly specular, and hence, scatters minimal energy outside of the reflection angle. On the other hand, a projector screen is highly diffuse, and the apparent brightness (radiance) of the screen is the same, regardless of viewing orientation.

Half of the battle in comprehending BRDF (and radiometry in general) is understanding the nomenclature and geometry. The nomenclature used is that recommended by Nicodemus (1970), which has subsequently been adopted by many authors. The National Bureau of Standards monograph by Nicodemus et al. (1977) is a seminal document on BRDF.

The BRDF is a function of the incident angle (θ_i), specified by the zenith and azimuth angles θ_i and ϕ_i; the reflected angle (θ_r), similarly specified by zenith and azimuth angles θ_r and ϕ_r, and finally the wavelength (λ). The zenith angles are defined relative to the local surface normal, which is $\theta_i = 0$ deg. Most materials have azimuthal or rotational symmetry about the surface normal. This reduces the degrees of freedom by one, enabling the azimuth angle to be characterized by only the difference between ϕ_i and ϕ_r, $\phi = \phi_r - \phi_i$. By convention, ϕ_i will be designated as $\phi = 0$ deg and the reflected or scattering azimuth angle defined relative to this orientation, increasing counterclockwise when looking down on the surface. Forward scattering is therefore $\phi = 180$ deg. This reduces the BRDF specification for rotationally symmetric materials to a three-dimensional (3-D) angular specification of $f_r(\theta_i; \theta_r, \phi; \lambda)$. The geometry is illustrated in Fig. 6.7.

Note from Fig. 6.7 that the source and detector occupy a solid angle ($d\omega$). BRDF is theoretically specified for a point source and detector, as well as an in-

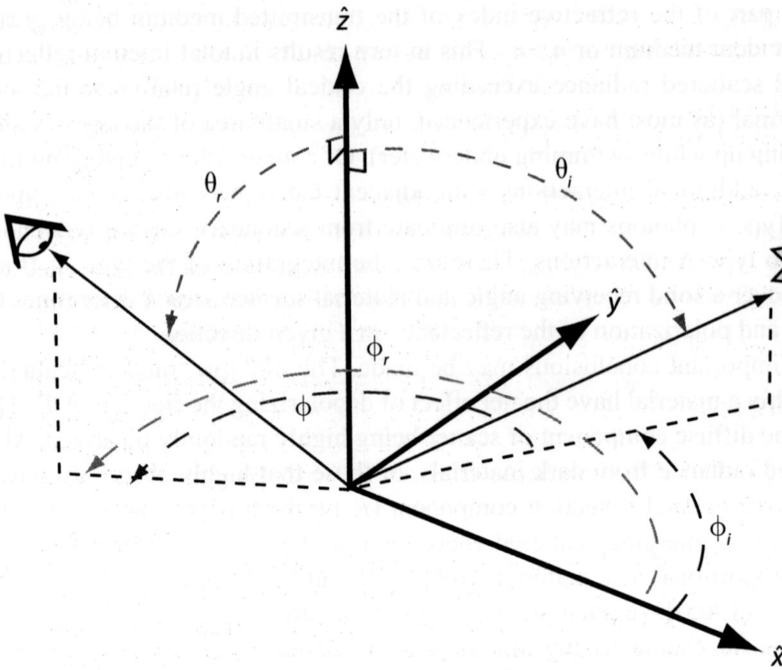

Figure 6.7 The BRDF geometry is uniquely specified by four angles corresponding to the source zenith and azimuth angles θ_i and ϕ_i and the reflected zenith and azimuth angles θ_r and ϕ_r. Most materials have azimuthal symmetry, in which case only a relative azimuth angle ϕ is required where $\phi = \phi_r - \phi_i$.

finitesimal surface area (*dA*) but practical measurement considerations result in averaging over the source and detector solid angles (ω_i) and (ω_s) and surface area (*A*). The averaging is most critical when the BRDF varies greatly as a function of angle, such as is the case with a highly specular or mirror-like material around the scattered specular lobe.

BRDF is actually a subset of the more general *bidirectional scattering distribution function* (BSDF). Accompanying BRDF are the transmissive (BTDF) and volume (BVDF) scattering functions that apply to materials having those scattering features [Stover (1995)]. The discussion here will be limited to BRDF, but it is worth noting that radiance contributions in what remote sensing ascribes to BRDF have elements from these other scattering sources (e.g., vegetative canopies).

In general, manmade surfaces are likely to have a higher BRDF value in the forward scattering plane ($\phi = 180$ deg) near a reflectance angle equal to the incidence angle, per the law of reflectance. However, this is generally not the case for natural surfaces with significant structure, such as vegetation. The so-called "hot spot" is present in the backscattering direction of the illuminating source, which may produce BRDF two to ten times that at diffuse reflection angles. The source of the hot spot is primarily due to self-shadowing not being visible when looking at a surface from the same orientation as the illumination angle. As the view angle moves away from the illumination position, self-shadowing by the material, such as from leaves of vegetation, results in decreased radiance. Coherent backscatter is also responsible for the hot-spot phenomenon, but only dominates when the structure size of the material is on the order of the incident wavelength [Hapke et al. (1996)].

Reflectance, or the ratio of incident energy to that reflected, is properly defined only through the BRDF. This fact is often forgotten, as it is common to use a scalar value as introduced in Sec. 6.1 for a material's reflectance. Reflectance spectra "truth" databases typically contain only a scalar value as a function of wavelength. These values are actually the *directional-hemispherical reflectance* ρ_{DHR}, which is the total reflectance for a specific angle of incidence (see Fig. 6.3). In terms of BRDF, ρ_{DHR} is given by

$$\rho_{\mathrm{DHR}}(\theta_i,\phi_i)=\int_{2\pi} f_r(\theta_i,\phi_i;\theta_r,\phi_r;\lambda)\cos(\theta_r)d\Omega_r. \tag{6.20}$$

Note that if f_r is a constant, this results in ρ_{DHR} being equal to $f_r\cdot\pi$.

Polarimetric BRDF, termed pBRDF, is the more generalized case of the scalar BRDF. In addition to quantifying the magnitude of the directional scattering, the polarization of the scattering is characterized. It is often overlooked that only the pBRDF correctly predicts the total reflectance magnitude when the incident irradiance is partially polarized. As described in Sec. 6.1, the radiometric quantities of Eq. (6.6) become Stokes vectors, and the BRDF becomes a Mueller matrix. The generalized *polarimetric BRDF* ($\mathbf{F}_r$) is thus represented as

$$\mathbf{F}_r(\theta_i,\phi_i;\theta_r,\phi_r;\lambda)=\frac{d\vec{L}_r(\theta_r,\phi_r)}{d\vec{E}(\theta_i,\phi_i)}. \tag{6.21}$$

Mueller matrix notation is most often used to describe transmissive mediums (such as optics), which results in unitless Mueller matrices. Also, the matrix is frequently normalized such that the m_{00} element of $\mathbf{M}$ is 1 and the multiplicative constant is dropped—this notation readily represents the medium's polarization characteristics at the expense of losing absolute radiometric values. When representing BRDF using Mueller matrices, the matrix has units of sr^{-1} as expected, and multiplicative constants must be maintained. In this manner, the f_{00} element of $\mathbf{F}_r$ remains equivalent to the scalar BRDF value such that

$$\rho_{\mathrm{DHR}}(\theta_i,\phi_i)=\int_{2\pi} f_{00}(\theta_i,\phi_i;\theta_r,\phi_r;\lambda)\cos(\theta_r)d\Omega_r. \tag{6.22}$$

A good review of polarized BRDF representations is provided by Flynn and Alexander (1995).

Invoking the assumption that circular polarization is not present in a significant amount upon reflection from most natural surfaces, Coulson (1998) reduces the Mueller matrix to a 3×3 matrix and the Stokes vector to a three-element vector. With this reduction in dimensionality, Eq. (6.21) may be explicitly written as

$$\begin{bmatrix} L_0 \\ L_1 \\ L_2 \end{bmatrix} = \begin{bmatrix} f_{00} & f_{01} & f_{02} \\ f_{10} & f_{11} & f_{12} \\ f_{20} & f_{21} & f_{22} \end{bmatrix} \begin{bmatrix} E_0 \\ E_1 \\ E_2 \end{bmatrix}. \tag{6.23}$$

We will often use this simplification since for passive remote sensing of natural surfaces we expect to see very little circularly polarized energy.

6.3 Reflectance Variability or Texture

The formal definition of BRDF requires the measurement of an infinitesimal surface area (dA) with an illumination source and detector that subtend infinitesimal solid angles. It is obvious that each of these three areas must have a finite size for practical measurement purposes. It is actually desirable to have a surface area of sufficient size that adequately represents the material.

For example, consider characterizing the scatter from a "painted metal plate." Close inspection of the painted plate may reveal small defects such as paint bubbles or chips. If the BRDF measurement area was small and a defect occupied a significant fraction of the measurement area, it would significantly impact the scattering measurement. However, if a sufficiently large area of the plate would be measured, the microscopic variability would be averaged out, and a more accurate BRDF measurement would result.

Local scattering variability within a material class is often called "texture," and may be quantified as the *bidirectional reflectance variance function* (BRVF) [Ni et al. (1999)] or the bidirectional texture function, as it is commonly called in the computer graphics community [Dana et al. (1999)]. Note that this may be considered semantics—for the metal plate, one could also quantify the BRDF values for "pristine paint," "paint bubbles," and "paint chips." From these three subclasses, the BRDF of the entire painted metal plate could be generated from a linearly weighted combination of these surfaces.

Such approaches using fundamental material BRDF values quickly become impractical, since subclass divisions may be continued indefinitely; for instance, a subdivision of "paint chips" may be "paint chips with metal indentation," etc. The fundamental material approach toward constructing "macro" BRDF values is also difficult with complex materials, such as a tree canopy, which has significant transmittance and interaction among the leaves, ground, etc. The linear superposition of such complex objects becomes impossible with BRDF data of only the individual constituent materials. A BRDF measurement of a whole tree canopy is often more attractive; alternately, nonlinear scene simulation techniques may be employed (see Chapter 10).

Note that BRDF measurement of such macromaterials enables averaging of local variabilities but increases the necessity of assigning adequate qualitative descriptors of the material. For instance, when pulling the BRDF of grass from a database of BRDF measurements, one would likely also want to know such parameters as the grass height, density of coverage or the amount of ground visible, the health of the grass, time of year, etc.

BRVF is a function of the surface area considered. If a remote sensing payload has a *ground sample distance* (GSD) of 1 ft, then there will be essentially no pixel-to-pixel variability due to BRDF when viewing the metal plate previously described. However, if the GSD is 1 in, then some pixel-to-pixel variability will likely be manifested from the material defects. Therefore, the BRVF may be defined as the BRDF probability density function given a measurement area (A), according to

$$BRVF(A) = p(f_r \mid A). \tag{6.24}$$

Often the BRVF distribution is unimodal and approximately Gaussian, in which case the variance is an adequate means of quantifying the BRVF. It is also noted that the mean value of the BRVF is the BRDF.

BRVF has led to low-pass spatial filtering of high spatial resolution hyperspectral data cubes for target detection algorithms. If the target is resolved, then filtering down to the GSD of the projected target area may increase the signal to noise in detection algorithms due to the decreased background variability. Similarly, specular reflections from individual leaves in a tree canopy may have significant polarization imparted; however, when integrated at the level of a tree stand, the net polarized radiance is not so easily determined.

Before continuing our discussion of pBRDF and ways to characterize the pBRDF of a surface, we will briefly review methods to measure scalar BRDF, since pBRDF approaches build directly on them.

6.4 BRDF Measurement

A means of quantifying the BRDF, or more generally the pBRDF, is needed to generate *a priori* BRDF databases of target and background materials that may be applied to remote sensing algorithms. One means of generating the data is through BRDF models that may use physics-based principles to derive the directional reflectance (these will be discussed in Sec. 6.6). However, it will be seen that for practical purposes, measurements are required as inputs for most BRDF models.

The key elements of any optical scatter measurement are the sample material or object to be measured, the illumination source, and the detector. Most BRDF measurement devices employ one or more goniometric arms that provide angular positioning of the source and/or detector element. In some cases, the sample orientation may also be changed in order to achieve the full hemispherical range of source and detector orientations.

When high angular resolution is required to resolve the specular peak of mirror-like materials, the solid angle subtended by the detector may be minimized by increasing the material-to-detector distance or decreasing the detector size. For diffuse materials, the angular resolution is not as critical, since there are usually only modest changes in BRDF with reflection angle. The detector signal to noise can become an issue as one makes spectral BRDF measurements where a $\Delta\lambda$ of 10 nm may be desired, commensurate with the spectral bias of many hyperspectral sensors. Signal strength may also become problematic when measuring highly specular materials outside the specular lobe. However, in this circumstance the low signal is usually not of interest in remote sensing applications.

Commercial BRDF measurement systems have been developed and are available. However, most measurement needs are satisfied with systems customized to the user's unique application. It is for this reason, in part, that very few BRDF databases exist. Measurements taken by a particular group often have inadequate material and experimental conditions described, and have tailored features that are not easily adaptable to a new user's interest. One exception is the *nonconventional exploitation factors* (NEF) database, which contains BRDF information for a number of materials [NEF (1996)].

Newer approaches in BRDF measurement often incorporate imaging techniques that enable the simultaneous sampling of multiple angles, greatly decreasing the required number of measurements. Imaging systems also readily enable characterization of the BRVF. However, many of the techniques are not polarization friendly. Other novel techniques have also been developed and will be briefly explored. The impetus for most of the newer measurement approaches is improved rendering in computer animation and simulation, for which there is a significant commercial market.

Outdoor BRDF measurements are common for remote sensing due to the large spatial scales of the materials involved, as well as the inability to bring representative materials, such as undisturbed live vegetation, into the lab. Approaches toward outdoor BRDF measurements will be reviewed, as well as the means to handle some of the challenges outdoor measurements present.

Finally, the measurements required to capture the most general form of BRDF, the polarimetric BRDF, will be reviewed (see Sec. 6.5.4). The foregoing measurement techniques may all be adapted to polarimetric measurements, with varying levels of complexity.

6.4.1 Conventional laboratory measurements

The most common and traditional means of measuring BRDF is to use an illumination source of small angular extent and a corresponding radiometer to measure the scattered radiance. Several means of acquiring the necessary source and detector angular sampling are invoked by using a goniometer. For most systems, it is easiest to fix the source position and vary the detector location to sample θ_r and ϕ_r. The incident angle θ_i is sampled by moving the target sample, which is usually a relatively small, planar sample. With a large detector system, such as a spectrometer, the detector position is fixed and the source and material are moved to sample the hemisphere [Feng et al. (1993)].

Illumination sources may be either lasers or a broad-band source coupled with spectral filters at the source or detector to enable spectral measurements.

Often the data acquisition process is automated, whereby the angular position of the detector and material is changed to cover the prescribed BRDF measurement sampling density. The number of required measurements is significant. For an isotropic material (no azimuth dependency) and sampling at 10-deg increments in both θ_i, θ_r and ϕ, the number of required measurements exceeds 1500 per spectral band: 9 for 0 deg$\leq\theta_i\leq$80 deg, 9 for 0 deg$\leq\theta_r\leq$80 deg, and 19 for 0 deg$\leq\phi\leq$180 deg ($9\times9\times19$). This simple calculation illustrates the challenge in adequately measuring BRDF and motivates the modeling discussion in Sec. 6.6.

Lab measurements on materials of interest to remote sensing are particularly challenging. The heterogeneity or texture of most natural materials occurs at a spatial scale much larger than the typical sample size that is used in the laboratory. For this reason, natural materials are best measured over larger spatial scales and in their natural, undisturbed states by outdoor measurement techniques (see Sec. 6.5.3). However, BRDF measurements of manmade materials, which often constitute "targets" in spectral detection algorithms, may be more accurately measured in the controlled lab environment. A review of BRDF lab measurements with a remote sensing perspective is provided by Sandmeier and Strahler (2000).

6.4.2 Camera-based measurements

The use of focal planes to make BRDF measurements greatly increases measurement efficiency. Rather than having a single detector element, and hence a single bistatic angle for each measurement, multiple reflection angles may be simultaneously acquired by the individual focal plane photo sites. Several permutations on this concept may be employed. BRDF measurement techniques using focal planes may be categorized into three basic approaches:

(1) wide field of view (FOV) imaging to simultaneously sample many reflecting angles,
(2) tailored optics imaging systems that uniquely sample the material (many variants), and
(3) narrow FOV imaging used in a manner similar to a single element detector.

The wide FOV systems rely on a large uniform material area for making measurements. Discrete scattering angles are obtained from each pixel of the imaging system, which enables an efficient, dense sampling of scattering angles for a single incident angle. Of course, spatial inhomogeneities in the material erroneously manifest themselves as a BRDF change, so caution must be used. For pBRDF measurements using an optical system with polarization filters, the high incident angles make this approach challenging. A few outdoor systems make use of this measurement approach and will be addressed separately in Sec. 6.5.3.

The second basic imaging configuration, the tailored optics systems, encompasses a number of measurement concepts and is among the most creative. The overall approach is to re-image the material surface in a manner that enables efficient changes to the system, such as varying the incident angle of illumination or acquiring multiple viewing geometries. One such approach images an infinitesimal surface point [Dana (2001) and Dana and Wang (2004)], and another employs a kaleidoscope that provides multiple discrete scattering angles while resolving the surface [Han and Perlin (2003)]. The most significant disadvantages of these systems are the limitations imposed on the illuminating source and the sample size—outdoor measurements using the sun would be difficult. Also, since these systems use reflective optics having multiple reflections or varying reflectance angles, measuring the polarimetric BRDF is problematic due to the polarization dependency of the system.

Finally, a narrow FOV imaging system may be used in a manner analogous to the way a single element detector is used. Implicit in this measurement technique is the ability to quantify BRVF from the image data. However, as with a single detector, many measurements or images must be acquired to cover the scattering hemisphere. Therefore, this technique must heavily rely on BRDF models to inter/extrapolate the data. This technique is adaptable to both the lab and field. For field use, calibration and stray light mitigation are readily employed. Systems using this approach have not been widely noted in the literature, likely due to the inefficiency of hemispherical sampling. These three basic imaging approaches to BRDF measurement, along with their relative merits, are illustrated in Fig. 6.8.

The following approaches are those of the "tailored optics systems," with the wide FOV systems addressed in Sec. 6.5.3. Discussion of the narrow FOV camera based measurement will be postponed until Chapter 10 where it is used in an example study linking pBRDF measurement and modeling approaches.

A few novel BRDF measurement techniques using imaging are briefly reviewed here. Marschner et al. (1999) report on a system that images an object of known shape, such as a sphere or a cone that is covered with a desired material to be measured. The shape of the object inherently provides the multiple viewing geometries, rather than using optics. Viewing the object, while having a single illumination source, enables the direct measurement of a large number of incident and scattering angles with a single image. The technique is readily adaptable to pBRDF measurements, but only for a relatively small class of materials, such as painted surfaces. Measurement of background materials could not be accomplished using the technique.

Dana and Wang (2004) use an off-axis parabolic mirror to image a single point on a material surface that provides multiple view angles. Multiple image points on the material surface are obtained by translating the parabolic mirror above the surface. The multiple image points enable BRVF or texture measurements. Again, this measurement concept is ill-adapted toward pBRDF measurement due to the high incident angles on the parabolic optic. A similar approach is also reported by Apel et al. (2001).

Finally, Han and Perlin (2003) image through a kaleidoscope that enables the simultaneous measurement of BRDF and BRVF. A tapered kaleidoscope with front-surface mirrors is used to image a material, creating a virtual sphere consisting of multiple tapered facets that correspond to different viewing zenith angles

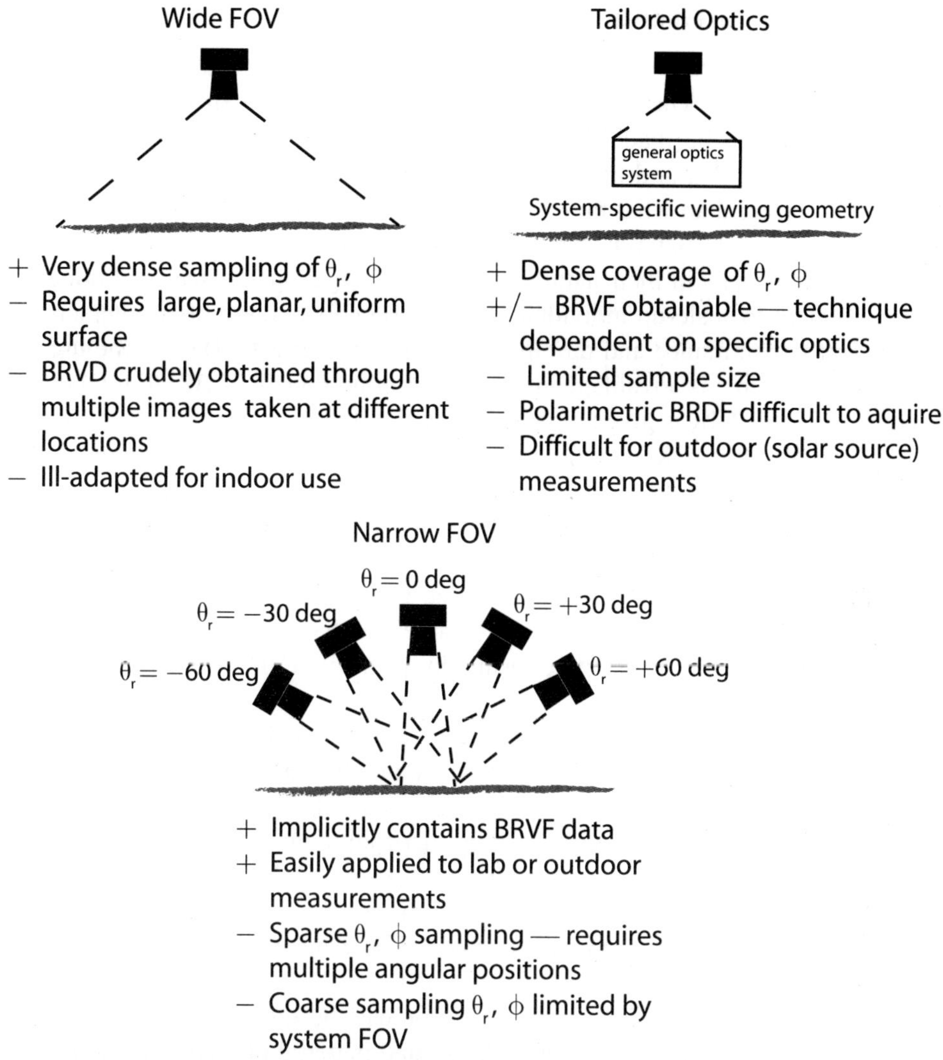

Figure 6.8 Three fundamental approaches toward focal-plane-based BRDF measurements, along with their advantages (+) and disadvantages (–).

of the object. The effect is equivalent to having multiple camera angles imaging the same surface area. A digital projector provides the light source, and the incident illumination angles are controlled by selectively turning on groups of pixels in the digital projector. The kaleidoscope is one of the most efficient measurement approaches, but again is not easily adapted for pBRDF measurements, nor is it very suitable for measurement of natural materials of large spatial extent. This leads us to consideration of field instruments which, though cumbersome in many ways, are almost always necessary for characterizing natural surfaces.

6.4.3 Field measurements

Portable BRDF devices suitable for outdoor measurements are attractive for a number of reasons. The use of portable devices arises out of necessity when measurements must be made that are extremely difficult, if not impossible, to replicate in the lab. Natural materials may be heterogeneous over spatial extents significantly larger than what may be measured in the lab. Vegetation is a classic example of one such material, whether it is grass or a leaf canopy. Direct measurement of materials in their natural state and at larger spatial scales eliminates the requirement to scale-up individual material BRDFs that are often interactive, such as leaf transmittance and multiple leaf adjacency effects. Having the use of the sun as the source is advantageous as well. A good review of BRDF field measurements in the VNIR is given by Walthall et al. (2000).

Full polarimetric BRDF field measurements also have an additional concern—the source must have a generator producing various polarization states. For practical reasons, this is impossible. Placing an appropriate filter over the sun while making a measurement would be difficult and would require a large aperture filter, depending on the sample size being measured and the stand-off distance of the filter. As will be seen in Chapter 10, having the ability to change only the analyzer polarization state results in quantifying the first column of the $\mathbf{F}_r$ scattering matrix.

An obvious challenge to outdoor measurements is cooperative weather and stray light. Good weather may eventually be found, but the downwelled sky radiance is always an error source in the measurements. In addition, the magnitude and distribution of this error source changes depending on local atmospheric conditions, such as extent of cloud cover. This error source obviously has a spectral dependence, as the blue sky testifies. A good discussion of outdoor measurement errors and minimization techniques is provided by Sandmeier (2000) with some quantitative assessments provided by Lyapustin and Privette (1999) and Epema (1991). A technique for minimizing this error will be discussed in Chapter 10 when addressing an approach toward background material pBRDF measurement. Finally, the source zenith position is not easily adjustable. In most circumstances, outdoor measurements are made over a sample size of area A that is greater than that made with lab measurements. A sample area must be sufficiently large to average out high spatial frequency inhomogeneities or texture in the material, as discussed in Sec. 6.4. Adequate sample size is indicated when the resulting BRDF value is insensitive to changes in the sample area in the FOV of the instrument, or $(df_r/dA) \rightarrow 0$.

A highly relevant challenge, though outside the scope of this treatment, is generating a sufficiently accurate and meaningful descriptive characterization of the material, which is critical for natural materials. It is by these descriptive labels that the material type will be selected and used in subsequent analysis, synthetic image generation, etc. A simple descriptor such as "Paint XYZ on Aluminum" is not sufficient when ascribing BRDF to inhomogeneous targets. (Actually,

Figure 6.9 An example of field goniometers for BRDF measurements. FIGOS is shown on the left and the SFG system in the middle and right [Reprinted with permission from Elsevier, courtesy of Sandmeier (2000) (left and right) and Schill (middle)].

adequately describing "simple" materials is also very challenging. Added to the description of "Paint XYZ on Aluminum" should be information such as application method, surface condition and paint thickness—a picture doesn't hurt!) It is suggested that a robust meta-data set always accompany such measurements. This meta-data should include photographs of various viewing geometries of the sample, as well as detailed verbal descriptors.

We now move to a brief review of some field devices reported in the literature. Two fundamental designs may be used: a traditional "lab-like" system in which the sensor is moved around a hemisphere above the target, or one in which the sensor does not translate, but acquires different view angles from the fixed position. With the latter, the target area must be sufficiently uniform such that views of each area are representative of one another.

The most direct approach toward field BRDF measurements is to emulate a laboratory setup by using a goniometer. With the illumination source (the sun) and target orientation on the ground fixed, the goniometer serves to move the detector to sampling positions throughout the hemisphere.

One such system is FIGOS (field goniometer system), built by the Remote Sensing Lab of the University of Zurich [Sandmeier et al. (1995) and Sandmeier and Itten (1999)]. The system consists of a "zenith" arc of 2-m radius that rests on a circular frame of 4-m diameter—the azimuthal arc (Fig. 6.9). A nearly identical goniometer, the Sandmeier Field Goniometer (SFG) was constructed by NASA Ames based on the FIGOS design. However, this field goniometer is fully automated and the acquisition time for the same angular sampling scheme as FIGOS ($\Delta\theta_r = 15$ deg, $\Delta\phi_r = 30$ deg) is completed in less than 10 min [Sandmeier (2000)]. Figure 6.9 pictures the SFG and FIGOS systems.

Another goniometer advertised as having outdoor measurement capability was constructed by ONERA in France. The target area is imaged with a bundle of 59 fiber optics and a fore optic [Serrot et al. (1998) and Boucher et al. (1999)]. The fiber optics mixes the incident polarization of the scattered radiance, thus eliminating the polarization dependency of the diffraction grating in the spectrometer and making it suitable for pBRDF measurements.

The previously described goniometer systems provide high angular precision and rapid sampling of the scattering hemisphere and are suitable for highly accurate characterization of field materials. However, both systems require significant support for transport and setup, which is exacerbated by having to time the weather conditions for suitable measurement periods. A simpler measurement technique is often warranted that still provides meaningful BRDF data. Representing this other extreme are simple measurements made with a radiometer attached to a hand-held boom. The angular position of such a device may be estimated based on trigonometry of the height and distance from the measured area. Measurements of only a few geometric positions may provide an understanding of the BRDF anisotropy.

An alternative approach to a sensor being repositioned around the hemisphere is a fixed sensor that changes the view angle over a large homogeneous measurement area. One such BRDF measurement device is PARABOLA (Portable Apparatus for Rapid Acquisition of Bidirectional Observations of Land and Atmosphere), which has been used in various forms by NASA Goddard since the mid-1980s [Deering and Leone (1986)]. In an attempt to average out spatial inhomogeneities, such a sensor is often mounted high on a mast or a lift in order for the small FOV to image at an adequate GSD (see Fig. 6.10).

As noted earlier, diffraction gratings are highly polarization sensitive, and for pBRDF measurements, the incident radiance on the diffraction grating should first be randomly polarized to provide consistent results. An equivalent approach may be made with an imaging system. Rather than scanning a radiometer to acquire the multiple view angles, a wide FOV camera lens may be used. The University of Arizona uses such a system that assists in the vicarious radiance calibration of Landsat (Nandy et al. (1999), Nandy et al. (2001), and Czapla-Myers et al. (2002)). Linear CCDs may also be used to make a conical push-broom scan around the target area [Radke et al. (1999) and Demircan et al. (2000)].

6.4.3.1 Overhead BRDF measurement

Finally, new payloads have enabled BRDF measurement from satellites and aircraft. In these instances the atmosphere provides an additional measurement uncertainty in deriving the surface-leaving radiance. One such instrument is *POLDER* (POLarization and Directionality of the Earth Reflectances), which has a wide field of view (GSD of 6 km) and is flown on the ADEOS satellite [Deschamps et al. (1994)]. Derivation of POLDER BRDF products is described in Leroy et al. (1997) and Nadal and Bréon (1999).

Similar large GSD data, though nonpolarimetric, is provided by NASA's MODIS (Moderate Resolution Imaging Spectroradiometer) instruments, flown on Terra (EOS AM-1) and Aqua (EOS PM-1), having a GSD of 250–1000 m, depending on the spectral band. MODIS scans ±55-deg, thus enabling multiple angular views with successive passes. BRDF products from MODIS are described by Schaaf et al. (2002). The Terra satellite also hosts NASA's MISR (Multiangle

Figure 6.10 The Parabola III system showing the sensor (left) and the sensor mounted on a boom (right) for field measurements [NASA (2004)].

Imaging SpectroRadiometer) payload, which provides BRDF data using four spectral bands to acquire nine angular views spaced in the along-track direction.

6.4.4 Polarimetric BRDF measurement

As noted in Sec. 6.3, one quantifies the reflective BRDF Mueller matrix $\mathbf{F}_r$ by making polarimetric BRDF measurements using Eq. (6.21). In polarimetric BRDF measurements, the scattered or reflected Stokes radiance vector **L** must be quantified such that

$$\vec{\mathbf{L}}(\theta_r, \phi) = \mathbf{F}_r(\theta_i, \phi, \theta_r)\mathbf{E}(\theta_i). \tag{6.25}$$

However, without the use of polarization filtering, the detector measures only the magnitude of the irradiance and radiance, as in the case of the scalar BRDF:

$$L(\theta_r, \phi) = f_{00}(\theta_i, \phi, \theta_r)E_0(\theta_i), \tag{6.26}$$

where the "0" subscript denotes the first element of the Stokes vector, which is the total flux, and f_{00} is the upper left element of the BRDF matrix equivalent to the scalar BRDF f_r.

Clearly, additional measurements are needed to characterize the other 15 elements of the BRDF matrix. When considering linear polarization, this requirement is reduced to determining the remaining eight elements of the 3×3 BRDF matrix. These additional elements of the array may be determined by linear combinations of incident irradiance polarization states $\vec{\mathbf{E}}$ and received polarization radiance states $\vec{\mathbf{L}}$.

The most generalized means of acquiring the matrix elements is through presenting multiple incident polarization states, and measuring the polarized output for each incident state, thus building a system of linear equations. The polarization filters that create incident polarization states are termed *generators*, while those that filter the output are called analyzers. The presentation of i incident polarization states onto the sample and their polarized radiance measurements may be represented as

$$\mathbf{F}_r\left[\vec{\mathbf{E}}_1\,\vec{\mathbf{E}}_2\cdots\vec{\mathbf{E}}_{i-1}\,\vec{\mathbf{E}}_i\right]=\left[\vec{\mathbf{L}}_1\,\vec{\mathbf{L}}_2\cdots\vec{\mathbf{L}}_{i-1}\,\vec{\mathbf{L}}_i\right], \tag{6.27}$$

where $[\vec{\mathbf{E}}_1\vec{\mathbf{E}}_2\cdots\vec{\mathbf{E}}_{i-1}\vec{\mathbf{E}}_i]$ is a $4\times i$ matrix consisting of irradiance column Stokes vectors and $[\vec{\mathbf{L}}_1\vec{\mathbf{L}}_2\cdots\vec{\mathbf{L}}_{i-1}\vec{\mathbf{L}}_i]$ is the corresponding reflected radiance representation. Rewriting these terms as matrix quantities **E** and **L**, the new expression is

$$\mathbf{F}_r\mathbf{E}=\mathbf{L}, \tag{6.28}$$

where it is seen that

$$\mathbf{F}_r=\mathbf{L}\mathbf{E}^{-1}. \tag{6.29}$$

However, inversion of **E** is possible only when considering a nonsingular square matrix. For the general case where $i>4$, the pseudo inverse of **E** is sought, $\mathbf{E}^{\#}$, which provides a least squares estimate in the presence of random noise. The pseudo inverse is given by

$$\mathbf{E}^{\#}=\mathbf{E}^T(\mathbf{E}\mathbf{E}^T)^{-1}, \tag{6.30}$$

where ^{T} is the transpose of the matrix. The Mueller matrix is therefore solved by

$$\mathbf{F}_r=\mathbf{L}\mathbf{E}^{\#}. \tag{6.31}$$

In this manner the full BRDF Mueller matrix may be determined for each permutation of θ_i, θ_r, ϕ, and λ, as the scalar BRDF would be measured.

For practical measurement considerations, one would like an efficient set of input and output polarization states in order to minimize the number of measurements. The equation describing this measurement setup is given as

$$\vec{L}=\mathbf{T}_A\mathbf{F}_r\mathbf{T}_G\vec{E}, \tag{6.32}$$

where $\mathbf{T}_G$ is the transmissive generator filter over the source and $\mathbf{T}_A$ is the transmissive analyzer filter over the detector. Note that the generator and analyzer Mueller matrices have no units, but the BRDF Mueller matrix $\mathbf{F}_r$ has BRDF units, sr^{-1}. Referencing the polarization filters provided in Chapter 5, a simple example is constructed for generator and analyzer linear horizontal filters. The equation is given by

$$\vec{L}=\mathbf{T}_{\ominus}\mathbf{F}_r\mathbf{T}_{\ominus}\vec{E}, \tag{6.33}$$

or explicitly as

$$\begin{bmatrix} L_0 \\ L_1 \\ L_2 \end{bmatrix} = \frac{1}{2}\begin{bmatrix} 1 & 1 & 0 \\ 1 & 1 & 0 \\ 0 & 0 & 0 \end{bmatrix}\begin{bmatrix} f_{00} & f_{01} & f_{02} \\ f_{10} & f_{11} & f_{12} \\ f_{20} & f_{21} & f_{22} \end{bmatrix}\frac{1}{2}\begin{bmatrix} 1 & 1 & 0 \\ 1 & 1 & 0 \\ 0 & 0 & 0 \end{bmatrix}\begin{bmatrix} E_0 \\ E_1 \\ E_2 \end{bmatrix}, \tag{6.34}$$

which reduces to

$$\begin{bmatrix} L_0 \\ L_1 \\ L_2 \end{bmatrix} = \frac{1}{4}\begin{bmatrix} (f_{00}+f_{01}+f_{10}+f_{11})(E_0+E_1) \\ (f_{00}+f_{01}+f_{10}+f_{11})(E_0+E_1) \\ 0 \end{bmatrix}. \tag{6.35}$$

However, as always, it is only the first Stokes component that the detector will be measuring. If the original source is highly randomly polarized, then $E_1 \ll E_0$ and the measurement yields

$$L_0 = \frac{(f_{00}+f_{01}+f_{10}+f_{11})E_0}{4}. \tag{6.36}$$

In a similar manner, other permutations of generator and analyzer polarization states produce additional linear combinations of the Mueller matrix elements. A summary of such combinations is provided by Bicket and Bailey (1985). To quantify the 3×3 subset of $\mathbf{F}_r$ that relates to linear polarization, a total of nine measurement permutations is required including the three generator and analyzer states of horizontal, +45 deg, and no (or random) polarization. These states are represented symbolically as ⊖, ⊘, and ⊛, respectively. Using this symbolic representation, Eq. (6.36) may be recast as

$$\ominus\ominus = \frac{L_0}{E_0} = \frac{f_{00}+f_{01}+f_{10}+f_{11}}{4}, \tag{6.37}$$

where the first "⊖" represents the generator state and the second "⊖" is the polarization of the analyzer. Using this notation, the Mueller matrix elements may be shown to equal

$$f_{00} = \circledast\circledast \tag{6.38a}$$

$$f_{01} = 2\ominus\circledast - \circledast\circledast \tag{6.38b}$$

$$f_{02} = 2\oslash\circledast - \circledast\circledast \tag{6.38c}$$

$$f_{10} = 2\circledast\ominus - \circledast\circledast \tag{6.38d}$$

$$f_{11} = 4\ominus\ominus - 2\circledast\ominus - 2\ominus\circledast + \circledast\circledast \tag{6.38e}$$

$$f_{12} = 4\oslash\ominus - 2\circledast\ominus - 2\oslash\circledast + \circledast\circledast \tag{6.38f}$$

$$f_{20} = 2 \circledast \ominus - \circledast \circledast \tag{6.38g}$$

$$f_{21} = 4 \ominus \oslash - 2 \circledast \oslash - 2 \ominus \circledast + \circledast \circledast \tag{6.38h}$$

$$f_{22} = 4 \oslash \oslash - 2 \circledast \oslash - 2 \oslash \circledast + \circledast \circledast . \tag{6.38i}$$

Often the symmetry of the material results in $f_{01} = f_{10}$, $f_{02} = f_{20}$ and $f_{12} = -f_{21}$.

Careful error analysis must also accompany this measurement process as errors may be introduced from several factors. The illuminating source may have some inherent polarization and the detector may have a polarization-dependent response. Some errors are always present from polarization filters, which are not perfect. All filters have a finite extinction coefficient, or the transmittance along one polarization axis relative to the other axis. This amounts to some leakage of the opposite polarization state, which becomes an error source. This leakage is also spectrally dependent. Finally, the fidelity of filter alignment results in an error source. Propagation of Mueller matrix element errors has been addressed by several authors [Peterson et al. (2000), Chenault et al. (1991), and Hayes (1997)]. To generate an estimate of the pBRDF Mueller matrix, this process must be repeated for each source-sensor geometry of interest.

6.5 BRDF Models

The complexity of BRDF measurement as complicated by pBRDF measurement leads us to consider BRDF models as a way to describe BRDF behavior. The goal is to describe BRDF in terms of physical phenomena and potentially reduce the number of measurements required to describe the full BRDF behavior of a surface.

6.5.1 Torrance-Sparrow model

Torrance and Sparrow (1967) presented one of the first BRDF models to capture such phenomena as the off-specular peak, as well as providing good predictions as $\theta_r \rightarrow 90$ deg. The Torrance-Sparrow model is developed on the basis of geometrical optics, and as such, requires the root mean square (rms) surface roughness (σ_m) to be comparable to or greater than the wavelength considered ($\sigma_m/\lambda \gtrsim 1.0$). As with many BRDF models, the contributions of individual microfacet reflections to the overall material BRDF is considered. Each microfacet of area A_f is treated as a specular surface for which the surface normal angular positions (α) are distributed according to a Gaussian probability distribution ($P(\alpha)$). The diffuse BRDF component of the BRDF arises from multiple microfacet reflections or internal scattering. Therefore, the reflected radiance (L_r) may be expressed as the sum of the specular and diffuse components

$$L_r = L_{r,s} + L_{r,d}, \tag{6.39}$$

with the diffuse component given in terms of the incident radiance (L_i) by

$$L_{r,d} = aL_i \cos\theta_i, \tag{6.40}$$

where a is a constant.

The specular reflection is obtained by considering the Fresnel reflection from each microfacet. The significant advancement made by the Torrance-Sparrow model was the introduction of a *geometric attenuation factor* G, which enables masking and shadowing. Masking is the blockage of specular reflections by adjacent microfacets, while shadowing is the blockage of the illumination source onto a microfacet by adjacent microfacets. The resulting BRDF from the Torrance-Sparrow model (see Fig. 6.11) is given as

$$f_r = \frac{F(\theta_i, \hat{n}) A_f G(\theta_{i,p}, \theta_{r,p}) P(\alpha)}{4\cos\theta_i \cos\theta_r} + \frac{a}{d\omega_i}, \tag{6.41}$$

where the second term is the diffuse component and the specular reflectance coordinate system is relevant to the microfacet normal, the $\theta_{X,p}$ coordinates result from projections of θ_i and θ_r onto the plane determined by the facet and surface normals, and $F(\theta_i, \hat{n})$ is the Fresnel reflectance associated with flux incident from the θ_i direction.

So, which parameters are required for producing Torrance-Sparrow BRDF predictions? To obtain the Fresnel reflectance, the index of refraction ($\hat{n}$) is required. A roughness parameter (c) that relates the distribution of facet slopes relative to the normal plane is required. Note that c is contained in $P(\alpha)$:

$$P(\alpha) = ce^{-c^2\alpha^2}. \tag{6.42}$$

Torrance and Sparrow used a value of $c = 0.05$, which was justified based on fitting the data to experimentally determined BRDF. While Torrance-Sparrow makes use of first principles to model the BRDF, it nonetheless requires parameters (c, a, and possibly $\hat{n}$) that Torrance and Sparrow fit to experimental data.

6.5.2 Maxwell-Beard model

The development of the *Maxwell-Beard* BRDF model was originally motivated for use on painted surfaces [Maxwell et al. (1973)]. The model development emphasizes BRDF prediction from IR laser sources (1–4 μm) with varying polarization states. As with the Torrance-Sparrow model, separate specular and diffuse contributions to the BRDF are considered, which Maxwell and Beard term surface and volume contributions.

With the surface model, only single reflections from the microfacet surface are considered (see Fig. 6.12). The distribution of the microfacets are obtained through a *"zero angle" bistatic scan* (ZBS) in which the detector and illumination source are co-located, or as close to the same position as possible without subtending each other. The surface normals of each microfacet are defined as being oriented in the (θ_N, ϕ_N) direction. The measured signal of the ZBS scan may then be related to the density of microfacets that fall within the detector solid angle,

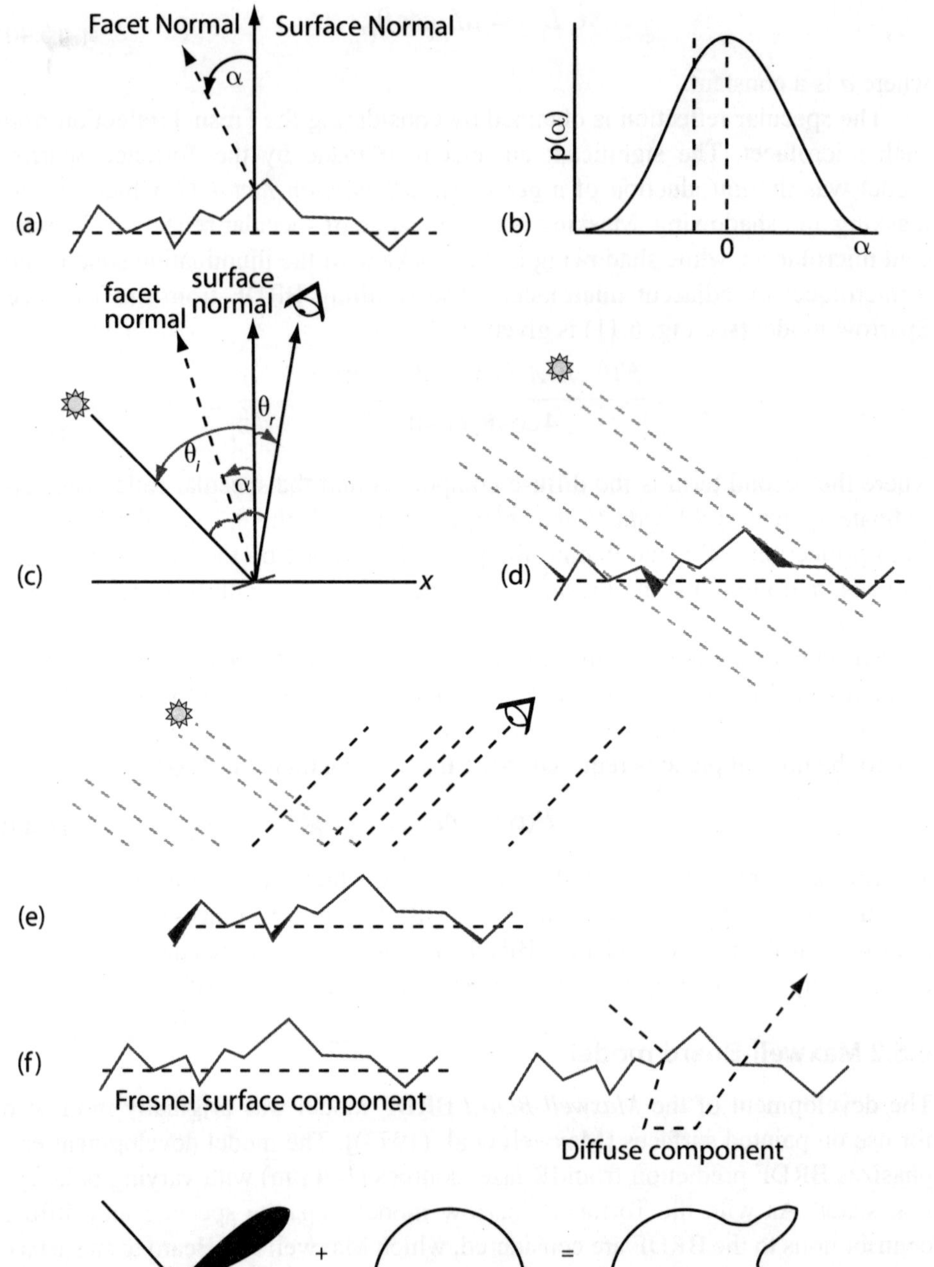

Figure 6.11 Illustration of terms used in the Torrance-Sparrow BRDF model (note that azimuthal effects are ignored to simplify the illustration but are included in the model). (a) Facetized surface; (b) Gaussian probability distribution of facet normals; (c) For a given source-sensor geometry, only one angle α will result in a specular reflection and that angle has a probability of occurring as shown in (b); (d) shadowing effects (i.e., these facets will not contribute to final radiance); (e) masking effects (i.e., shaded facets will not contribute to final radiance); and (f) BRDF is the sum of specular and diffuse components.

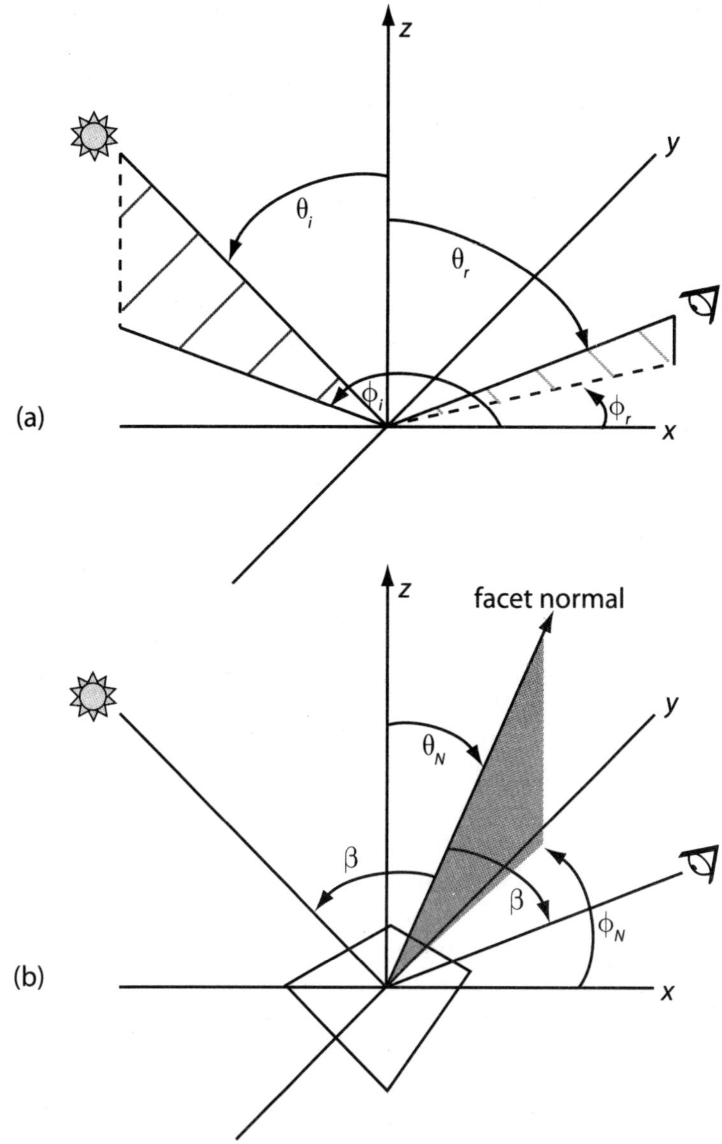

Figure 6.12 Illustration of the geometric parameters used in the Maxwell-Beard model. θ_N, ϕ_N defines the facet normal relative to the surface geometry described in (a) global geometry defined relative to the plane of the surface. (b) The sun-target-sensor defines a plane β that is the half angle in this plane between the sun and the sensor. The facet normal required to generate a specular reflection must be in the plane and at an equal angle β from the sun and the sensors.

giving a density of $\Xi\ (\theta_N, \phi_N)$ that has units of sr^{-1}. Reflection from the microfacets is given by the Fresnel reflectance. This provides an empirical way to describe the facet probability distribution instead of the Gaussian assumption used in the Torrance-Sparrow model.

In terms of these experimentally measured parameters, the surface model component of the BRDF may be expressed as

$$f_{r_{\mathrm{surf}}}(\theta_i,\phi_i;\theta_r,\phi_r)=\frac{R_F(\beta)}{R_F(0)}\frac{f_{ZBS}(\theta_N)\cos^2\theta_N}{\cos\theta_i\cos\theta_r}, \tag{6.43}$$

where R_F is the Fresnel reflectance, expressed in terms of half the angle between the source and receiver, and 2β is the bistatic angle or angle between the source and receiver. $f_{ZBS}(\theta_N)$ is the BRDF from the ZBS scan through the zenith position (*i.e.*, $-90\text{ deg}\leq\theta_i=\theta_r\leq 90\text{ deg}$). It is given by

$$f_{ZBS}(\theta_N)=\frac{R_F(0)\Xi(\theta_N,\phi_N)}{4\cos\theta_i\cos\theta_r}, \tag{6.44}$$

from which the microfacet density function is obtained.

All of the information needed for Eq. (6.43) is experimentally obtained. However, the Fresnel reflectance requires the complex index of refraction $\hat{n}$ of the material. Maxwell and Beard assumed that the surfaces were dielectrics, a reasonable assumption for the paint samples they were modeling, making $k\approx 0$ or $\hat{n}\approx n$. A value of n in their study was estimated as $n=1.65$ and was based on experience with paint samples. As an alternative, Maxwell-Beard indicates the value of n may be calculated based on Brewster's angle θ_B or the angle of incidence where the *P*-polarization component is minimum.

Using Eq. (6.43), Maxwell and Beard derived what the in-plane BRDF should be with a fixed incident angle. They found systematic variations that were attributed to shadowing and masking of the microfacets, previously addressed in the Torrance-Sparrow model discussion. However, Maxwell and Beard developed their own empirically derived function to account for shadowing and obscuration (SO), which they found superior to the Torrance-Sparrow function. The SO function has two free parameters, τ and Ω, and is given by

$$\mathrm{SO}(\tau,\Omega)=\frac{1+\frac{\theta_N}{\Omega}e^{-2\beta/\tau}}{1+\frac{\theta_N}{\Omega}}\left(\frac{1}{1+\frac{\phi_N}{\Omega}\frac{\theta_i}{\Omega}}\right), \tag{6.45}$$

where ϕ_N is a "factor calculated from the geometry, which adjusts the falloff rate of the shadowing and obscuration function in the forward-scattered direction." With this modification, the Maxwell-Beard surface BRDF is given by

$$f_{r_{\mathrm{surf}}}(\theta_i,\phi_i;\theta_r,\phi_r)=\frac{R_F(\beta)}{R_F(0)}\frac{f_{ZBS}(\theta_N)\cos^2\theta_N}{\cos\theta_i\cos\theta_r}\mathrm{SO}(\tau,\Omega). \tag{6.46}$$

Maxwell and Beard then developed a volume component of the model. The non-Lambertian volume component development was motivated by experimental observation that the diffuse scatter component was in fact not Lambertian, due to both the angular dependency and the lack of complete depolarization. The non-Lambertian volume component accounts for subsurface scatter, or the type-B and

-C photons in Fig. 6.6. Derivation of this volume component considers the exponential loss via scattering of energy as the light propagates into the medium, as well as the exponential loss of energy as the light propagates back to the surface. It is assumed that there is no net transmission of energy through the surface, and absorption in the medium is not explicitly considered. Given these considerations, the parametric volume component of the BRDF is given as

$$f_{r_{\text{vol}}} = \frac{2\rho_v f(\beta) g(\theta_N)}{\cos\theta_i + \cos\theta_r}, \tag{6.47}$$

where $f(\beta)$ and $g(\theta_{\hat{N}})$ collectively include the β and θ_N dependencies, and are treated as free parameters for adjustment based on the empirical data. However, the computer model implemented by Maxwell and Beard kept $f(\beta) = g(\theta_{\hat{N}}) = 1$, and simply states that these parameters may provide flexibility in future model development. ρ_V is a constant that may be seen to equal $f_{r_{\text{vol}}}$ when $\theta_i = \theta_r = 0$ deg and with $f(\beta) = g(\theta_{\hat{N}}) = 1$. ρ_V is experimentally obtained by measuring the BRDF at $\theta_i = \theta_r = 0$ deg with the incident light polarized orthogonally to the detector filter.

The complete Maxwell-Beard BRDF model is given by the sum of the surface and volume components, or

$$\begin{aligned} f_r(\theta_i,\phi_i;\theta_r,\phi_r) &= f_{r_{\text{surf}}} + f_{r_{vol}} \\ &= \frac{R_F(\beta)}{R_F(0)} \frac{f_{ZBS}(\theta_N)\cos^2\theta_N}{\cos\theta_i\cos\theta_r} SO(\tau,\Omega) + 2\frac{\rho_v f(\beta) g(\theta_N)}{\cos\theta_i + \cos\theta_r}. \end{aligned} \tag{6.48}$$

So, how is the model implemented? The monostatic scan is necessary for determining the microfacet surface normal distribution function. For the microfacet Fresnel reflectance, an estimate of $\hat{n}$ is required that may be estimated based on Brewster's angle derived from experimental data. Using these as inputs, three parameters are fit to empirically measured BRDF; two of these parameters model the shadowing and obscuration, τ and Ω, and one gives the volume component of the scatter, ρ_V. Values of these parameters used in the Maxwell-Beard paper for a green and tan paint were $\tau = 15$ [radians], $\Omega=40$ [radians], and $\rho_V=0.007$ and 0.05 [sr^{-1}].

The *Nonconventional Exploitation Factors Data System* (NEFDS) uses a modified version of the Maxwell-Beard model [NEF (1996)]. The SO function is simplified and does not include the term in parentheses in Eq. (6.45). The volume scattering parameters $f(\beta)$ and $g(\theta_{\hat{N}})$ are also dropped. However, the NEF version allows the simultaneous inclusion of a Lambertian (ρ_D) as well as the non-Lambertian volume component of scatter. These modifications result in a form of the Maxwell-Beard model given by

$$f_r(\theta_i,\phi_i;\theta_r,\phi_r)$$
$$=\frac{R_F(\beta)}{R_F(0)}\frac{f_{ZBS}(\theta_N)\cos^2\theta_N}{\cos\theta_i\cos\theta_r}\left(\frac{1+\frac{\theta_N}{\Omega}e^{-2\beta/\tau}}{1+\frac{\theta_N}{\Omega}}\right)+\rho_D+\frac{2\rho_\upsilon}{\cos\theta_i+\cos\theta_r}. \quad (6.49)$$

The Maxwell-Beard model is addressed in more detail in Sec. 6.5.3.1 as part of the target material pBRDF model development. The models discussed to this point have focused on the scalar BRDF. In the next section we will introduce pBRDF models that will be treated in more depth in Chapters 9 and 11.

6.5.3 Polarimetric BRDF models

Polarimetric BRDF (pBRDF) models are required for predicting the reflected polarized radiance given an incident irradiance having arbitrary polarization. There has been minimal development of pBRDF models. As with the scalar or intensity-only conventional BRDF models, a distinction is made between homogeneous (target) materials and inhomogeneous (background) materials. For target materials, polarized versions of scalar BRDF target models have been created by incorporating the Fresnel reflectance contributions from the microfacet surface representation. The Mueller matrix for each microfacet is considered and related back to the global macrogeometry, and a superposition of the individual microfacet polarized radiance contributions is made. Background material pBRDF models have been developed that crudely approximate landcover classes at large GSDs.

6.5.3.1 Target material pBRDF models

A late 1990s industry survey concluded that no existing pBRDF model represented pBRDF signatures with the required fidelity [Hess and Priest (1999)]. However, some historical scalar BRDF models such as He (1991) provide an intrinsic means of modeling polarization.

Like He's model, a new physical optics model by Duncan et al. (2003) also provides polarization information. Other historical scalar BRDF models derive polarized reflectance values as an intermediary to calculating the scalar radiant intensity L or the L_0 Stokes vector component. However, few efforts have been made toward implementing fully polarized versions of these models.

Recently, Priest and Germer (2000) and Priest and Meier (2002) provided a general polarized formulation for a microfacet BRDF model. The microfacets are represented as a 2-D Gaussian distribution function from which the polarized radiance may be calculated. A polarized version of the Sandford-Robertson BRDF model has been developed by Conant and Iannarilli (2002), where the volumetric scattering component is considered to be completely depolarizing. Finally, a polarized variant of the Torrance-Sparrow BRDF model has been reported by Fetrow et al. (2002). Meyers (2002) implemented a hybrid model using the Priest microfacet specular reflectance and the volumetric scattering component of the Torrance-Sparrow model.

In pBRDF models, it is common to assume that the volumetric scattering is completely depolarizing (cf. type-B photons in Fig. 6.6). However, as reported by Ellis (1996), this assumption is not always accurate.

In summary, most of the pBRDF target models employ a fully polarized Mueller matrix representation of the Fresnel specular term and assume that the scalar form of the volumetric and shadowing terms suffice. As a result they look mathematically identical to Eqs. (6.41) and (6.49) with the Fresnel reflectance terms $F(\theta_i, \hat{n})$ and $R_F(\beta)$ replaced with the Fresnel Mueller matrix introduced in Sec. 6.2.1.

6.5.3.2 Background material pBRDF models

Even fewer pBRDF models for background materials exist; however, there is a parameterized model that supports the POLDER mission. Data collected over large, homogeneous land areas was analyzed to produce two expressions for the pBRDF of land cover. pBRDF representations for general "vegetation" and "soil" classes have been developed [Rondeaux and Herman (1991) and Bréon et al. (1995)]. The models are used as a linear combination with the relative weighting based on a normalized difference vegetation index (NDVI) calculation [Nadal and Bréon (1999)]. The models are given by

$$\rho_p^{veg} = \frac{F_p(\alpha)}{4(\cos\theta_i + \cos\theta_r)}, \tag{6.50}$$

$$\rho_p^{soil} = \frac{F_p(\alpha)}{4\cos\theta_i \cos\theta_r}, \tag{6.51}$$

where α is the incident angle and $\alpha = (\pi - \gamma)/2$, where γ is given by

$$\cos\gamma = -\cos\theta_i \cos\theta_r - \sin\theta_i \sin\theta_r \cos\phi. \tag{6.52}$$

$F_p(\alpha)$ is the polarized fraction of the Fresnel reflectance given by

$$F_p(\alpha) = \frac{1}{2}\left(\frac{\hat{n}\cos\alpha_t - \cos\alpha}{\hat{n}\cos\alpha_t + \cos\alpha}\right)^2 - \left(\frac{\hat{n}\cos\alpha - \cos\alpha_t}{\hat{n}\cos\alpha + \cos\alpha_t}\right)^2, \tag{6.53}$$

where α_t is the transmitted angle solved via Snell's law.

This model provides a baseline by which the pBRDF of natural materials may be represented—however, only at a GSD that integrates out the BRDF variability. For this reason even if it were highly accurate, it is inadequate for our purposes. Existing scalar BRDF models for background materials are not readily amenable to a polarized adaptation. A viable background pBRDF representation will likely be stochastic in nature due to the high variability of these materials at GSDs of interest (GSD $\approx$ 0.3 m). We will return to this issue in Chapter 10.

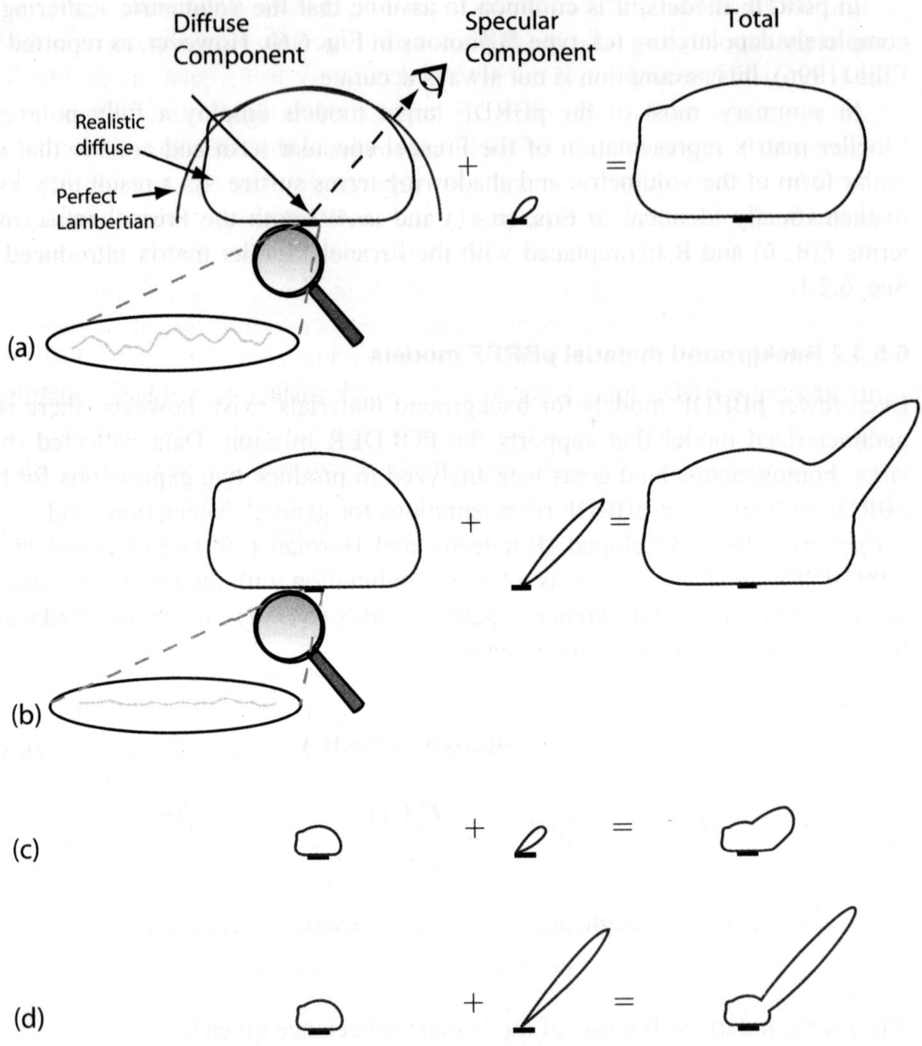

Figure 6.13 Illustrations showing conceptual BRDF for various materials. The plots show the magnitude of the radiance for reflectance angles in the principle plane for targets illuminated as shown. (a) Approximately diffuse white surface, (b) white surface with strong specular component, (c) approximately diffuse black surface, and (d) black surface with strong specular component.

6.6 Summary of pBRDF Concepts

It is always valuable to have an intuitive sense of the dominant parameters that can control the phenomenon we are trying to understand. The mathematics of BRDF, and pBRDF in particular, often does not generate this intuitive sense. To help with this first-order conceptualization, consider the illustration of two surfaces shown in Figs. 6.13(a) and 6.13(b) and the simplified principle plane BRDF cross-section model associated with each. The BRDF model assumes that there is a multiple scattered approximately Lambertian term (diffuse) additively combined with a single scattered first surface reflection term (specular). Shadowing and obscuration at grazing angles cause the diffuse term to deviate from the true Lambertian behavior, which would cause the scattered radiance to be equal in all directions. As our intuition tells us, the smoother surface has a significantly larger specular component. These two surfaces might approximate the behavior of a white automobile hood (see Fig. 6.13(b)) and relatively rough white construction paper (see Fig. 6.13(a)). They have approximately the same reflectivity when illuminated at 45 deg and viewed from overhead. But when viewed from the specular direction, the construction paper appears roughly the same as when viewed from overhead, while the car hood appears much brighter (the common effect of reflected solar glare from the smooth finish on an automobile). Figures 6.13(c) and 6.13(d) show similar simple BRDF models for a diffuse black surface (e.g., black construction paper) and a specular black surface (e.g., black automobile hood). Note that again the vertical views of these two black targets would produce similar signal levels. From the specular view angle the contrast would be exaggerated because at the specular view angle, the specular (first surface) component is a larger fraction of the overall signal.

The treatment thus far has dealt only with the magnitude of the radiance. Since our visual system is polarization insensitive, this is to first order what we would see and is in keeping with our intuitive sense of the behavior of surfaces. When attempting to build an intuitive sense of the polarized behavior of materials, we need to consider the impact of properties such as surface roughness and absorption on the reflected (and absorbed) polarized radiance. To help with this process we have reproduced Fig. 6.13 as Fig. 6.14, adding the polarized components. To make the figures more comparable, we are showing twice the polarized radiance in the BRDF illustrations so that the average value represents the magnitude of the unpolarized radiance in each direction and should reproduce the values in Fig. 6.13, i.e.,

$$L_{\text{TOT}} = L_{\perp} + L_{\parallel} = \frac{2L_{\perp} + 2L_{\parallel}}{2}, \tag{6.54}$$

where L_{TOT} represents the total radiance (or reflectance factor) shown in Fig. 6.13, and $L_{\perp}$ and $L_{\parallel}$ are the perpendicular and parallel components of the reflected radiance (or reflectance factors), respectively.

Let's begin by considering the multiple scattered (diffuse) component of the BRDF in Fig. 6.14. The randomly polarized incident flux will potentially become partially polarized on reflection. However, after undergoing multiple reflections from the randomly oriented microfacets that make up the surface, the orientation of the aggregate polarization is expected to again be random such that we expect the diffuse (multiple scattered) component of the polarization to be random. Thus, the parallel and perpendicular components of the diffuse terms in Fig. 6.14 are approximately equal. To understand the single scattered (specular) component, it is often useful to consider absorbed flux as well. In Fig. 6.14, we have included an

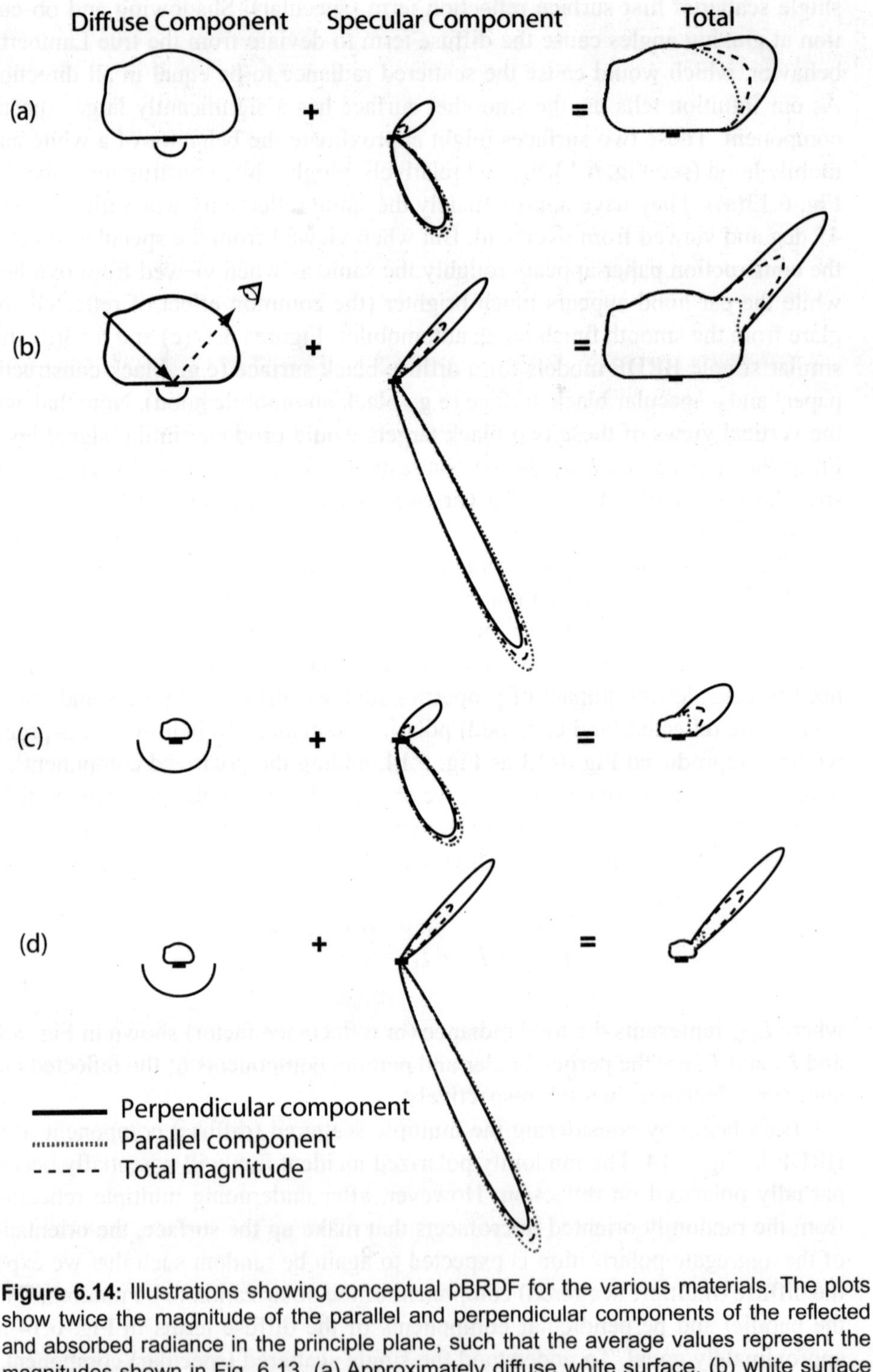

Figure 6.14: Illustrations showing conceptual pBRDF for the various materials. The plots show twice the magnitude of the parallel and perpendicular components of the reflected and absorbed radiance in the principle plane, such that the average values represent the magnitudes shown in Fig. 6.13. (a) Approximately diffuse white surface, (b) white surface with strong specular component, (c) approximately diffuse black surface, and (d) black surface with strong specular component.

illustration showing the direction and magnitude of the energy absorbed at each polarization below the target. This figure shows that because of the microfacet orientations, some energy will be transmitted through the surface at essentially all angles and absorbed. Because the most probable orientation of a microfacet is horizontal, most of the transmitted (and therefore absorbed) flux will be headed into the directions of refracted beams associated with nearly horizontal surfaces. The EM energy oscillating in the plane of incidence (||) (and therefore perpendicular to the surface) is more likely to penetrate the microfacets and be absorbed. Conversely, the EM energy oscillating perpendicular to the plane of incidence ($\perp$) (and therefore parallel to the near-horizontal microfacets) is less likely to be transmitted and more likely to be reflected. As we see in the simplified model shown in Fig. 6.14, this results in significantly more in-plane (||) energy absorbed (leaving less to be specularly reflected) than perpendicular ($\perp$) energy, with the net result that the specular lobe is dominated by perpendicular (i.e., horizontally polarized radiation). This logic suggests, as seen in Fig. 6.14a, that while some polarization may be induced at many angles, the most significant polarization will appear in the specular direction. Furthermore, the more specular surfaces will be strongly polarized (i.e., have larger DoP values).

Recognize that in the principle plane for a horizontal surface, the linear polarization will be almost exclusively either horizontal or perpendicular (since symmetry dictates that polarization at angles either side of vertical will be balanced by polarization on the other side of vertical). Thus, we can define the first order DoP as

$$\text{DoP} \simeq \frac{S_1}{S_0} = \frac{|L_\perp - L_{||}|}{L_\perp + L_{||}}. \tag{6.55}$$

To use the visualization in Fig. 6.14, the DoP is equal to half the difference between the $\perp$ and || components (recall that we are plotting twice the value for comparison purposes) divided by the average value. This is very telling when we compare the white specular target to the black specular target. Here we see that the high absorption by the black target has a significant impact on the denominator of Eq. (6.55), resulting in much higher DoP values. In fact, even though the more diffuse black sample induces less polarization, it still has a higher DoP than the diffuse white sample. In general, the percentage of reflection due to first surface reflection is larger for dark objects; therefore, they will tend to exhibit more polarized behavior (i.e., have higher DoP values).

Note that the treatment presented here has been simplified for clarity. It is intended to provide an intuitive sense of some of the parameters that impact the polarized behavior of materials relative to the diffuse and specular behavior of which we already have an intuitive sense through our daily observations of the world. Once again, it is important to note that the Fresnel reflection behavior is a function of the complex index of refraction (that is not fully captured in this simplified treatment) and that the effective roughness of a surface is a function of wavelength (i.e., surfaces that appear smooth relative to flux at 2.5 μm will appear somewhat rougher to flux at 0.4 μm).

This section has presented a framework for describing the polarimetric reflectance properties of materials. In practice, there are relatively few materials whose pBRDF values have been characterized. Essentially all of the models have unknown parameters that require rather extensive measurements to generate an estimate of these unknowns. As a result, much analysis is forced to proceed on the basis of generalizations about the relative behavioral properties of materials. When more quantitative analysis is required, the existing database can be searched and, where necessary, augmented with additional measurements. One approach to such measurements in the reflective regime is described in Chapter 10.

As to the generalizations, we will summarize some of them here.

(1) Nadir view/nadir illumination tends to induce no polarization difference.

(2) Polarization from specular surfaces (as expressed by the DoP) tends to increase with view angle away from the zenith and then decrease even though the total amount of reflected energy increases.

(3) Umov's effect indicates that the DoP of dark objects will tend to be high compared to the DoP of bright objects of similar composition.

(4) It is the specular component of the reflectance that tends to induce polarization.

  (4a) Thus, objects viewed in the specular direction are more likely to have polarimetric signatures.

  (4b) Objects that are smooth relative to the wavelength are more likely to have first surface (i.e., specular) returns and therefore, exhibit polarized behavior.

(5) The electric field reflected perpendicular to the plane of incidence (reflectance) is typically larger than the field parallel to the plane of incidence (reflectance). Thus, the angle of the polarization tends to be oriented in the plane parallel to the prevailing plane of the surface.

(6) Most naturally occurring objects and first surface reflectance from man-made objects tend not to exhibit circular polarization. As a result, much polarimetric remote sensing focuses on analysis of linear polarization.

Our discussion of polarization to this point has tended to focus on measurement or observation of the behavior of materials in a controlled environment (e.g., an object illuminated from a direction with either completely random or linearly polarized radiation). Our interest of course is in viewing and understanding the polarimetric behavior of the world in the much more complicated scenario of the natural radiation field. To this end, the next chapter will review the governing equation for scalar remote sensing of reflected radiance and then develop an equivalent expression incorporating polarization effects.

References

Apel, O., Goerling, C., Leinhos, U., Mann, K.R., & Schaefer, B. (2001). "CHARISMA: a new way for angular-resolved scattering measurements." *Proceedings SPIE*, Vol. 4347, pp. 569–578.

Bicket, W.S., & Bailey, W.M. (1985). "Stokes vectors, Mueller matrices, and polarized scattered light." *American Journal of Physics*, Vol. 53, No. 5, pp. 468–478.

Boucher, Y., Cosnefroy, H., Petit, A.D., Serrot, G., & Briottet, X. (1999). "Comparison of measured and modeled BRDF of natural targets." *Proceedings SPIE*, Vol. 3699, pp. 16–26.

Bréon, F.M., Tanré, D., Lecomte, P., & Herman, M. (1995). "Polarized reflectance of bare soils and vegetation: measurements and models." *IEEE Transactions on Geoscience and Remote Sensing*, Vol. 33, No. 2, pp. 487–499.

Chenault, D.B., Pezzaniti, J.L., & Chipman, R.A. (1992). "Mueller matrix algorithms." *Proceedings SPIE*, Vol. 1746, pp. 231–246.

Conant, J.A., & Iannarilli, J.F.J. (2002). "Development of a combined bidirectional reflectance and directional emittance model for polarization modeling." *Proceedings SPIE*, Vol. 4481, pp. 206–215.

Coulson, K.L. (1988). *Polarization and Intensity of Light in the Atmosphere*. A. Deepak Pub., Hampton, VA.

Czapla-Myers, J.S., Thome, K.J., & Biggar, S.F. (2002). "Optical sensor package for multiangle measurements of surface reflectance." *Proceedings SPIE*, Vol. 4480, pp. 326–333.

Dana, K.J., Ginneken, B.V., Nayar, S.K., & Koenderink, J.J. (1999). "Reflectance and texture of real-world surfaces." *ACM Transactions on Graphics*, Vol. 18, No. 1, pp. 1–34.

Dana, K.J. (2001). "BRDF/BTF measurement device." *IEEE, Eighth International Conference on Computer Vision,* Volume 2, pp. 460–466.

Dana, K.J., & Wang, J. (2004). "Device for convenient measurement of spatially varying bidirectional reflectance." *Journal of the Optical Society of America A*, Vol. 21, No. 1, pp. 1–12.

Deering, D.W., & Leone, P. (1986). "A sphere-scanning radiometer for rapid directional measurements of sky and ground radiance." *Remote Sensing of Environment*, Vol. 19, No. 1, pp. 1–24.

Demircan, A., Schuster, R., Radke, M., Schnermark, M., & Rser, H.P. (2000). "Use of a wide angle CCD line camera for BRDF measurements." *Infrared Physics & Technology*, Vol. 41, pp. 11–19.

Deschamps, P.Y., Bréon, F.c.M., Leroy, M., Podair, A., Bricaud, A., Buriez, J.C., & Sèze, G.e. (1994). "The POLDER mission: Instrument characteristics and scientific objectives." *IEEE Transactions on Geoscience and Remote Sensing*, Vol. 32, No. 3, pp. 598–615.

Duncan, D.D., Hahn, D.V., & Thomas, M.E. (2003). "Physics-based polarimetric BRDF models." *Proceedings SPIE*, Vol. 5192, pp. 129–140.

Ellis, K.K. (1996). "Polarimetric bidirectional reflectance distribution function of glossy coatings." *Journal of the Optical Society of America A*, Vol. 13, No. 8, pp. 1758–1762.

Epema, G.F. (1991). "Studies of errors in field measurements of the bidirectional reflectance factor." *Remote Sensing of Environment*, Vol. 35, pp. 37–49.

Feng, X. (1990). "Comparison of Methods for Generation of Absolute Reflectance Factor Measurements for BRDF Studies." Master's thesis, Rochester Institute of Technology, Rochester.

Feng, X., Schott, J.R., & Gallagher, T.W. (1993). "Comparison of methods for generation of absolute reflectance factor values for BRDF studies." *Applied Optics*, Vol. 32, No. 7, pp. 1234–1242.

Fetrow, M.P., Wellems, D., Sposato, S.H., Bishop, K.P., Caudill, T.R., Davis, M.L., & Simrell, E.R. (2002). "Results of a new polarization simulation." *Proceedings SPIE*, Vol. 4481, pp. 149–162.

Flynn, D.S., & Alexander, C. (1995). "Polarized surface scattering expressed in terms of a bidirectional reflectance distribution function matrix." *Optical Engineering*, Vol. 34, pp. 1646–1650.

Goldstein, D.H. (2003). *Polarized Light*. 2nd Ed., Marcel Dekker Inc., New York.

Han, J.Y., & Perlin, K. (2003). "Measuring bidirectional texture reflectance with a kaleidoscope." *ACM Transactions on Graphics*, Vol. 22, No. 3, pp. 741–748.

Hapke, B., DiMucci, D., Nelson, R., & Smythe, W. (1996). "The cause of the hot spot in vegetation canopies and soils: Shadow-hiding versus coherent backscatter." *Remote Sensing of Environment*, Vol. 58, No. 1, pp. 63–68.

Hayes, D.M. (1997). "Error propagation in decomposition of Mueller matrices." *Proceedings SPIE*, Vol. 3121, pp. 112–123.

He, X., Torrance, K., Sillon, F., & Greenberg, D. (1991). "A comprehensive physical model for light reflection." *Proceedings of the 18th Annual Conference on Computer Graphics and Interactive Techniques*, (*SIGGRAPH*), pp.175–186.

Hess, M., & Priest, R. (1999). "Comparison of polarization bidirectional reflectance distribution function (BRDF) models." *IEEE Aerospace Conference Proceedings*, Vol. 4, pp. 95–102.

Leroy, M., Deuzé, J.L., Bréon, F.M., Hautecoeur, O., Herman, M., Buriez, J.C., Tanré, D., Bouffiès, S., Chazette, P., & Roujean, J.L. (1997). "Retrieval of atmospheric properties and surface bidirectional re-flectances over the land from POLDER (processing algorithms)." *Journal of Geophysical Research*, Vol. 102, No. D14, pp. 7023–7037.

Lyapustin, A.I., & Privette, J.L. (1999). "A new method of retrieving surface bidirectional reflectance from ground measurements: Atmospheric sensitivity study." *Journal of Geophysical Research*, Vol. 104, No. D6, pp. 6257–6268.

Marschner, S.R., Westin, S.H., Lafortune, E.P.F., Torrance, K.E., & Greenberg, D.P. (1999). "Image-based BRDF measurement including human skin." *Proceedings from Tenth Eurographics Workshop on Rendering,* pp. 139–152.

Maxwell, J.R., Beard, J., Weiner, S., Ladd, D., & Ladd, S. (1973). "Bidirectional reflectance model validation and utilization." *Technical Report AFAL-TR-73-303*, Environmental Research Institute of Michigan (ERIM).

Meyers, J.P. (2002). "Modeling Polarimetric Imaging Using DIRSIG." Doctoral dissertation, Rochester Institute of Technology, Rochester.

Nadal, F., Nadal, F., & Breon, F.M. (1999). "Parameterization of surface polarized reflectance derived from POLDER spaceborne measurements." *IEEE Transactions on Geoscience and Remote Sensing*, Vol. 37, No. 3, pp. 1709–1718.

Nandy, P., Thome, K.J., & Biggar, S.F. (1999). "Laboratory characterization of a CCD camera system for retrieval of bi-directional reflectance distribution function." *Proceedings SPIE*, Vol. 3870, pp. 243–253.

Nandy, P., Thome, K., & Biggar, S. (2001). "Characterization and field use of a CCD camera system for retrieval of bidirectional reflectance distribution function." *Journal of Geophysical Research*, Vol. 106, No. D11, pp. 11957–11966.

NASA MODIS land team. (2004). "Grassland PROVE (prototype validation exercise)." http://modarch.gsfc.nasa.gov/MODIS/LAND/VAL/prove/grass/prove.html.

NEF. (1996). "Nonconventional Exploitation Factors (NEF) Modeling. Technical Report." ORD 257–96 (Limited distribution).

Ni, W., Woodcock, C.E., & Jupp, D.L.B. (1999). "Variance in bidirectional reflectance over discontinuous plant canopies." *Remote Sensing of Environment*, Vol. 69, No. 1, pp. 1–15.

Nicodemus, F.E. (1970). "Reflectance nomenclature and directional reflectance and emissivity." *Applied Optics*, Vol. 9, No. 6, pp. 1474–1475.

Nicodemus, F.E., Richmond, J.C., Hsia, J.J., Ginsberg, I.W., & Limperis, T. (1977). "Geometrical considerations and nomenclature for reflectance." *NBS Monograph 160*, U.S. Dept. of Commerce, National Bureau of Standards, Washington, DC.

Peterson, J.Q., Jensen, G.L., & Kristl, J.A. (2000). "Imaging polarimetry capabilities and measurement uncertainties in remote sensing applications." *Proceedings SPIE*, Vol. 4133, pp. 221–232.

Priest, R.G., & Germer, T.A. (2002). "Polarimetric BRDF in the microfacet model: Theory and measurements." *Proceedings of the 2000 Meeting of the Military Sensing Symposia Specialty Group on Passive Sensors*, Vol. 1, pp. 169–181.

Priest, R.G., & Meier, S.R. (2002). "Polarimetric microfacet scattering theory with applications to absorptive and reflective surfaces." *Optical Engineering*, Vol. 41, No. 5, pp. 988–993.

Rondeaux, G., & Herman, M. (1991). "Polarization of light reflected by crop canopies." *Remote Sensing of Environment*, Vol. 38, No. 1, pp. 63–75.

Radke, M., Roser, H.P., & Demircan, A. (1999). "Bidirectional reflectance measurements using a CCD-line camera on a rotating device." *IEEE, Geoscience and Remote Sensing Symposium*, Vol. 1, pp. 589–591.

Sandmeier, S., Sandmeier, W., Itten, K.I., Schaepman, M.E., & Kellenberger, T.W. (1995). "The Swiss field goniometer system (FIGOS)." *IEEE, International Geoscience and Remote Sensing Symposium*, Vol. 3, pp. 2078–2080.

Sandmeier, S.R., & Itten, K.I. (1999). "A field goniometer system (FIGOS) for acquisition of hyperspectral BRDF data." *IEEE Transactions on Geoscience and Remote Sensing*, Vol. 37, No. 2, pp. 978–986.

Sandmeier, S.R., & Strahler, A.H. (2000). "BRDF laboratory measurements." *Remote Sensing Reviews*, Vol. 18, No. 24, pp. 481–502.

Sandmeier, S.R. (2000). "Acquisition of bidirectional reflectance factor data with field goniometers." *Remote Sensing of Environment*, Vol. 73, No. 3, pp. 257–269. http://www.sciencedirect.com/.

Schaaf, C.B., Gao, F., Strahler, A.H., Lucht, W., Li, X., Tsang, T., Strugnell, N.C., Zhang, X., Jin, Y., & Muller, J.-P. (2002). "First operational BRDF, albedo nadir reflectance products from MODIS." *Remote Sensing of Environment*, Vol. 83, No. 1-2, pp. 135–148.

Schill, S. http://steve.schill.com/research.html.

Schott, J.R. (2007). *Remote Sensing: The Image Chain Approach*. 2nd Ed., Oxford University Press, New York.

Serrot, G., Bodilis, M., Briottet, X., & Cosnefroy, H. (1998). "Presentation of a new BRDF measurement device." *Proceedings SPIE*, Vol. 3494, pp. 34–40.

Shell, J.R. (2005). "Polarimetric Remote Sensing in the Visible to Near Infrared." Doctoral dissertation, Rochester Institute of Technology, Rochester.

Stover, J.C. (1995). *Optical Scattering Measurement and Analysis*. 2nd Ed., SPIE Press, Bellingham, WA.

Torrance, K.E., & Sparrow, E.M. (1967). "Theory for off-specular reflection from roughened surfaces." *Journal of the Optical Society of America A*, Vol. 57, No. 9, pp. 1105–1114.

Umov, N. (1905). "Chromatische depolarisation durch Lichtzerstreuung." *Zeitschrift für Physik A Hadrons and Nuclei.*, Vol. 6, pp. 674–676.

Walthall, C., Roujean, J.L., & Morisette, J. (2000). "Field and landscape BRDF optical wavelength measurements: Experience, techniques and the future." *Remote Sensing Reviews*, Vol. 18, No. 24, pp. 503–531.

James R. Shell II
Scott D. Brown
Chabitha Devaraj
David W. Messinger
David Pogorzala
Adam Goodenough
John R. Schott

Chapter 7
Polarized Form of the Governing Equation Including Atmospheric Scattering Terms

In this chapter we will look at all the energy sources that contribute to the polarimetric radiance reaching the sensor. In Sec. 7.1 we introduce the radiometric terms of interest in the form of a governing equation. To better understand the polarimetric nature of these terms, we delve into the polarized behavior of atmospheric scattering in Sec. 7.2. The radiometric terms and concepts used throughout this section draw heavily on the radiometry fundamentals introduced in Chapter 2.

7.1 Governing Polarized Radiance Equation

In order to analyze remotely sensed polarimetric data, we need to develop a governing equation describing all the terms that contribute to the polarimetric radiance reaching the sensor. First, the radiometric equation for the unpolarized radiance is introduced and nomenclature is established. Then, the polarimetric representation of these equations is derived. This representation highlights the role of the polarimetric BRDF and guides a simplified field measurement technique introduced in Chapter 10. The polarized radiance governing equation forms the basis for all subsequent remote sensing studies. The approach presented here follows that of Shell and Schott (2005).

7.1.1. Scalar representation of the governing equation

The total radiance in the visible to near infrared (VNIR) portion of the spectrum (i.e., that of solar origin) reaching a sensor aperture (L_s) may be approximated as the sum of three radiance sources (see Schott (2007) for a more complete derivation of the terms in the governing equation):

(1) direct solar reflection from the target (L_r)
(2) *upwelled* atmospheric *radiance* resulting from solar scatter along the target to sensor path (L_u) and
(3) target-reflected *downwelled* radiance from the skydome (L_d).

The order of the radiance terms above is that of typically decreasing magnitude, though the ground or target reflectance and atmospheric conditions greatly influence their relative values (cf. Fig. 4.12 and Table 4.1 of Schott (2007)). These radiance terms are functions of the incident and reflected zenith angles (θ_i, θ_r) and reflected azimuth angle (ϕ).

An expression for the radiance from the direct solar reflection (L_r) is obtained by first considering the *exoatmospheric solar irradiance* (E_s) that propagates through the atmosphere along the solar-to-target path having a transmittance of τ_i. When incident upon a surface, it is then reflected, and again attenuated by the atmosphere along the ground-to-sensor atmospheric path by τ_r. We can use the bidirectional reflectance distribution function (f_r) introduced in Chapter 6 to relate the reflected radiance to the incident irradiance. Assembling these terms, (L_r) may therefore be expressed as

$$L_r = \tau_r(\theta_r) f_r(\theta_i, \theta_r, \phi) \cos\theta_i \; \tau_i(\theta_i) E_s(\theta_i). \tag{7.1}$$

Care must be used with the coordinate systems in Eq. (7.1). BRDF is defined relative to the material surface normal, which generally is not coincident with the zenith direction. This requires rotation of the coordinate systems to account for the local surface normal's deviation from the normal to the earth. However, for purposes of introducing this approach, we consider only zenith-facing materials such that Eq. (7.1) is adequate. (Secondary illumination from adjacent surfaces and shadowing are also important, but are considered secondary effects and not necessary for this discussion.)

In a similar fashion, target-reflected radiance from the sky (L_d) may be derived. The downwelled radiance distributed over the entire sky hemisphere ($L_d^{\Omega i}$) is integrated to sum irradiance contributions onto the target from the sky, which is modified by the cosine of the incident angle from the surface normal. As before, each of these irradiance contributions is then reflected by the surface BRDF, which is then attenuated by the target-to-sensor atmospheric transmittance. Replacing the BRDF by an isotropic reflectance factor not having angular dependency greatly simplifies the expression, as the reflectance factor may be placed outside the integral. However, the more stringent BRDF must be retained, as it is essential to polarimetry. An appropriate expression for L_d is therefore

$$L_d = \tau_r(\theta_r) \iint_{\Omega_i} f_r(\theta_i, \theta_r, \phi) \cos\theta_i \; L_d^{\Omega_i}(\theta_i, \phi)\, d\Omega_i, \tag{7.2}$$

where $d\Omega_i = \sin\theta_i \, d\theta_i d\phi$[sr].

A full representation for the upwelled atmospheric radiance (L_u) will not be attempted, as it is rather complex and usually approximated by atmospheric scattering codes such as *MODTRAN* [Berk et al. (1999)], as is the downwelled sky radiance component ($L_d^{\Omega i}$) in Eq. (7.2). The upwelled radiance is given simply to show the geometry dependence as

$$L_u = L_u(\theta_r, \phi). \tag{7.3}$$

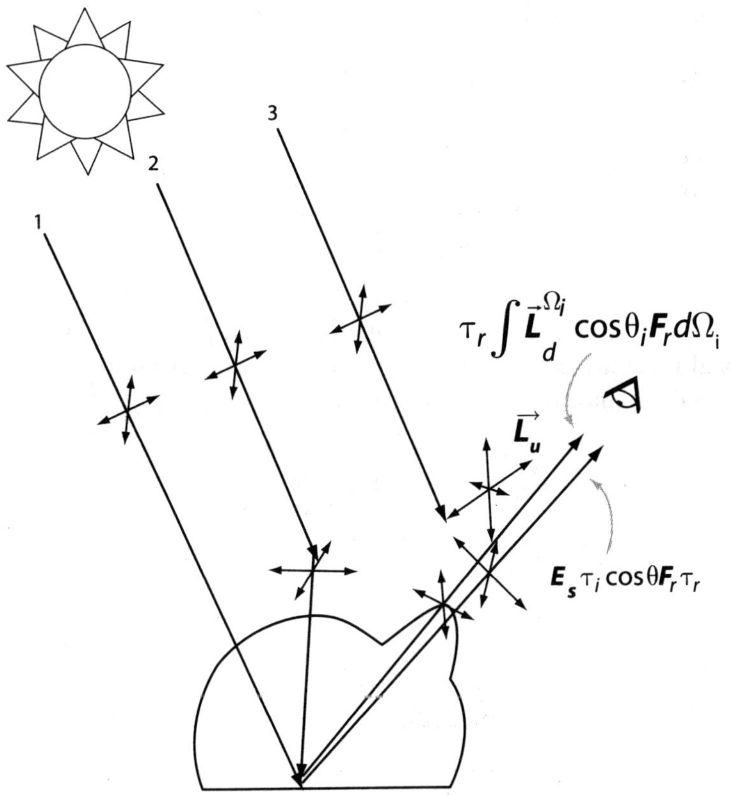

Figure 7.1 Illustration of key terms and energy paths in the governing equation. Path one shows the randomly polarized incident flux bidirectionally reflected and polarized by the target and propagated to the sensor. Path two shows randomly polarized solar illumination scattered and polarized by the atmosphere and progagated to the target where it is polarimetrically bidirectionally reflected, integrated over the hemisphere above the target, and propagated to the sensor. Path three shows randomly polarized solar illumination scattered and polarized by the atmosphere and propagated to the sensor.

7.1.2 Governing equation—Stokes representation

Transforming Eqs. (7.1) through (7.3) into the polarized representation is accomplished using the Mueller-Stokes formalism introduced in Chapters 4 and 5. In brief, all radiometric flux values are replaced by Stokes vectors and "transfer" functions such as atmospheric transmittance and reflectance (BRDF) are replaced by Mueller matrices [Shell and Schott (2005)]. Prior to making these substitutions, some simplifications are appropriate (see Fig. 7.1). First, the exoatmospheric solar irradiance may be considered randomly polarized, so only the scalar magnitude (or first Stokes component) of the direct solar irradiance needs to be considered. Second, the atmospheric transmittance values in Eqs. (7.1) through (7.3) all primarily represent absorption of forward scattering, which retains the incident polarization. Therefore, the scalar values for τ_i and τ_r may be used without resorting to a Mueller matrix representation. Eqs. (7.1) through (7.3) therefore become

$$\vec{L}_r = \tau_r(\theta_r)\, \mathbf{F}_r\, (\theta_i,\theta_r,\phi)\tau_i(\theta_i)\, \cos\theta_i\, E_s(\theta_i), \tag{7.4}$$

$$\vec{L}_d = \tau_r(\theta_r) \iint_{\Omega_i} \mathbf{F}_r(\theta_i,\theta_r,\phi)\, \cos\theta_i\, \vec{L}_d^{\Omega_i}\, (\theta_i,\phi_i)\, d\Omega_i, \tag{7.5}$$

and

$$\vec{L}_u = \vec{L}_u(\theta_r,\phi_r), \tag{7.6}$$

where $\mathbf{F}_r$ is now the polarimetric BRDF (pBRDF). Some knowledge of the upwelled polarized radiance ($\vec{L}_u$) along the target and sensor may be gained from Rayleigh scattering theory and other sources, such as Coulson et al. (1960) and Chandrasekhar (1950). However, knowledge of the polarized downwelled radiance ($\vec{L}_d^{\Omega_i}$) is more problematic since this term often has a high spatial variability, e.g., varying cloud cover. We will take a more complete look at these terms in Sec. 7.2.

The total polarized radiance reaching a sensor aperture is then

$$\vec{L}_s = \vec{L}_r + \vec{L}_d + \vec{L}_u. \tag{7.7}$$

Atmospheric scattering, generally proportional to λ^{-4}, results in $\vec{L}_d$ and $\vec{L}_u$ having relatively large magnitudes at shorter wavelengths compared to $\vec{L}_r$, especially from orbital altitudes. Polarimetric remote sensing of the atmosphere uses this phenomenon to minimize ground-reflected polarization signatures to better extract atmospheric water vapor and aerosol properties [Leroy et al. (1977)].

Conversely, for polarimetric remote sensing of land features, one often wants the magnitude of the direct solar reflected radiance to be large compared to the reflected radiance from the downwelled sky and upwelled atmospheric scattering, i.e., $\vec{L}_r > \vec{L}_d, \vec{L}_u$. This provides optimal conditions for estimating the polarimetric BRDF, $\mathbf{F}_r$. Rigorously exploiting polarimetric signatures in a manner analogous to the way spectral signatures are exploited requires estimating ($\mathbf{F}_r$), given the polarized radiance reaching the aperture ($\vec{L}_s$), just as an estimate of a material's spectral reflectance factor is desired in magnitude-only remote sensing. Estimating $\mathbf{F}_r$ given the radiance at the sensor aperture proceeds as

$$\vec{L}_r = \vec{L}_s - \vec{L}_d - \vec{L}_u, \tag{7.8}$$

whereupon substitution and rearrangement yields

$$\tau_r\, \mathbf{F}_r\, \tau_i\, \cos\theta_i\, E_s = \vec{L}_s - \tau_r \iint_{\Omega_i} \mathbf{F}_r \cos\theta_i\, \vec{L}_d^{\Omega_i}\, d\Omega_i - \vec{L}_u. \tag{7.9}$$

Since the exoatmospheric irradiance is randomly polarized, we can often assume that only the first column of the pBRDF Mueller matrix is of concern in the $\vec{L}_r$ expression when the specular component of reflected flux is dominated by direct solar reflection (i.e., we are viewing close to the principle plane). In fact, overhead polarimetric remote sensing is usually restricted to the first column of the polarimetric BRDF matrix. (Solving for other matrix elements requires illumination by varying polarization states, which can be difficult if we restrict ourselves to passive sensing.) However, recognize that in certain cases the incidence flux from the sky can be highly polarized, as discussed in Sec. 7.2. With this consideration, Eq. (7.9) may be expressed as

$$\tau_r \begin{bmatrix} f_{00} \\ f_{10} \\ f_{20} \end{bmatrix} \tau_i \cos\theta_i \, E_s = \vec{L}_s - \tau_r \iint_{\Omega_i} \mathbf{F}_r \cos\theta_i \, \vec{L}_d^{\Omega_i} \, d\Omega_i - \vec{L}_u, \tag{7.10}$$

with the first column of the pBRDF given by

$$\begin{bmatrix} f_{00} \\ f_{10} \\ f_{20} \end{bmatrix} = \frac{\vec{L}_s - \tau_r \iint_{\Omega_i} \mathbf{F}_r \cos\theta_i \, \vec{L}_d^{\Omega_i} \, d\Omega_i' - \vec{L}_u}{\tau_r \tau_i \cos\theta_i \, E_s}. \tag{7.11}$$

Solving for $\mathbf{F}_r$ is complicated by its inclusion in the integral of the $\vec{L}_d$ term, which also contains the highly spatially variable and generally ill-known downwelled radiance component ($\vec{L}_d^{\Omega_i}$). However, under nominal sky conditions, the magnitude of the direct solar irradiance for $\lambda > 600$ nm is $5\times$ that of the integrated sky dome irradiance, increasing to $10\times$ for $\lambda > 1000$ nm. This makes it reasonable (particularly when operating close to the principle plane) to approximate the polarized radiance contribution of the downwelled sky radiance as an error term:

$$\begin{bmatrix} f_{00} \\ f_{10} \\ f_{20} \end{bmatrix} = \frac{\vec{L}_s - \vec{L}_u}{\tau_r \tau_i \cos\theta_i E_s} - \frac{\tau_r \iint_{\Omega_i} F_r \cos\theta_i \vec{L}_d^{\Omega_i} d\Omega_i}{\tau_r \tau_i \cos\theta_i \, E_s} \tag{7.12}$$

$$= \frac{\vec{L}_s - \vec{L}_u}{\tau_r \tau_i \cos\theta_i \, E_s} - \begin{bmatrix} \epsilon_0 \\ \epsilon_1 \\ \epsilon_2 \end{bmatrix}. \tag{7.13}$$

Therefore, when operating near the principle plane, polarimetric remote sensing may recover the first column of the polarimetric BRDF Mueller matrix to within the error resulting from downwelled sky radiance, presented as

$$\begin{bmatrix} f_{00} + \epsilon_0 \\ f_{10} + \epsilon_1 \\ f_{20} + \epsilon_2 \end{bmatrix} = \frac{\vec{L}_s - \vec{L}_u}{\tau_r \tau_i \cos\theta_i \, E_s}. \tag{7.14}$$

Table 7.1 Maximum DoP for the Rayleigh atmosphere [Coulson (1988), © A. Deepak Publishing] and fraction of skylight to total irradiance [see Shell and Schwarting (2004)].

λ(μm)	DoPmax	dsky
0.3120	0.55	—
0.3715	0.72	0.47
0.4365	0.82	0.38
0.5460	0.91	0.28
0.8090	0.97	0.18

Note that ϵ_0 is always positive, and while termed an "error" may be approximated with some certainty (Sec. 7.2.2), reducing the error in the retrieved pBRDF. For diffuse surfaces, the ratio of ϵ_0/f_{00} is equivalent to the ratio of the downwelled sky irradiance to the direct solar irradiance. The linear polarization terms ϵ_1 and ϵ_2 may be either positive or negative and represent the polarization resulting from the downwelled sky radiance. The polarimetric downwelled radiance terms may be estimated using radiation propagation models, as discussed in Sec. 7.2.

Situations in which the total radiance (L_s) is not dominated by the direct solar reflectance component (L_r) should be recognized. For instance, consider the case of viewing water at a high incidence angle outside of the principle plane. In this situation, the dominant signal will be from the downwelled sky component (L_d), as the highly specular water surface will be reflecting the sky radiance (L_d^{Ω}) in the background. Furthermore, unlike the direct solar illumination component, the sky illumination source may itself be appreciably polarized depending on the relative orientation of the background sky to the sun and the spectral band (see Table 7.1).

In this section we have derived the framework for a governing equation incorporating the polarimetric characterization of the radiation. In order to better understand the implications of this equation, we need to look briefly at the polarized nature of the natural radiation field.

7.2 Atmospheric Scattering and the Polarized State of the Terms in the Governing Equation

In this section, we first describe the polarized nature of the radiation from the sky (Sec. 7.2.1) and then briefly look at a validation study of a radiative transfer code that will be used in later chapters to model the polarized behavior of the atmospheric terms in the governing equation. This section draws on Shell and Schott (2005) and Devaraj et al. (2007).

7.2.1 Characterization of the polarized state of the incident radiative field

In this section we examine in more detail the polarized nature of the atmospheric terms in the governing equation. Specifically, the downwelled and upwelled radiance components, $\overrightarrow{L_d}$ and $\overrightarrow{L_u}$, must be considered. For intensity-only remote sensing, ($\overrightarrow{L_d}$) or equivalently L_{0d} provides additional signal (reflectance) from the target. This is particularly true when the Lambertian reflectance approximation is considered. However, in polarimetric remote sensing, this term is a source of uncertainty, as the $\overrightarrow{L_d}$ polarization is dependent on the geometric location in the sky dome.

Upwelled radiance ($\overrightarrow{L_u}$) or the solar energy that is scattered in the atmosphere in the direction toward the sensor, is an additive term that increases the uncertainty in both intensity and polarimetric remote sensing. It must be subtracted from the sensor-reaching radiance when recovering the reflectance factor or the first column of the pBRDF Mueller matrix (Eq. (7.12)). For intensity-only remote sensing, it serves as a contrast reduction term. The effects of $\overrightarrow{L_u}$ in polarimetric remote sensing are more complex, since the upwelled radiance is, in general, polarized.

Conservation of energy is observed with radiance in the atmosphere, as in any other medium. Atmospheric transmittance along the incident or solar-to-target path (τ_i) and along the reflected or target-to-sensor path (τ_r) were previously introduced as factors that attenuate the energy along that path. From the conservation of energy, it is noted that

$$\tau = 1 - \rho - \alpha, \tag{7.15}$$

where ρ is reflectance or scattering and α is absorptance. τ may be expressed in terms of the *optical depth* (δ) as

$$\tau = e^{-\delta} = e^{-(\delta_s + \delta_\alpha)}, \tag{7.16}$$

where δ_s and δ_α are the optical depths for the scattered (reflected) and absorbed components. Generally, absorption results in photons being lost to thermal energy conversion by atmospheric constituents. It is the reflectance or scattering that is of most interest here, as it is these photons that are responsible for the $\overrightarrow{L_u}$ and $\overrightarrow{L_d}$ components.

Atmospheric scattering is fundamentally governed by the interaction of electromagnetic energy with molecules and particles. Solutions for the interaction of electromagnetic waves with these molecules and particles are complex and governed by Maxwell's equations. It is convenient to approximate the scattering effect based on the size of the scattering center relative to the wavelength of incident radiation. *Rayleigh scatter* results from interaction with molecules or particles that are small in comparison to λ. *Mie* or aerosol *scattering* theory applies to particles whose size is on the same order as that of λ, and finally, nonselective scattering results from particles that are large compared to λ. Using these three categorizations, δ_s may be represented as the sum of these individual scattering terms, resulting in atmospheric transmittance expressed as

$$\tau = e^{-\delta} = e^{-(\delta_r + \delta_a + \delta_{ns} + \delta_\alpha)}, \tag{7.17}$$

where δ_r, δ_a, and δ_{ns} are the optical depths resulting from the Rayleigh, aerosol, and nonselective scattering, respectively. This expression provides an understanding of the source of atmospheric losses, but does not provide information on the direction of scatter—other than out of the propagation direction along which τ is determined.

The direction of the scatter and in particular the polarization of the scattered energy must be determined in order to quantify $\vec{L}_d$ and $\vec{L}_u$. This information is captured by the phase function of the scattering. Each of the three scattering components and their phase functions are now examined in more detail.

7.2.1.1 Rayleigh scatter

Rayleigh scattering applies when the particle size is small relative to the wavelength, or $[(2\pi a)/\lambda] \langle\langle 1$, where a is the radius of a spherical scatterer [Kokhanovsky (2001)]. Coulson (1988) indicates that $(a/\lambda) \leq 0.03$ is required to meet the small-particle criterion. Rayleigh scatter explains why the sky is blue, since the magnitude of the scattering is proportional to λ^{-4}. (Actually the "blue" is also a result of the spectral response of the human eye, combined with the λ-dependent scattering.) This also explains the red color associated with a sunrise and sunset, since the long solar path length through the atmosphere preferentially scatters the blue out of the propagation path. Rayleigh scatter is independent of particle size once you are below the $a/\lambda < 0.03$ threshold, which significantly simplifies the mathematical description. First, it is noted that the Rayleigh optical depth δ_r may be expressed in terms of the Rayleigh scattering coefficient (β_r) which is the magnitude of scatter per unit length of propagation (z).

$$\delta_r = \beta_r z. \tag{7.18}$$

Without further derivation β_r

$$\beta_r = \frac{32\pi^3 (\hat{n}(\lambda) - 1)^2}{3\lambda^4 m} \left[\mathrm{m}^{-1}\right], \tag{7.19}$$

where $\hat{n}(\lambda)$ is the complex index of refraction and m is the number density or molecules per cubic meter [Rayleigh (1871)]. From the scattering coefficient β_r, the attenuation along the propagation direction is therefore determined as a function of the wavelength, refractive index, and density.

The scattering out of the propagation path ($\beta_r(\theta)$) may be expressed in terms of the scattering coefficient and a *phase function* ($p(\theta)$), which provides the angular scattering distribution function,

$$\beta_r(\theta) = \frac{\beta_r}{4\pi} p(\theta)[sr^{-1}m^{-1}], \tag{7.20}$$

where the scattering angle (θ) is the angle between the direction of the incident photon and the scattered photon.

The Rayleigh phase function for randomly oriented particles [Kokhanovsky (2001)] is

$$p(\theta) = \frac{y + \cos^2\theta}{y + \frac{1}{3}}, \tag{7.21}$$

with y being a sphericity or molecular anisotropy parameter typically ranging from 1 to 13, with $y = 1$ for spherical scatterers. The *Rayleigh scattering function* for incident randomly polarized radiance and $y = 1$ is given by [Schott (2007)]:

$$\beta_r(\theta) = \frac{8\pi^2(n(\lambda)-1)^2}{3\lambda^4 m}\left[\frac{3}{4}(1+\cos^2\theta)\right]. \tag{7.22}$$

Furthermore, the DoP is given by Eq. (7.23), where it is seen for spherical scatters ($y = 1$) that the radiance becomes completely polarized as $\theta \to 90$ deg or DoP = 1 for $\theta = 90$ deg [Kokhanovsky (2001)]

$$\mathrm{DoP} = \frac{1-\cos^2\theta}{y+\cos^2\theta}. \tag{7.23}$$

The maximum DoP is always at $\theta = 90$ deg (or very close to 90 deg for actual sky conditions) and for this reason, the sky has a maximum DoP in an arc 90 deg from the sun, with the polarization composed of the *S*-polarization (i.e., at right angles to the sun-scattering center-observer plane). The location of maximum polarization is easily verified by viewing the sky radiance ($\vec{L}_d$) in different θ_i locations with a linear polarization filter. Of course, the same is true for the upwelled ($\vec{L}_u$) component, as will be seen from overhead polarization images. From Eq. (7.23), it is also seen that $\mathrm{DoP}_{max} = y^{-1}$.

The polarization of the scattered radiance is understood if the scattering geometry of dipole radiation is visualized. Incident randomly polarized radiance scattered in the forward direction continues to be randomly polarized. However, in accordance with Eq. (7.23), the polarization increases with scattering angle.

Based on Rayleigh scattering theory, Chandrasekhar (1950) derived expressions using a "discrete ordinate method" for the polarized radiance leaving the top and bottom of the atmosphere, or $\vec{L}_u$ and $\vec{L}_d$, respectively. From these expressions, Coulson et al. (1960) published tables of calculated results.

Although the magnitude of skylight decreases with increasing λ per the λ^{-4} scattering dependency, the DoP actually increases with λ. This is due to multiple scattering, which has the effect of depolarizing shorter wavelengths. The maximum DoP for a nominal atmosphere as a function of wavelength is given in Table

7.1, which also includes the typical fraction of the diffuse sky irradiance (d_{sky}) relative to the total.

While the skylight polarization is predominantly *S*-polarization, there is a negative polarization branch, or *P*-polarization (polarization direction radially oriented with respect to the sun) observed near the solar point. Multiple Rayleigh scattering has been shown as a probable source of the negative polarization branch [Coulson (1988)].

7.2.1.2 Aerosol and nonselective scatter

As the scattering center size increases to the same order as that of the wavelength, Rayleigh scattering theory breaks down and aerosol scattering theory must be used. *Aerosol scattering* is often treated by *Mie scattering* theory and is predominantly in the forward direction, which retains the initial radiance polarization. The magnitude of $\vec{L}_d$ and $\vec{L}_u$, which results from scattering away from the propagation direction, is inherently low. Therefore, the polarization from aerosol scattering may be treated as a first-order correction to Rayleigh scattering [Coulson (1988)].

Nonselective scattering may be treated by geometric optics due to the large particle sizes. The net polarization effects from aerosol and nonselective scatter are low in comparison to the polarization from Rayleigh scatter.

7.2.2 Estimation of the atmospheric terms in the polarized governing equation

Given that $\vec{L}_d$ and $\vec{L}_u$ are polarized, a means of estimating these parameters is needed such that $\vec{L}_r$ and specifically $\mathbf{F}_r$ may be retrieved, given $\vec{L}_s$ (Eq. (7.11)). The magnitude or L_0 component of $\vec{L}_u$ is frequently estimated using atmospheric propagation computer codes such as MODTRAN [Berk et al. (1999)]. Recently, polarized versions of MODTRAN (MODTRAN-P) have been developed and may also be used to estimate the polarized atmospheric radiance [Egan (2004)]. An alternate technique uses the "Coulson tables," which provide estimates of the Rayleigh scattering polarization component [Coulson (1960)].

Interestingly, some have proposed using the land-reflected polarization signature ($\vec{L}_r$ and $\vec{L}_d$) to derive the atmospheric contribution ($\vec{L}_u$). At sufficiently large GSD and over uniform land cover regions, the $\vec{L}_r + \vec{L}_d$ component may be treated as relatively constant or as "truth" data [Bréon et al. (1995)]. The land-reflected radiance components are then derived by applying background polarimetric BRDF land cover models such as those discussed in Chapter 6. Obviously, if it is the polarimetric variation between materials within the broad background class that interests us, this is not an attractive option.

The degree of polarization due to Rayleigh scatter is depicted in Fig. 7.2, along with an example of direct measurement of the polarized state of the sky from Lee (1998). Since we will seldom have access to measurements of the sky such as shown in Fig. 7.2, we will often need to resort to models to help in visual-

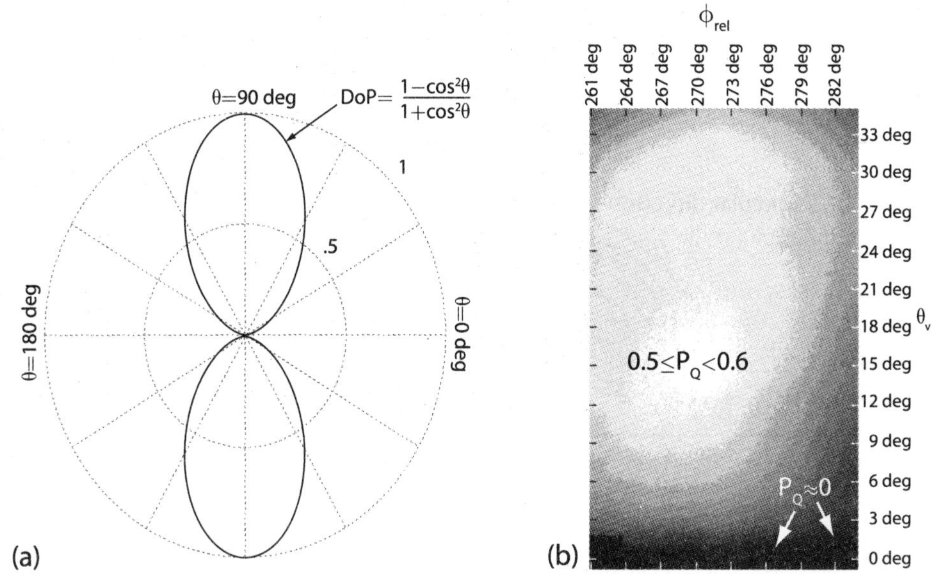

Figure 7.2 Polarization characteristics of scattered flux. (a) Polar plot of the DoP induced by Rayleigh scatter of randomly polarized flux incident on a scattering center. (b) Illustration of the relative polarization of a clear sky. The image is a grayscale representation produced from two images taken with linear polarizers oriented at right angels to each other such that the grayscale is proportional to PQ = [L(0 deg)−L(90 deg)]/[L(0 deg)+(90 deg)]. The sun is at an elevation of −0.46 deg and 0-deg azimuth. The grayscale quantization is set at DPQ = 0.05 [Courtesy of Lee (1998)].

izing the polarimetric contribution from sky light and in estimating terms in the governing equation.

7.2.2.1 Use of radiative transfer codes to estimate polarimetric atmospheric terms

This section focuses for convenience on the polarized version of MODTRAN. However as MODTRAN accounts for only Rayleigh-induced polarization, any radiative transfer code could be modified to include Rayleigh effects and achieve similar results [Fetrow et al. (2002)].

MODTRAN has been augmented to generate Stokes vectors for the radiance terms it calculates. These calculations include the polarizing influence due to single scatter by a Rayleigh atmosphere and the depolarizing effects due to multiple scatter. The solar irradiance is assumed to be randomly polarized. Furthermore, the beam transmittance along τ_i and τ_r are assumed to induce no change in the polarization. Thus, the primary sources of polarized radiance are assumed to be from the upwelled and downwelled radiance induced by Rayleigh scatter.

A critical part of understanding polarimetric signatures is understanding the relative magnitude and polarimetric state of the incident light field. The relevant terms can be estimated using the polarized version of MODTRAN. As described

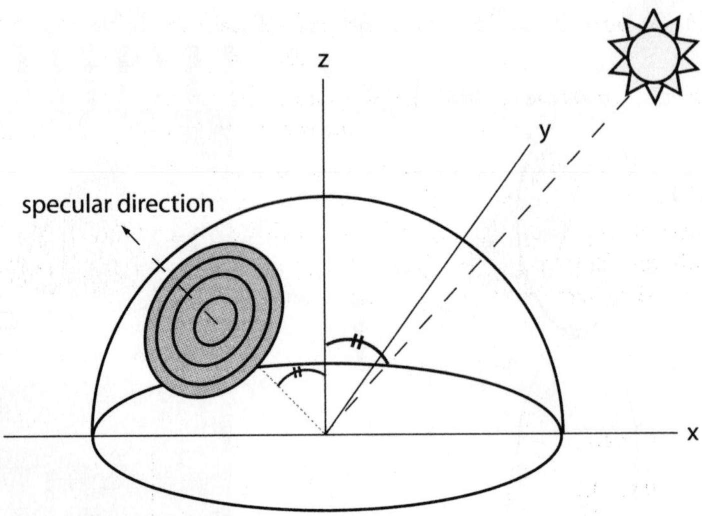

Figure 7.3 Illustration of the region in the sky (shaded) where near-specular viewing would result in approximately unpolarized radiation from both the sun and the sky for horizontal targets.

above, the direct insolation term from the sun is randomly polarized as is the forward scattered radiance from Rayleigh and Mie scatter. Thus, the largest source of incident radiance for most surfaces is randomly polarized. This is particularly true for objects viewed by a sensor in or near the principle plane of the sun, at the zenith angles near the specular angle (see Fig. 7.3). However, for specular surfaces, a significant fraction of the reflected energy can come from the downwelled sky radiation in the specular direction (cf. Fig. 7.4).

Since the specular component of the BRDF is most likely to maintain the degree of polarization of the incident flux, it is important to understand its DoP and polarization orientation. For relatively clear atmospheres, the downwelled radiance will be dominated by single scattered radiation observing the Rayleigh criteria. We can use MODTRAN to carefully predict the polarized state of the downwelled radiance as described above. However, an intuitive sense of the relative magnitude and orientation can be achieved by consideration of Fig. 7.5. This figure tells us that if we view the sky at right angles to the beam from the sun, we will have strongly polarized radiation and that the DoP falls off quite rapidly from this 90-deg value (with very small values from +30 deg to −30 deg and from 150 deg to 210 deg).

Figure 7.5 further shows that if we imagine concentric rings around the solar illumination line projected onto the sky hemisphere and envision where our sky light comes from (i.e., where it would intersect the projected rings), the polarized energy scattered from that region will be oriented along the tangent to the ring (e.g., the primary axis of polarization for the scattered energy is oriented perpendicularly to the plane containing the source, the scattering center, and the sensor). This is illustrated in Fig. 7.6 with two photos of a pair of linear polarizers

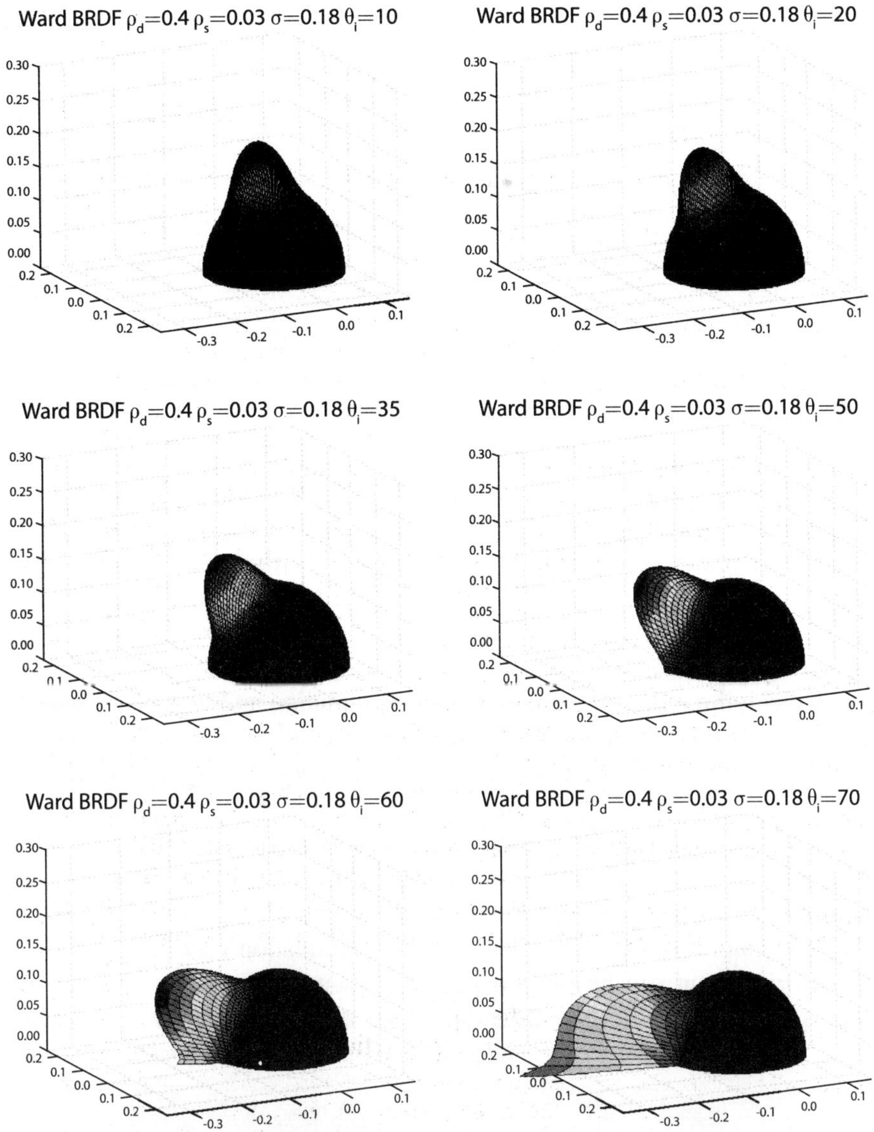

Figure 7.4 Example of BRDF functions for somewhat specular surfaces, viewed at various angles, illustrating the relative importance of the reflected energy from the specular direction. (See color plate following page 133.)

oriented at 90 deg to each other. The polarizers are transmitting the flux from the southern sky just above the horizon. In Fig. 7.6(a) the sun is low in the eastern sky and vertical polarization dominates. In Fig. 7.6(b) the sun is near the zenith and horizontal polarization dominates from the same region of the sky. Thus, one can imagine cases where the sun is low in the sky (i.e., early morning sun in the east) and we are looking at the world from the south, facing north with a large zenith angle (see Fig. 7.7). The specular reflection will be low in the northern sky

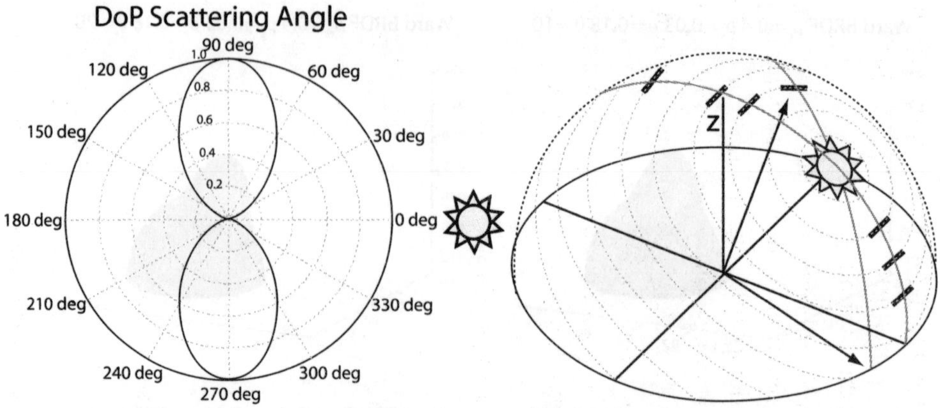

Figure 7.5 Visualizations of DoP and AoP from scattering.

and at right angles to the illumination line, so the DoP will be large. The polarization from that region of the sky will have a large vertical component. However, as we see from an assessment of how Fresnel reflectance drives BRDF (see Chapter 6), a flat level surface viewed in this fashion will tend to preferentially reflect horizontally polarized radiation. Thus, the surface when viewed in this fashion has competing phenomena. It wants to reflect mostly horizontally polarized radiation but is receiving mostly vertically polarized radiation and as a result may not have a strong polarization signature. On the other hand, if the sun were high in the southern sky (15-deg zenith) and we looked from west to east at a target with a relatively high view angle, we would again have a high DoP but this time the scattered energy would be horizontally polarized and we might expect a high DoP in the Fresnel component of the reflected beam. Thus, we see that the same target can exhibit significantly different polarization signatures depending on the sun-target-camera angle. Because the interplay of illumination/view angles, BRDF, and target orientation can be quite complex, it is useful to have a model such as MODTRAN-P to predict the behavior of the atmosphere and a visualization tool to help understand the target energy interaction. In the next section, we will

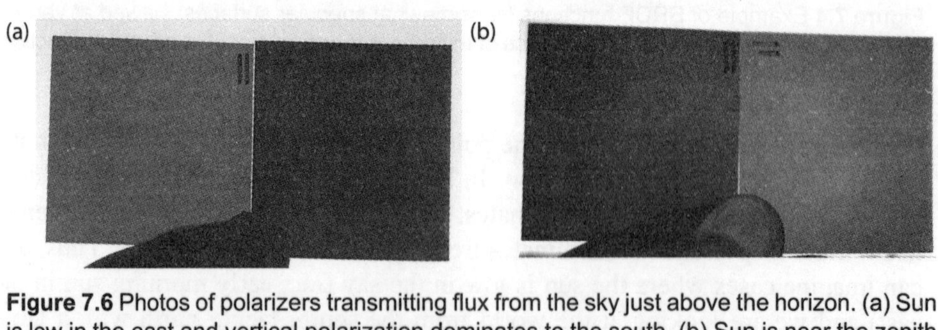

Figure 7.6 Photos of polarizers transmitting flux from the sky just above the horizon. (a) Sun is low in the east and vertical polarization dominates to the south. (b) Sun is near the zenith and horizontal polarization dominates to the north.

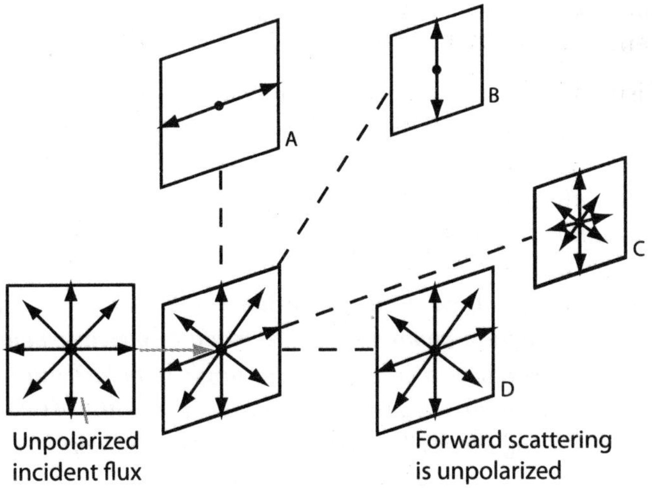

(a) Polarization from a scattering center.

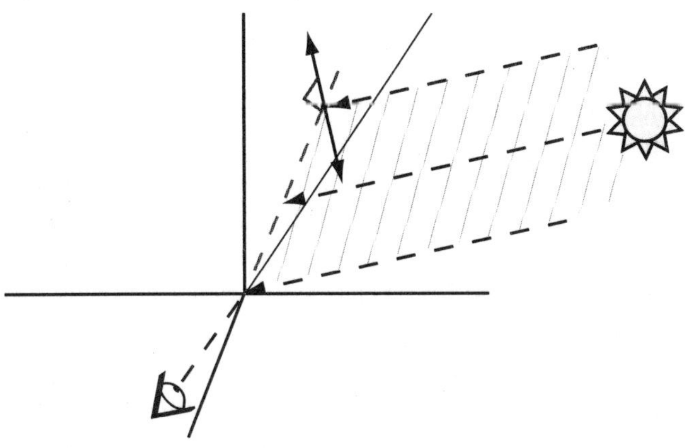

(b) Illustration of how polarization axis is oriented perpendicularly to source scattering center - observer plane. In this case, the observed sky light would have a strong vertical polarization.

Figure 7.7 Polarization orientation of a single scattered beam. (a) Unpolarized flux can generate oscillations of the electric field in all directions perpendicular to the beam. This leads to unpolarized radiation scattered into the forward direction (D), or fully polarized flux. Scattered at right angles (A and B) and partially polarized flux at other angles (C), (b) shows the polarization orientation of flux scattered from the sky and reflected by the surfaces on the earth.

briefly introduce the use of a visualization tool that will be used in Chapters 10 and 12 and is used here to help visualize the polarized state of the sky.

7.2.2.2 Visualization of sky polarization and validation of the DIRSIG implementation of MODTRAN-P

In order to visualize the polarimetric behavior of the sky, we will use the Digital Imaging and Remote Sensing (DIRS) Image Generation (*DIRSIG*) model [Schott (2007) Chapter 14]. The DIRSIG modeling code is designed to generate high fidelity synthetic images and has been upgraded to use MODTRAN-P to support radiation propagation of polarized beams. This section discusses the visualization of the sky using DIRSIG and the validation of the MODTRAN-P implementation in DIRSIG, which will be used for further visualization in Chapters 12 and 14. *Note that in this section comparisons are made to measurement results from Coulson (1988). Coulson uses a convention for angle of polarization (AoP) that is different from the convention used in the rest of the text, with vertical AoP being 0 deg and horizontal being 90 deg. We define* C_{omp} *to be the compliment of the AoP:*

$$C_{omp} = 90 - \text{AoP}. \tag{7.24}$$

We compare this to AoP values as defined by Coulson, which adjust for the naming convention difference. To be consistent in comparison with Coulson, the Coulson results are presented as $\mathrm{C_{omp}}$ values. These results are drawn from Devaraj et al. (2007).

DIRSIG has historically utilized the Air Force Research Lab's (AFRL) atmospheric radiative transport codes (MODTRAN [Berk et al. (1989)] and FASCODE [Smith et al. (1978)]) for all solar, lunar, sky, and path contributions. For these polarized simulations, an experimental version of MODTRAN that predicts polarized scattered radiance (referred to as MODTRAN-P) was utilized. In order to verify that the output from MODTRAN-P is being correctly incorporated into DIRSIG, we must be able to visualize where any given pixel is located. While this ability is currently available in DIRSIG in the form of zenith and azimuth angle maps, it is still difficult to get a qualitative understanding of where any given pixel is located, particularly when the sensor is pointed at the sky. As DoP and AoP are heavily dependent on the angle formed between the sun, the scattering object (in this case, a "piece of sky"), and the sensor, it is important to have a scene that both contains the entire sky dome and also gives us an explicit understanding of where any given pixel is located in the sky. For these reasons, a test scene was created that consisted of large alphabetic letters constructed as physical 3-D objects in a computer-aided design (CAD) environment. The letters corresponded to the cardinal compass directions, as well as to the X and Y directions within the DIRSIG environment. A cube was suspended in mid-air above the center of the scene to indicate a zenith angle of 0 deg. The geometry was then placed on a large flat plate to represent the ground and to create a horizon. The materials attributed to each object were basic materials drawn from the DIRSIG database; Fig. 7.8(a) depicts an overhead view of the scene.

Image data for the polarized atmospheric validation studies were rendered by a VNIR/SWIR pushbroom sensor, which was oriented vertically and swept

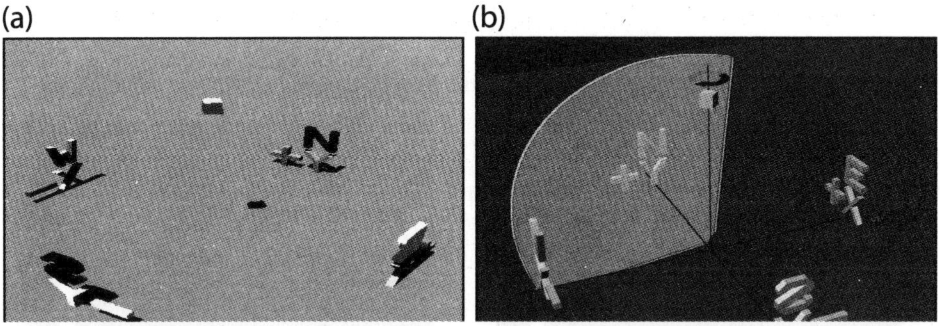

Figure 7.8 (a) Oblique rendering of the DIRSIG scene used for atmospheric validation. (b) Illustration of the pushbroom sensor used in the atmospheric validation study. Note how the FOV extends beyond a zenith of 0 deg.

360 deg about the z-axis. The sweep started and ended facing north (+Y). The sampling rate was configured such that there are three pixels for every degree of rotation, resulting in images that are 1080 pixels across. The sensor was 1000 pixels in the vertical dimension and was configured with a field of view that extends from below the horizon to beyond a 0-deg zenith angle, such that the sensor is seeing the sky behind itself. An illustration of the pushbroom sensor imaging the scene is shown in Fig. 7.8 (b). An RGB rendering of this 360-deg panoramic image is shown in Fig. 7.9. The elongated object across the top of the scene is the bottom of the floating cube. The sun (which has been suppressed) is located due south, and can be seen above the large "S" object. The shadow of the cube is seen due north, which is on the left and right edges of the scene as shown in Fig. 7.9.

This test scene was used in the simulations with a 40-km visibility for the atmosphere in MODTRAN-P to explore the variability of DoP and AoP across

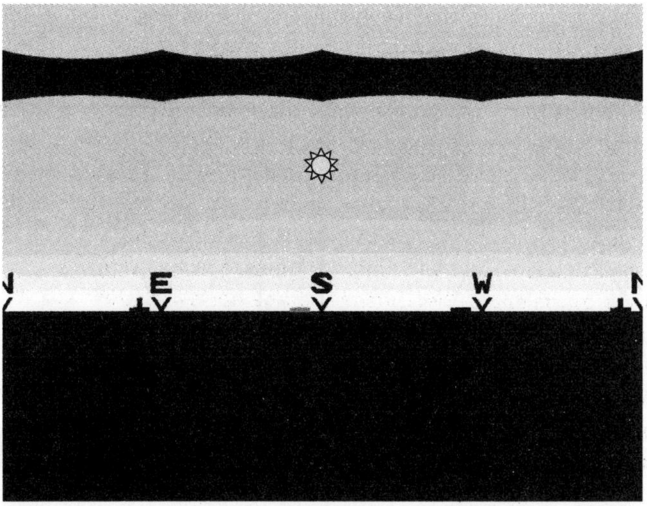

Figure 7.9 Panoramic rendering of the DIRSIG scene used for atmospheric validation (sun added for clarity).

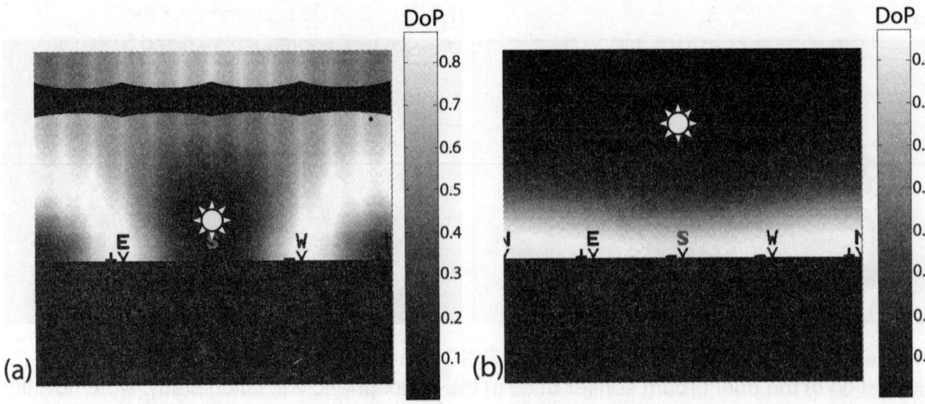

Figure 7.10 DoP distribution for (a) high and (b) low solar zenith.

the atmosphere. By changing the latitude of the simulation, a qualitative comparison of the DoP distribution for high and low solar zenith is shown (Fig. 7.10). It can be noticed that the DoP distribution varies in accordance with the theoretical model discussed earlier. When the solar zenith is high (or for low solar elevation in the sky), the DoP minima occurs above "S" and "N" objects corresponding to the solar and antisolar minima. In the low solar zenith case only the solar minima is shown because the antisolar minima occurs below the horizon. Also, in both cases the DoP maxima occurs at 90-deg scattering angle. The artifacts in Fig. 7.10(a) are attributed to the discrete sampling of the sky and the bilinear interpolation currently used. User control over the sky sampling and interpolation will be introduced in future DIRSIG releases.

To perform quantitative analysis, DIRSIG-generated skylight polarization was compared with the data obtained from Coulson et al. (1960). Figure 7.11 presents the DoP distribution on the solar meridian at different times of day at 0.65 μm. The plot illustrates that the DoP value reaches a maximum value at 90-deg

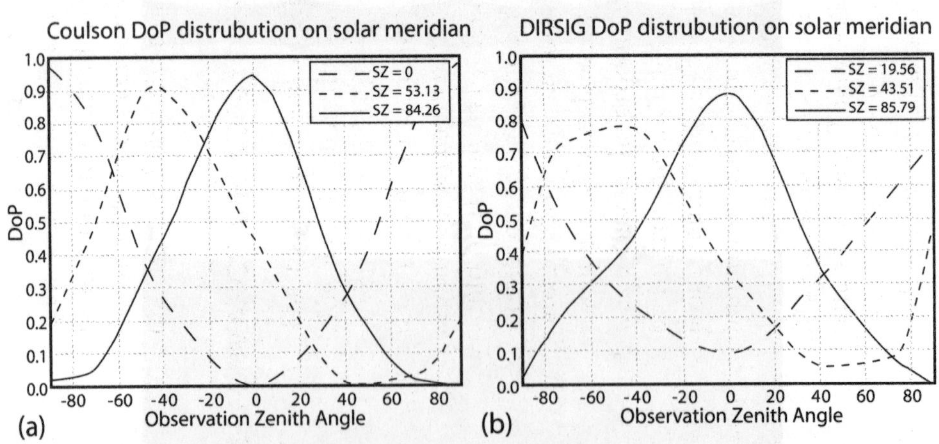

Figure 7.11 DoP distribution of (a) Coulson and (b) DIRSIG data on the solar meridian for different times of day (λ = 0.65 μm).

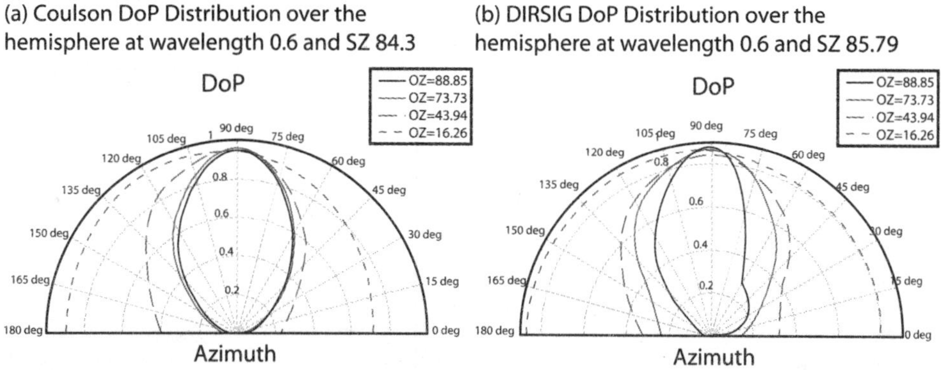

Figure 7.12 DoP distribution of (a) Coulson and (b) DIRSIG data over half of the hemisphere for different observation zeniths (OZ) for high solar zenith.

scattering angle for all three solar zenith (SZ) cases. Even though the absolute maximum value of DoP from DIRSIG data is found to be slightly lower than the Coulson data, the desired DoP variability for different observation zenith angles is observed. Any mismatch between the atmosphere used in the simulations and the Coulson data can lead to such deviations in the resulting absolute value differences.

In addition, the DoP azimuth distribution over the hemisphere for different observation zenith angles for a high solar zenith case was investigated and the result is shown in Fig. 7.12. DIRSIG data was simulated at 0.65 μm with the time of day at 6 a.m. The plot illustrates the variability of DIRSIG-generated DoP at different observation zenith angles such as 88 deg, 74 deg, 44 deg, and 16 deg and the data from Coulson observed at approximately the same observation zenith angles. It can also be seen that the DIRSIG-predicted DoP values linearly increase with the observation azimuth and have a maximum value when the observation azimuth is 90 deg relative to the solar azimuth, thus demonstrating its high correlation with the trends seen in Coulson data. When the observation zenith angle becomes smaller, it can be seen that the DoP values are higher because the observation locations move farther from the solar location. Due to the rotational symmetry of DoP, the data is plotted over only half of the hemisphere.

The DoP variation as a function of wavelength is illustrated using the data generated between 0.4 and 0.7 μm for 6 a.m., 8 a.m., 10 a.m., and 12 p.m. cases. The results were compared with the Coulson data for different solar zenith angles ranging from low sun to high sun. Figure 7.13 illustrates the maximum DoP as a function of wavelength. First, it can be observed that the DIRSIG data is accurate in following a linearly increasing trend across the spectral bands at all times, since the DoP maximum is expected to increase with increasing wavelength. Multiple scattering effects dominate the shorter wavelength region as compared to larger wavelengths. Again, absolute differences in the values between Coulson and DIRSIG in Figs. 7.11 through 7.13 are due to the fact that the exact same atmospheres were not modeled for the two cases.

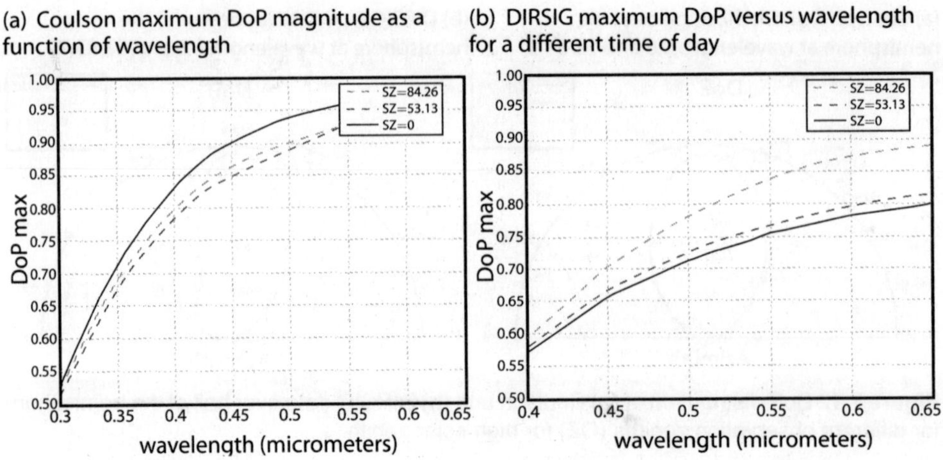

Figure 7.13 Maximum DoP versus wavelength of (a) Coulson and (b) DIRSIG data for different times of day.

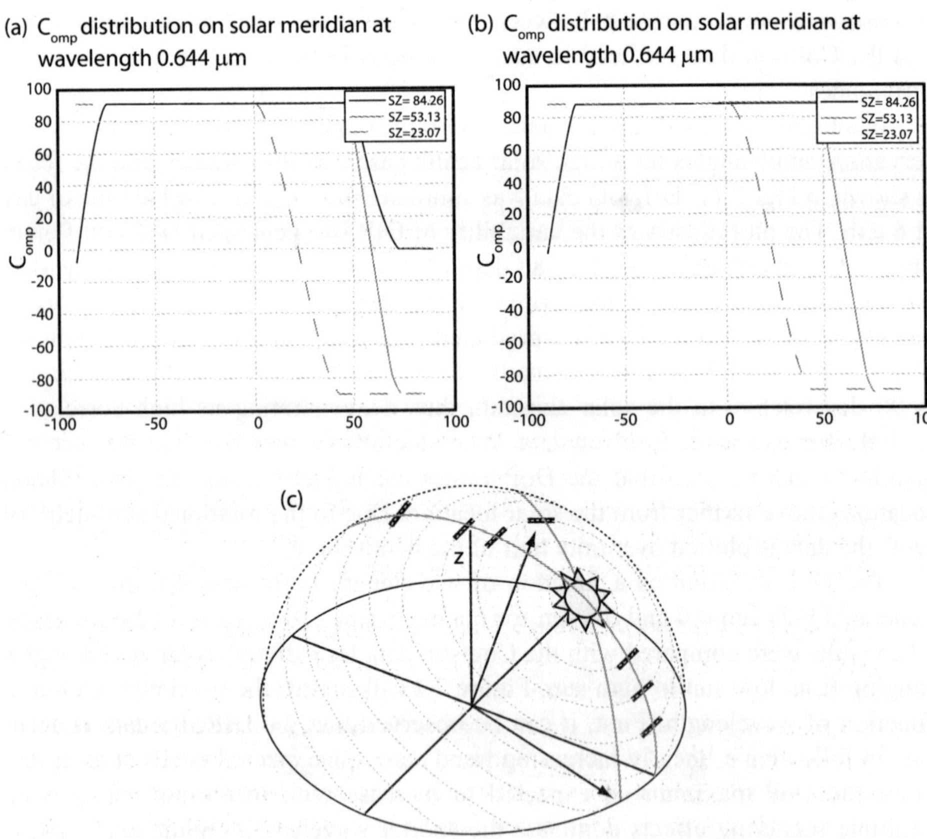

Figure 7.14 C_{omp} distribution of (a) Coulson and (b) DIRSIG data on the solar meridian for different times of day. (c) Sampling concept for (a) and (b). Note that the C_{omp} convention used is shown in Fig. 7.16.

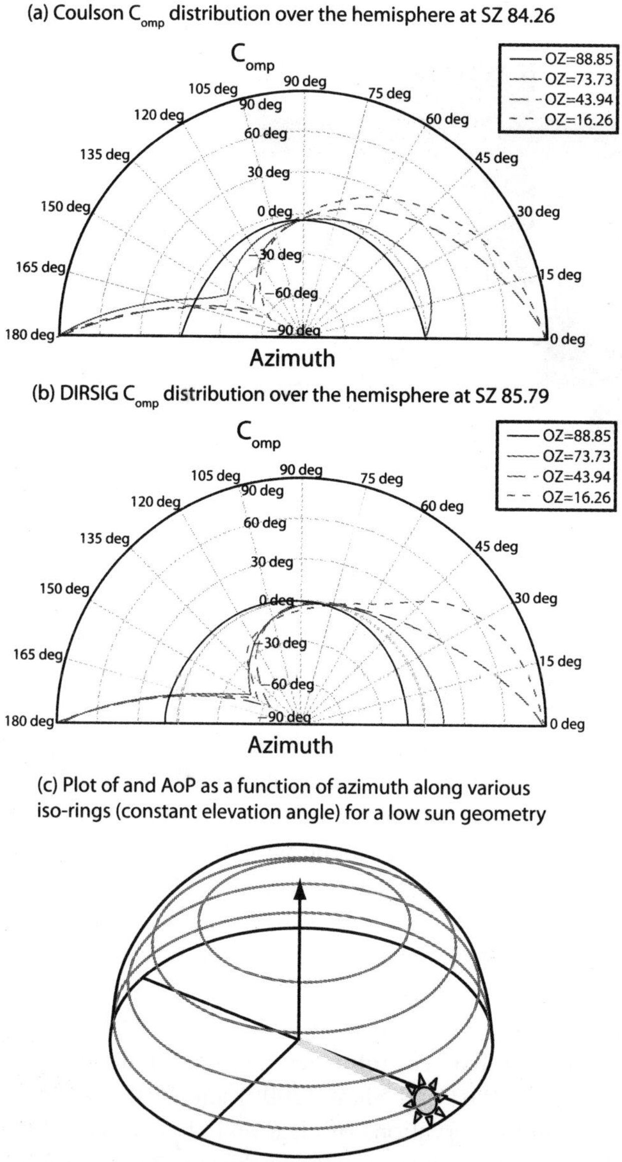

Figure 7.15 C_{omp} distribution of (a) Coulson and (b) DIRSIG data over the hemisphere for different observation zenith angles for high solar zenith. (c) Sampling concept for (a) and (b). Note that the C_{omp} convention used is shown in Fig. 7.16.

In order to verify the AoP prediction capability, an analysis was performed to show the distribution of the C_{omp} angle on the solar meridian for different times of day. It can be seen from Fig. 7.14 that DIRSIG is accurate in predicting the C_{omp} values at all observation zenith angles on the solar meridianal plane. The C_{omp} values at all points above the sun location remain about 89 deg, while the C_{omp} has a sign change below the sun.

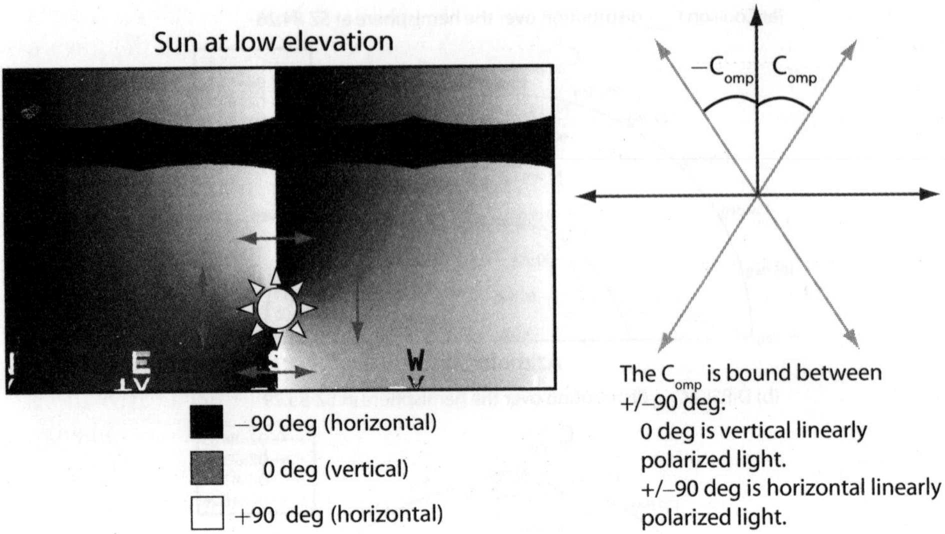

Figure 7.16 Visualization of the C_{omp} values for the DIRSIG scene shown in Fig. 7.10.

The C_{omp} azimuth distribution over the hemisphere for different observation zenith angles was also investigated. The results presented in Fig. 7.15 indicate the C_{omp} azimuthal variation across the entire hemisphere observed at solar zenith of 84.26 deg with the corresponding DIRSIG data generated at 6 a.m. It can be noticed that the C_{omp} at lower observation zenith tends to gradually decrease from 90 deg and crosses 0 deg at about 90-deg relative azimuth and increases to 90 deg when observed on the solar meridian plane with 180-deg relative azimuth angle. However, when observed at zenith angle of 80 deg, both Coulson and DIRSIG C_{omp} values have smaller values throughout the observation hemisphere. A visualization of the C_{omp} values as rendered by DIRSIG can be seen in Fig. 7.16.

It is important to note that this treatment has emphasized the effect of clear sky scattering on the downwelled polarization field. In many (most) cases, clouds will be present in the sky that will influence the magnitude and character of the downwelled polarization. Pust and Shaw (2006) and Pust and Shaw (2007) discuss instrumentation and observations of clear and cloudy skies that confirm that clouds in general reduce the polarization from the sky due to multiple scattering. However, they also suggest that clouds can influence the angle of polarization and be indicators of variations in the polarimetric behavior of clear sky regions from what would be predicted for severely clear cases.

7.3 Predicting the Polarimetric Radiance at the Sensor

Based on either experimental measurements or use of MODTRAN-P, we can estimate the atmospheric terms in the polarimetric form of the governing equation (cf. Sec. 7.1). The reflectance terms will use some form of the polarized BRDF discussed in Chapter 6. However, an important but easily overlooked issue arises in effectively implementing the merger of the polarized Stokes vector representation (from a code such as MODTRAN) with pBRDF values through the governing equation. This is due to the three frames of reference in use along the radiation propagation paths. The incident Stokes vector is typically defined in the *Global Coordinate System* and relative to the plane of primary incident illumination (as is each Stokes vector associated with downwelled radiance from a location in the sky), as shown in Fig. 7.17.

The pBRDF models, on the other hand, are typically defined relative to the surface normal and assume the incident flux is defined in terms of the source-target-target-normal plane. Thus, except when the target is in the plane tangent to the earth, the incident Stokes vector in the Global Coordinate System must be transformed into the pBRDF system prior to making the reflectance calculations. Similarly, the sensor typically analyzes the data relative to the plane containing the normal to the earth and the sensor. However, the pBRDF typically defines an output Stokes vector in the target-normal-target-sensor plane which again, unless the target is in the plane of the earth, will not coincide with the sensor geometry. Thus, before analysis, the reflected Stokes vector from the pBRDF calculation must be transformed into the earth-normal-sensor plane. Since the direction of propagation is common, this simply requires us to first rotate the incident Stokes vector into the pBRDF incident plane and then rotate from the pBRDF output plane into the sensor plane. Recall that the rotation of a Stokes vector is easily done with a Mueller matrix if we know the rotation angle (see Fig. 7.18 and discussion of Fig. 4.5). The orientation of linearly polarized light is defined with respect to the propagation direction and a reference axis that typically has some context in the real world (e.g., the "up" direction). The BRDF for a material is a function of the incident and reflected directions relative to the surface. In the case of a polarized BRDF, the polarization state (e.g., vertical linearly polarized light) is also assumed to use the surface relative coordinate space as the reference (meaning the "up" direction is parallel to the surface normal). Once we attempt to model a surface in the context of a global coordinate system, we must resolve the effects of the surface orientation within that system. Consider vertical linearly polarized light (in the global coordinate system) incident on a surface that is tilted at 45 deg about an axis in-plane with the incident light. In the context of the tilted surface, the incident light is linearly polarized but the orientation is −45 deg rather than 0 deg (vertical).

To correctly reflect the radiation off of a surface arbitrarily oriented in a global coordinate system, we must address two effects. First, the global incident and reflected directions must be projected into the local coordinate space so that they can be used to access the BRDF. Second, the Stokes geometry of the global incident and reflected polarizations must be translated into and out of the local coordinate space. The global-to-local vector projections required to evaluate the BRDF are common to any radiative transfer problem. However, the translation of the Stokes geometry is unique to polarized radiative transfer.

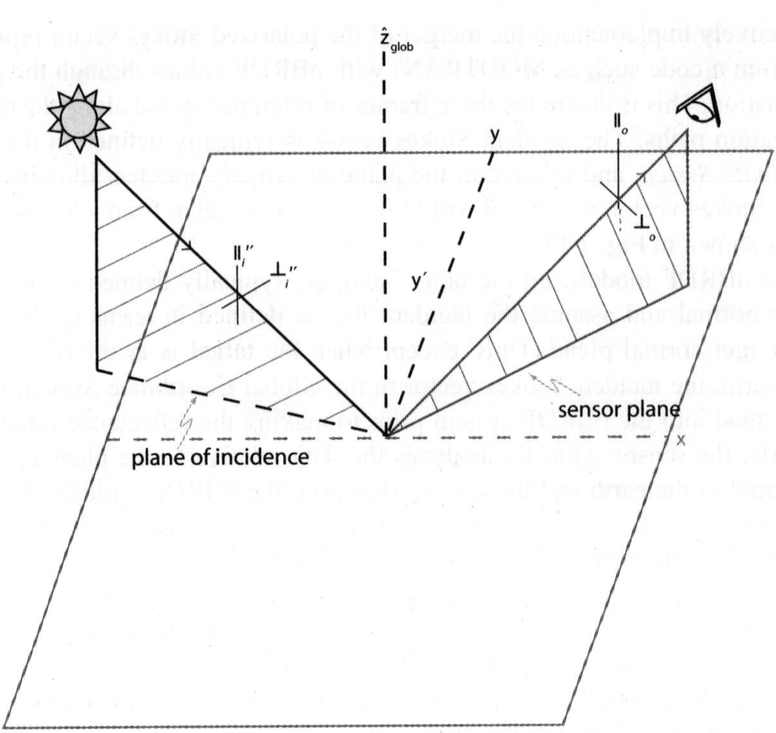

Figure 7.17 Illustration of the definition of global orientation angles to define the Stokes vector in the plane of incidence (*i*) and the sensor plane (*o*). Note that the axis labeled $||_i$ is in the plane of incidence and is perpendicular to the direction of propagation (*P* polarization state) and that the axis $\perp_i$ is perpendicular to $||_i$ and the direction of propagation (*S* polarization state). Similar logic follows for $||_o$ and $\perp_o$, relative to the sensor plane.

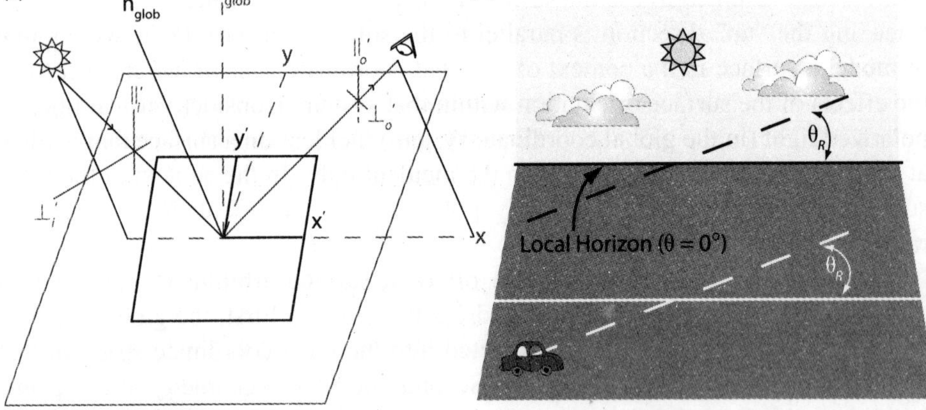

Figure 7.18 (a) Geometry of imaging system alignment or the rotation of a given Stokes vector. (b) Illustration of incident and output (sensor) angles relative to a target tipped relative to the plane of the earth. The pBRDF model uses the primed angles shown in (a). Thus, we need to rotate the global Stokes vectors into this frame and then out of it, after reflection back into the global sensor frame.

To resolve the relative versus global Stokes geometry problem, we need to establish a rotation that will translate the polarization state into and out of a surface relative coordinate system defined by the surface normal in the global coordinate system ($\hat{n}_{glob}$). For a light path traveling in the direction $\vec{v}_i$, the P (vertical) and S (horizontal) polarization orientations will be defined so that the P polarization state is perpendicular to $\vec{v}_i$, in the plane of the global "up" vector and its projection on $\hat{z}_{glob}$ is positive. The S polarization state is orthogonal to both the propagation direction and P, such that $\vec{v}_P \perp \vec{v}_S \perp \vec{v}_i$.

The rotation for incident light ($\vec{v}_i$) can be determined by computing the rotation of the vertical orientation from the global coordinate system into the local coordinate system. This is accomplished by computing the angle between the surface "up" direction (defined by the surface normal, $\hat{n}_{glob}$) and the global "up" direction ($\hat{z}_{glob}$) in the plane orthogonal to the incident light. The calculation of this angle requires calculation of the S and P unit vectors of the incident light propagation direction, as well as the facet normal vector projected into the S-P plane of the incident light ($\vec{n}_{i_{SP}}$),

$$\vec{v}_s = \hat{z}_{glob} \times \vec{v}_i, \tag{7.25}$$

where $\vec{v}_s$ is a vector pointing in the direction of the perpendicular polarization axis ($\perp_1$ in Fig. 7.15) and $\hat{v}_s$ is a unit vector, i.e., the magnitude-normalized version of $\vec{v}_s$

$$\vec{v}_p = \vec{v}_i \times \vec{v}_s, \tag{7.26}$$

where $\vec{v}_p$ is a vector pointing in the direction of the parallel polarization axis ($\|_i$ in Fig. 7.15) and $\hat{v}_p$ is the corresponding unit vector. The facet normal projected on the S-P plane is given by

$$\vec{n}_{i_{SP}} = \vec{v}_i \times (\hat{n}_{glob} \times \vec{v}_i). \tag{7.27}$$

The incident rotation angle (α_i) can be computed as the inverse tangent of the ratio of the S and P components of the vector $\vec{n}_{i_{SP}}$,

$$\alpha_i = \tan^{-1}\left(\frac{\vec{n}_{i_{SP}} \cdot \vec{v}_S}{\vec{n}_{i_{SP}} \cdot \vec{v}_P}\right). \tag{7.28}$$

This angle can be used to construct a Mueller matrix that will rotate the incident Stokes vector from the global Stokes geometry into the surface relative Stokes geometry:

$$\boldsymbol{M}_{\alpha_i} = \begin{bmatrix} 1 & 0 & 0 & 0 \\ 0 & \cos(2\alpha_i) & \sin(2\alpha_i) & 0 \\ 0 & -\sin(2\alpha_i) & \cos(2\alpha_i) & 0 \\ 0 & 0 & 0 & 1 \end{bmatrix}. \tag{7.29}$$

The surface relative to global rotation angle for a similar exittent (output) geometry (α_o) can be computed using the same approach. However, the rotation angle is opposite in sign compared to the similar incident geometry. The reflected polarized radiance (L_r) for polarized incident light is then

$$\boldsymbol{L}_r = \boldsymbol{M}_{\alpha_o} \cdot [\boldsymbol{M}_{\mathrm{BRDF}} \cdot (\boldsymbol{M}_{\alpha_i} \cdot \boldsymbol{E}_i)], \tag{7.30}$$

where $\boldsymbol{M}_{\alpha_o}$ is the local-to-global (exittent) Stokes rotation matrix, $\boldsymbol{M}_{\mathrm{BRDF}}$ is the Mueller matrix from the polarized BRDF for the incident/exittent reflected geometry, $\boldsymbol{M}_{\alpha_i}$ is the global-to-local (incident) Stokes rotation matrix, and $\boldsymbol{E}_i$ is the incident irradiance defined in the global Stokes coordinate system.

Using the pBRDF concepts presented in the last chapter and the governing equation and polarimetric radiative transfer mechanisms presented in this chapter, we can describe the Stokes vector incident on a remote sensing system. The next chapter addresses the sensors that can be used to capture this polarimetric signal.

References

Berk, A., Berstein, L.S., & Robertson, D.C. (1989). "MODTRAN: a moderate resolution model for LOWTRAN 7." *GL-TR-89-0122, Spectral Sciences*, Burlington, MA.

Berk, A., Anderson, G.P., Acharya, P.K., Chetwynd, J.H., Bernstein, L.S., Shettle, E.P., Matthew, M.W., & Adler-Golden, S.M. (1999). "MODTRAN4 User's Manual." *01731-3010*, Air Force Research Lab, Hanscom AFB.

Bréon, F.M., Tanré, D., Lecomte, P., & Herman, M. (1995). "Polarized reflectance of bare soils and vegetation: measurements and models." *IEEE Transactions on Geoscience and Remote Sensing*, Vol. 33, No. 2, pp. 487–499.

Chandrasekhar, S. (1950). *Radiative Transfer*. Clarendon Press, Oxford.

Coulson, K., Jitendra, D., & Sekera, Z. (1960). *Tables Related to Radiation Emerging from a Planetary Atmosphere with Rayleigh Scattering*. University of California Press, Berkeley.

Coulson, K.L. (1988). *Polarization and Intensity of Light in the Atmosphere*. A. Deepak Pub., Hampton, VA.

Devaraj, C., Brown, S., Messinger, D., Goodenough, A., & Pogorzala, D. (2007). "A framework for polarized radiance signature prediction for natural scenes." *Proceedings SPIE*, Vol. 6565, 65650Y.

Egan, W.G. (2004). *Optical Remote Sensing Science and Technology*. Marcel Dekker Inc., New York.

Kokhanovsky, A.A. (2001). *Optics of Light Scattering Media: Problems and Solutions*. 2nd Ed., Springer-Verlag Telos, Santa Clara.

Leroy, M., Deuzé, J.L., Bréon, F.M., Hautecoeur, O., Herman, M., Buriez, J.C., Tanré, D., Bouffiès, S., Chazette, P., & Roujean, J.L. (1997). "Retrieval of atmospheric properties and surface bidirectional reflectances over the land from POLDER (processing algorithms)." *Journal of Geophysical Research*, 102(D14):17023–17037.

Lee, R.L., Jr. (1998). "Digital imaging of clear-sky polarization." *Applied Optics*, Vol. 37, No. 9, pp. 1465–1476.

Lord Rayleigh (J.W. Stratt). (1871). *Philosophical Magazine*, Vol. 41, pp. 107–120, 274–279.

Pust, N.J., & Shaw, J.A. (2006). "Imaging spectropolarimetry of cloudy skies." *Proceedings SPIE,* Vol. 6240, 624006.

Pust, N.J., & Shaw, J.A. (2007). "All-sky polarization imaging." *Proceedings SPIE,* Vol. 6682, 668204.

Shell, J.R., & Schott, J.R. (2005). "A polarized clutter measurement technique based on the governing equation for polarimetric remote sensing in the visible to near infrared." *Proceedings SPIE*, Vol. 5811, pp. 34–45.

Shell, J.R., & Schwarting, T. (2004). "Derivation of atmospheric transmittance and diffuse sky irradiance fraction using ASD measurements." Technical report, Digital Imaging and Remote Sensing Laboratory, Rochester Institute of Technology, Rochester.

Schott, J.R. (2007). *Remote Sensing: The Image Chain Approach*, 2nd Ed., Oxford University Press, New York.

Smith, H.J.P., Dube, D.J., Gardner, M.E., Clough, S.A., Kneizys, F.X., & Rothman, L.S. (1978). "FASCODE: Fast Atmospheric Signature Code (Spectral Transmittance and Radiance)." *Air Force Geophysics Laboratory Technical Report AFGL-TR-78-0081*, Hanscom AFB.

Color Plate Section

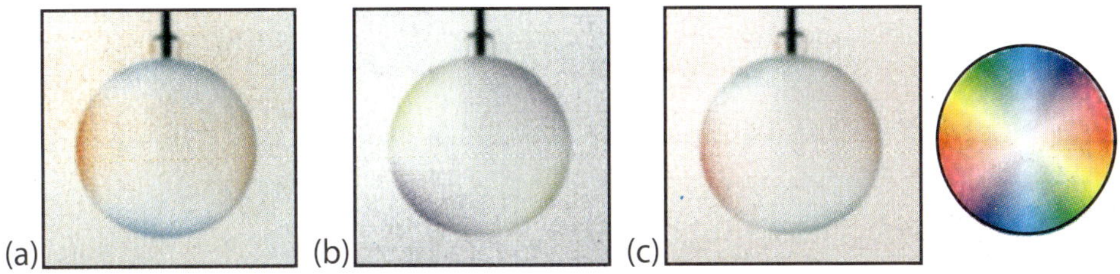

Figure 9.4 Two-parameter colorimetric polarization-difference imaging (2C-PDI) images of back-illuminated dielectric sphere at an effective distance of 0.13 attenuation lengths. Images (a), (b), and (c) were obtained with the analyzer oriented at the angles of 0 deg, 36 deg, and 72 deg with respect to the vertical, respectively. 2C-PDI highlights areas that are polarized parallel to the PDI axes and has blind spots where the light is polarized at 45 deg with respect to the PDI axes. The key at the right reveals how the colors in the images map into polarization direction; for example, red represents an excess of horizontal polarization and cyan represents an excess of vertical polarization [Tyo et al. (1998)].

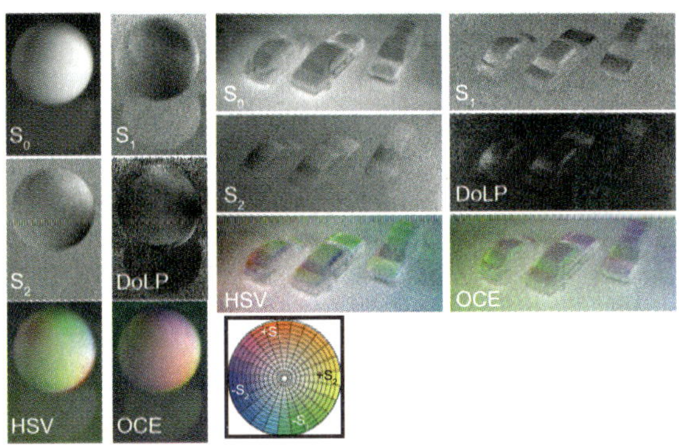

Figure 9.5: Illustration of opponent color encoding (OCE) (i.e., Eqs. (9.4) through (9.7)) and hue saturation and value encoding (i.e., Eqs. (9.15) through (9.17)) applied to longwave infrared polarimetric images.

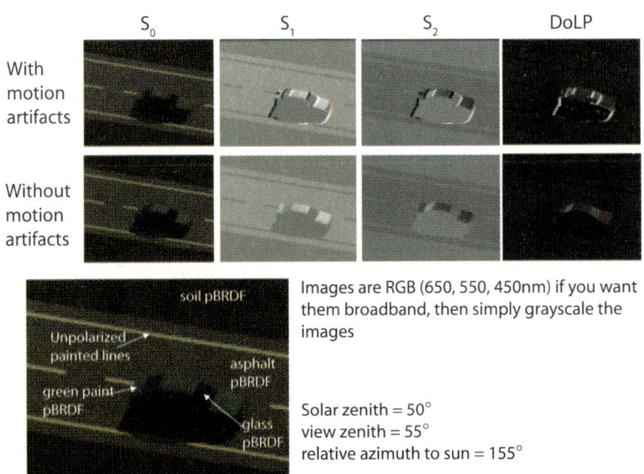

Figure 9.8 Illustration of artifacts introduced by pushbroom and DoTP imagers. Top shows image with artifacts, middle shows same target with no motion, and bottom shows optical properties of materials simulated in DIRSIG.

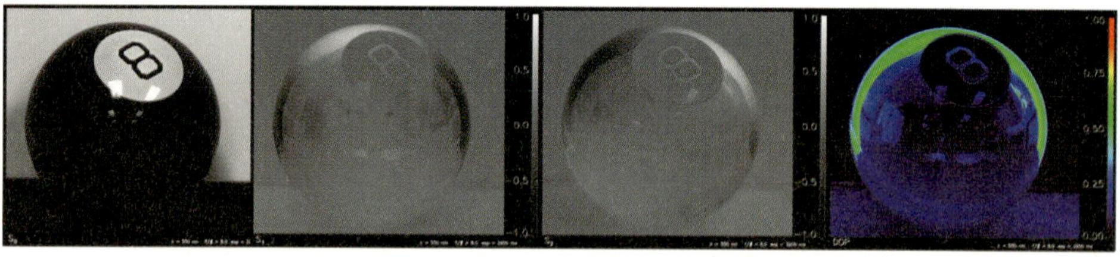

Figure 10.5 The Stokes and DoP images of a "magic 8-ball" under ambient lighting conditions at 550 nm. S0 (left), S1 (middle left), S2 (middle right), and color-encoded DoP (right).

Figure 10.6 The polarization angle information from "magic 8-ball" image. Green corresponds to $\psi = 0$ deg while the red-black transition is the transition point from $\psi = 90$ deg to -90 deg.

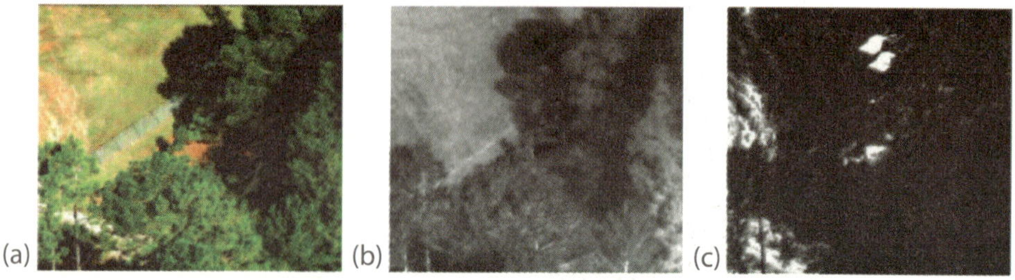

Figure 11.11 (a) Multispectral visible, (b) unpolarized MWIR, and (c) degree of polarization MWIR image of vehicles in tree shadows [Courtesy of Tyo et al. (2006)].

John R. Schott

Chapter 8
Sensors for Measuring the Polarized State of a Beam

We have throughout the earlier chapters made the assumption that we could observe and record the polarized state of the EM energy reaching a sensor. In this chapter we will present some of the basic methods for sensing polarized radiation. We begin with simple intuitive approaches (Sec. 8.1) and then introduce full Stokes vector sensors in Sec. 8.2. Section 8.3 extends the principles of the first two sections to imaging sensors, which are of the most interest for direct remote sensing applications. Finally in Sec. 8.4, we introduce some of the sensor-related issues associated with polarimetric imaging for remote sensing. Throughout this chapter we emphasize the general issues of sensing as they relate to understanding the nature of the remotely sensed signal. The details of sensors and sensor design are beyond the scope of this treatment, so for a more thorough treatment the reader should consult the references for this chapter and the current literature.

8.1 Sensing of Polarization Contrast

For cases where linear polarization dominates the polarized portion of a partially polarized beam, it is possible to use very simple methods to capture some of the polarimetric character of the signal. Consider the case shown in Fig. 8.1(a) of partially polarized flux incident on an extremely simple sensor. The sensor is made up of a linear polarizer followed by an aperture that controls the field of view of a detector. A more efficient design is shown in Fig. 8.1(b) where a lens is used to more effectively gather the flux and control the field of view. To deal rigorously with the design in Fig. 8.1(b), we would need to introduce the polarimetric Mueller matrix of the optic, so we will continue with the simple design in Fig. 8.1(a) for the present.

Assume that the linear polarizer is oriented with its transmissive axis along the horizontal axis. The Stokes vector associated with the flux incident on the detector can be expressed as

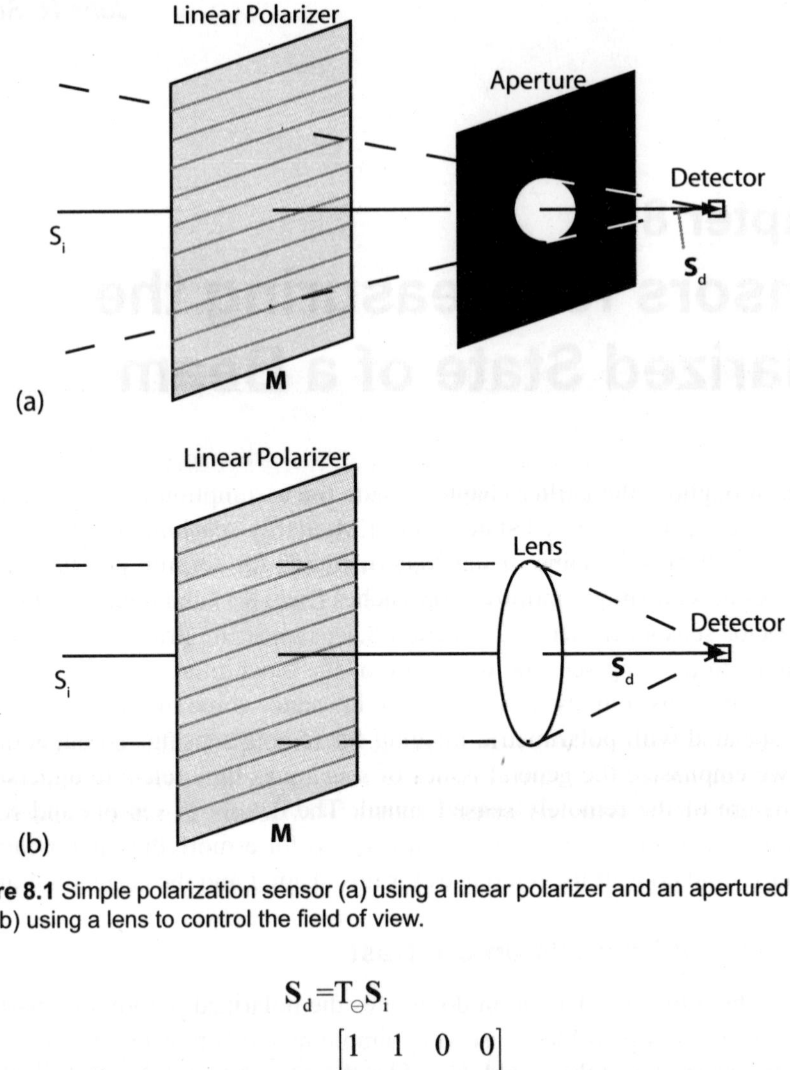

Figure 8.1 Simple polarization sensor (a) using a linear polarizer and an apertured detector and (b) using a lens to control the field of view.

$$\mathbf{S}_d = \mathbf{T}_{\ominus}\mathbf{S}_i = \frac{1}{2}\begin{bmatrix} 1 & 1 & 0 & 0 \\ 1 & 1 & 0 & 0 \\ 0 & 0 & 0 & 0 \\ 0 & 0 & 0 & 0 \end{bmatrix}\mathbf{S}_i, \tag{8.1}$$

where $\mathbf{S}_i$ is the Stokes vector associated with the incident flux, $\mathbf{T}_{\ominus}$ is the Mueller matrix associated with a horizontal polarizer (see Chapter 5), and $\mathbf{S}_d$ is the Stokes vector incident on the detector. If we assume that the detector is insensitive to the orientation of the electrical field (this is a good assumption for most detectors if the beam is incident on the detector along the direction normal to the surface), then only the S_0 component of $\mathbf{S}_d$ can be isolated (measured) to generate an electrical signal in the detector. Thus, it is only the first row of $\mathbf{T}_{\ominus}$ that impacts the final sensed signal. To use our simple sensor to characterize the polarization state

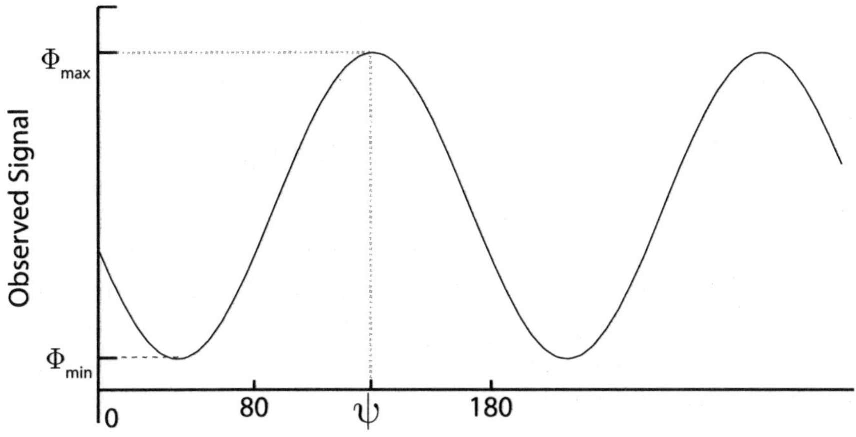

Figure 8.2 Response of a simple linear polarimeter (see Fig. 8.1) to rotation of the linear polarizer when viewing partially linear polarized radiation.

of a beam, we rotate the polarizer and record the detector output. An identical result could be obtained by rotating the entire sensor. This yields the more general equation for the sensor

$$\mathbf{S}_{d\theta} = \mathbf{M}_{\theta} \cdot \mathbf{S}_{i}, \tag{8.2}$$

where $\mathbf{S}_{d\theta}$ is the Stokes vector onto the detector when the linear polarizer is rotated through an angle θ from the horizontal and $\mathbf{M}_{\theta}$ is the Mueller matrix for the rotated ideal linear polarizer, which Collett (1993) shows can be expressed as

$$\mathbf{M}_{\theta} = \frac{1}{2}\begin{bmatrix} 1 & \cos 2\theta & \sin 2\theta & 0 \\ \cos 2\theta & \cos^2 2\theta & \sin 2\theta \cos 2\theta & 0 \\ \sin 2\theta & \sin 2\theta \cos 2\theta & \sin^2 2\theta & 0 \\ 0 & 0 & 0 & 0 \end{bmatrix}. \tag{8.3}$$

A quick verification of Eq. (8.3) can be accomplished by inserting the angles 0 deg, 45 deg, and 90 deg and verifying that the Mueller matrices for ideal horizontal, +45 deg, and vertical polarization are returned.

The sensor will respond to the S_0 component of $\mathbf{S}_{d\theta}$ and generate a sinusoidal output as a function of the angle θ in response to partially polarized radiation as shown in Fig. 8.2. Wolff (1994) defines the partial polarization (equal to the DoP for partially linearly polarized flux (i.e., the DoLP)) derived from such an instrument as

$$P_{P} = \frac{\Phi_{max} - \Phi_{min}}{\Phi_{max} + \Phi_{min}}, \tag{8.4}$$

where Φ_{max} and Φ_{min} are the minimum and maximum flux observed by the polarimeter as the polarizer is rotated. Note that the form of Eq. (8.4) will cancel any multiplicative terms, so the polarimeter output can be expressed in any unit as long as it has zero bias and is linearly proportional to the energy reaching the detector. Bowers et al. (2008) discuss the importance of this linearity assumption and the impact of nonlinearity on calibration of polarimetric sensors. The angle of polarization (ψ) associated with the polarized contribution to the flux is simply the angle associated with the maximum flux (see Fig. 8.2). Note that randomly polarized flux would have a constant flux value with angle and that fully linearly polarized flux would have $\Phi_{min} = 0$ in Fig. 8.2. This approach to polarimetric sensing is very intuitive. Indeed, rotating a linear polarizer held in front of your eye provides a visualization of this type of measurement. In practice however, acquiring data over a wide range of angles and maximizing the response for each point of interest is impractical. Luckily, as we will see in the next section, the necessary information can be acquired with just a few measurements.

8.2 Generalized Stokes Vector Polarimeters

As discussed in the previous section, a rotating linear polarizer and many samples can be used to characterize the polarized state of a beam. In fact, restricting ourselves to linearly polarized radiation, it is clear from Fig. 8.2 that if we sample the polarized signal at any three nonredundant angles, we should be able to reconstruct the sinusoidal response shown. This in fact is the basis for the three filter orientations described in the generation of the linear Stokes vector introduced in Chapter 4 (see Fig. 4.2). Indeed, *Pickering's method* and *Fessenkov's method* are two of the many methods that can be used to characterize the linear polarization state of a beam by orienting filters at different angles in the polarimeter. Recall that the unnormalized linear Stokes vector can be obtained using three angular samples according to Pickering's method to yield [Solomon (1981)]

$$S_0 = \Phi_0 + \Phi_{90} \tag{8.5}$$

$$S_1 = \Phi_0 - \Phi_{90} \tag{8.6}$$

$$S_2 = 2\left[\Phi_{45} - (S_0/2)\right], \tag{8.7}$$

or using Fessenkov's method to yield [Prosch (1983)]

$$S_0 = \frac{2}{3}\left(\Phi_0 + \Phi_{60} + \Phi_{120}\right) \tag{8.8}$$

$$S_1 = \frac{2}{3}\left(2\Phi_0 - \Phi_{60} - \Phi_{120}\right) \tag{8.9}$$

$$S_2 = \frac{-2}{\sqrt{3}}\left(\Phi_{120} - \Phi_{60}\right), \tag{8.10}$$

or more intuitively, using the modified Pickering's method and four filters to yield [Walraven (1981)]

$$S_0 = \frac{\Phi_0 + \Phi_{45} + \Phi_{90} + \Phi_{-45}}{2} \tag{8.11}$$

$$S_1 = \Phi_0 - \Phi_{90} \tag{8.12}$$

$$S_2 = \Phi_{45} - \Phi_{-45}. \tag{8.13}$$

Furthermore, as described in Chapter 4, the angle of polarization can be recovered from the linear Stokes vector using

$$\psi = \frac{1}{2}\tan^{-1}\left(\frac{S_2}{S_1}\right) \tag{8.14}$$

and the degree of polarization from a partially linearly polarized beam using

$$\text{DoP} = \frac{\sqrt{S_1^{\,2} + S_2^{\,2}}}{S_0}. \tag{8.15}$$

Thus, we see that for partially linearly polarized radiation, the polarimetric nature of the beam can be fully characterized with three samples made with a linear polarizer. Tyo (1998) demonstrates that the optimum angular sampling scheme (i.e., minimal correlation between channels) is to spread the angles equally over the 180-deg angular sampling range of the linear polarizers. Fessenkov's method represents one example of this approach. However, Tyo (1998) points out that the maximum decorrelation in the sampled data can be obtained by generating three channels expressed as

$$C_1 = \frac{1}{\sqrt{3}}\left(\Phi_0 + \Phi_{60} + \Phi_{120}\right) \tag{8.16}$$

$$C_2 = \frac{1}{\sqrt{2}}\left(\Phi_0 - \Phi_{120}\right) \tag{8.17}$$

$$C_3 = \frac{1}{\sqrt{6}}\left(\Phi_0 - 2\Phi_{60} + \Phi_{120}\right). \tag{8.18}$$

These channels, referred to as the sum (C_1) and difference (C_2 and C_3), can be used to display polarimetric image data from an appropriate three-channel sensor (see Chapter 9).

The discussion above has focused on the special case where we can assume that the contribution due to circular polarization is significant. While this is a common though not universally true assumption for earth remote sensing, we want to

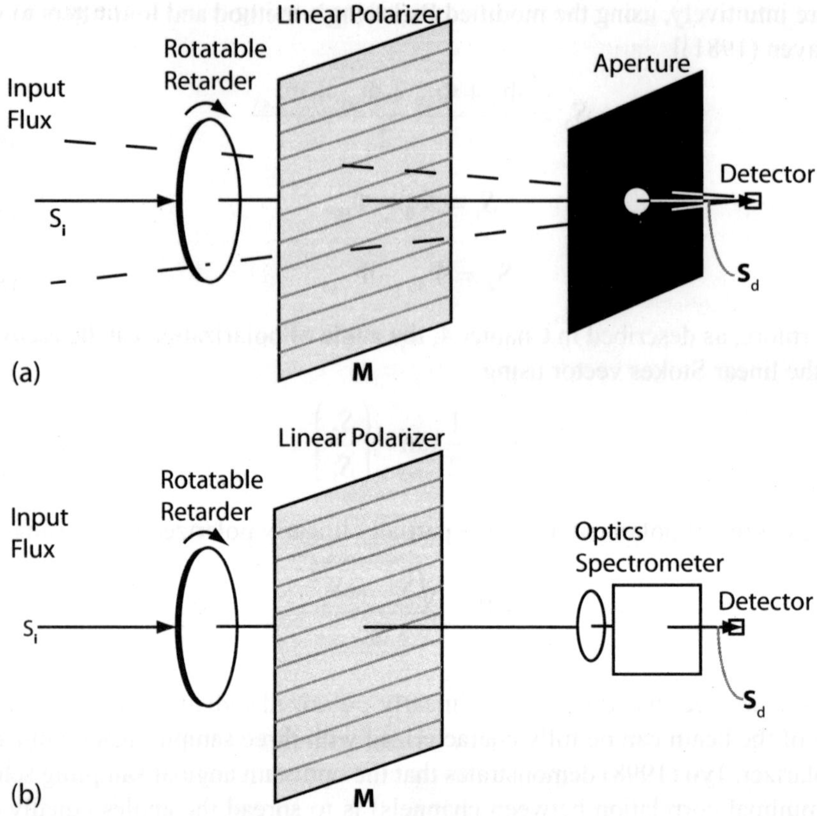

Figure 8.3 Conceptual illustration of full Stokes vector polarimeters. (a) Elementary polarimeter and (b) more practical polarimeter using optical elements to shape field of view and sample spectrum.

develop a more general formalism for characterizing the full Stokes vector using a polarimeter. It is important to recognize that the full Stokes vector formalism developed here can easily be simplified to the case of a linear Stokes vector (i.e., when $S_3 = 0$).

Conceptually, the simplest way to build a full Stokes vector polarimeter would be to use the definition of the Stokes parameters and take measurements with six filters in front of our detector. These would consist of four linear polarizers located at 0 deg, 45 deg, 90 deg, and −45 deg and a right and left circular polarizer (see Eq. (5.29) and related discussion). This approach requires three polarizing elements and six measurements and in general is not commonly used in polarimeters. Stokes vector polarimeters can take on many forms, with perhaps the simplest shown in Fig. 8.3. In this case, we have a rotatable retarder in front of a fixed linear polarizer (analyzer) leading into the radiometer. In practice, the radiometer will contain optical elements to control the field of view and often to isolate the spectral region sampled (spectral polarimetry). For the moment, we can work with the simple conceptual instrument shown in Fig. 8.3(a). The governing equation for such a polarimeter can be expressed as

$$\begin{aligned}\mathbf{S}_{\mathrm{d}} &= \mathbf{M}_{\mathrm{P}} \cdot \mathbf{M}_{\mathrm{R}} \cdot \mathbf{S}_{\mathrm{i}} \\ &= \mathbf{M}_{\mathrm{I}} \cdot \mathbf{S}_{\mathrm{i}},\end{aligned} \tag{8.19}$$

where $\mathbf{M}_R$ is the Mueller matrix for the retarder, $\mathbf{M}_P$ is the Mueller matrix for the linear polarizer, $\mathbf{S}_i$ and $\mathbf{S}_d$ are the Stokes vectors of the incident flux and the flux on the detector, respectively, and $\mathbf{M}_I$ is the composite Mueller matrix of the instrument produced from the product $\mathbf{M}_P \cdot \mathbf{M}_R$.

We can express the *instrument Mueller matrix* containing four four-element-row matrices as

$$\mathbf{M}_{\mathrm{I}} = \begin{bmatrix} \mathbf{m}_0^{\mathrm{T}} \\ \mathbf{m}_1^{\mathrm{T}} \\ \mathbf{m}_2^{\mathrm{T}} \\ \mathbf{m}_3^{\mathrm{T}} \end{bmatrix}, \tag{8.20}$$

where $\mathbf{m}_0^{\mathrm{T}}$ represents the transpose of $\mathbf{m}_0$ (i.e., $\mathbf{m}_0^{\mathrm{T}}$ is the first row of $\mathbf{M}_I$).

Our treatment of the analysis of the instrument governing Eq. (8.19) is drawn from Tyo et al. (2006) and Chipman (1995). Recalling that the detector responds only to the S_0 component of $\mathbf{S}_d$, we can write an expression proportional to the observed signal from the jth measurement as

$$\mathrm{S}_{0j} = \mathbf{m}_{0j}^{\mathrm{T}} \cdot \mathbf{S}_i, \tag{8.21}$$

where $\mathbf{m}_{0j}^{\mathrm{T}}$ $[m_{00j}, m_{01j}, m_{02j}, m_{03j}]$ is the vector made up of the first row of $\mathbf{M}_I$ associated with the jth orientation of the retarder-polarizer. Thus, Eq. (8.21) can be expressed as the simple linear equation

$$\mathrm{S}_{0j} = m_{00j}\,\mathrm{S}_{0i} + m_{01j}\,\mathrm{S}_{1i} + m_{02j}\,\mathrm{S}_{2i} + m_{03j}\,\mathrm{S}_{3i}. \tag{8.22}$$

If we know $\mathbf{m}_{0j}$, then Eq. (8.22) contains four unknowns (i.e., the input Stokes vector). In general, if we can write four or more independent equations of the form of Eq. (8.22), we should be able to solve for the input Stokes vector ($\mathbf{S}_i$).

By rotating the retarder in our polarimeter (Fig. 8.3) or in general changing the instrument matrix ($\mathbf{M}_I$) in a way that changes $\mathbf{m}_{0j}$, we generate as many equations of the form of Eq. (8.22) as desired. Since we have four unknowns, we must acquire four or more samples. This can be expressed in matrix form as

$$\mathbf{X} = \mathbf{A} \cdot \mathbf{S}_{\mathrm{i}}, \tag{8.23}$$

where $\mathbf{X}$ is the $N \times 1$ vector of observed signals for the N samples (i.e., retarder angles) and $\mathbf{A}$ is the $N \times 4$ *system matrix* made up of the $\mathbf{m}^{\mathrm{T}}_{0j}$ vectors as rows. To solve for $\mathbf{S}_i$, we use the pseudo-inverse of $\mathbf{A}$, which can be expressed as

$$\mathbf{A}^{\#} = \left(\mathbf{A}^{\mathrm{T}}\mathbf{A}\right)^{-1}\mathbf{A}^{\mathrm{T}}, \tag{8.24}$$

which, when applied to Eq. (8.23) yields

$$\mathbf{A}^{\#}\cdot\mathbf{X} = \mathbf{A}^{\#}\left(\mathbf{A}\cdot\mathbf{S}_{\mathrm{i}}\right) = \left(\mathbf{A}^{\mathrm{T}}\mathbf{A}\right)^{-1}\left(\mathbf{A}^{\mathrm{T}}\mathbf{A}\right)\mathbf{S}_{\mathrm{i}} = \hat{\mathbf{S}}_{\mathrm{i}} \tag{8.25}$$

where $\hat{\mathbf{S}}_{\mathrm{i}}$ is the best estimate of $\mathbf{S}_{\mathrm{i}}$ in a least-squared error sense. $\mathbf{A}^{\#}$ is referred to as the *data reduction matrix*. It is clear that to reduce errors, care must be taken to select the analyzer characteristics that form the $\mathbf{m}_{0j}$ vectors such that **A** can be solved for. For linear polarizers, **A** must be of rank 3 to allow recovery of the Stokes vector and of rank 4 for a full Stokes polarimeter.

Let's look at an example for the case where our retarder ($\mathbf{M}_{\mathrm{R}}$) is a quarter wave plate and our linear polarizer ($\mathbf{M}_{\mathrm{p}}$) is an ideal horizontal polarizer. Collett (1993) expresses the Mueller matrix for a rotated quarter wave plate as

$$\mathbf{M}_{\lambda/4}(\theta) = \frac{1}{2}\begin{bmatrix} 1 & 0 & 0 & 0 \\ 0 & \cos^2 2\theta & \sin 2\theta\cos 2\theta & \sin 2\theta \\ 0 & \sin 2\theta\cos 2\theta & \sin^2 2\theta & -\cos 2\theta \\ 0 & -\sin 2\theta & \cos 2\theta & 0 \end{bmatrix}. \tag{8.26}$$

Recall that the ideal horizontal polarizer can be represented as

$$\mathbf{T}_{\ominus} = \frac{1}{2}\begin{bmatrix} 1 & 1 & 0 & 0 \\ 1 & 1 & 0 & 0 \\ 0 & 0 & 0 & 0 \\ 0 & 0 & 0 & 0 \end{bmatrix}. \tag{8.27}$$

Thus, the governing equation for our polarizer would be of the form

$$\mathbf{S}_{\mathrm{d}} = \mathbf{M}_{\mathrm{I}}\cdot\mathbf{S}_{\mathrm{i}} = \mathbf{T}_{\ominus}\cdot\mathbf{M}_{\lambda/4}(\theta)\cdot\mathbf{S}_{\mathrm{i}} \tag{8.28}$$

and the $\mathbf{m}_{0j}^{\mathrm{T}}$ vectors making up the systems matrix would be of the form

$$\mathrm{M}_{0j}^{\mathrm{T}} = \frac{1}{2}\left[1, \cos^2 2\theta_j, \sin 2\theta_j \cos 2\theta_j, \sin 2\theta_j\right]. \tag{8.29}$$

Ambirajan and Look (1995) solve for the set of four rotator angles that would yield a near-optimum solution to the data reduction matrix for a rotatable quarter wave plate and a horizontal polarizer. They recommend that rotation angles of −45 deg, 0 deg, 30 deg, and 60 deg or −90 deg, −45 deg, 30 deg, and 60 deg be used, as they are near optimal and the simple values of the trigonometry functions yield a simple data reduction matrix. Sabatke et al. (2000) look at the case of optimizing the retardance and rotation angles and find that an improvement over the quarter wave plate could be obtained using retarders close to one-third of a wave. Tyo and Wei (2006) address the question of allowing the retardance of the retarder to vary in the presence of error.

The approach presented above for characterization of an instrument governing equation can be generalized to include any combination of retarders and polarizer used in a polarimeter. Furthermore, it can be simplified to deal with linear polarizers where only the first three elements of the Stokes vector are required.

The discussion above has implied that the system matrix (**A**) in Eq. (8.23) could be known. In fact, the retarder and linear polarizers used are never ideal and the other optical elements in the polarimeter can introduce additional character variability to the instrument Mueller matrix, making it difficult to generate an analytical form for **A.** It is much more common to solve for **A** empirically during the calibration process. Calibration of the polarimeter is accomplished by inputing known Stokes vectors and observing the output signals. For the jth polarization state, this can be expressed as

$$\mathbf{S}_{\text{d}j} = \hat{\mathbf{M}}_{\text{I}j} \cdot \mathbf{S}_i, \tag{8.30}$$

where $\hat{\mathbf{M}}$ is the unknown instrument Mueller matrix. In practice, recall that we observe only the first Stokes parameter of $\mathbf{S}_{\text{d}j}$ and hence need only the first row of $\hat{\mathbf{M}}_{\text{I}j}$, which we term $\hat{\mathbf{m}}_{0j}^{\text{T}}$. The system matrix for the instrument is then made up of N row vectors $\hat{\mathbf{m}}_{0j}^{\text{T}}$, one for each of the N polarization states of the instrument. In matrix form, this can be expressed as

$$\mathbf{X} = \mathbf{A} \cdot \mathbf{S}_{\text{i}}, \tag{8.31}$$

where **X** is an $(N \times 1)$ vector of signals observed for the N states of the polarimeter, **A** is the $(N \times 4)$ system matrix, and $\mathbf{S}_{\text{i}}$ is the input Stokes vector. If we now consider the case where we input a number (Q) of Stokes vectors, we can write a matrix representation of the process as

$$\mathbf{Y} = \mathbf{A} \cdot \mathbf{T}, \tag{8.32}$$

where **Y** is the $(N \times Q)$ matrix made up of column vectors ($\mathbf{X}_{\text{q}}$) of observed signals for each input Stokes vector ($\mathbf{S}_{\text{q}}$) and **T** is the $(4 \times Q)$ matrix made up of each input Stokes vector ($\mathbf{S}_{\text{q}}$) as columns. To solve for **A**, we use the pseudo-inverse of **T** to yield

$$\mathbf{Y} \cdot \mathbf{T}^{\#} = \mathbf{A} \cdot \mathbf{T} \cdot \mathbf{T}^{\#} = \hat{\mathbf{A}}, \tag{8.33}$$

where $\hat{\mathbf{A}}$ is the best (in a least-squared error sense) estimate of **A.**

Clearly, we must use caution in selecting the Stokes vectors that make up **T** to ensure that **T** is invertible. This process incorporates the instrument unknowns into the solution for $\hat{\mathbf{A}}$ via calibration with input flux with known Stokes vectors. Any unknown flux can then be analyzed using Eq. (8.25) and the estimated system matrix $\hat{\mathbf{A}}$.

Our discussion to this point has been simplified by focusing on single-detector or point polarimeters, rather than on imaging polarimeters, which are of more interest for remote sensing. Point polarimeters are widely used in the laboratory and field to characterize the Mueller matrices or pBRDFs of materials of interest. More importantly, the approach introduced here for a point polarimeter can to first order be generalized to imaging polarimeters by treating each pixel (or group of pixels) as a point radiometer, often with its own system matrix that must be obtained through calibration.

8.3 Polarimetric Imaging Sensors

A wide range of imaging polarimeters has been designed based on expanding the principles of the point radiometer described in Sec. 8.2 to two dimensions. In this section we will introduce a small sampling of the potential methods for acquiring polarimetric images. Because a serious treatment requires an understanding of optical principles beyond what we have developed here and beyond what remote sensing scientists need, we restrict ourselves to largely conceptual designs and encourage the reader to delve more deeply into the literature for a more complete understanding. In general, we will emphasize approaches to imaging remote sensing that are readily available for ground truth or simple laboratory experiments or systems that are in use today for remote sensing of the earth. Many more types of instruments are in various stages of development and test in research and development labs and will hopefully become sources for new streams of data available to the remote sensing community.

The simplest form of polarimetric imaging is that used in polarized sunglasses. The same principle has long been used in photography to increase contrast under conditions where a strongly polarized background signal is present. In both cases, a linear polarizer is oriented roughly orthogonally to the polarized background component of the flux to cancel that component and increase the contrast from the rest of the scene (see Fig. 8.4). When looking through a scattering medium that has a polarized component to the scattering (e.g., the atmosphere), we can increase the contrast in a distant object using a polarizer oriented orthogonally to the polarization angle of the scattered flux (see Fig. 8.5).

This single polarizer approach was extended to a two polarizer approach that was used from space to generate some of the earliest polarimetric images of earth [Egan et al. (1991)]. This approach used two cameras equipped with linear cross-polarized filters. The photographer (astronaut) rotates the camera pair until the contrast is maximized (as seen through the lens viewfinder) and then snaps the simultaneous shutters. To analyze the images, they are digitized (the early cameras were film cameras) if necessary and then registered to each other. The sum of the two images provides the S_0 component of the Stokes vector and the difference provides an estimate of the polarimetric contrast (which, depending on the filter orientation, may approximate the S_1 or S_2 Stokes parameters). Note that rotating the cameras will not optimize the contrast between all objects simultaneously, so this approach must focus either on a particular target or more often on the average scene contrast.

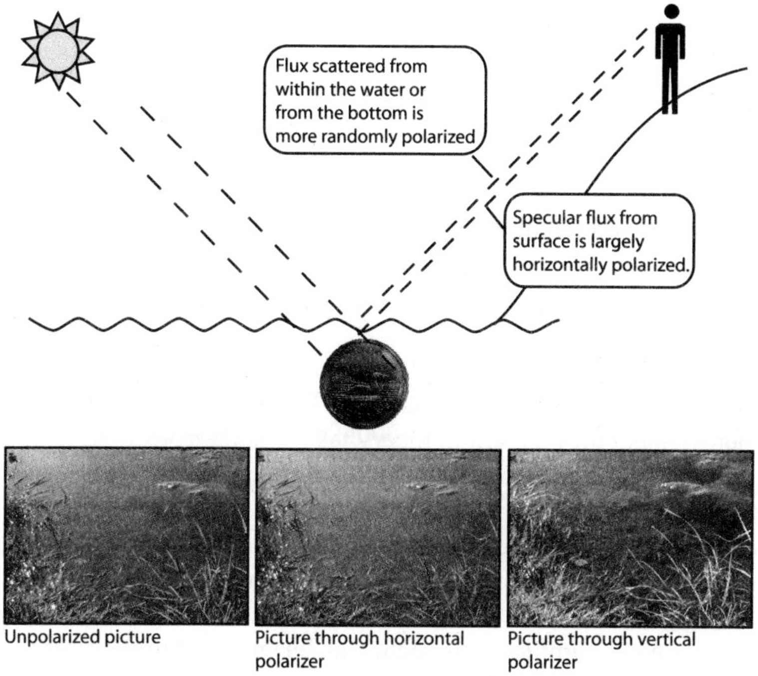

Figure 8.4 Simple polarimetric imaging system employing a single linear polarizer. (See color plate.)

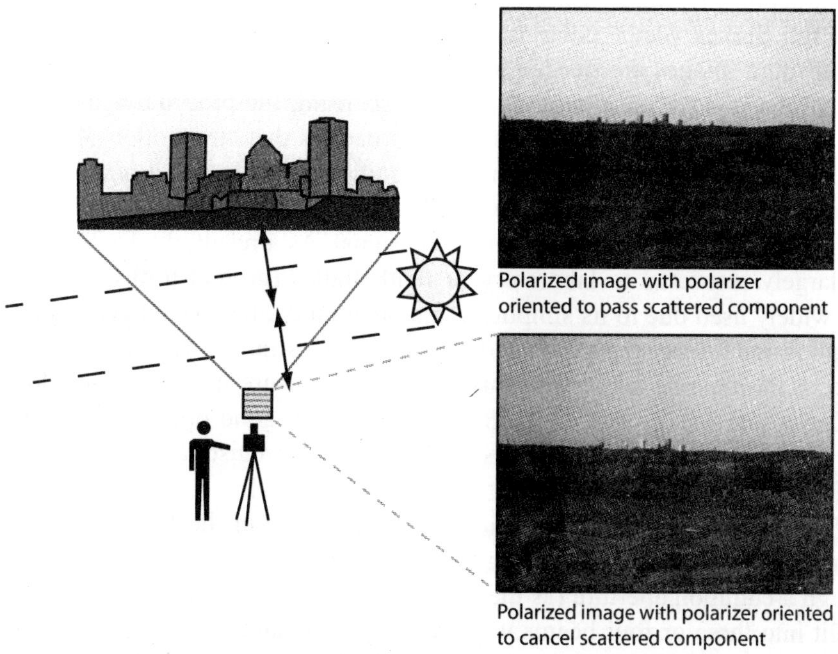

Figure 8.5 Use of polarizer oriented orthogonally to the orientation of the scattered polarization to increase contrast when imaging through a scattering medium. (See color plate.)

These early approaches were followed by a number of methods that attempt to capture the full state of linear polarization (i.e., the first three Stokes parameters) or the full Stokes vector. Most of the systems in use or likely to be used in the near future for earth remote sensing are linear polarization imagers. This is in part due to the relative simplicity of designs that need only linear polarization filters and in part because the remotely sensed signatures from a passively illuminated earth show little or no circular polarization. Tyo et al. (2006) in a review of polarimetric remote sensing introduce a taxonomy of polarimetric sensing methods that we will draw on here in describing both linear and full Stokes vector imaging polarimeters.

One common method employed for early multispectral and polarimetric imaging was to use multiple cameras, each filtered independently. If the cameras are boresighted, they should in theory take simultaneous images of the same scene at the same time. In practice, the slight differences in optics, location, and alignment result in misregistered images that must in general be registered and resampled to form each Stokes vector image. The cost of multiple cameras and post-processing and errors due to residual misregistration have led to a variety of alternate designs.

One of the most common approaches to imaging polarimetry uses the *division of time polarimeter* (DoTP), shown in Fig. 8.6. These imagers use sequential images taken with the analyzer rotated to different orientations. For a linear polarimeter, three or more orientations of a linear polarizer are sufficient to allow reconstruction of a linear Stokes vector as described in Sec. 8.2 (see Fig. 8.7). For a full Stokes vector polarimeter, a retarder is required in the analyzer and four or more images are needed to reconstruct the Stokes vector. In either case the analysis is done on a pixel by pixel basis using the procedures discussed in Sec. 8.2. The obvious limitation of this approach is that any motion of the target or sensor resulting in a translation of a significant fraction of a pixel before all frames of imagery are acquired invalidates the implicit assumption that common pixels in all frames are sampling the same signal. As a result, the DoTP approach was largely restricted to laboratory or field studies (ground truth) where it has been widely used due to its simplicity and quantitative integrity. Recent advances in high frame rate systems have led to early demonstrations in dynamic environments. Care must be taken with this approach to ensure that the image does not wander on the focal plane as the filters rotate. With good optical alignment and rigid mounts, the sequential images can be very well registered, resulting in very precise measurements of the Stokes vector of each pixel.

Division of amplitude polarimeters (DoAmP) avoid the DoTP timing issue by taking all of the images simultaneously. In this case the images are acquired through a common aperture (as they are with the DoTP approach), then the beam is split into three or four beams with beam splitters and analyzers and refocused onto three or four focal planes [Azzam (1985)]. Each focal plane forms a full resolution image of the incident beam, often passing through an analyzer formed by the beam splitter (which is also a linear polarizer) and a retarder. The result is

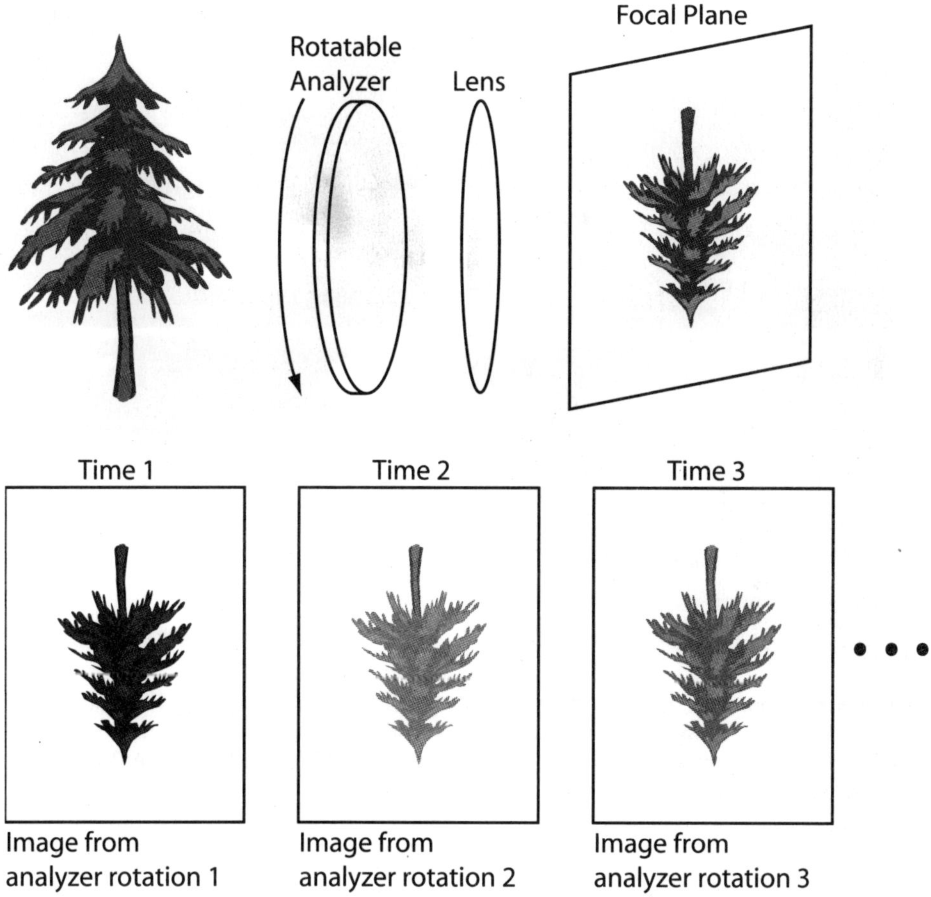

Figure 8.6 Imaging division of time polarimetry concept. Note that the analyzer may be a single rotatable linear polarizer in a linear polarimeter on a rotatable retarder and a fixed linear polarizer in a full Stokes vector polarimeter.

three or four (three for linear, four for full Stokes vector) simultaneously acquired full resolution polarimetrically filtered images from which Stokes vectors can be computed on a pixel by pixel basis using the procedures described in Sec. 8.2. This approach suffers from difficulty in aligning the images on the focal planes after the different complex optical paths. As a result, the images must in general be registered and resampled in post-processing.

If we look to methods traditionally used by the remote sensing community to acquire multispectral data, most of them are applicable to polarimetric imaging. The traditional multispectral line scanning approaches [Schott (2007)] could be employed with polarimetric analyzers replacing the spectral filters. To increase signal to noise, many modern multispectral systems use filtered linear arrays. A polarimetric version of this *pushbroom* concept is shown in Fig. 8.8. These approaches require careful timing of the scan rates relative to the detector sampling to ensure good spatial registration of the filtered data.

Figure 8.7 Polarimetric images showing strong polarization of sky and reflection of sky in upper windows. Lower windows, which reflect the adjacent building, show much less polarimetric character. (Courtesy of R.C. Olsen, Lt. Phil Smith, and Ms. Angie Puetz, Naval Postgraduate School.)

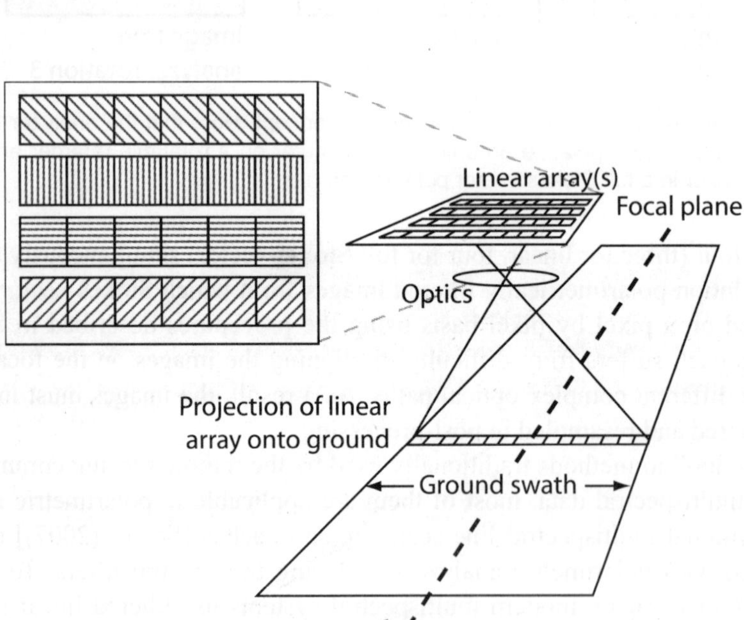

Figure 8.8: Pushbroom sensor concept employing polarizing filters.

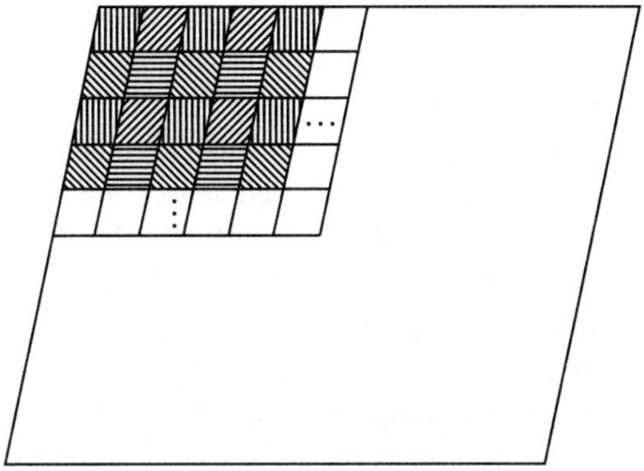

Figure 8.9 Illustration of linear polarization filter pattern used in a division of focal plane imaging polarimeter.

Division of focal plane (DoFP) array polarimeters use conceptually the same technology used in commercial digital color cameras. An array of linear polarizers is fabricated onto the focal plane array in a pattern such as the pattern shown in Fig. 8.9. In order to form a polarimetric image, we must interpolate the expected response to each filter for the locations where no sample was taken for that filter. This results in lower spatial resolution data; however, because of advances in focal plane array technology, large arrays with small pixel size can be fabricated. Nonetheless, even if resolution issues can be overcome with this approach, there are still issues at edges or with high spatial frequency targets, due to interpolation artifacts. Despite these limitations, the simplicity of this design and its effectiveness (if the polarimetric spatial frequencies of the scene are lower than the pixel sampling frequencies) make it very popular. Modern micro-fabrication techniques have made it possible to manufacture DoFP devices across the spectral range commonly used for remote sensing (0.4–14 μm).

8.4 Issues Related to Polarimetric Imaging Sensors

One concern with all imaging sensors is nonuniformity of response. This includes simple flat field nonuniformities associated with variable bias, gain, and linearity between detector elements (pixels). Imaging polarimeters suffer from all of these nonuniformities and must be calibrated and corrected using conventional approaches. In addition, it is common for the polarimetric response to change across the focal plane. This means that in general the system matrix (**A**) in Eq. (8.23) and therefore the data reduction matrix ($\mathbf{A}^{\#}$) may be different for every pixel in the imager. As a result, the calibration procedures discussed in Sec. 8.2 may need to be applied on a pixel by pixel basis to achieve acceptable results.

A second major concern with imaging polarimeters is spatial *registration* between the various filtered images. Essentially all of the approaches have registration issues. With some designs, the misregistration may be fixed so that we can characterize it and then apply a relative fixed resampling process. In other cases, the user must compute the extent of misregistration and develop a new correction for every acquisition. Persons et al. (2002) discuss a method to post-process polarimetric images to achieve image registration at approximately the 0.1-pixel level, which they suggest is the level required for misregistration errors to be compatible with noise levels for the thermal infrared sensor they were studying. Ratliff et al. (2006) discuss issues and methods to mitigate the misregistration inherent in DoFP systems. It is difficult to over-emphasize the importance of registration. Because the Stokes parameters (other than S_0) involve differences, they accentuate misregistration artifacts. This means that misregistration artifacts are amplified and can easily be mistaken as polarimetric signatures.

Another important consideration for polarimetric imaging systems is achieving acceptable *signal to noise* levels. The filtration process associated with forming polarimetric images typically reduces the signal to approximately 50% for approximately randomly polarized flux and significantly more for some filter orientations if the flux is strongly polarized. For the first Stokes parameter, the signal to noise is improved by summing several filtered images. For the other parameters, this is not the case and if the polarization of the beam is not optimally filtered (optimal retardance and rotation angles for the analyzer), the signal to noise can suffer [Bowers et al. (2008)]. Other factors affecting signal to noise and errors in polarimetric images include alignment and precision of repositioning of polarizing elements, as well as integrity of polarizers. Much of our discussion in previous chapters assumed ideal filters. In fact, all filters are less than ideal and this impacts the performance of our instruments. Two of the most common measures of performance of linear polarizers are the *diattenuation*, which can be expressed as

$$D = \frac{\Phi_{max} - \Phi_{min}}{\Phi_{max} + \Phi_{min}} = \frac{\tau_{max} - \tau_{min}}{\tau_{max} + \tau_{min}} \tag{8.34}$$

and the *extinction ratio*, expressed as

$$R = \frac{\tau_{max}}{\tau_{min}}, \tag{8.35}$$

where Φ_{max} and Φ_{min} are the maximum and minimum flux associated with cross-polarized states of a linear polarizer, and τ_{max} and τ_{min} are the associated transmission values. If we have linearly polarized incident flux, it is clear that

$$R = \frac{D+1}{1-D}. \tag{8.36}$$

In the visible region, extinction ratios of 100 or more are common. However, in other spectral regions or with stressing designs, this level is not always achieved and leakage of cross-polarized radiation can introduce errors in our analysis. Tyo and Wei (2006) discuss at greater depth than we can address here some of the issues associated with errors due to optical elements in polarimeters. For our purposes, it is important to recognize that these issues exist, that careful calibration of instruments is necessary to characterize them, and that some, but by no means all, of the issues can be compensated for by careful design and calibration of the instrument.

References

Ambirajan, A., & Look, D.C. (1995). "Optimum angles for a polarimeter: part I." *Optical Engineering,* Vol. 34, pp. 1651–1655.

Azzam, R.M.A. (1985). "Arrangement of four photodetectors for measuring the state of polarization of light." *Optical Letters*, Vol. 10, pp. 309–311.

Bowers, D.L., Boger, J.K., Wellems, L.D., Ortega, S.E., Fetrow, M.P., Hubbs, J.E., Black, W.T., Ratliff, B.M., & Tyo, J.S. (2008). "Unpolarized calibration and nonuniformity correction for LWIR microgrid imaging polarimeters." *Optical Engineering*. Vol. 47, 046403.

Collett, E. (1993). *Polarized Light: Fundamentals and Applications*. 2nd Ed., Marcel Dekker, New York.

Chipman, R.A. (1995). "Polarimetry." *Handbook of Optics*, Vol. 2, Chap. 22, McGraw-Hill, New York.

Egan, W.G., Johnson, W.R., & Whitehead, V.S. (1991). "Terrestrial polarization imagery obtained from the Space Shuttle: characterization and interpretation." *Applied Optics,* Vol. 30, No. 4, pp. 435–442.

Fetrow, M.P., Wellems, D.L., Sposato, S.H., Bishop, K.P., Caudill, T.R., Davis, M.L. & Simrell, E.R. (2002). "Results of a new polarization simulation." *Proceedings SPIE*, Vol. 4481, pp. 149–162.

Persons, C.M., Chenault, D.B., Jones, M.W., Spradley, K.D., Gulley, M.G., & Farlow, C.A. (2002). "Automated registration of polarimetric imagery using Fourier transform techniques." *Proceedings SPIE,* Vol. 4819, pp. 107–117.

Prosch, T., Hennings, D., and Raschke, E. (1983). "Video polarimetry: a new imaging technique in atmospheric science." *Applied Optics*, Vol. 22, pp. 1360–1363.

Ratliff, B.M., Boger, J.K., Fetrow, M.P., Tyo, J.S., & Black, W.T. (2006). "Image processing methods to compensate for IFOV errors in microgrid imaging polarimeters." *Proceedings SPIE*, Vol. 6240, 62400E.

Sabatke, D.S., Descour, M.R., Dereniak, E., Sweatt, W.C., Kemme, S.A., & Phipps, G.S. (2000). "Optimization of retardance for a complete Stokes polarimeter." *Optical Letters,* Vol. 25, No. 11, pp. 802–804.

Schott, J.R. (2007). *Remote Sensing: The Image Chain Approach*. 2nd Ed., Oxford University Press, New York.

Solomon, J.E. (1981). "Polarization imaging." *Applied Optics*, Vol. 20, No. 9, pp. 1537–1544.

Tyo, J.S. (1998). "Optimum linear combination strategy for an N-channel polarization-sensitive vision or imaging system." *Journal of the Optical Society of America A,* Vol. 15, No. 12, pp. 359–366.

Tyo, J.S., Goldstein, D.L., Chenault, D.B., & Shaw, J.A. (2006). "Review of passive imaging polarimetry for remote sensing applications." *Applied Optics,* Vol. 45, No. 22, pp. 5453–5469.

Tyo, J.S., & Wei, H. (2006). "Optimizing imaging polarimeters constructed with imperfect optics." *Applied Optics,* Vol. 45, No. 22, pp. 5497–5503.

Walraven, R. (1981). "Polarization imagery." *Optical Engineering*, Vol. 20, No. 1, pp. 14–18.

Wolff, L.B. (1994). "Polarization camera for computer vision with a beam splitter." *Journal of the Optical Society of America A,* Vol. 11, No. 11, pp. 2935–2945.

John R. Schott

Chapter 9
Processing and Display Algorithms

Relatively little research on processing of polarimetric remotely sensed image data has been published. In part this is because high-resolution polarimetric image data has not been widely available for operational sensors to spur application scientists to develop and publish processing algorithms. It is also partially due to the fact that most of the algorithms developed for processing multispectral data can also be applied to polarimetric data. For example, Wolff (1990) used simple gray level thresholding of the polarization ratio to separate metals from nonmetals and Thilak et al. (2005) show that standard multiband material classification techniques can be used to classify materials using Stokes vector images of simple targets. These multiband processing methods are well treated in the literature and will not be covered here [Schowengerdt (2006), Richards (1999), and Schott (2007)]. Some image processing and display approaches particular to polarimetric image data have been developed and will be introduced here.

In processing polarimetric images, the first issue to recall is that essentially all of the processing steps involve image differences that will exaggerate any misregistration between the images. Thus, careful registration of the raw filtered images before any further processing is a critical first step. Because the filtered images are highly correlated, most conventional registration methods relying on correlation are applicable and will not be addressed here [Schowengerdt (2006) and Schott (2007)]. However, the reader is cautioned that high levels of subpixel registration are required, particularly if per-pixel quantitative analysis is planned.

9.1 Display of Polarimetric Images

The first possible way to view polarimetric images is to look at the raw filtered images. However, these data are so highly correlated that they tend not to accentuate the polarimetric properties of the scenes. The next step is typically to compute the *Stokes vector images* and to display the Stokes vector (see Fig. 9.1). The Stokes vector images can be combined using color techniques to allow simultaneous viewing of the Stokes parameters. In the simplest case, this would

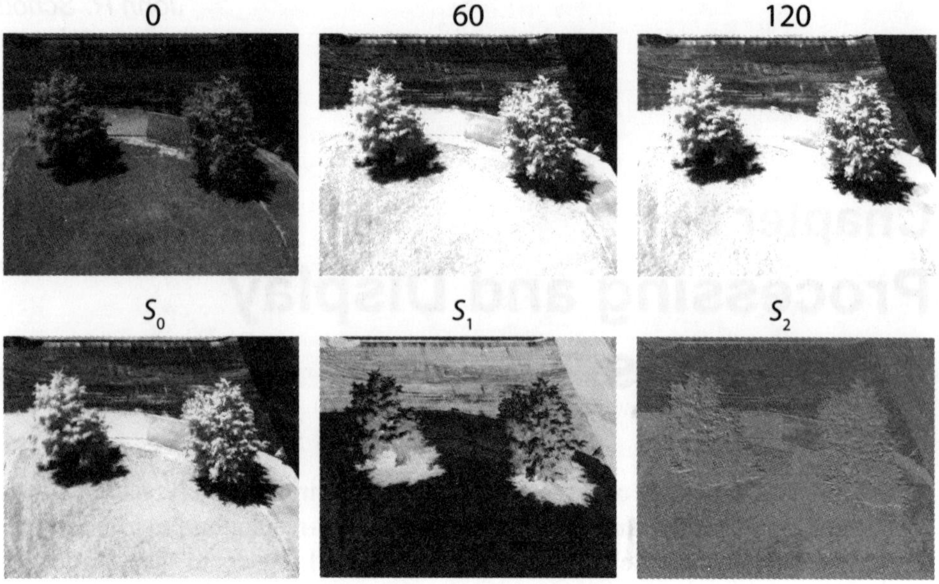

Figure 9.1 Comparison of raw filtered images and Stokes vector images.

involve displaying each Stokes vector as a driver for each color display channel. For example, for the common case where we assume $S_3 = 0$, we set

$$\begin{aligned} S_0 &\Rightarrow \text{Green} \\ S_1 &\Rightarrow \text{Red} \\ S_2 &\Rightarrow \text{Blue} \end{aligned} \tag{9.1}$$

This requires us to scale S_0 over the display range and to bias S_1 and S_2 such that 0 values fall roughly in the middle of the display range (see Fig. 9.2). Simple display methods such as this one often may fail to accentuate the polarization state of the data, which is often very low, i.e., Stokes vectors have most S_1 and S_2 values near zero. As a result, it is in these cases desirable to generate mean level red, green, and blue values to provide reference gray images when the Stokes parameter is near zero and to accentuate the S_1 and S_2 values where they deviate from zero. There are many possible ways to accomplish this.

Tyo et al. (1998) suggest an approach that takes advantage of the roughly orthogonal response of the visual system to the Value (brightness), Hue (color), and Saturation (purity of color, i.e., low saturations are pastel shades) (HSV) axes of color display. More specifically, *value* is the brightness of the scene and typically spans a range from zero to the maximum brightness displayable, *hue* is the angle in color space (ranging from 1 to 360 deg) used to select the equiluminance color, and *saturation* [ranging from 0 (neutral gray) to 1 (pure color)] describes the purity of the color (see Fig. 9.3). Note that there are simple transforms that

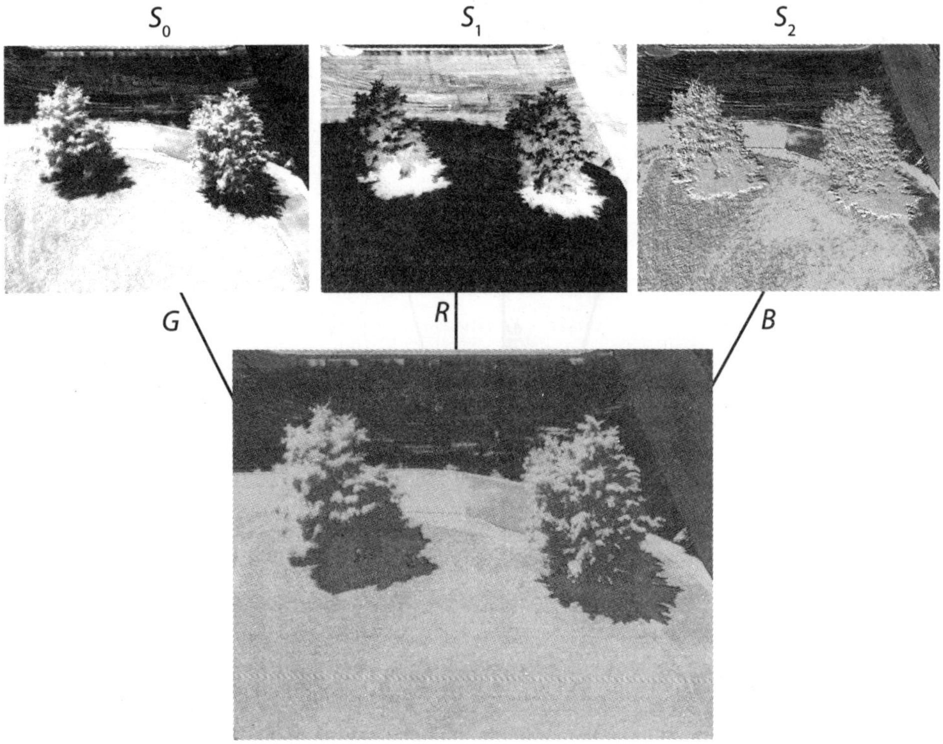

Figure 9.2 Color combination of Stokes vectors $R \rightarrow S_1$, $G \rightarrow S_0$, $B \rightarrow S_2$. (See color plate.)

relate red (R), green (G), and blue (B) display brightness to HSV values and HSV values to RGB;

$$\begin{bmatrix} R \\ G \\ B \end{bmatrix} = F \begin{bmatrix} H \\ S \\ V \end{bmatrix} \tag{9.2}$$

or

$$\begin{bmatrix} H \\ S \\ V \end{bmatrix} = F^{-1} \begin{bmatrix} R \\ G \\ B \end{bmatrix} \tag{9.3}$$

where F and F^{-1} represent the HSV-to-RGB transform and the RGB-to-HSV transform, respectively [Foley et al. (1995)].

Tyo et al. (1998) display the S_0 component as brightness (V) and the difference between cross-polarized components as saturation(s). They select two opponent hues (colors) to represent the positive and negative values of the polarization-difference image. This can be expressed as

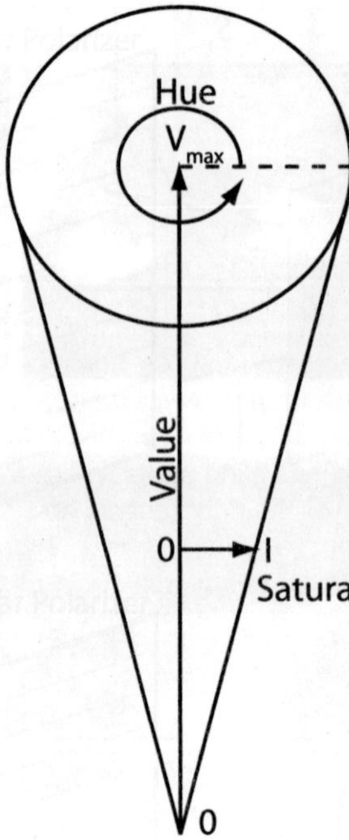

Figure 9.3 Illustration of the hue, saturation, and value color space.

$$DC_{\parallel} + DC_{\perp} \rightarrow V \tag{9.4}$$

$$| DC_{\parallel} - DC_{\perp} | \rightarrow S \tag{9.5}$$

$$DC_{\parallel} - DC_{\perp} > \underline{0} \rightarrow H_1 \tag{9.6}$$

$$DC_{\parallel} - DC_{\perp} < 0 \rightarrow H_2, \tag{9.7}$$

where $DC_{\parallel}$ and $DC_{\perp}$ are the image brightness values associated with the orthogonal polarization axis of the linear polarizer and H_1 and H_2 represent two opponent colors (hues). They point out that several sets of opponent colors could be used to display different initial reference angles for the linear polarizer (i.e., a family of images can be produced). Tyo et al. (1998) show examples of this approach (referred to as two-color polarimetric-difference imaging (2C-PDI)) applied to polarimetric imaging in turbid media (see Fig. 9.4).

Note that this approach can be applied simultaneously to a linear Stokes vector image as follows

$$S_0 \rightarrow V \tag{9.8}$$

$$|S_1| \rightarrow S \tag{9.9}$$

$$|S_2| \rightarrow S \tag{9.10}$$

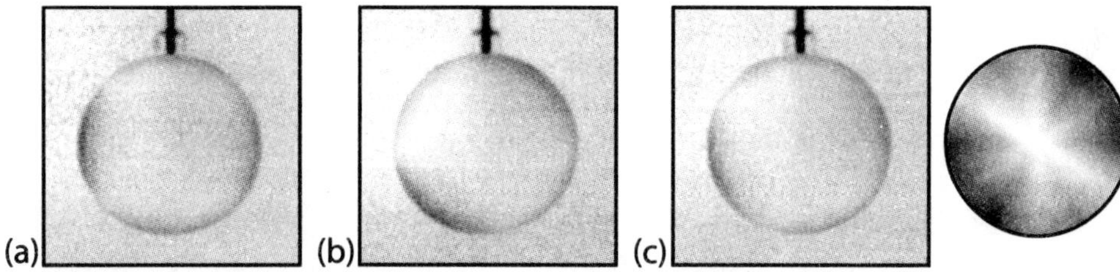

Figure 9.4 Two-parameter colorimetric polarization-difference imaging (2C-PDI) images of back-illuminated dielectric sphere at an effective distance of 0.13 attenuation lengths. Images (a), (b), and (c) were obtained with the analyzer oriented at the angles of 0 deg, 36 deg, and 72 deg with respect to the vertical, respectively. 2C-PDI highlights areas that are polarized parallel to the PDI axes and has blind spots where the light is polarized at 45 deg with respect to the PDI axes. The key at the right reveals how the colors in the images map into polarization direction; for example, red represents an excess of horizontal polarization and cyan represents an excess of vertical polarization [Tyo et al. (1998)]. (See color plate.)

$$S_1 \geq 0 \rightarrow H_1 \tag{9.11}$$

$$S_1 < 0 \rightarrow H_2 \tag{9.12}$$

$$S_2 \geq 0 \rightarrow H_3 \tag{9.13}$$

$$S_2 < 0 \rightarrow H_4, \tag{9.14}$$

where H_1 and H_2 are opponent colors (e.g., red and cyan) and H_3 and H_4 are another pair of opponent colors (e.g., green and magenta). However, visual discrimination when both S_1 and S_2 signals are strong can be difficult.

Bernard and Wehner (1977) propose using the HSV space to visualize the polarization character of a pixel according to

$$S_0 \rightarrow V \tag{9.15}$$

$$\text{DoP} \rightarrow S \tag{9.16}$$

$$2\psi \rightarrow H, \tag{9.17}$$

where DoP and ψ are the degree of polarization and the angle of polarization as introduced in Chapter 4. Figure 9.5 shows an example using Eqs. (9.15) through (9.17). Tyo et al. (1998) point out that this approach may suffer when applied to scenes with low polarization when the angle of polarization can vary rapidly from pixel to pixel. This motivated their development of the approach captured in Eqs. (9.4) through (9.7) for turbid media.

In some cases the interpretation of polarimetric data may be difficult due to a polarization bias across the image. This might occur if viewing through a long atmospheric path that was at an angle where significant polarization was induced (see Fig. 9.6). It might also occur if the camera were rotated. In this case, there

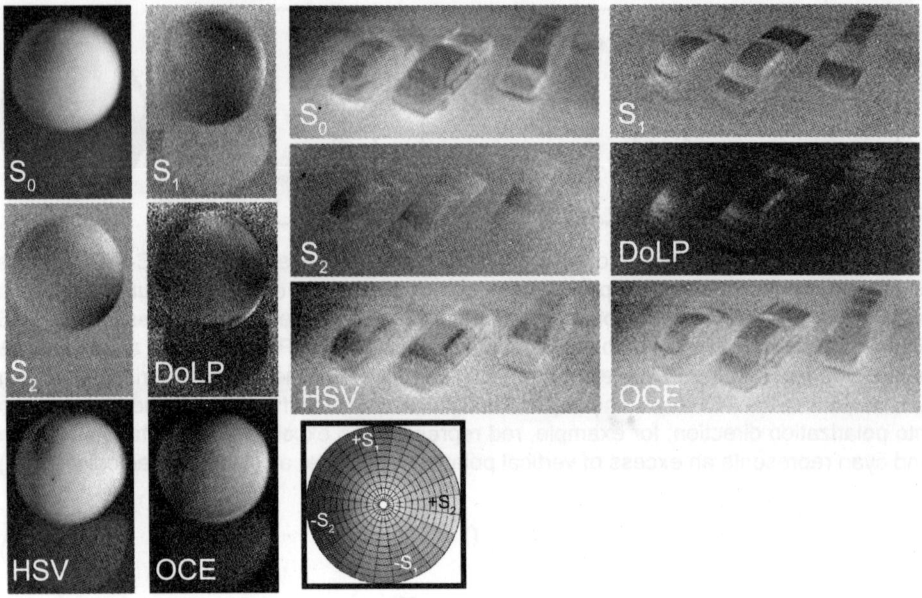

Figure 9.5 Illustration of opponent color encoding (OCE) (i.e., Eqs. (9.4) through (9.7)) and hue, saturation, and value encoding (i.e., Eqs. (9.15) through (9.17)) applied to longwave infrared polarimetric images. (See color plate.)

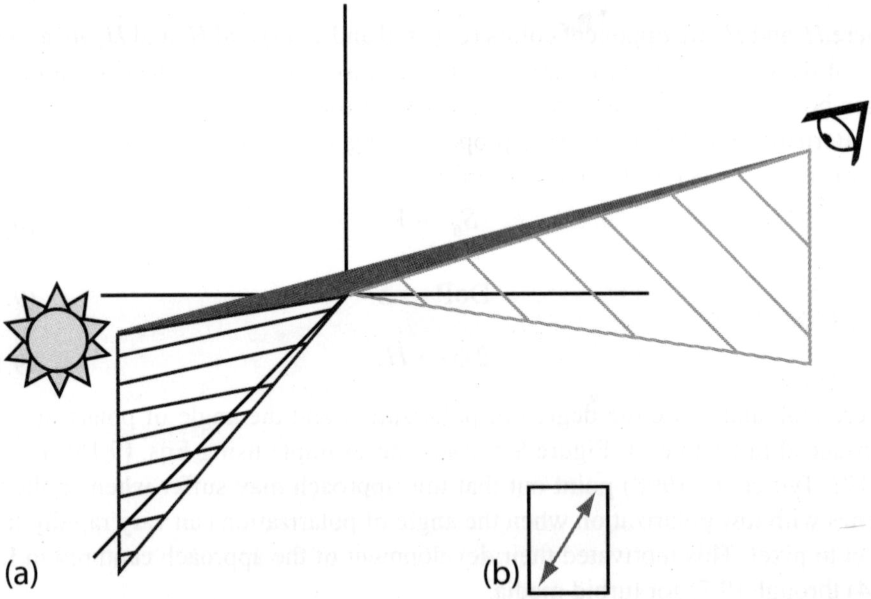

Figure 9.6 Illustration of how the atmosphere can induce polarization bias. (a) The scattering in the atmosphere will introduce polarization at right angles to the sun-scattering center-sensor plane (dark grey). In this case, the sun-scattering center-sensor angle is near 90 deg so the DoP will be large and the angle of polarization as seen by the sensor will introduce significant S_2 signal (b).

would be no increase in polarization; however, the orientation of the polarization (i.e., the AoP) would be changed. Of course, both of these effects can occur simultaneously. In addition, more subtle effects such as widespread reflection of strongly polarized downwelled radiance can also introduce image-wide effects. Because we are often interested in variations in a scene, it is often valuable to display data such that the reference levels or backgrounds appear the same. Thus, image-wide bias in the DoP or AoP may introduce variations in the display that make interpretation more difficult. This might manifest as an image-wide hue or saturation shift in a color visualization, making color-based interpretation more difficult. To compensate for these effects, standard image processing methods can be applied to the final DoP and AoP images. This would involve evaluating the DoP and AoP histograms. Since we expect there to be a significant number of objects in a scene with near-zero DoP, a bias of the minimum DoP from zero can indicate an atmosphere-induced bias that can be subtracted out. Similarly, when looking at the reflected signals, we usually expect the mean AoP to be zero deg because we assume that the average surface orientation in the scene is horizontal. Thus, on average, the AoP induced by reflection from objects in the scene will be near zero deg. Inspection of the AoP histogram can identify whether the mean value is significantly different from zero and any bias can be removed before display. An alternative approach must be employed if the display approach is based on the Stokes parameters. In this case, AoP bias must be removed by rotation of the Stokes vectors using the appropriate Mueller matrix rotation (see Eq. (7.29) and related discussion) for the image-wide AoP bias. The resulting images will have a mean AoP of zero deg and should yield more consistent display results. Note that the rotation process will not change the DoP; the rotation will only determine which Stokes parameter carries the DoP information. Therefore, if a DoP bias adjustment is desired, it must be performed after the rotation. For scenes where a significant fraction of the pixels have DoP values near zero, using a scene average or histogram-based approach to compute an AoP bias can lead to significant errors. This is because AoP calculations based on S_2/S_1 values can vary widely as both terms approach zero. An alternative approach involves plotting S_1 versus S_2. If the bulk of the pixels fall along a line, then the slope of the line (S_2/S_1) represents AoP bias, which can be removed by rotations. Note that the bias adjustments discussed above are designed to improve consistency of display for visual interpretation and may remove data useful for more detailed quantitative analysis.

The approaches presented in this section have emphasized methods to process polarimetric imagery for visual display and analysis. We reiterate that to be effective, these methods require good registration and are only applicable to three-band data sets due to the 3-D nature of the human visual system. In the next section we briefly review some data processing methods used specifically for analysis of polarimetric image data.

9.2 Data Processing and Analysis

Much of the processing of polarimetric image data is aimed at generating images for display and visual analysis as described in the previous section. In addition, standard single-band or multispectral processing techniques can be applied to individual bands or multiband data sets comprised of images acquired either through multiple analyzers or Stokes vector images. The methods employed at this stage include thresholding and edge detection/enhancement of individual images and a host of scene segmentation/classification, anomaly detection, and target detection approaches applied to multidimensional images. We do not want to downplay the value of these techniques to PI image analysis. However, because they are well treated in the general remote sensing literature, we will not review them here. In contrast, only a relatively small number of techniques have been developed that are specific to polarimetric data. Much of the PI-specific analysis has focused on the potential to take advantage of the angular variation in the Fresnel reflectance to capture the orientation of the surface [cf. Sadjadi and Chun (2004) and Morel et al. (2006)], with the ultimate goal of performing 3-D reconstruction of targets. Reid et al. (2006) describe an approach to estimate the surface normal vector from the degree of linear polarization (DoLP) and the angle of polarization (AoP) derived from each pixel of an LWIR imaging polarimeter. Their approach assumes that the user can estimate the index of refraction and surface roughness through some other means. The method involves comparison of a forward model with observed values to compute an estimate of the local surface normal. Their results, based on simulated data for roughened glass, indicate that recovery of the surface normal to within a few degrees requires knowledge of the roughness constant (σ) to within 0.025 and the index of refraction to within 0.05. For many applications, a rather involved material classification may be required to achieve the level of precision required.

Thilak et al. (2007) describe an approach to recover the complex index of refraction and the view angle from the surface normal. Their approach requires multiple image acquisitions using reflective polarimetric sensors when the source is at different locations (see Fig. 9.7). The approach assumes that the source and sensor are in the principle plane and uses a minimization technique (nonlinear least squares) to minimize the differences between a model of the pBRDF behavior of the surface (see Chapter 6) and the observed DoP values. The model fit yields an estimate of the effective complex index of refraction (i.e., n and k), which can then be used in a second optimization to estimate the view angle from the surface normal. The authors point out that the values of n and k recovered using this approach do not need to be physically correct; rather, as long as comparable values are retrieved each time, they can be used in subsequent material mapping. Model and laboratory results suggest that the approach is applicable over a relatively large range of incident illumination angles and that results improve if more incident angles over a larger range are available (five or more image acquisitions were commonly used). This approach shows some of the potential

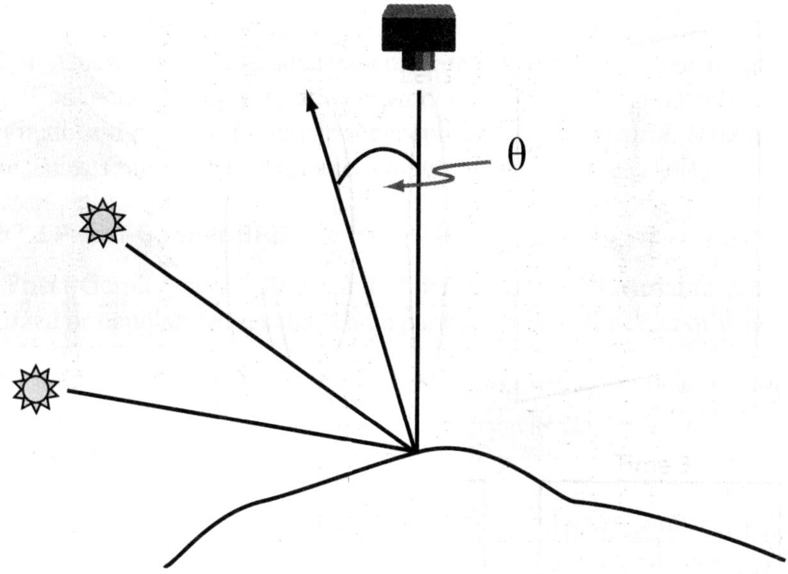

Figure 9.7 Illustration of the image acquisition procedure described by Thilak et al. (2007).

for polarimetric analysis, but is limited by the principle plane assumption and the operational strain associated with multiple acquisitions.

At the start of this chapter we pointed out the importance of image registration. Moving objects in an image can introduce localized misregistration in pushbroom or division-of-time polarimeters, even when the full frame is on average well registered. This results in false polarization signatures as shown in Fig. 9.8. These artifacts can aid in moving-object detection, but require object-specific registration algorithms if polarimetric analysis of the moving object is required.

We have not spent much time discussing how polarimetric signatures vary with wavelength. Because polarimetric signatures are heavily influenced by surface properties, generally they do not vary rapidly with wavelength. On the other hand, the effective surface roughness is directly related to wavelength. Thus, a surface that is somewhat smooth in the visible may appear to be quite smooth (specular) in the SWIR and near mirror-like in the LWIR. Zhao and Zhang (2006) suggest that PI image data acquired at multiple wavelengths can provide incremental data that is available due to spectral and polarimetric differences over broad spectral bands. Their results focus on methods to fuse multiband PI data for display. However, these data once registered can be processed with a variety of multidimensional processing algorithms for classification and target detection. Shaw (1999) also discusses how spectral polarization signatures over wide spectral ranges can carry data beyond what is available in a single spectral band.

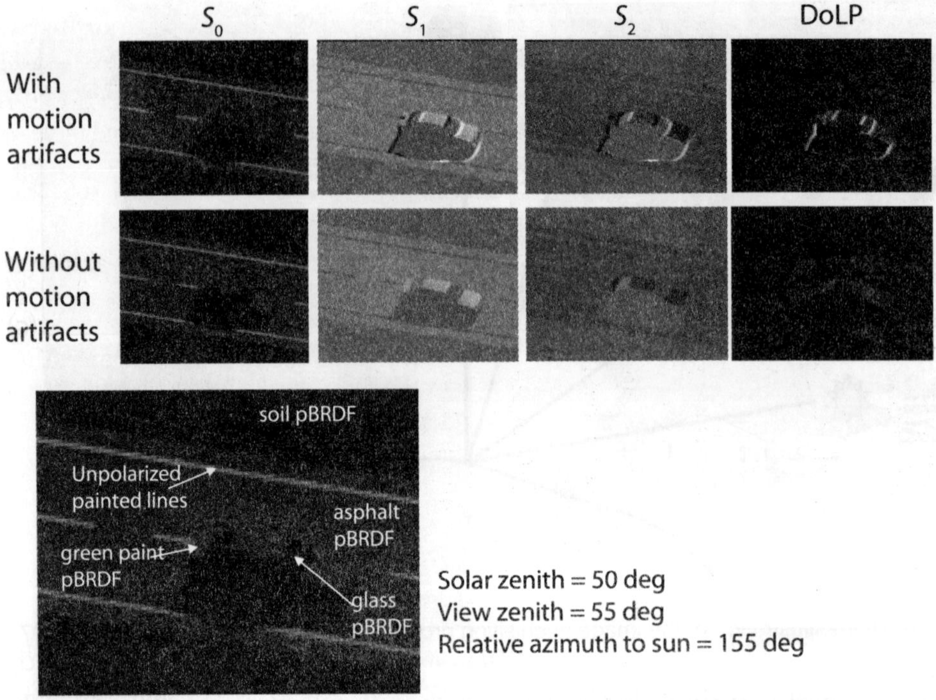

Figure 9.8 Illustration of artifacts introduced by pushbroom and DoTP imagers. Top shows image with artifacts, middle shows same target with no motion, and bottom shows optical properties of materials simulated in DIRSIG. (See color plate.)

References

Bernard, G.D. & Wehner, R. (1977). "Functional similarities between polarization vision and color vision." *Vision Research,* Vol. 17, pp. 1019–1028.

Foley, J.D., Dam, A.v., Feiner, S.K., & Hughes, J.F. (1995). *Computer Graphics: Principles and Practice in C.* 2nd Ed., Addison-Wesley Professional, Boston.

Morel, O., Stolz, C., Meriaudeau, F., & Gorria, P. (2006). "Active lighting applied to three-dimensional reconstruction of specular metallic surfaces by polarization imaging." *Applied Optics*, Vol. 45, No. 17, pp. 4062–4068.

Reid, R.B., Oxley, M.E., Eismann, M.T., & Goda, M.E. (2006). "Quantifying surface normal estimation." *Proceedings SPIE*, Vol. 6240, 624001.

Richards, J.A. (1999). *Remote Sensing Digital Image Analysis, An Introduction*. 3rd Ed., Springer, New York.

Sadjadi, F.A., & Chun, C.S.L. (2004). "Remote sensing using passive infrared Stokes parameters." *Optical Engineering*, Vol. 43, pp. 2283–2291.

Schott, J.R. (2007). *Remote Sensing: The Image Chain Approach*, 2nd Ed., Oxford University Press, New York.

Schowengerdt, R.A. (1997). *Remote Sensing. Models and Methods for Image Processing.* 2nd Ed., Academic Press, Burlington, MA.

Schowengerdt, R.A. (2006). *Remote Sensing: Models and Methods for Image Processing.* 3rd Ed. Academic Press, Burlington, MA.

Shaw, J. (1999). "Degree of linear polarization in spectral radiances from water-viewed infrared polarimeters." *Applied Optics*, Vol. 38, pp. 3157–3165.

Thilak, V., Saini, J., Voelz, D.G., & Creusere, C.D. (2005). "Pattern recognition for passive polarimetric data using nonparametric classifiers." *Proceedings SPIE*, Vol. 5888, 588816.

Thilak, V., Voelz, D.G., & Creusere, C.D. (2007). "Polarization-based index of refraction and reflection angle estimation for remote sensing applications." *Applied Optics*, Vol. 46, No. 30, pp. 7527–7536.

Tyo, J.S., Pugh, E.N., Jr., & Engheta, N. (1998). "Colorimetric representations for use with polarization-difference imaging of objects in scattering media." *Journal of the Optical Society of America A*, Vol. 15, No. 2, pp. 367–374.

Wolff, L.B. (1990). "Polarization-based material classification from specular reflection." *Pattern Analysis and Machine Intelligence, IEEE Transactions on*, Vol. 12, No. 11, pp. 1059–1071.

Zhao, Y., Pan, Q., & Zhang, H. (2006). "Material classification based on multiband polarimetric images fusion." *Proceedings SPIE*, Vol. 6240, 624007.

James R. Shell II
Scott D. Brown
Michael G. Gartley
John R. Schott

Chapter 10
Measurements and Modeling of the pBRDF of Materials

To this point we have focused on the underlying phenomenology that governs the formation and observation of polarimetric signatures in remotely sensed images. In this chapter we will introduce a simple method to measure the primary terms impacting linear pBRDF (Sec. 10.1) and an approach to modeling polarimetric imaging phenomenology in the reflective region (0.4–2.5 μm) of the spectrum (Sec. 10.2). Many devices and approaches have been developed to measure pBRDF and the variation in pBRDF. A variety of these are described in Chapter 6. To keep our treatment here manageable, we have chosen to present only one approach, due to its simplicity (i.e., nearly anyone could use the approach with minimum instrumentation) and the author's familiarity with the data. We have chosen to limit the discussion to the linear polarization terms, due to the small contribution from circular polarization for most passive sensing of the earth.

10.1 Polarimetric BRDF Measurement Approach

Ideally, BRDF measurements are made in a lab environment using a "point" illumination source with careful control and minimization of stray light. However, many materials such as vegetation do not lend themselves to easy indoor measurements, due to alteration of their natural state or simply because of their physical size (e.g., a tree canopy). Outdoor BRDF measurements of such materials become a necessity and, as described in Chapter 6, many approaches have been successfully employed [Deering and Leone (1986), Walthall et al. (2000), Sandmeier and Itten (1999), and Sandmeier (2000)]. Wide field-of-view (FOV) imaging systems may be used that efficiently enable the simultaneous measurement of multiple scattering angles [Czapla-Myers (2002), Han and Perlin (2003), and Dana and Wang (2004)].

10.1.1 Measurement approach

One simple approach described by Shell and Schott (2005) for measurement of background materials will be presented here. It uses a narrow FOV ($\approx$10 deg) imaging system to make BRDF measurements. Each image pixel is approximately at the same scattering angle as that at the center of the image, such that the average radiance across the focal plane enables determination of the BRDF. Such an approach limits the scattering angle resolution to the FOV; however, this is not a concern for most natural surfaces that are not appreciably specular and hence do not have rapid BRDF changes over the 10-deg FOV of the system. The impetus for this technique is the ability to quantify the BRDF variability as well as the pBRDF. Multiple scattering angles are sampled by repositioning the camera in the hemisphere above the measurement surface.

This technique may be used at any distance from the measurement surface—the only prerequisite is that the ground FOV (GFOV) is large enough that it adequately integrates the spatial variability or texture of the material. For instance, a GFOV of 1 ft may be adequate for grass, asphalt, and aggregate; but measurements of tree canopies and shrubs would require a larger GFOV. For easy field use not requiring elevated platforms or other positioning devices, an operating distance for the measurements discussed here was 2 m, providing a GFOV of approximately 0.3 m.

A successful technique for outdoor BRDF measurements may be developed by considering the radiance contributions to a sensor (cf. Eq. (7.7)). It is first noted that imaging surfaces at a distance of 2 m results in negligible atmospheric scattering along the surface-to-sensor path, such that $\vec{L}_u \approx 0$. The surface radiance is therefore composed of the direct solar and downwelled sky reflectance, or $\vec{L}_r$ and $\vec{L}_d$. The measurement made when the surface is illuminated by the sun and downwelled sky radiance will be referred to as image C (see Fig. 10.1).

The downwelled sky radiance is a stray light source for the purpose of BRDF measurements. It may be directly measured and eliminated via an image subtraction technique. $\vec{L}_d$ is measured by occluding only the sun (see Fig. 10.2), and imaging the shadowed surface (image D in Fig. 10.1). In this manner, it is seen that

$$\vec{L}_r = (\vec{L}_r + \vec{L}_d) - (\vec{L}_d) \propto C - D. \tag{10.1}$$

The error terms shown in Eq. (7.14) are therefore eliminated by the "shadow" image. This is quite valuable, as comparison of the C and C−D data quantifies the change to the linear Stokes components resulting from the sky polarization.

The "digital counts" recorded by the imaging system may be normalized into absolute BRDF values by use of a *Spectralon* calibration target. Spectralon has a highly Lambertian, approximately angular-invariant BRDF of ρ/π, with a nearly randomly polarized reflectance of $\rho \geq 0.97$ across most of the VNIR spectrum [Goldstein (1999)]. As with the surface measurement, images of the calibration target are taken both in sun and in shadow (images A and B, respectively).

When acquiring multiple images over a short time period such that the atmospheric conditions and solar zenith position (θ_i) do not change appreciably, the BRDF may be determined by the ratio of the known calibration target BRDF to that of the unknown surface or

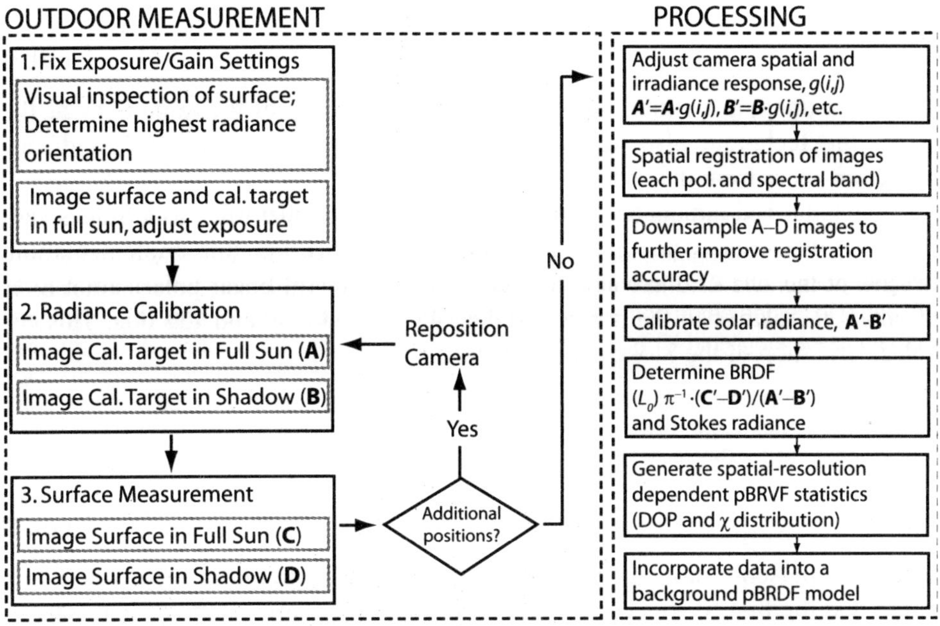

Figure 10.1 Measurement and process flow for making polarimetric BRDF and BRVF measurements with the camera system.

$$\frac{L_r^{cal}}{L_r^{sur}} = \frac{\frac{\rho}{\pi}}{f_r} \rightarrow f_r = \frac{\rho}{\pi}\frac{L_r^{sur}}{L_r^{cal}}. \tag{10.2}$$

In terms of the digital counts of the pixels in each of the four images A through D, the BRDF is simply

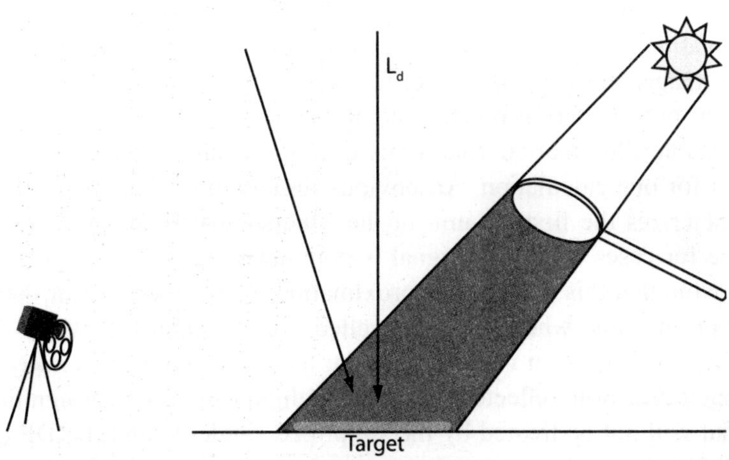

Figure 10.2 Illustration of measurement system with sun blocked to acquire reflected sky radiance measurement (image D in Fig. 10.1).

$$f_r = \frac{\rho}{\pi}\left[\frac{C-D}{A-B}\right]. \tag{10.3}$$

When imaging a calibration target such that it occupies the same FOV as the target, this technique also self corrects for the so-called "lens falloff" irradiance reduction away from the center of the focal plane.

The polarized radiance leaving the surface may be quantified as a Stokes vector using well-established approaches (see Chapter 4). For this implementation, images of the surface were acquired under four different linear polarization filter orientations relative to the horizon: 0 deg, 45 deg, 90 deg, and 135 deg. This enables derivation of the Stokes vector according to

$$\begin{bmatrix} S_0 \\ S_1 \\ S_2 \end{bmatrix} = \begin{bmatrix} \frac{I_0+I_{90}+I_{45}+I_{135}}{2} \\ I_0 - I_{90} \\ I_{45} - I_{135} \end{bmatrix}, \tag{10.4}$$

where I_x represents an image acquired with the polarization filter set at x deg. It is noted that the first Stokes component is derived using an average of both sets of cross-polarized images to reduce noise.

In terms of the images using the calibration target, it is seen from Eqs. (10.2) and (10.3) that the polarimetric BRDF is therefore

$$\begin{bmatrix} f_{00} \\ f_{10} \\ f_{20} \end{bmatrix} = \frac{\rho}{\pi(A_{\text{arb}} - B_{\text{arb}})} \begin{bmatrix} \frac{1}{2}[(C_0 - D_0)+(C_{90} - D_{90})+(C_{45} - D_{45})+(C_{135} - D_{135})] \\ (C_0 - D_0)-(C_{90} - D_{90}) \\ (C_{45} - D_{45})-(C_{135} - D_{135}) \end{bmatrix}, \tag{10.5}$$

where arb indicates an arbitrary polarization filter orientation for imaging the calibration target, since this radiance is approximately randomly polarized.

To summarize, for each hemispherical scattering position, a total of eight images is acquired of the target surface: four polarization orientations, each with two illumination conditions (full sun and shadow). A minimum of two calibration target images must be taken, one for each illumination condition. Therefore, a data set at one scattering position comprises ten images. Care must be taken to ensure stable illumination conditions during the time required to acquire all of the data for one calculation. An obvious limitation of this approach is that it only characterizes the first column of the Mueller matrix and is therefore only appropriate for cases where the signal is dominated by randomly polarized illumination. Note that this is a good approximation when viewing near the specular direction, or any time when the downwelled term is small relative to the direct solar term. However, when viewing specular targets at angles well away from the solar specular direction, reflected polarized skylight can become a significant contributor that will not be treated by the simplified single-column BRDF described by Eq. (10.5).

10.1.2 BRDF probability distribution (BRVF) calculation

Thus far, only the average digital count values over the entire image have been considered in deriving the BRDF. However, one impetus for using a technique that employs a digital camera is the ability to quantify the BRDF variability, or BRVF. The *BRVF* is important as it characterizes not only the range of BRDF values that might be associated with a material, but for background modeling it helps characterize the magnitude and spatial distribution of the clutter field in which we might search for a target. The variability is obviously a function of the ground sample distance (GSD), as a larger GSD results in greater averaging of texture within a pixel, and hence decreased pixel-to-pixel variability within a single-material class. The high-resolution images acquired with the BRDF measurement system may then be used to generate the BRVF, given the anticipated GSD of a remote sensing sensor. Generating the BRVF is accomplished by convolving the image $f[x,y]$ with a convolution kernel $h[x,y]$ sized to the GSD of interest. The result is a lowpass filtered image $g[x,y]$ with the spatial texture representative of the GSD of $h[x,y]$. This is presented mathematically as

$$g[x,y]=\frac{1}{X^2}\sum_{i=0}^{m-1}\sum_{j=0}^{n-1} f[x,y]h[x-i,y-j], \tag{10.6}$$

where X^2 is a weighting factor such that the average magnitude of $g[x,y]$ is that of the original image $f[x,y]$. Ideally, $h[x,y]$ is the point spread function of the remote sensing platform in question, but for quick processing, a simple function with a unit magnitude and square spatial extent is used (termed a RECT function by some [Gaskill (1979)]). Figure 10.3 illustrates the effect using a simple color (RGB) image of grass taken with a commercial digital camera.

Unlike the polarimetric BRDF determination (which can use image-wide averages), the accuracy of the BRVF depends on the degree of the spatial registration of the four sets of polarized C and D images (Fig. 10.1). When the size of the convolution kernel is commensurate with the spatial registration accuracy, significant errors result. The same is true of movement of measurement surfaces while acquiring the four polarization orientations, e.g., grass blowing in the wind. This requires the C and D image sets to be spatially registered prior to performing BRVF calculations. For most applications, the resolution of the ground-based camera is significantly higher than that of the remote sensors of interest, and registration issues can be minimized by the convolution operation in Eq. (10.6).

A summary of the general measurement steps for this technique was previously presented as Fig. 10.1. Depending on the polarimetric imaging system used to make the measurements, this process should be modified accordingly, with modifications such as spectral filter changes, etc.

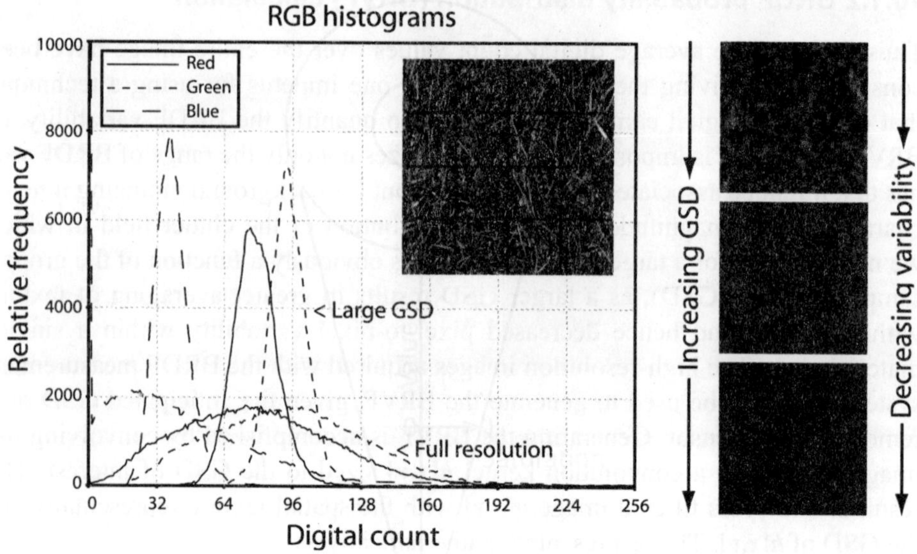

Figure 10.3 The RGB BRDF distributions or BRFV for a grass measurement. Histograms are shown for the full image resolution and at a larger GSD. The averaging of the texture as a function of GSD is illustrated at right.

10.1.3 Imaging system description and characterization

The imaging system used for the measurement presented here consists of a SenSys 1602E camera having a 1536×1024 thermo-electric-cooled 12-bit silicon CCD with a response nonlinearity ≤ 0.5%. A filter wheel located between the lens and the CCD is used to mount 25-mm diameter bandpass filters. The spectral filter

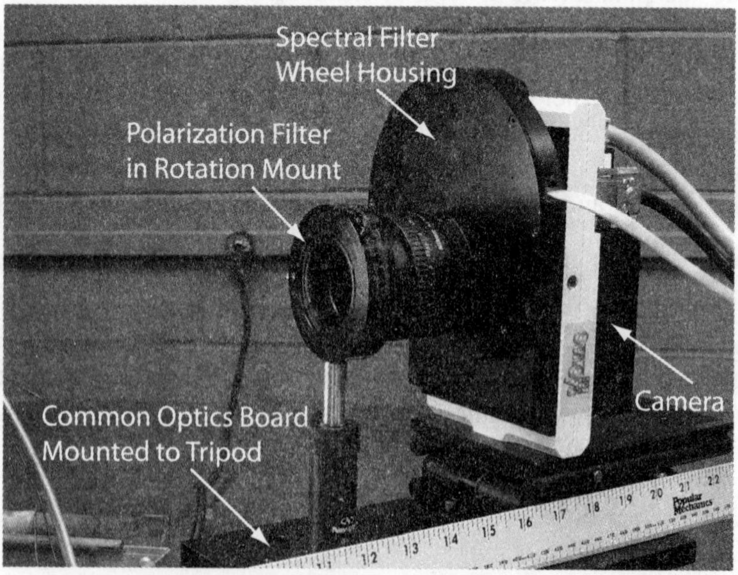

Figure 10.4 The assembled imaging system mounted on a tripod.

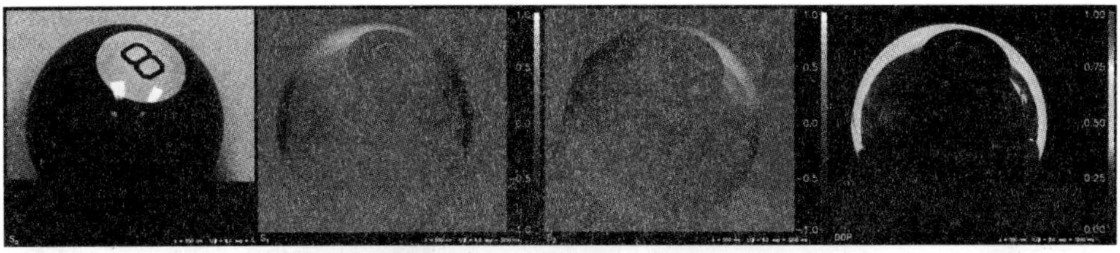

Figure 10.5 The Stokes and DoP images of a "magic 8-ball" under ambient lighting conditions at 550 nm. S_0 (left), S_1 (middle left), S_2 (middle right), and color-encoded DoP (right). (See color plate.)

wheel housing accepts a standard F-mount lens, to which a Nikon 50-mm, f/1.8 lens is attached. A linear polarization filter is mounted external to the lens on an optics post in a precision rotary mount, which is mounted to a common optics board with the camera. This assembly is then mounted on a tripod. To demonstrate the technique, data is presented for only two spectral bands, 550 $\pm$ 5nm and 750 $\pm$ 12nm. An overview of the system is shown in Fig. 10.4.

The imaging system was characterized in order to gain an understanding of the measurement uncertainties and limitations. First, it was noted that "dark" images of the camera were highly repeatable and had negligible error contribution to the series of images used to make measurements.

The *lens falloff* (or focal plane irradiance decrease away from the center of the array) was also quantified by imaging into an integrating sphere that provided a uniform radiance field. At an aperture setting of f/8.0, where the system is usually operated, the irradiance at the edge of the focal plane is 0.94 $\pm$ 0.01 of that relative to the center. Correction to the lens falloff is necessary only under circumstances where the calibration target may not be imaged over the full FOV of the system. A dark subtraction and gain (falloff) correction was applied where appropriate before further processing.

To illustrate the system performance, a data set was acquired by imaging a "magic 8-ball." The ball is well-suited for demonstrating polarization phenomenology, as it has a highly smooth, specular surface, including regions of black and white that have very low and very high diffuse (randomly polarized) reflectance. In addition, the curvature of the ball provides multiple specular view angles. The ball was imaged under ambient lighting conditions in front of a Spectralon panel. The images were processed according to Eq. (10.4), providing the Stokes vectors from which the DoP and AoP were calculated (Figs. 10.5 and 10.6). The DoP image provides a good demonstration of expected results—reflectance from the Spectralon panel off the edges of the ball provides a DoP commensurate with that expected from Fresnel reflectance, with a peak magnitude reached near Brewster's angle. In addition, the DoP is larger for the black regions as predicted by Umov's effect (see Chapter 6). Finally, the AoP image shows how the AoP changes with the orientation angle of the tangent to the sphere.

Figure 10.6 The polarization angle information from "magic 8-ball" image. Green corresponds to $\psi = 0$ deg, while the red-black transition is the transition point from $\psi = 90$ deg to -90 deg. (See color plate.)

10.1.4 Example measurement results

Indoor laboratory measurements of pea gravel at 550 nm are presented to demonstrate the technique, along with field results for soil, asphalt, and grass. A quartz-halogen lamp was used as a source that illuminated the gravel at an incident angle of $\theta_i \approx 37.5$ deg. Polarimetric BRDF measurements were made in the forward ($\phi \approx 180$ deg) and side ($\phi \approx 90$ deg) scattering positions. The scattering zenith angle at the center of the images was $\theta_r \approx 30.3$ deg for the forward scattering case and $\theta_r \approx 29.1$ deg for the side scattering angle.

The standoff distance was such that the full FOV covered 26.7 cm, resulting in a GSD of 174 μm. The images were processed using Eq. (10.3), with the exception that "shadow" images were not required in the lab. BRVF statistics were calculated for GSD pixel sizes of 1, 13, 41 and 101 pixels, or 0.017, 0.226, 0.713, and 1.757 cm. Obviously, these are not GSDs of interest for most overhead remote sensing applications, but serve to illustrate the technique, which is easily scaled. Figure 10.7 presents the results. The polarization components of the BRVF may be presented as the distribution of Stokes components or by the DoP. DoP is chosen here, as it is insensitive to rotational alignment of the camera system about the optical axis.

Unlike outdoor conditions, the irradiance was not uniform across the entire FOV; therefore, the BRDF intensity measurement should be considered only an approximation. However, the DoP measurement is independent of irradiance uniformity. In the forward scattering case, the average BRDF is 0.0250 sr^{-1}. Similar results are obtained for the side scattering $\phi \approx 90$ deg sensor orientation where the average BRDF is 0.0291 sr^{-1}. In both cases, the mean BRDF is independent of GSD due to linearity. The decreased radiance in the forward scattering direction

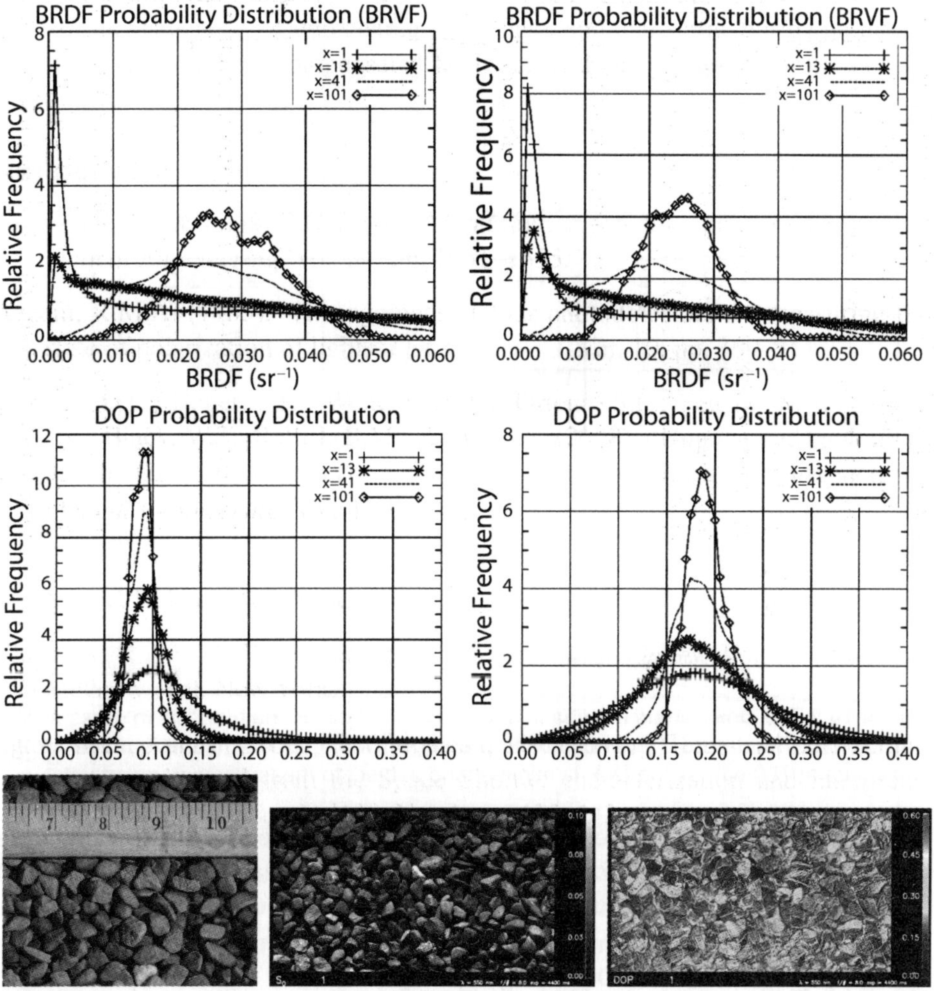

Figure 10.7 The BRDF and DoP probability distributions for the side (left column) and forward (right column) scattering orientations. A photo of the gravel is shown at bottom left with a ruler (in inches) along with the forward scattering images of the intensity S_0 (bottom middle) and color-encoded DoP (bottom right) which is scaled from $0.0 \leq \text{DoP} \leq 0.6$.

is attributed to a higher fraction of the surface being shadowed, which is common with many natural materials.

There is a marked difference in the DoP between the forward- and side-viewing sensor orientations. For forward scattering, the mean DoP for the 1, 13, 41, and 101 averaging kernels is 0.1973, 0.1860, 0.1931, and 0.1929. The same results for the side scattering are 0.1300, 0.0976, 0.0922, and 0.0917, where the higher value for the 1×1 kernel is attributed to residual spatial misregistration of the raw images. Investigation of the data reveals expected reflective polarization phenomenology: materials with lower reflectance typically have a higher DoP due

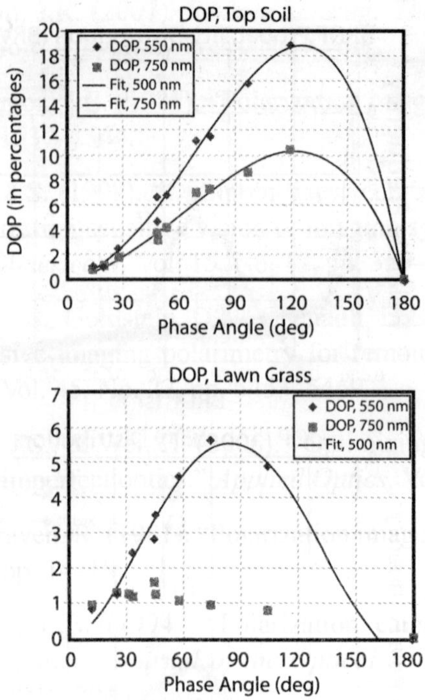

Figure 10.8 The DoP versus the phase angle ξ for top soil, asphalt, and lawn grass at 550 and 750 nm. Fourth-order polynomial fits are shown with the data. No fit is made for the grass data at 750 nm, as the DoP is minimal and subject to measurement uncertainty.

to a higher fraction of surface Fresnel reflectance relative to diffuse, volumetric scatter. In addition, the polarization orientation (AoP) for the forward scatter is ≈ 0 deg while that of the side scatter is ≈ -45 deg, consistent with surface microfacet Fresnel reflectance. Similar measurements of highly reflective diffusely scattering marble chips resulted in a DoP ≈ 0.02 for both the side- and forward-scattering locations.

The DoP calculation is not linear, as the S_1 and S_2 Stokes components are summed in quadrature. When there is variability in the pixel-to-pixel polarization orientation, the net result is a decreased DoP when averaging those pixels. This generally results in a decreasing DoP changing with increasing GSD until the GSD is sufficiently large to average out the texture variability.

Shell (2005) used the method described above to develop pBRDF estimates of a number of background materials using natural illumination. These values were used to develop pBRDF models (see Fig. 10.8). The fitted pBRDF models for backgrounds were then used together with target pBRDF models (see Chapter 6) in synthetic scene generation models (see DIRSIG discussion in Chapter 7 and Sec. 10.2). The results shown in Fig. 10.8 are expressed in terms of the source-target-sensor angle (ξ), which is related to the zenith and azimuth angles through

$$\cos\xi = \cos\theta_i \cos\theta_r + \sin\theta_i \sin\theta_r \cos\phi. \tag{10.7}$$

10.2 Incorporation of pBRDF Models in Synthetic Scene Generation Models

In this section we show how pBRDF models can be used with synthetic scene simulation tools to visualize polarimetric phenomena. To accomplish this, we will briefly review the DIRSIG model introduced in Chapter 7 and then illustrate how it uses pBRDF concepts previously introduced.

10.2.1 Introduction to DIRSIG

The initial development of the Digital Imaging and Remote Sensing Image Generation (DIRSIG) model was begun at Rochester Institute of Technology (RIT) in the late 1980s as a 3-D simulation environment for predicting images that would be produced by thermal infrared systems. Since that time, the model has been expanded to cover the 0.35- to 20.0-μm region of the spectrum [Schott (2007)]. The model is designed to produce passive broadband, multispectral, and hyperspectral imagery through the integration of a suite of first-principles-based radiation propagation modules. These object-oriented modules address tasks ranging from BRDF predictions of a surface, to time- and material-dependent surface temperature predictions, to the dynamic viewing geometry of scanning imaging instruments on agile platforms. In addition to the myriad of DIRSIG-specific objects that have been created, there is a suite of interface objects that leverage externally developed components (e.g., MODTRAN [Anderson et al. (1995)] and FASCODE [Anderson et al. (1995)]) and are modeling workhorses for the remote sensing community. The software is employed internally at RIT and externally within the user community as a tool to aid in the evaluation of sensor designs and to produce imagery for algorithm testing purposes. Key components of the model and some aspects of the model's overall performance have been gauged by several validation reports at various stages of the model's evolution [Brown et al. (1996) and Mason et al. (1994)]. The initial modification of the DIRSIG radiometry framework to support fully spectropolarimetric radiation propagation was completed in 2002 [Meyer (2002)].

The DIRSIG model is an image-generation tool that utilizes a complex computational radiometry subsystem to predict absolute fluxes within a 3-D scene description. The model uses $[1\times4]$ Stokes vector and $[4\times4]$ Mueller matrix calculus to propagate, reflect, transmit, etc. fluxes within the simulated scene environment. When modeling signatures in the midwave infrared (MWIR) region (3–5 μm), the daytime illumination from the sun is proportional to the emitted radiation from ambient (approximately 300 K) materials. Furthermore, many manmade materials have moderate reflectance values (e.g., $\rho > 0.2$) in the MWIR region; therefore, we must consider both the reflected and the self-emission contributions to the surface leaving flux. The DIRSIG radiometry engine utilizes a single governing equation across all wavelength regions such that reflected and self-emitted contributions are always included unless explicitly disabled.

The DIRSIG model has a flexible radiometry sub-system for computing radiance values for arbitrary paths within the defined scene. The primary mechanism used to predict images is reverse ray-tracing where rays originate from the imaging detectors and are propagated into the scene. When a ray intersects the scene geometry, the associated radiometry solver is run to compute the surface leaving radiance. DIRSIG has a handful of radiometry solvers used for opaque surfaces; the most flexible is the Generic Radiometry Solver, which computes the reflected radiance by sampling the hemisphere above the target. The distribution of these samples is based on the shape and magnitude of the associated BRDF. The nominal hemispherical sampling is cosine projected and has user-defined sampling parameters (e.g., total number of samples, etc.). The incident load for those samples is determined by tracing higher generation rays that intersect other surfaces and trigger other instances of the radiometry solver. The fidelity of the sampling for higher generation bounces can be decreased using a bounce-dependent decay rate that modifies the sampling parameters. The total number of bounces that are tracked is also user controllable. The incident loads from the sampled hemisphere are numerically integrated using the geometry-specific reflectance (BRDF) and the solid angle of the sample. The incident illumination from the sun, moon, and sky are provided by MODTRAN-P, which has been integration tested with DIRSIG (see Chapter 7) against Coulson's polarized sky measurements [Coulson et al. (1960)]. Since the pBRDF is accessed via surface relative incident and reflected angles, the polarization orientation of the incident sources must be projected into the surface coordinate system, and the surface leaving radiance must be projected into the polarization coordinates of the sensor (see Sec. 7.3).

10.2.2 Surface radiometry solvers

The *Radiometry Solver* is a fundamental component of DIRSIG's radiative transfer engine. An instance is assigned to each surface material and bulk material. The solver determines the energy propagating in any given direction by sampling the environment. This sampling includes the sun or moon, manmade light sources, the atmosphere, and other scene geometry. The classic radiometry solver has been utilized within DIRSIG since the 1980s. It is the most computationally efficient radiometry solver, but may not always be the most accurate one. The classic radiometry solver assumes surface reflectance to be composed of a diffuse and a specular reflectance value based on the spectral emissivity of the material being modeled and a user-supplied value of specularity. These user-supplied values make up a simplified BRDF model for the material that is utilized to sample incident radiance onto the surface of interest and to determine the quantity of radiance reflected toward the sensor. The *Generic Radiometry Solver* supports a large suite of analytical BRDF models, as well as a large range of user-configurable parameters, permitting a more accurate solution to the surface radiometry problem. This solver allows the user to specify the number of samples from which to sample the radiance incident on a surface from the hemisphere above it. A Monte-Carlo im-

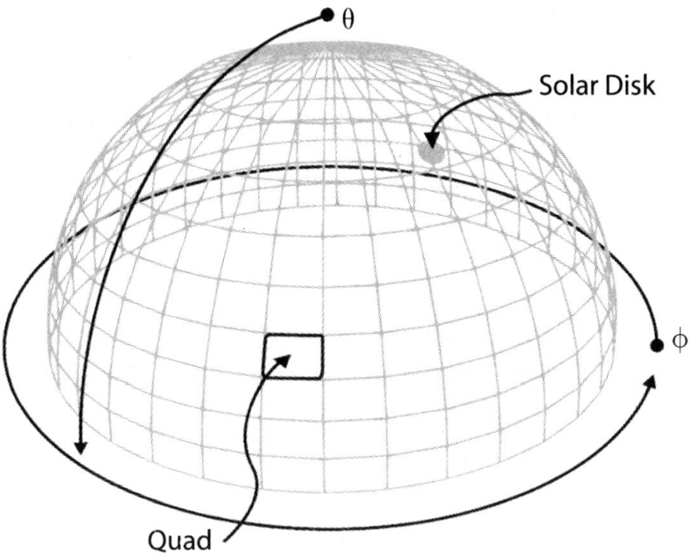

Figure 10.9 An illustration of the quad segmented concept of the BRDF hemisphere. A somewhat exaggerated projection of a solar disk onto the dome is shown.

portance sampling approach is utilized to determine which portions of the hemisphere to sample more densely. In some cases, the BRDF value at a particular position in the hemisphere may be small but the incident radiance from that direction may be large. For these cases, the user can force the entire hemisphere above the material surface to be sampled. To achieve this, the user specifies the number of azimuthal and zenith quadrants (see Fig. 10.9) from which at least one incident radiance sample is determined. In addition to importance sampling and minimum quadrant sampling, one sample is also taken for each important radiance source in the scene (such as the sun, moon, and any manmade light source). The result is a rigorous radiometric sampling of the light incident on and reflected from each material surface. In the polarized mode, each radiance sample is represented by a Stokes vector.

10.2.3 Supported polarimetric BRDF models

DIRSIG supports a wide variety of polarimetric BRDF models commonly found in the remote sensing literature. Although many of the models are actually quite similar, DIRSIG supports many specific forms to aid the user in leveraging model parameters found in the literature.

10.2.3.1 Generalized microfacet-based target model

The generalized microfacet-based *polarized BRDF* target model is useful for materials that are homogeneous at spatial scales of interest to remote sensing (typically manmade materials). The form of this BRDF is the following:

$$f = f_s + f_d, \tag{10.8}$$

where the diffuse component (f_d) is similar to the diffuse component utilized within the NEF database and the specular component (f_s) is a generalized form containing a Fresnel reflection Mueller matrix, a shadowing and obscuration function, and a surface slope probability distribution function:

$$f_s = \frac{P(\alpha,\sigma,B)F'(\theta_i,\theta_r,\phi,n,k)}{4\cos\theta_i\cos\theta_r}S. \tag{10.9}$$

DIRSIG currently supports only the NEF database v9.45 shadowing and obscuration function [NEFDS (2004)] and the Gaussian and Cauchy surface slope probability distribution functions. The unpolarized diffuse scattering term has a purely Lambertian term and a geometrically dependent diffuse term

$$f_d = f_{d1} + \frac{f_{d2}}{\cos\theta_i\cos\theta_r}, \tag{10.10}$$

where f_{d1} and f_{d2} are arbitrary constants. This form of a diffuse, multiple scatter term is purely empirical, but was found to fit measured material properties quite well.

This polarized BRDF model is also capable of spectral interpolation utilizing a supplied spectral reflectance curve with a higher spectral resolution than what is available for BRDF parameters. The spectral interpolation linearly interpolates the specular (polarized) component of the BRDF and scales the diffuse portion relative to the higher fidelity spectral reflectance data.

10.2.3.2 Polarized Roujean background model

The polarized Roujean background model is geared toward naturally occurring background materials such as grass and soil. The magnitude of the BRDF is described by the *Roujean* model [Roujean (1992)] and takes the form

$$f = [k_0 + k_1 g_1(\theta_i,\theta_r,\phi) + k_2 g_2(\theta_i,\theta_r,\phi)]\frac{1}{100\pi}, \tag{10.11}$$

where k_0, k_1, and k_2 are experimentally derived constants and g_1 and g_2 are geometric functions of the zenith angle of incidence (θ_i), the zenith angle of reflection (θ_r), and the relative azimuth (ϕ) between them. The polarization signature of this model is derived from a polynomial fit of experimentally measured values to the total angular extent between the incident and view directions given by

$$\cos\xi = \cos\theta_i\cos\theta_r + \sin\theta_i\sin\theta_r\cos\phi. \tag{10.12}$$

The polynomial fit is simply a fourth-order polynomial with no bias of the form

$$\mathrm{DoP}(\xi) = p_1\xi + p_2\xi^2 + p_3\xi^3 + p_4\xi^4. \tag{10.13}$$

The orientation of the polarization between S_1 and S_2 components of the pBRDF Mueller matrix is determined by the relative view and reflection directions. This model is also capable of introducing statistical variability into both the magnitude and polarization components of the Mueller matrix. Example configurations of this model were presented in Sec. 10.1.

10.2.3.3 Priest-Germer BRDF

The Priest-Germer model [Priest and Meier (2002)] can be used to generate either polarized or unpolarized results. Three parameters as a function of wavelength are used for model input:

(1) Complex index of refraction, real part (n)
(2) Complex index of refraction, imaginary part (k)
(3) Surface roughness (σ)

The complex index of refraction is used to compute the Fresnel reflectance. For the diffuse portion of this microfacet model, the DHR (directional-hemispherial reflectance) is needed. A high-resolution precomputed table of this information is computed and loaded from an external file. (Note that we can precompute this table because of the limited set of input parameters).

10.2.3.4 Torrance-Sparrow BRDF

Torrance and Sparrow described a reflectance model [Torrance and Sparrow (1967)] utilizing the concept of treating a material surface as a series of connected microfacets (i.e., perfectly flat Fresnel reflectors) (see Sec. 6.5.1). Their model contains a specular component resulting from Fresnel reflection and a diffuse component resulting from multiply scattered and subsurface scattered light. The Torrance and Sparrow pBRDF model takes on the form

$$f_r = \frac{F(\theta_i, \hat{n}) A_f G(\theta_{i,p}, \theta_{r,p}) P(\alpha)}{4\cos\theta_i \cos\theta_r} + \frac{a}{d\omega_i}, \tag{10.14}$$

where θ_i is the angle of incidence relative to the microfacet normal, the angles $\theta_{r,p}$ and $\theta_{i,p}$ are the zenith angles of incidence and reflection in the plane determined by the facet and surface normals, G is a geometric attenuation factor incorporating masking and shadowing effects, F is the Fresnel reflectivity given the material's complex index of refraction n, and P is the surface slope probability function. The Torrance and Sparrow pBRDF assumes a Gaussian surface slope distribution of the form

$$P(\alpha) = ce^{-c^2\alpha^2}. \tag{10.15}$$

10.2.3.5 Stokes vector orientation considerations

All of the previously mentioned BRDF models produce Mueller reflection matrices that assume that the target material is parallel to the ground (e.g., the target

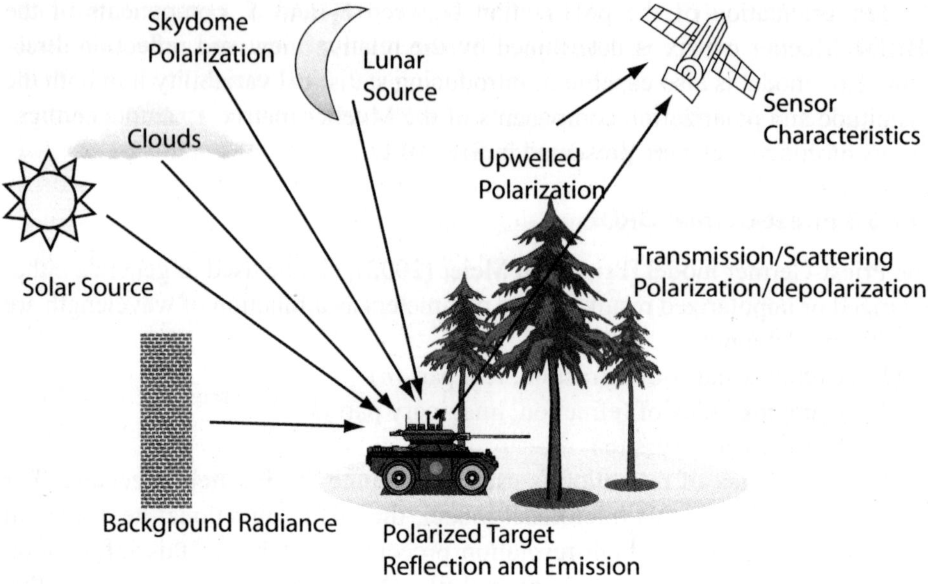

Figure 10.10 DIRSIG considers a variety of radiance sources, including: solar, lunar, sky, scene background, and path contributions that determine the sensed polarized signature coming from the direction of a target in a simulated scene.

normal points directly up in the +z direction). To correctly reflect the radiation from a surface arbitrarily oriented in a global coordinate system, we must address two effects. First, the global incident and reflected directions must be projected into the local coordinate space so that they can be used to access the BRDF. Second, the Stokes geometry of the global incident and reflected polarizations must be translated into and out of the local coordinate space. The global-to-local vector projections required to evaluate the BRDF are common to any radiative transfer problem. However, the translation of the Stokes geometry is unique to polarized radiative transfer. The mathematical approach to accomplishing this correction is described in Section 7.3.

10.3 End-to-End Passive Polarimetric Scene Simulation

DIRSIG operates as a full end-to-end spectropolarimetric light propagation code to simulate remotely sensed scenes. Photons originating from a variety of sources (Fig. 10.10), such as the sun, the skydome, the moon, and manmade sources (such as headlights and street lamps) are traced through the simulated scene geometry until they arrive at the focal plane. Once at the focal plane, the radiance values may be converted to sensor digital count values.

10.3.1 Polarized atmosphere

DIRSIG primarily utilizes MODTRAN for simulating solar, lunar, downwelled, and upwelled sources of radiance. For polarimetric scene simulations, *MOD-*

TRAN-P is utilized [Egan and Liu (2002)]. MODTRAN-P simulates the sky polarization and has been demonstrated to match values measured and published by Coulson et al. (1960) as discussed in Chapter 7. This atmospheric radiative transfer code treats both the sun and the moon as completely unpolarized sources of irradiance; however, the Rayleigh component of the upwelled and downwelled radiance terms are polarized. Polarization and depolarization of the target-sensor path transmission are not currently modeled in MODTRAN-P. The utility of a MODTRAN-P based atmosphere is also enhanced by the ability to modify deviations in the source and path contributions, based on user-supplied vertical atmospheric profiles, visibility conditions, aerosol models, and time-of-day and day-of-year effects.

If the user does not have access to MODTRAN, or requires less radiometric fidelity, DIRSIG may be configured with a "Simple" atmosphere. This atmosphere simulates the sun based on published exoatmospheric spectral solar irradiance and assumes a sky temperature of 240 K with no path radiance contributions or transmission losses. The DIRSIG Simple atmosphere does not currently support a polarized skydome.

10.3.2 Polarized manmade sources

Manmade light sources, such as car headlights, street lamps, and indoor lighting may be included within a scene configuration. Typically, the user defines the source radiant intensity as a spectrally dependent Stokes vector. In addition to the spectropolarimetric properties, the orientation of the light source may be defined, along with an angular intensity distribution function.

10.3.3 Surface leaving radiance

The radiance leaving a particular surface in a scene is a combination of the polarized radiance reflected from background sources, as well as the polarized thermally emitted radiance. For each material facet within a scene, the user supplies a material configuration. The material configuration identities which radiometry solver should be utilized, as well as the physical material properties such as BRDF, transmission, extinction, and thermal inertia. The most accurate radiometry solver utilized is the Generic Radiometry Solver, which allows the user to determine how many background samples are taken, how many generation light bounces are considered, and the method with which the background samples are spatially distributed. This solver permits sampling for sources of radiance over the entire hemisphere above a sample, which is important for considering both shadowing and background clutter effects. This capability is especially critical for simulating scenes in the thermal infrared when the primary sources of radiance are not the sun and sky, but objects in the scene around the target.

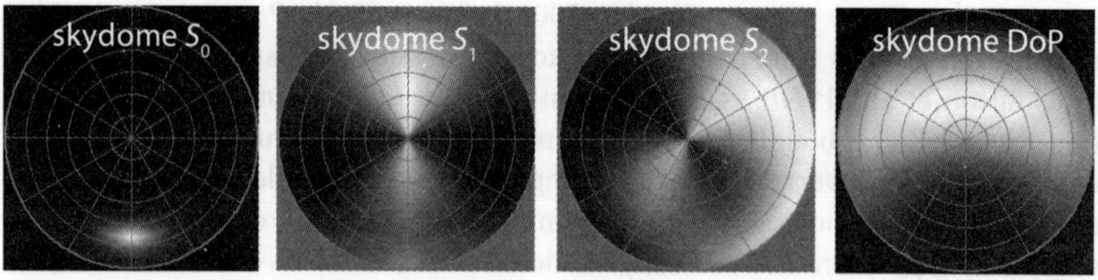

Figure 10.11 Illustration of the polarized downwelled radiance field (0.4–0.9 μm) used in generation of Tables 10.1–10.3.

10.3.4 Platform and sensor modeling

DIRSIG contains a highly configurable sensor and platform model. The user has the ability to assemble an imaging system with multiple focal planes, each having its own pointing direction, master clock rate, and spectral bandpass. In addition, DIRSIG is capable of integrating user-supplied jitter profiles and platform motion ephemeris data. DIRSIG is also capable of simulating active imaging systems such as LIDAR and DIAL. In active mode, DIRSIG can track multiple transmitted pulses in flight, as well as incorporate user-supplied source transmission characteristics such as spectral, spatial, and temporal variability.

10.3.5 Simulation examples

Before we introduce image examples, we will consider some numerical examples derived from DIRSIG listed in Tables 10.1–10.3. The three examples are for a glossy green paint (Table 10.1), a less glossy green paint (Table 10.2), and a matte finish tan paint (Table 10.3). All three examples include a 90 deg, 180 deg, 0 deg azimuth case at a range of wavelengths from the blue, where atmospheric scatter can be expected to play a strong role, to the near infrared, where scattering effects should be significantly smaller. The solar zenith angle for all these examples is 60 deg, producing a polarized downwelled skylight radiance field as shown in Fig. 10.11. The sensor zenith in all cases is at 66 deg so that Table B in each figure is roughly in the specular direction and Table C in each case is in the backscatter direction. Note that for all cases, the sensor is in space and the targets are horizontal. A wealth of data can be explored in these tables; we will point out only a few of the interesting themes. First, note that in the backscatter direction for all targets, neither the target nor the atmosphere induce appreciable polarization. Second, we observe that for all these targets, the DoP tracks with specularity (i.e., higher DoP with glossier surfaces), as expected at the near-specular direction. However, there is a considerable variation among wavelengths; much of the total DoP for less specular surfaces is contributed by the DoP of the upwelled radiance. Finally, note that at the 90-deg azimuth angle, most of the observed DoP for all targets is induced by the upwelled radiance and thus for these cases, the final DoP carries limited information about the target.

Table 10.1 Effective Aperture-Reaching Stokes radiance values for green paint (glossy). All radiance values have units of W/cm²/sr/μm, except for band-integrated value, which has units of W/cm²/sr, assuming a unity sensor response function.

Table A Sensor zenith = 60 deg, solar zenith = 66 deg, and relative azimuth of 90 deg beween sun and sensor.

	Solar reflected from target				Skydome reflected from target				Solar scattered from atm (upwelled)				Total				Reflected[1]	Upwelled	Total[2]
λ (μm)	S_0	S_1	S_2	S_3	S_0	S_1	S_2	S_3	S_0	S_1	S_2	S_3	S_0	S_1	S_2	S_3	DoP	DoP	DoP
0.40	3.13E-05	-9.43E-07	-8.44E-07	-1.85E-23	9.67E-05	1.38E-05	-1.17E-06	1.38E-07	5.66E-03	1.72E-03	1.46E-03	0.00E+00	5.78E-03	-1.70E-03	-1.46E-03	1.38E-07	10%	40%	39%
0.50	3.38E-04	-4.86E-06	-4.35E-06	9.81E-23	4.63E-04	2.76E-05	-5.80E-06	3.78E-07	4.71E-03	1.47E-03	1.25E-03	0.00E+00	5.51E-03	-1.45E-03	-1.26E-03	3.78E-07	3%	41%	35%
0.60	4.16E-04	-7.33E-06	-6.56E-06	2.28E-22	3.86E-04	2.25E-05	-7.64E-06	3.80E-07	2.43E-03	-7.39E-04	-6.29E-04	0.00E+00	3.24E-03	-7.24E-04	-6.43E-04	3.80E-07	3%	40%	30%
0.70	4.44E-04	-8.93E-06	-7.99E-06	-2.86E-57	3.15E-04	1.75E-05	-8.04E-06	3.62E-07	1.53E-03	-4.57E-04	-3.89E-04	0.00E+00	2.29E-03	-4.49E-04	-4.05E-04	3.62E-07	2%	39%	26%
0.80	2.05E-03	-8.63E-06	-7.72E-06	-5.30E-22	1.05E-03	1.13E-05	-6.68E-06	2.97E-07	9.04E-04	-2.76E-04	-2.35E-04	0.00E+00	4.00E-03	-2.73E-04	-2.49E-04	2.97E-07	0%	40%	9%
0.90	1.37E-03	-6.00E-06	-5.37E-06	6.07E-23	5.85E-04	5.83E-06	-4.07E-06	1.86E-07	5.18E-04	-1.67E-04	-1.42E-04	0.00E+00	2.47E-03	-1.67E-04	-1.51E-04	1.86E-07	0%	42%	9%
band-integrated	4.65E-04	-3.67E-06	-3.28E-06	-1.62E-23	2.89E-04	9.85E-06	-3.34E-06	1.74E-07	1.58E-03	-4.82E-04	-4.10E-04	0.00E+00	2.33E-03	-4.76E-04	-4.17E-04	1.74E-07	1%	40%	27%

Table B Sensor zenith = 60 deg, solar zenith = 66 deg, and relative azimuth of 180 deg beween sun and sensor (forward scattering).

	Solar reflected from target				Skydome reflected from target				Solar scattered from atm (upwelled)				Total				Reflected[1]	Upwelled	Total[2]
λ (μm)	S_0	S_1	S_2	S_3	S_0	S_1	S_2	S_3	S_0	S_1	S_2	S_3	S_0	S_1	S_2	S_3	DoP	DoP	DoP
0.4	1.51E-03	1.36E-03	2.22E-05	-1.88E-22	5.17E-04	4.06E-04	5.23E-06	-3.89E-09	7.90E-03	1.65E-03	-2.88E-05	0.00E+00	9.92E-03	3.42E-03	-1.39E-06	-3.89E-09	87%	21%	34%
0.5	8.17E-03	7.20E-03	1.17E-04	1.91E-57	2.28E-03	1.71E-03	2.10E-05	-1.79E-08	8.39E-03	1.52E-03	-2.66E-05	0.00E+00	1.88E-02	1.04E-02	1.12E-04	-1.79E-08	85%	18%	55%
0.6	1.26E-02	1.11E-02	1.81E-04	1.61E-21	2.82E-03	2.27E-03	2.67E-05	-2.65E-08	5.53E-03	8.80E-04	-1.54E-05	0.00E+00	2.09E-02	1.43E-02	1.92E-04	-2.65E-08	87%	16%	68%
0.7	1.55E-02	1.38E-02	2.24E-04	2.11E-56	3.01E-03	2.51E-03	2.81E-05	-3.21E-08	4.17E-03	6.28E-04	-1.10E-05	0.00E+00	2.27E-02	1.69E-02	2.41E-04	-3.21E-08	88%	15%	75%
0.8	1.69E-02	1.36E-02	2.21E-04	1.94E-21	3.46E-03	2.20E-03	2.35E-05	-2.95E-08	2.80E-03	4.27E-04	-7.46E-06	0.00E+00	2.31E-02	1.62E-02	2.37E-04	-2.95E-08	78%	15%	70%
0.9	1.18E-02	9.59E-03	1.56E-04	1.36E-21	2.16E-03	1.44E-03	1.46E-05	-2.00E-08	1.74E-03	2.77E-04	-4.84E-06	0.00E+00	1.57E-02	1.13E-02	1.66E-04	-2.00E-08	79%	16%	72%
band-integrated	6.65E-03	5.66E-03	9.21E-05	4.72E-22	1.42E-03	1.05E-03	1.19E-05	-1.30E-08	3.05E-03	5.38E-04	-9.40E-06	0.00E+00	1.11E-02	7.25E-03	9.46E-05	-1.30E-08	83%	18%	65%

Table C Sensor zenith = 60 deg, solar zenith = 66 deg, and relative azimuth of 0 deg beween sun and sensor (backscattering).

	Solar reflected from target				Skydome reflected from target				Solar scattered from atm (upwelled)				Total				Reflected[1]	Upwelled	Total[2]
λ (μm)	S_0	S_1	S_2	S_3	S_0	S_1	S_2	S_3	S_0	S_1	S_2	S_3	S_0	S_1	S_2	S_3	DoP	DoP	DoP
0.4	3.04E-05	4.35E-09	5.20E-10	4.69E-25	1.03E-04	1.85E-05	-5.97E-08	5.01E-10	8.03E-03	9.22E-07[3]	-1.10E-07	0.00E+00	8.17E-03	1.85E-05	-1.69E-07	5.01E-10	14%	0%	0%
0.5	3.34E-04	2.26E-08	2.70E-09	8.50E-24	4.92E-04	3.67E-05	-3.19E-07	4.76E-10	6.80E-03	-2.88E-05	3.44E-06	0.00E+00	7.62E-03	7.86E-06	3.12E-06	4.76E-10	4%	0%	0%
0.6	4.10E-04	3.42E-08	4.08E-09	1.79E-23	4.11E-04	2.85E-05	-3.98E-07	-9.84E-11	3.45E-03	-2.94E-05	3.51E-06	0.00E+00	4.27E-03	-8.73E-07	3.11E-06	-9.84E-11	3%	1%	0%
0.7	4.37E-04	4.20E-08	5.02E-09	-8.16E-24	3.34E-04	2.14E-05	-3.73E-07	-3.86E-10	2.13E-03	-2.54E-05	3.03E-06	0.00E+00	2.90E-03	-3.93E-06	2.66E-06	-3.86E-10	3%	1%	0%
0.8	2.04E-03	4.12E-08	4.92E-09	-1.67E-23	1.14E-03	1.38E-05	-2.80E-07	-4.24E-10	1.22E-03	-1.74E-05	2.08E-06	0.00E+00	4.40E-03	-3.61E-06	1.80E-06	-4.24E-10	0%	1%	0%
0.9	1.36E-03	2.90E-08	3.46E-09	9.67E-24	6.39E-04	7.18E-06	-1.49E-07	-2.75E-10	6.81E-04	-1.09E-05	1.30E-06	0.00E+00	2.68E-03	-3.66E-06	1.15E-06	-2.75E-10	0%	2%	0%
band-integrated	4.62E-04	1.73E-08	2.07E-09	1.17E-24	3.12E-04	1.26E-05	-1.58E-07	-2.07E-11	2.23E-03	-1.12E-05	1.32E-06	0.00E+00	3.00E-03	1.43E-06	1.17E-06	-2.07E-11	2%	1%	0%

1. Reflected DoP is degree of polarization due to solar reflected and skydome reflected contributions.

2. Total DoP is degree of polarization due to solar reflected, skydome reflected, and solar scattered (upwelled) contributions.

3. There is a sign difference in the solar scattered S_1 component of radiance that is output by MODTRAN4-P, most likely the sign change is because the refraction of light at 400nm is more severe than for the other wavelengths resulting in a slightly different effective phase angle (bouncing around zero) between the observer and the sun at this wavelength relative to the longer wavelengths (there is a sign change in the S_1 upwelled component about the solar point in the sky).NEF material 0358UUUPNT: $\sigma = 0.02$ rad $= 1°$, glossy green paint.

Table 10.2 Effective Aperture-Reaching Stokes radiance values for green paint (less glossy). All radiance values have units of W/cm²/sr/μm, except for band-integrated value, which has units of W/cm²/sr, assuming a unity sensor response function.

Table A Sensor zenith = 60 deg, solar zenith = 66 deg, and relative azimuth of 90 deg beween sun and sensor.

	Solar reflected from target				Skydome reflected from target				Solar scattered from atm (upwelled)				Total				Reflected[1]	Upwelled	Total[2]
λ (μm)	S_0	S_1	S_2	S_3	S_0	S_1	S_2	S_3	S_0	S_1	S_2	S_3	S_0	S_1	S_2	S_3	DoP	DoP	DoP
0.40	2.17E-05	-3.05E-06	-2.73E-06	2.02E-22	6.86E-05	4.85E-06	-4.72E-06	4.29E-07	5.66E-03	-1.72E-03	-1.46E-03	0.00E+00	5.75E-03	-1.71E-03	-1.47E-03	4.29E-07	9%	40%	39%
0.50	1.79E-04	-1.87E-05	-1.68E-05	-2.50E-21	2.68E-04	-9.24E-07	-2.12E-05	1.33E-06	4.71E-03	-1.47E-03	-1.25E-03	0.00E+00	5.16E-03	-1.49E-03	-1.29E-03	1.33E-06	10%	41%	38%
0.60	1.81E-04	-3.28E-05	-2.93E-05	5.51E-21	2.14E-04	-1.35E-05	-2.98E-05	1.51E-06	2.43E-03	-7.39E-04	-6.29E-04	0.00E+00	2.83E-03	-7.85E-04	-6.88E-04	1.51E-06	19%	40%	37%
0.70	1.83E-04	-4.56E-05	-4.08E-05	-6.25E-21	1.85E-04	-2.16E-05	-3.47E-05	1.58E-06	1.53E-03	-4.57E-04	-3.89E-04	0.00E+00	1.90E-03	-5.24E-04	-4.65E-04	1.58E-06	27%	39%	37%
0.80	7.41E-04	-4.95E-05	-4.43E-05	1.74E-21	4.25E-04	-2.28E-05	-3.17E-05	1.38E-06	9.04E-04	-2.76E-04	-2.35E-04	0.00E+00	2.07E-03	-3.48E-04	-3.11E-04	1.38E-06	9%	40%	23%
0.90	4.91E-04	-3.82E-05	-3.42E-05	5.94E-57	2.42E-04	-1.60E-05	-2.11E-05	8.96E-07	5.18E-04	-1.67E-04	-1.42E-04	0.00E+00	1.25E-03	-2.21E-04	-1.97E-04	8.96E-07	11%	42%	24%
band-integrated	1.80E-04	-1.88E-05	-1.68E-05	-1.30E-22	1.40E-04	-6.99E-06	-1.43E-05	7.13E-07	1.58E-03	-4.82E-04	-4.10E-04	0.00E+00	1.90E-03	-5.08E-04	-4.42E-04	7.13E-07	13%	40%	36%

Table B Sensor zenith = 60 deg, solar zenith = 66 deg, and relative azimuth of 180 deg beween sun and sensor (forward scattering).

	Solar reflected from target				Skydome reflected from target				Solar scattered from atm (upwelled)				Total				Reflected[1]	Upwelled	Total[2]
λ (μm)	S_0	S_1	S_2	S_3	S_0	S_1	S_2	S_3	S_0	S_1	S_2	S_3	S_0	S_1	S_2	S_3	DoP	DoP	DoP
0.4	1.30E-04	1.00E-04	1.63E-06	-4.94E-23	1.25E-04	5.35E-05	-3.41E-06	3.91E-09	7.90E-03	1.65E-03	-2.88E-05	0.00E+00	8.16E-03	1.80E-03	-3.05E-05	3.91E-09	60%	21%	22%
0.5	7.59E-04	5.39E-04	8.77E-06	-8.17E-56	5.17E-04	2.11E-04	-1.52E-05	6.72E-08	8.39E-03	1.52E-03	-2.66E-05	0.00E+00	9.67E-03	2.27E-03	-3.30E-05	6.72E-08	59%	18%	24%
0.6	1.10E-03	8.45E-04	1.37E-05	-4.24E-22	5.52E-04	2.72E-04	-2.19E-05	1.43E-07	5.53E-03	8.80E-04	-1.54E-05	0.00E+00	7.18E-03	2.00E-03	-2.35E-05	1.43E-07	68%	16%	28%
0.7	1.41E-03	1.13E-03	1.84E-05	-5.77E-22	5.78E-04	3.09E-04	-2.59E-05	2.03E-07	4.17E-03	6.28E-04	-1.10E-05	0.00E+00	6.16E-03	2.07E-03	-1.84E-05	2.03E-07	73%	15%	34%
0.8	2.07E-03	1.22E-03	1.99E-05	6.36E-22	7.91E-04	2.83E-04	-2.39E-05	2.15E-07	2.80E-03	4.27E-04	-7.46E-06	0.00E+00	5.65E-03	1.93E-03	-1.15E-05	2.15E-07	53%	15%	34%
0.9	1.51E-03	9.39E-04	1.53E-05	4.99E-22	4.90E-04	1.91E-04	-1.59E-05	1.51E-07	1.74E-03	2.77E-04	-4.84E-06	0.00E+00	3.74E-03	1.41E-03	-5.46E-06	1.51E-07	57%	16%	38%
band-integrated	6.97E-04	4.78E-04	7.78E-06	8.42E-24	3.05E-04	1.32E-04	-1.06E-05	7.84E-08	3.05E-03	5.38E-04	-9.40E-06	0.00E+00	4.06E-03	1.15E-03	-1.22E-05	7.84E-08	61%	18%	28%

Table C Sensor zenith = 60 deg, solar zenith = 66 deg, and relative azimuth of 0 deg beween sun and sensor (backscattering).

	Solar reflected from target				Skydome reflected from target				Solar scattered from atm (upwelled)				Total				Reflected[1]	Upwelled	Total[2]
λ (μm)	S_0	S_1	S_2	S_3	S_0	S_1	S_2	S_3	S_0	S_1	S_2	S_3	S_0	S_1	S_2	S_3	DoP	DoP	DoP
0.4	1.91E-05	1.48E-08	1.77E-09	-5.11E-23	6.93E-05	1.02E-05	4.66E-08	-3.15E-08	8.03E-03	9.22E-07[3]	-1.10E-07	0.00E+00	8.12E-03	1.02E-05	-6.16E-08	-3.15E-08	12%	0%	0%
0.5	1.63E-04	9.16E-08	1.09E-08	8.54E-23	2.62E-04	2.07E-05	6.99E-07	-1.03E-07	6.80E-03	-2.88E-05	3.44E-06	0.00E+00	7.22E-03	-8.03E-06	4.15E-06	-1.03E-07	5%	0%	0%
0.6	1.54E-04	1.61E-07	1.92E-08	1.97E-22	1.95E-04	1.63E-05	9.74E-07	-1.17E-07	3.45E-03	-2.94E-05	3.51E-06	0.00E+00	3.80E-03	-1.30E-05	4.50E-06	-1.17E-07	5%	1%	0%
0.7	1.45E-04	2.24E-07	2.68E-08	8.26E-23	1.56E-04	1.29E-05	9.18E-07	-1.19E-07	2.13E-03	-2.54E-05	3.03E-06	0.00E+00	2.43E-03	-1.23E-05	3.97E-06	-1.19E-07	4%	1%	1%
0.8	7.00E-04	2.43E-07	2.90E-08	1.20E-22	4.08E-04	8.75E-06	6.89E-07	-1.05E-07	1.22E-03	-1.74E-05	2.08E-06	0.00E+00	2.32E-03	-8.45E-06	2.80E-06	-1.05E-07	1%	1%	0%
0.9	4.60E-04	1.87E-07	2.23E-08	-2.92E-23	2.29E-04	4.80E-06	3.73E-07	-6.84E-08	6.81E-04	-1.09E-05	1.30E-06	0.00E+00	1.37E-03	-5.88E-06	1.69E-06	-6.84E-08	1%	2%	0%
band-integrated	1.64E-04	9.21E-08	1.10E-08	4.05E-23	1.32E-04	7.36E-06	3.70E-07	-5.44E-08	2.23E-03	-1.12E-05	1.32E-06	0.00E+00	2.53E-03	-3.74E-06	1.70E-06	-5.44E-08	3%	1%	0%

1. Reflected DoP is degree of polarization due to solar reflected and skydome reflected contributions.

2. Total DoP is degree of polarization due to solar reflected, skydome reflected, and solar scattered (upwelled) contributions.

3. There is a sign difference in the solar scattered S_1 component of radiance that is output by MODTRAN4-P, most likely the sign change is because the refraction of light at 400nm is more severe than for the other wavelengths resulting in a slightly different effective phase angle (bouncing around zero) between the observer and the sun at this wavelength relative to the longer wavelengths (there is a sign change in the S_1 upwelled component about the solar point in the sky).

NEF material 0998UUUPNT: $\sigma = 0.40$ rad $= 23°$, green paint on aluminum.

Table 10.3: Effective Aperture-Reaching Stokes radiance values for tan paint (matte). All radiance values have units of W/cm²/sr/μm, except for band-integrated value, which has units of W/cm²/sr, assuming a unity sensor response function.

Table A Sensor zenith = 60 deg, solar zenith = 66 deg, and relative azimuth of 90 deg beween sun and sensor.

	Solar reflected from target				Skydome reflected from target				Solar scattered from atm (upwelled)				Total				Reflected[1]	Upwelled	Total[2]
λ (μm)	S_0	S_1	S_2	S_3	S_0	S_1	S_2	S_3	S_0	S_1	S_2	S_3	S_0	S_1	S_2	S_3	DoP	DoP	DoP
0.40	1.07E-04	-4.87E-06	-4.36E-06	2.41E-22	2.43E-04	-1.44E-07	-6.46E-06	2.74E-07	5.66E-03	-1.72E-03	-1.46E-03	0.00E+00	6.01E-03	-1.72E-03	-1.47E-03	2.74E-07	3%	40%	38%
0.50	8.84E-04	-2.36E-05	-2.11E-05	-3.02E-21	1.05E-03	-7.50E-06	-2.21E-05	7.17E-07	4.71E-03	-1.47E-03	-1.25E-03	0.00E+00	6.64E-03	-1.50E-03	-1.29E-03	7.17E-07	3%	41%	30%
0.60	2.11E-03	-3.32E-05	-2.97E-05	2.07E-21	1.73E-03	-1.16E-05	-2.48E-05	6.89E-07	2.43E-03	-7.39E-04	-6.29E-04	0.00E+00	6.28E-03	-7.84E-04	-6.83E-04	6.89E-07	2%	40%	17%
0.70	3.23E-03	-4.59E-05	-4.11E-05	5.92E-21	2.04E-03	-1.57E-05	-2.78E-05	8.71E-07	1.53E-03	-4.57E-04	-3.89E-04	0.00E+00	6.80E-03	-5.19E-04	-4.58E-04	8.71E-07	2%	39%	10%
0.80	3.73E-03	-5.34E-05	-4.78E-05	-4.38E-21	1.87E-03	-1.70E-05	-2.60E-05	9.62E-07	9.04E-04	-2.76E-04	-2.35E-04	0.00E+00	6.50E-03	-3.46E-04	-3.09E-04	9.62E-07	2%	40%	7%
0.90	2.44E-03	-4.22E-05	-3.78E-05	1.08E-58	1.03E-03	-1.24E-05	-1.73E-05	7.15E-07	5.18E-04	-1.67E-04	-1.42E-04	0.00E+00	3.98E-03	-2.21E-04	-1.97E-04	7.15E-07	2%	42%	7%
band-integrated	1.25E-03	-2.03E-05	-1.82E-05	8.33E-23	7.97E-04	-6.43E-06	-1.25E-05	4.23E-07	1.58E-03	-4.82E-04	-4.10E-04	0.00E+00	3.62E-03	-5.09E-04	-4.41E-04	4.23E-07	2%	40%	19%

Table B Sensor zenith = 60 deg, solar zenith = 66 deg, and relative azimuth of 180 deg beween sun and sensor (forward scattering).

	Solar reflected from target				Skydome reflected from target				Solar scattered from atm (upwelled)				Total				Reflected[1]	Upwelled	Total[2]
λ (μm)	S_0	S_1	S_2	S_3	S_0	S_1	S_2	S_3	S_0	S_1	S_2	S_3	S_0	S_1	S_2	S_3	DoP	DoP	DoP
0.4	1.53E-04	4.90E-05	7.98E-07	2.40E-23	2.77E-04	3.26E-05	-2.19E-07	7.69E-09	7.90E-03	1.65E-03	-2.88E-05	0.00E+00	8.33E-03	1.73E-03	-2.82E-05	7.69E-09	19%	21%	21%
0.5	1.10E-03	2.33E-04	3.80E-06	-1.14E-54	1.17E-03	1.13E-04	-1.94E-07	2.71E-08	8.39E-03	1.52E-03	-2.66E-05	0.00E+00	1.07E-02	1.87E-03	-2.30E-05	2.71E-08	15%	18%	18%
0.6	2.41E-03	3.23E-04	5.25E-06	3.03E-22	1.86E-03	1.27E-04	1.36E-07	3.23E-08	5.53E-03	8.80E-04	-1.54E-05	0.00E+00	9.80E-03	1.33E-03	-9.97E-06	3.23E-08	11%	16%	14%
0.7	3.60E-03	4.05E-04	6.60E-06	3.33E-22	2.17E-03	1.35E-04	2.07E-07	5.21E-08	4.17E-03	6.28E-04	-1.10E-05	0.00E+00	9.94E-03	1.17E-03	-4.16E-06	5.21E-08	9%	15%	12%
0.8	4.10E-03	4.11E-04	6.69E-06	-5.73E-22	1.98E-03	1.16E-04	1.28E-07	7.46E-08	2.80E-03	4.27E-04	-7.46E-06	0.00E+00	8.88E-03	9.54E-04	-6.43E-07	7.46E-08	9%	15%	11%
0.9	2.68E-03	2.84E-04	4.61E-06	-6.98E-22	1.10E-03	7.03E-05	-3.79E-08	6.72E-08	1.74E-03	2.77E-04	-4.84E-06	0.00E+00	5.52E-03	6.31E-04	-2.60E-07	6.72E-08	9%	16%	11%
band-integrated	1.41E-03	1.71E-04	2.77E-06	-6.11E-23	8.56E-04	5.93E-05	1.93E-09	2.61E-08	3.05E-03	5.38E-04	-9.40E-06	0.00E+00	5.31E-03	7.68E-04	-6.62E-06	2.61E-08	10%	18%	14%

Table C Sensor zenith = 60 deg, solar zenith = 66 deg, and relative azimuth of 0 deg beween sun and sensor (backscattering).

	Solar reflected from target				Skydome reflected from target				Solar scattered from atm (upwelled)				Total				Reflected[1]	Upwelled	Total[2]
λ (μm)	S_0	S_1	S_2	S_3	S_0	S_1	S_2	S_3	S_0	S_1	S_2	S_3	S_0	S_1	S_2	S_3	DoP	DoP	DoP
0.4	1.03E-04	2.60E-08	3.11E-09	5.33E-23	2.54E-04	4.73E-06	8.89E-08	-4.88E-09	8.03E-03	9.22E-07[3]	-1.10E-07	0.00E+00	8.39E-03	4.76E-06	-1.80E-08	-4.88E-09	1%	0%	0%
0.5	8.67E-04	1.26E-07	1.51E-08	-1.73E-22	1.11E-03	7.39E-06	2.89E-07	-1.95E-08	6.80E-03	-2.88E-05	3.44E-06	0.00E+00	8.78E-03	-2.13E-05	3.74E-06	-1.95E-08	0%	0%	0%
0.6	2.09E-03	1.78E-07	2.13E-08	-2.01E-22	1.86E-03	4.35E-06	2.95E-07	-2.46E-08	3.45E-03	-2.94E-05	3.51E-06	0.00E+00	7.40E-03	-2.49E-05	3.82E-06	-2.46E-08	0%	1%	0%
0.7	3.20E-03	2.55E-07	3.05E-08	-2.33E-22	2.21E-03	2.42E-06	3.52E-07	-3.76E-08	2.13E-03	-2.54E-05	3.03E-06	0.00E+00	7.54E-03	-2.27E-05	3.41E-06	-3.76E-08	0%	1%	0%
0.8	3.69E-03	3.12E-07	3.72E-08	2.57E-22	2.04E-03	6.82E-07	3.66E-07	-4.87E-08	1.22E-03	-1.74E-05	2.08E-06	0.00E+00	6.94E-03	-1.64E-05	2.48E-06	-4.87E-08	0%	1%	0%
0.9	2.40E-03	2.59E-07	3.09E-08	-2.77E-22	1.13E-03	-1.83E-07	2.62E-07	-4.02E-08	6.81E-04	-1.09E-05	1.30E-06	0.00E+00	4.21E-03	-1.08E-05	1.59E-06	-4.02E-08	0%	2%	0%
band-integrated	1.23E-03	1.16E-07	1.38E-08	-5.74E-23	8.61E-04	1.94E-06	1.65E-07	-1.76E-08	2.23E-03	-1.12E-05	1.32E-06	0.00E+00	4.33E-03	-9.14E-06	1.50E-06	-1.76E-08	0%	1%	0%

1. Reflected DoP is degree of polarization due to solar reflected and skydome reflected contributions.

2. Total DoP is degree of polarization due to solar reflected, skydome reflected, and solar scattered (upwelled) contributions.

3. There is a sign difference in the solar scattered S_1 component of radiance that is output by MODTRAN4-P, most likely the sign change is because the refraction of light at 400nm is more severe than for the other wavelengths resulting in a slightly different effective phase angle (bouncing around zero) between the observer and the sun at this wavelength relative to the longer wavelengths (there is a sign change in the S_1 upwelled component about the solar point in the sky).

NEF material 1000UUUPNT: $\sigma = 0.80$ rad $= 46°$, tan paint on aluminum.

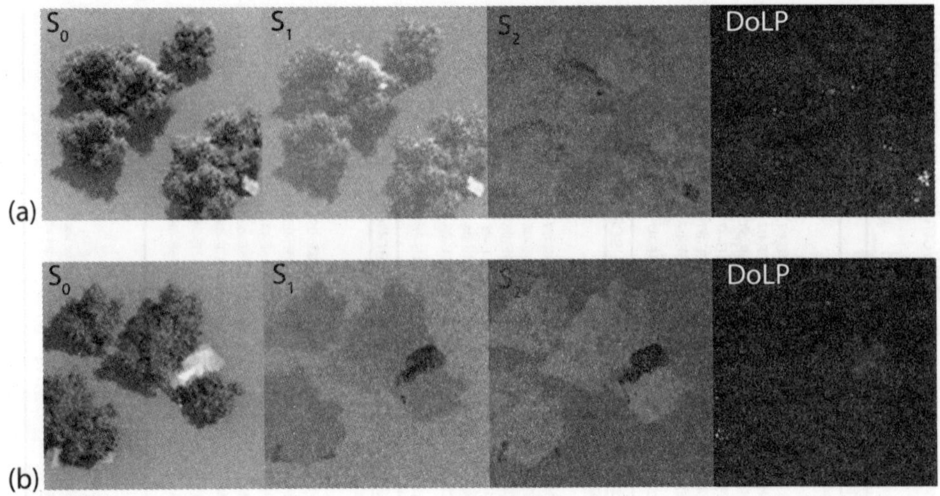

Figure 10.12 An example of a DIRSIG Stokes image set of a scene containing grass, trees, and draped green tarps under the trees. The first configuration (a) shows the imaging platform oriented about 160 deg relative azimuth to the sun, while the second (b) is positioned at about 90 deg relative azimuth to the sun.

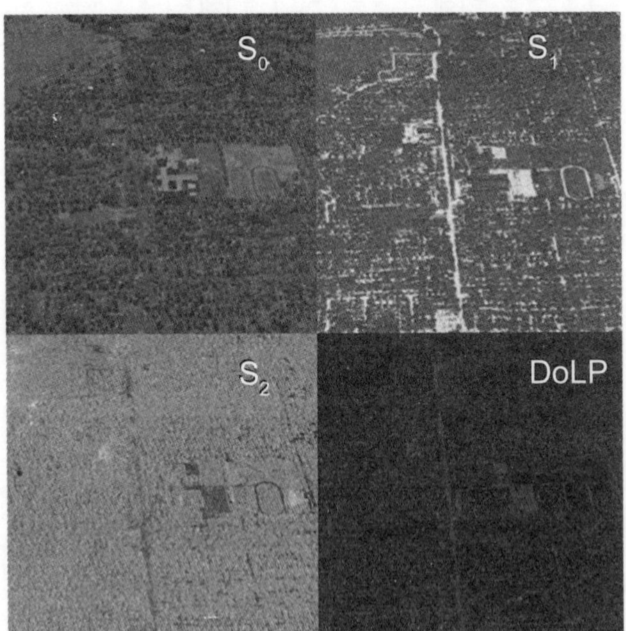

Figure 10.13 A portion of a DIRSIG Megascene attributed with polarized material BRDFs on selected background and target materials. An intensity band misregistration of 0.5 pixels was simulated to demonstrate registration artifacts in the resulting Stokes images.

The first polarized DIRSIG image simulation example consists of a scene geometry containing simply trees, grass, and two draped green tarps underneath the trees. In this configuration, we neglected atmospheric effects to concentrate on the underlying phenomenology present only in the scene. Figure 10.12(a) shows resulting Stokes images for the sun positioned at a zenith angle of 35 deg from nadir and at 160 deg in relative azimuth to the imaging platform. Figure 10.12(b) shows a second configuration where the imaging platform is moved to a position that is about 90 deg relative azimuth to the sun. The imaging platform was assumed to be static at a zenith angle of 40 deg and configured with four linear polarizers oriented at 0, 45, 90, and 135 deg. The resulting Stokes images (assuming perfect band-to-band registration) are shown in Fig. 10.12. In the forward-scattering imaging geometry, the tarps are slightly different in apparent brightness in the unpolarized S_0 image. The contrast between the tarps and the natural background is not significantly improved in the S_1 image. However, examination of the S_2 and DoLP images shows an enhancement in target-to-background contrast for the draped tarps.

The next example (see Fig. 10.13) shows a portion of a DIRSIG scene with polarized material properties. Specifically, the roofing, roadways, and grass have been attributed with a pBRDF, and the remainder of the materials are left with unpolarized BRDF models. The imaging platform was kept static and positioned at a zenith angle of about 50 deg. The sun was placed at a zenith angle of 40 deg and a relative azimuth to the sensor of 170 deg. In addition, a 0.5-pixel intensity band misregistration, sensor noise, and an optical MTF was applied to each simulated intensity image. The resulting Stokes images show both true polarization signatures and artifacts common in much polarimetric image data due to misregistration.

In closing this chapter, we note that synthetic modeling of the full polarimetric behavior of polarimetric imaging systems is a very recent advance that is likely to greatly aid in understanding PI images and phenomenology.

References

Anderson, G.P., Kneizys, F.X., Chetwynd, J.H., Wang, J., Hoke, M.L., Rothman, L.S., Kimball, L.M., McClatchey, R.A., Shettle, E.P., Clough, S.A., Gallery, W.O., Abreu, L.W., & Selby, J.E.A. (1995). "FASCODE/MODTRAN/LOWTRAN: past/present/future," *Proceedings of the 18th Annual Review Conference on Atmospheric Transmission Models*, Boston.

Brown, S.D., Schott, J.R., Raqueño, R.V., Kraska, T., & White, R. (1996). "Validation and analysis of the Digital Imaging and Remote Sensing Laboratory's synthetic image generation models." *Proceedings of the Seventh Annual Ground Target Modeling and Validation Conference.*

Chipman, R.A. (1995). "Polarimetry." *Handbook of Optics*, 2nd Ed., M. Bass, ed., Vol. 2, Chap. 22, McGraw-Hill, New York.

Czapla-Myers, J.S., Thome, K.J., & Biggar, S.F. (2002). "Optical sensor package for multiangle measurements of surface reflectance." *Proceedings SPIE,* Vol. 4480, pp. 326–333.

Coulson, K., Jitendra, D., & Sekera, Z. (1960). *Tables Related to Radiation Emerging from a Planetary Atmosphere with Rayleigh Scattering*. University of California Press, Berkeley.

Dana, K.J., & Wang, J. (2004). "Device for convenient measurement of spatially varying bidirectional reflectance." *Journal of the Optical Society of America A*, Vol. 21, No. 1, pp. 1–12.

Deering, D.W., & Leone, P. (1986). "A sphere-scanning radiometer for rapid directional measurements of sky and ground radiance." *Remote Sensing of Environment*, Vol. 19, No. 1, pp. 1–24.

Devaraj, C., Brown, S., Messinger, D., Goodenough, A., & Pogorzala, D. (2007). "A framework for polarized radiance signature prediction for natural scenes." *Proceedings SPIE*, Vol. 6565, 65650Y.

Egan, W. G. & Liu, Q. (2002). "Polarized MODTRAN 3.7 applied to characterization of ocean color in the presence of aerosols." *Proceedings SPIE,* Vol. 4481, pp. 228–241.

Gaskill, J.D. (1978). *Linear Systems, Fourier Transforms, and Optics*. Wiley, New York.

Goldstein, D.H., Chenault, D.B., & Pezzaniti, J.L. (1999). "Polarimetric characterization of Spectralon." *Proceedings SPIE*, Vol. 3754, pp. 126–136.

Han, J.Y., & Perlin, K. (2003). "Measuring bidirectional texture reflectance with a kaleidoscope." *ACM Transactions on Graphics*, Vol. 22, No. 3, pp. 741–748.

Mason, J.E., Schott, J.R., & Rankin-Parobek, D. (1994). "Validation analysis of the thermal and radiometric integrity of RIT's synthetic image generation model, DIRSIG," *Proceedings SPIE,* Vol. 2223, pp. 474–487.

Meyers, J.P. (2002). "Modeling Polarimetric Imaging Using DIRSIG." Doctoral dissertation, Rochester Institute of Technology, Rochester.

NEF9.4 (2004). Nonconventional Exploitation Factors (NEF) Modeling. *Tech. Rep. v9.5.*

Priest, R.G., & Meier, S.R. (2002). "Polarimetric microfacet scattering theory with applications to absorptive and reflective surfaces." *Optical Engineering*, Vol. 41, No. 5, pp. 988–993.

Roujean, J., Leroy, M., & Deshamps, P. (1992). "A bidirectional reflectance model of the earth's surface for the correction of remote sensing data," *Journal of Geophysical Research*, Vol. 97(D18), pp. 20455–20468.

Sandmeier, S.R., & Itten, K.I. (1999). "A field goniometer system (FIGOS) for acquisition of hyperspectral BRDF data." *IEEE Transactions on Geoscience and Remote Sensing*, Vol. 37, No. 2, pp. 978–986.

Sandmeier, S.R. (2000). "Acquisition of bidirectional reflectance factor data with field goniometers." *Remote Sensing of Environment*, Vol. 73, No. 3, pp. 257–269.

Schott, J.R. (2007). *Remote Sensing: The Image Chain Approach*, 2nd Ed., Oxford University Press, New York.

Shell, J.R., & Schott, J.R. (2005). "A polarized clutter measurement technique based on the governing equation for polarimetric remote sensing in the visible to near infrared." *Proceedings SPIE*, Vol. 5811, pp. 34–45.

Shell, J.R. (2005). "Polarimetric Remote Sensing in the Visible to Near Infrared." Doctoral dissertation, Rochester Institute of Technology, Rochester.

Torrance, K.E., & Sparrow, E.M. (1967). "Theory for off-specular reflection from roughened surfaces." *Journal of the Optical Society of America A*, Vol. 57, No. 9, pp. 1105–1114.

Walthall, C., Roujean, J.-L., & Morisette, J. (2000). "Field and landscape BRDF optical wavelength measurements: Experience, techniques and the future." *Remote Sensing Reviews*, Vol. 18, No. 24, pp. 503–531.

Michael G. Gartley
John R. Schott

Chapter 11
Longwave Infrared pBRDF Principles

To simplify the discussion of polarization concepts, we have for the most part avoided consideration of the emissive region of the EM spectrum. This chapter and the next specifically address the emissive region. In this chapter, we begin with a short review of some of the measurement and applications work involving polarimetric sensing in the thermal infrared. We then explain the fundamental concepts related to pBRDF models in the emissive region of the spectrum.

In the thermal infrared, we have two potential sources of polarized energy. The first is reflected energy, which will have behavioral phenomena similar to those in the VNIR-SWIR and are discussed in Chapters 2 through 10. The second involves the polarization state of the emitted energy. The final polarization state will depend on the degree of polarization due to each of these components and their relative magnitude. To begin this review we will briefly examine some of the literature describing measurements of the polarimetric emission from surfaces, as well as some papers that motivate consideration of the thermal infrared for polarimetric sensing.

11.1 Background on Polarimetric Remote Sensing in the Thermal Infrared

Although rare, polarimetric IR imaging-related topics have received some attention in the literature over the past 20 years. The experimental and theoretical work in polarimetric IR spans a range of applications, including but not limited to: astronomy, observations of space objects, characterization of polarized material emissivity, target cueing, and decoy discrimination. We will review a small sample of this work to introduce some of the principles and issues associated with sensing in this spectral region.

Jordan and Lewis (1994) describe experimental measurements of the *emission polarization* from glass and aluminum. Their work focused primarily on the wavelength region of 10 to 11 μm, dictated by their optical coatings and detector spectral response. They examined both smooth and sand-blasted versions of alu-

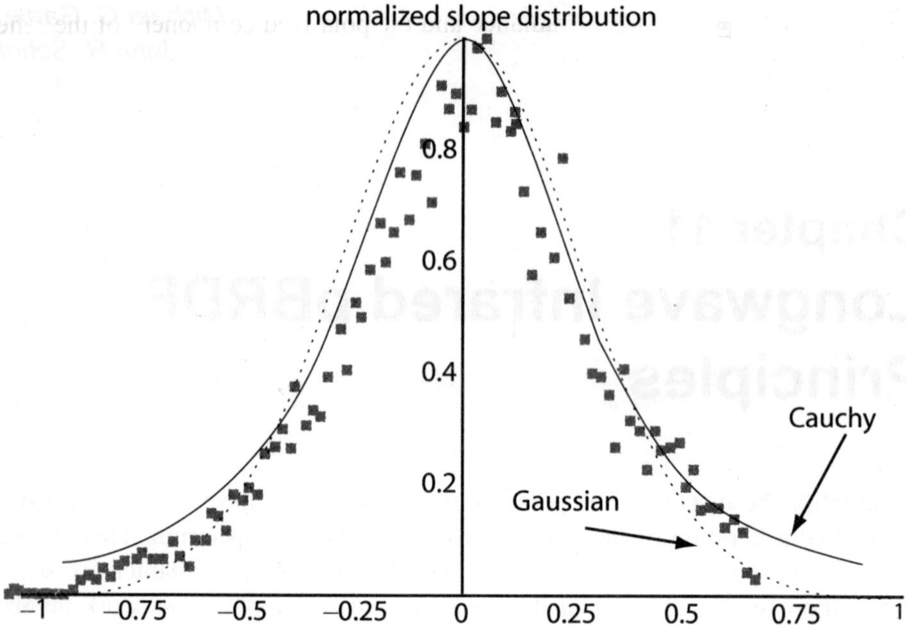

Figure 11.1 Measured surface slope distribution for a roughened glass sample [Courtesy of Jordan and Lewis (1994)].

minum and glass, mounted to a thermal bath to maintain a sample temperature of approximately 70°C. The intent of heating the sample was to keep the thermally emitted radiance level well above the ambient radiance that might be reflected from the sample surfaces. A combination of a rotatable linear polarizer and a quarter wave plate enabled measurements of all four Stokes parameters (S_0, S_1, S_2, and S_3). The surface roughness was measured utilizing a surface profilometer. The surface slope distributions for each sample were found to lie between a Gaussian and a Cauchy distribution (see Fig. 11.1).

The authors found the S_2 and S_3 Stokes components of the thermally emitted radiance to be zero within the noise level of the measurements. The partial polarization of all samples showed the S_1 radiance to always be negative, indicative of a partial *P* polarization.

Jordan et al. (1996) utilized the same polarized emission results. However, they also used an active technique to measure the complex index of refraction of their materials at 10.6 μm. In addition, this followup paper developed a model to estimate polarized emissivity of a material given the complex index of refraction and rms surface slope distribution as inputs. Figure 11.2 is taken from this work and shows excellent agreement between their model and the experimental results. The model is not presented here, but the reader is directed to the references for further details.

Gurtan and Dahmani (2005) describe more current work in the area of emission polarization. The authors built a polarimetric Fourier transform infrared

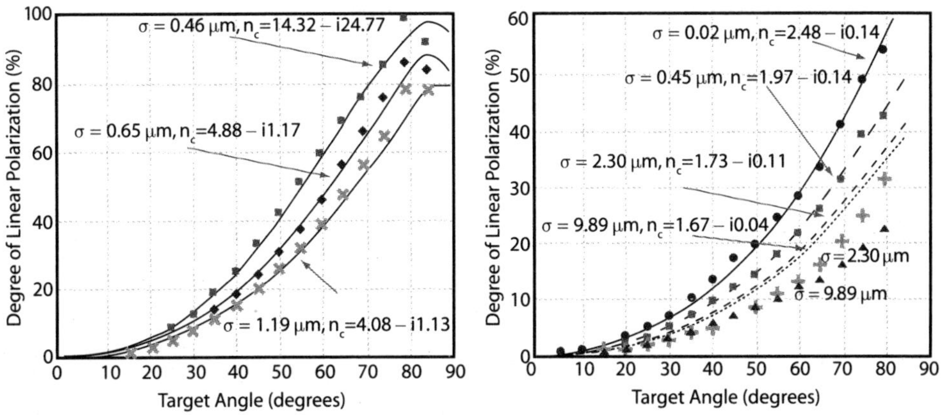

Figure 11.2 DoLP as a function of emission angle for various glass (left) and aluminum (right) surfaces [Courtesy of Jordan et al. (1996)].

(FTIR) spectrometer, enabling polarized spectral measurements. The FTIR instrument was outfitted with a wire grid polarizer and a quarter wave retarder plate. This spectrometer configuration enabled measurement of all four Stokes vector components between 4.5 and 13.0 μm.

The primary material examined by Gurtan and Dahmani was borosilicate glass. Included in their work was the complex index of refraction (n and k) values, over the same wavelength range that the FTIR covered (see Fig. 11.3), to facilitate evaluating a simple Fresnel model.

In order to examine the effect of surface roughness on the emission polarization, the authors sandblasted glass samples to various degrees. In addition to glass, they measured a Krylon black paint coating and a CARC green paint coating on smooth borosilicate glass substrates. The degree of roughness was quantified by a surface profilometer. From the profilometer traces, the authors calculated rms surface roughness (R_a) and rms surface slope roughness of all of the surfaces they examined. The authors found that the rms surface slope distribution followed a Gaussian distribution.

The polarized emission measurements showed that for all materials, the S_2 and S_3 components of the emitted Stokes radiance vector was zero to within the noise of the measurement. For the smooth glass samples, the authors found excellent agreement between measurement and Fresnel-predicted degree of emission polarization (see Fig. 11.4).

The emission polarization measurements were taken for emission angles between 10 and 80 deg. The authors found $\leq$2% DoLP for all samples at an emission angle of 10 deg. However, the DoLP reached about 55% for the smooth glass sample at an emission angle of 80 deg, and around 20% for all three of their sandblasted glass samples. The CARC green painted glass sample showed almost no emission polarization at most emission angles (max. 8% at 80 deg). The Krylon

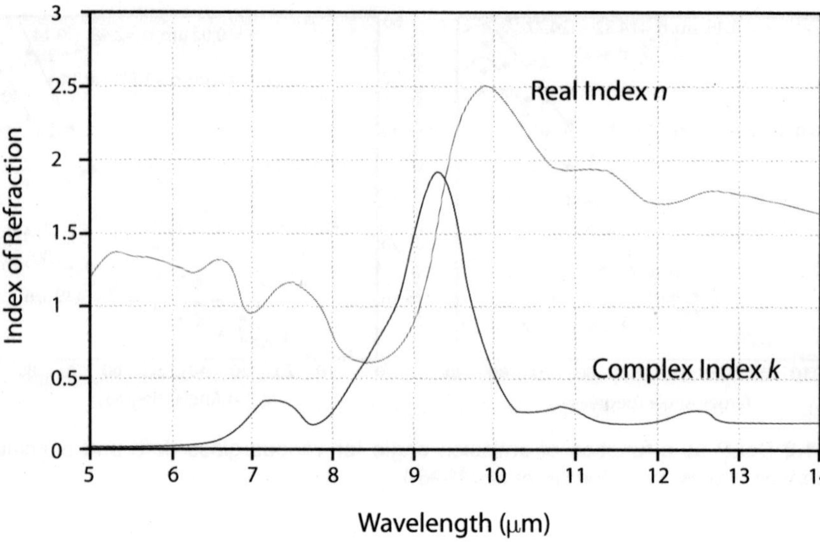

Figure 11.3 Index of refraction for borosilicate glass between 4.5 and 13.0 μm [Courtesy of Gurtan and Dahmani (2005)].

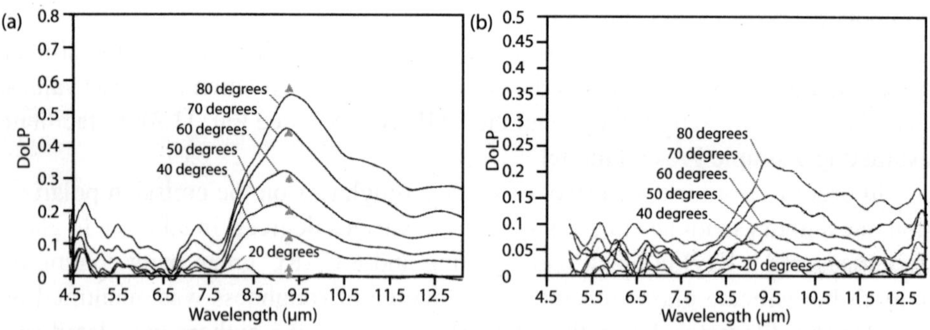

Figure 11.4 DoLP as a function of wavelength and emission angle for (a) smooth and (b) moderately rough surfaces. Triangles show the predicted values from the Fresnel reflectance for the smooth glass surface [Courtesy of Gurtan and Dahmani (2005)].

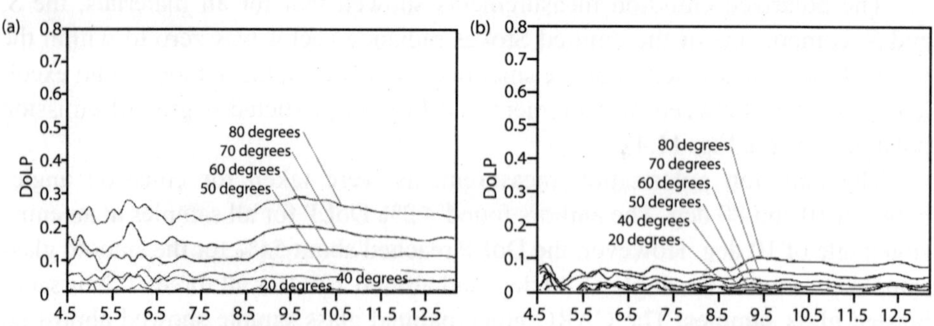

Figure 11.5 DoLP as a function of wavelength and emission angle for (a) Krylon black coated and (b) CARC green coated glass surfaces [Courtesy of Gurtan and Dahmani (2005)].

black painted sample showed an emission polarization increasing to about 25% at the max. emission angle of 80 deg (Fig. 11.5).

While only representing a sample of the thermal infrared emission data, these results are characteristic of the polarimetric behavior of materials in the thermal infrared. The emitted radiation is essentially unpolarized when viewed at nadir and has increasing polarization off nadir with vertical polarization dominating over horizontal. Furthermore, DoP is larger for smooth surfaces where Fresnel surface behavior dominates over multiple scattered radiation. The S_2 term is lacking in these studies because the measurements were oriented with the vertical polarizer in the principal plane (i.e., tilted surface or sensors will induce an S_2 contribution). The lack of an S_3 term is characteristic; as a result, much of our modeling and analysis will focus on the linear components.

11.2 Applications of Polarimetric Infrared Imaging

This section reviews a few examples of work intended to explore how polarimetric infrared imaging may be applied to operational scenarios. Pesses and Tan (2002) present work on polarimetric simulation of space objects in the longwave infrared. The intent of the work was to examine the potential utility of polarimetric LWIR imaging versus unpolarized LWIR imaging. The authors utilized a 3-D LWIR spectropolarimetric signature model called *Polar Heat.*

The first utility example presented polarimetric images of a spinning global positioning satellite (GPS). The images were rendered utilizing a computer-aided design (CAD) model of a GPS spacecraft containing over 10,000 individual facets. The solar array panels were assumed to be constructed of quartz glass, while the surfaces of the spacecraft bus and antennas were assumed to be constructed of aluminum and silver, respectively. The authors compared the utility of S_0, DoLP, and S_0/S_1 image products to aid in exploitation of the GPS spacecraft images (see Fig. 11.6). It was found that the DoLP image products showed the largest level of contrast as the GPS spacecraft spun, potentially providing more information to an image analyst looking to solve an intelligence problem.

Pesses and Tan (2002) also examined the case of imaging small objects in low earth orbit and objects in geosynchronous orbit. In both of these cases, the spacecraft cannot be spatially resolved. However, the authors generated a time-varying polarimetric signature model that algebraically combined the polarization effects of all portions of the target into one signal. A preliminary analysis showed that for space object identification, the polarimetric rotation signature will be more useful than the current hyperspectral rotation signatures.

Finally, Pesses and Tan present the challenging task that a ballistic missile defense system has of distinguishing between reentry vehicles and balloon decoys. The authors polarimetrically modeled these targets utilizing the Polar Heat model (Fig. 11.7). Polar Heat is outfitted with both Fresnel and BRDF reflectance models, as well as incoherent scattering effects. The authors discovered the

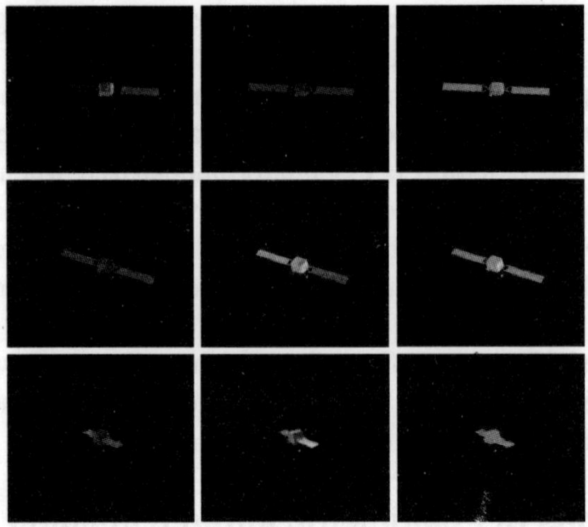

Figure 11.6 The left column shows three different false color views of a GPS at 10 μm (S_0). The middle column shows three different views of a GPS at 10 μm (DoLP). The right column shows three different views of a GPS at 10 μm S_0/S_1 [© IEEE, courtesy of Pesses and Tan (2002)].

actual reentry vehicles to have two to four times more DoLP signature than the aluminum-coated decoy balloons.

Polarization measurements in the infrared have demonstrated utility for the detection of manmade objects in natural backgrounds. One example that has been studied extensively, both with modeling and experimental collections, is the detection of surface-laid landmines and tripwires. Forssell (2001) examined the utility of polarized image collections in the infrared for detection of landmines and tripwires. He compared detection of these objects in a nonpolarized IR image against a DoLP image.

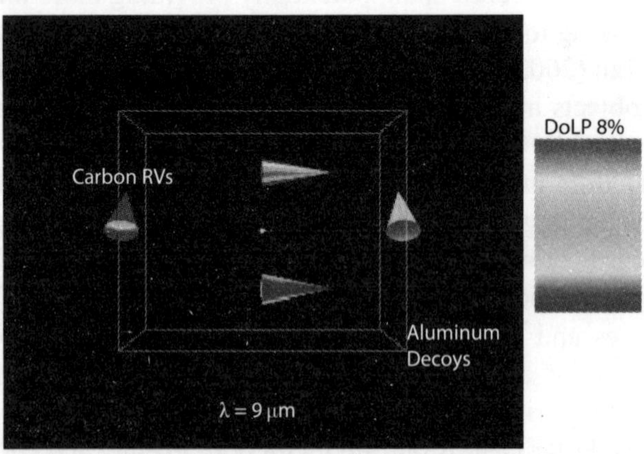

Figure 11.7 Comparison of modeled DoLP values for two carbon-coated reentry vehicles (RVs) and two aluminum-coated balloon decoys [© IEEE, courtesy of Pesses and Tan (2002)].

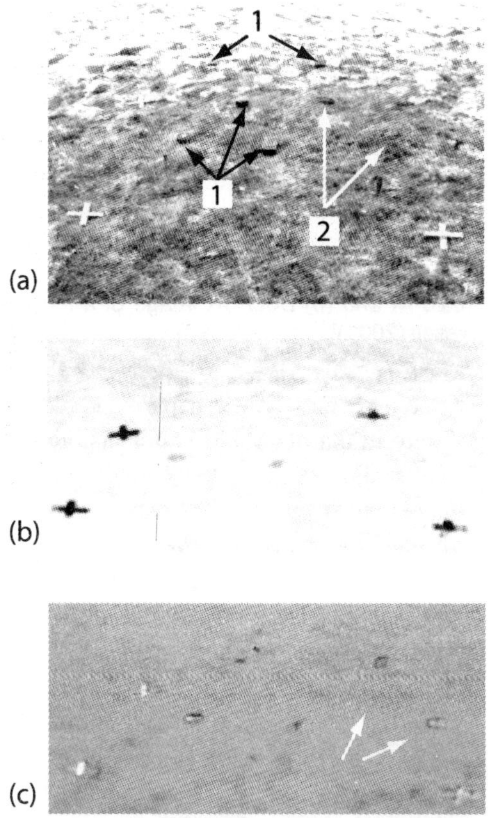

Figure 11.8 Visible contextual image (a) showing five surface-laid landmines and two landmines covered by dry grass. (b) Unpolarized IR and (c) DoLP images of the same scene [Courtesy of Forssell (2001)].

Although unpolarized thermal imagery can sometimes easily reveal surface-laid landmines, the detection becomes quite challenging after the mines begin to be covered by surrounding vegetation and dust from the ground (see Fig. 11.8). The problem of detecting tripwires is even more challenging, in that for most cases the wire width is much smaller than the ground sampling distance of the detector, making unpolarized radiance measurements (IR or visible) unproductive. As a test scenario, Forssell laid five mines on a dry grass ground with no covering and two mines covered with dry grass. The visible image (Fig. 11.8(a)) shows the uncovered mines designated by the number 1 and the covered mines designated by the number 2. The four crosses in the scene are placed as reference markers, but are not meant to actually be targets for detection. The unpolarized IR image (Fig. 11.8(b)) shows two of the five uncovered mines clearly visible above the background. However, all five of the uncovered mines are visible within the DoLP image (Fig. 11.8(c)). In addition, one of the covered mines is also visible within the DoLP image and one is not (white arrows).

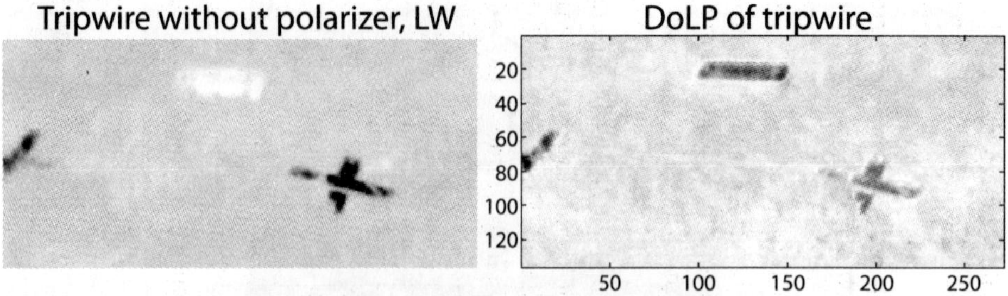

Figure 11.9 (a) Unpolarized IR and (b) DoLP IR image of a tripwire between two fiducal markers [Courtesy of Forssell (2001)].

Forssell also examined a scene where a tripwire is placed across a foot path. The tripwire is only 1.5 mm in diameter and is not visible within the unpolarized IR radiance image. However, Forssell is able to clearly detect the presence of the tripwire in the DoLP image (Fig. 11.9).

Cremer (2002) examines the utility of MWIR polarimetric measurements to solve the same problem. He presents an example where surface-laid landmines are difficult to detect with unpolarized MWIR radiance images. However, with the addition of a polarizer, he is able to easily detect the presence of landmines.

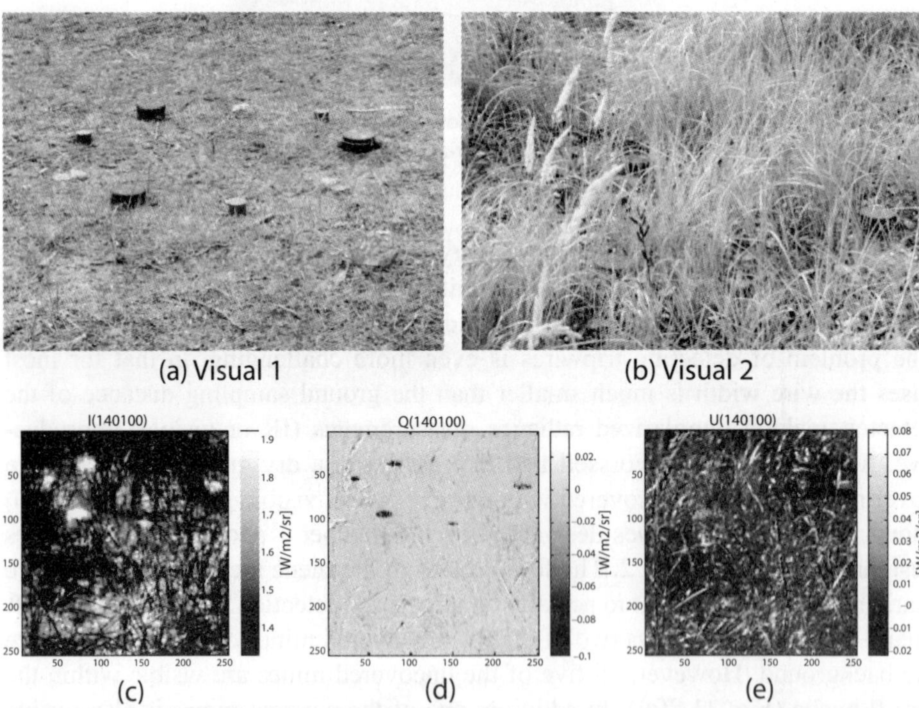

Figure 11.10 Visible images of mines (a) before and (b) after vegetation has grown around them. (c) S_0 IR image, (d) S_1 IR image, and (e) S_2 IR image of mines embedded in vegetation [Courtesy of Cremer (2002)].

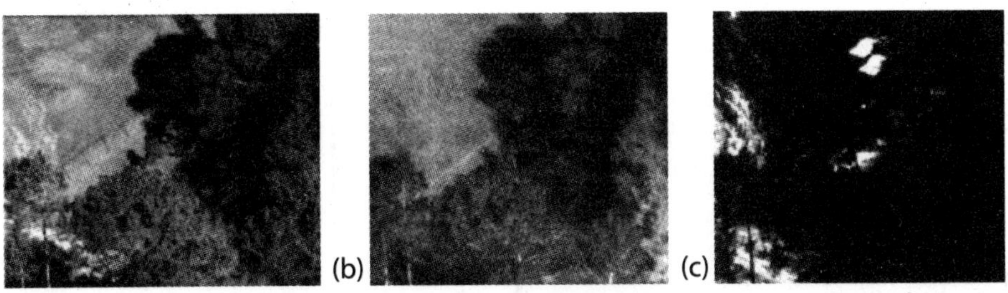

Figure 11.11 (a) Multispectral visible, (b) unpolarized MWIR, and (c) DoP MWIR image of vehicles in tree shadows [Courtesy of Tyo et al. (2006)]. (See color plate.)

In Fig. 11.10, two visible images show the location of the five mines before and after vegetation has grown around them. Next, the figure presents a broadband unpolarized MWIR image where three of the five mines are visible. The S_1 polarization image shows all five mines to have some polarimetric contrast, while the S_2 polarization image shows minimal contrast.

Another application of LWIR polarimetric imaging is detection of vehicles in a cluttered background. Tyo et al. (2006) show an example of two vehicles inside a shadow on the edge of a forest. The vehicle is not visible in the visible multispectral image or in the unpolarized LWIR image. However, adding LWIR polarization as another degree of freedom brings the vehicle out of the background and significantly enhances the ability for detection (see Fig. 11.11).

In summary, we find that polarized signatures in the thermal infrared offer some increased potential to improve the contrast between manmade targets and natural backgrounds.

11.3 Polarized BRDF and Emissivity Model

In order to describe the polarimetric behavior of materials in the emissive spectral region, we need to be able to describe the pBRDF in this spectral region. The polarized thermal BRDF models follow the same principles as the reflective BRDF models and take advantage of *Kirchoff's law* that

$$\varepsilon = 1 - r \tag{11.1}$$

for opaque surfaces in thermal equilibrium, where ε is emissivity and r is the reflectivity. A polarimetric BRDF model suitable for use in the LWIR is summarized here. This approach is drawn from Gartley et al. (2007) and Gartley (2007) and builds heavily on the BRDF models introduced by Maxwell et al. (1973) and Torrance and Sparrow (1967) and extended by Priest and Germer (2000). This reflectance and emissivity model is a generalization of the BRDF models introduced in Chapter 6. Upon close inspection, it is apparent that the Beard-Maxwell model, the Torrance-Sparrow model, and the Priest-Germer model all have the same general form.

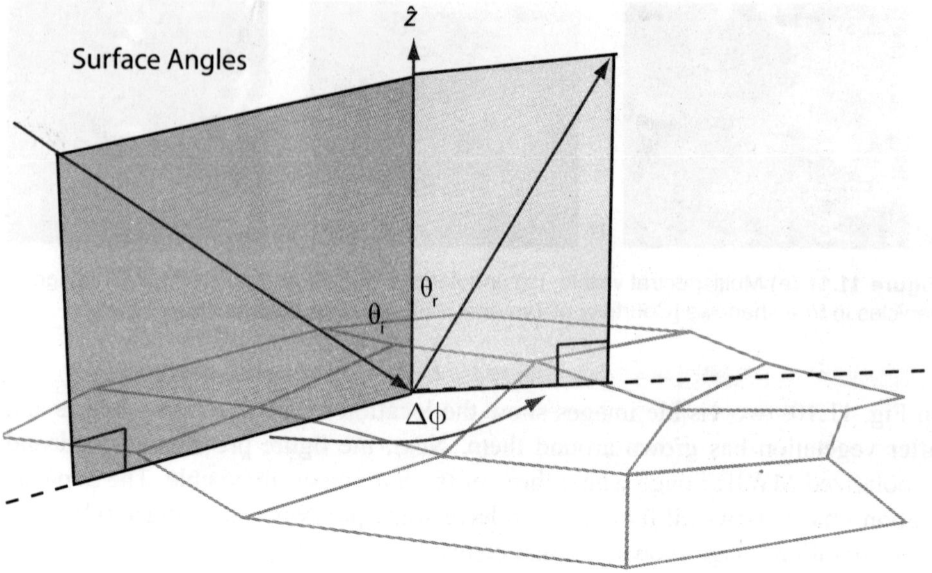

Figure 11.12 Polarized BRDF angles relative to macrosurface normal $\hat{z}$.

The polarized bidirectional reflection distribution function (pBRDF) can be generalized to include a polarized specular component and an unpolarized volume component. (Although in reality the volume component may contribute a small amount to the overall polarization of reflectance, this model treats the volume term as completely unpolarized.)

$$f_{pBRDF} = f_{spec} + f_{vol} = f_{polarized} + f_{unpolarized}. \tag{11.2}$$

The polarized component of the BRDF is a 4×4-element Mueller matrix as described in Section 11.3.1. The unpolarized component is a scalar value that is presented in Section 11.3.2.

11.3.1 Polarized specular reflection component of the pBRDF model

The specular component of the polarized BRDF is based on a statistical distribution ($P(\theta_N)$) of a Fresnel reflection Mueller matrix ($\boldsymbol{M}$) (see Eq. 6.12). In addition, we include a shadowing and obscuration function (SO (θ, β, τ, Ω)). These functions and associated inputs are discussed below.

$$f_{spec} = \frac{\mathbf{M}(\beta, \hat{n}, k)\mathrm{SO}(\theta, \beta, \tau, \Omega)P(\quad , \sigma, B)}{4\cos(\theta_i)\cos(\theta_r)}. \tag{11.3}$$

Since most of the surfaces we will encounter in our modeling efforts will not be perfectly flat, we can take advantage of a facet probability distribution function. A probability distribution allows us to express a nonflat surface in terms of flat microfacets that are oriented at an angle α relative to the macrosurface plane

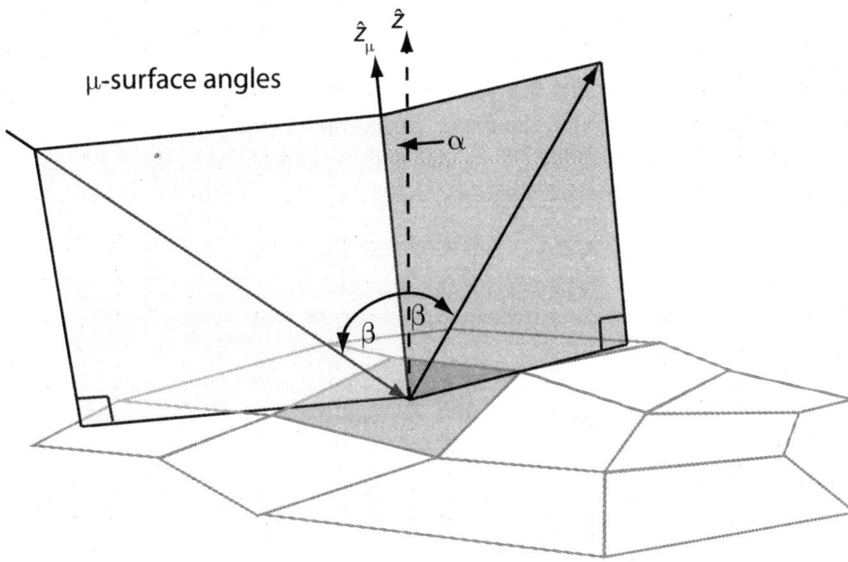

Figure 11.13 Polarized BRDF angles relative to microsurface normal $\hat{z}_\mu$ and macrosurface normal $\hat{z}$.

(see Fig. 11.12). Figure 11.13 illustrates how we can represent a roughened surface as a series of flat microfacets with different orientations.

As seen in the previous section, a common microfacet distribution function is the Gaussian distribution (Fig. 11.14). This function is given in terms of a bias parameter (B) and a roughness parameter (σ). Specifically, this distribution function is a Gaussian of the local surface slope ($\tan(\theta)$) with a variance of σ^2. It can be expressed as

$$P_G(\alpha,\sigma,B) = \frac{Be^{-\frac{\tan(\alpha)^2}{2\sigma^2}}}{2\pi\sigma^2\cos(\alpha)^3}. \tag{11.4}$$

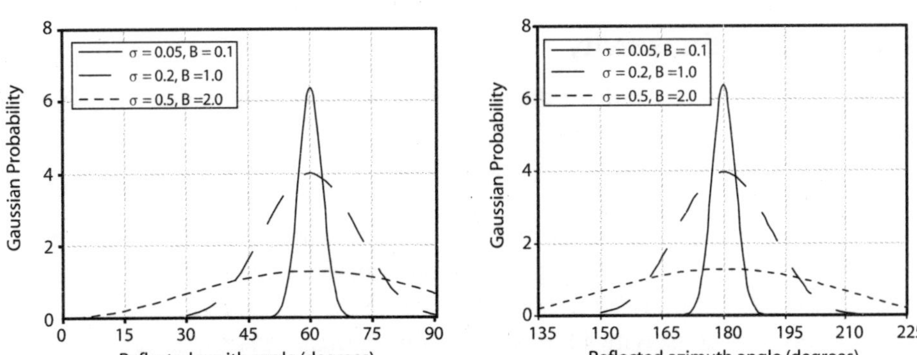

Figure 11.14 Examples of the Gaussian slope distribution function as a function of reflected zenith angle and relative azimuth between the incident and reflected directions, for flux incident at $\theta_i = 60$ deg and $\phi_i = 0$ deg and for various roughness and bias paramters.

The *shadowing and obscuration function* serves the purpose of accounting for shadowing and obscuration effects resulting from very rough surfaces. The particular function utilized by the Maxwell-Beard BRDF model is preferred due to its maturity within the NEF database. Equation 11.5 presents the function utilized by the Beard-Maxwell BRDF model and implemented in the NEF database. It is expressed as

$$\mathrm{SO}(\alpha,\beta,\tau,\Omega)=\frac{1+\frac{\alpha}{\Omega}e^{-2\beta/\tau}}{1+\frac{\alpha}{\Omega}}. \tag{11.5}$$

A *stronger* (smaller values of τ and Ω) shadowing and obscuration function reduces surface reflectance for higher roughness surfaces by considering that oblique incident and reflected angle scattering has a higher probability of being shadowed or re-reflected in another direction by a microfacet. Recall that β is the angle between the facet normal and the incident or Fresnel reflected flux (see Fig. 11.13).

11.3.2 Unpolarized reflection component

In addition to the polarized Fresnel component of the BRDF, there is also an unpolarized scattering component. This unpolarized component has a *volume* scattering term ρ_v and a *diffuse* scattering term ρ_d.

$$f_{vol}(\theta_i,\theta_r)=\rho_d+\frac{2\rho_v}{\cos(\theta_i)+\cos(\theta_r)}. \tag{11.6}$$

The diffuse scattering term is analogous to Lambertian reflectivity, where, by definition, there is no angular dependence on scattering and the result is completely unpolarized. The volume scattering term, also unpolarized, represents radiance that is absorbed and reflected immediately back out due to subsurface scattering.

11.4 Polarized Emissivity

The polarized emissivity utilizes the concept of energy conservation. Recall from Chapter 2 that

$$\rho+\tau+\varepsilon=1, \tag{11.7}$$

where ρ is the hemispherical reflectivity, τ is the transmission, and ε is the emissivity of a material. In developing a polarized emissivity model, we assume that the material does not transmit radiance ($\tau = 0$) in the infrared region of the spectrum and solve for emissivity in terms of *hemispherical reflectivity,* i.e.,

$$\varepsilon(\theta)=1-\int f_{pBRDF}(\theta,\theta_r,\Delta\phi)\cos(\theta_r)d\Omega. \tag{11.8}$$

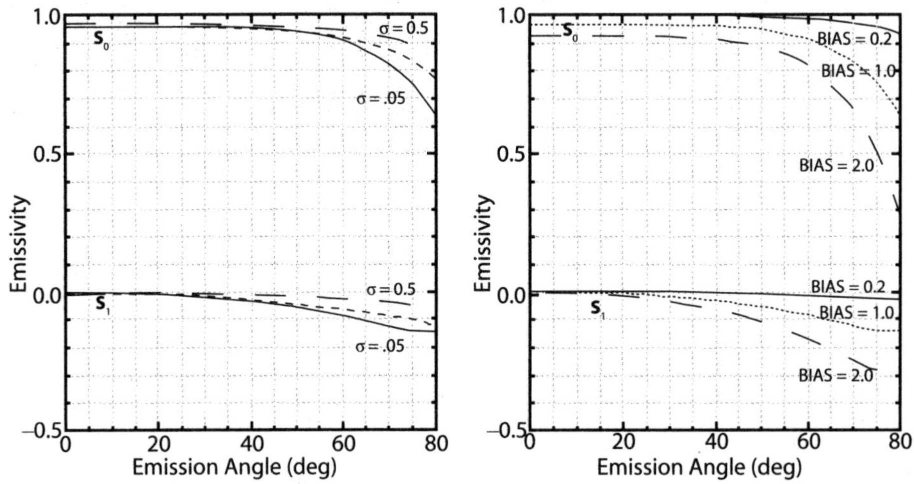

Figure 11.15 Plots showing effect of changing σ value (left) and *bias* value (right) of pBRDF function on S_0 and S_1 emissivity.

The above integral can be rewritten in terms of θ_r and ϕ_r as

$$\varepsilon(\theta) = 1 - \int_0^{2\pi}\int_0^{\pi/2} f_{pBRDF}(\theta,\theta_r,\Delta\phi)\cos(\theta_r)\sin(\theta_r)d\theta_r d\phi_r. \tag{11.9}$$

To understand how the different pBRDF inputs affect the behavior of the modeled emissivity, various examples are presented below.

As a baseline, a real-valued index of refraction value of 1.5 was chosen. For the shadowing and obscuration function, values of 5 and 10 were chosen for the τ and Ω parameters, respectively. The plot on the left of Fig. 11.15 shows the Stokes S_0 and S_1 emissivity values as a function of emission angle and three different values of surface roughness (σ). As expected, the S_0 emissivity is quite flat for zenith values less than about 45 deg. However, for the smoother surface (σ = 0.05), S_0 falls off much faster at larger emission angles than for the moderately and severely rough surfaces.

The plot on the right of Fig. 11.15 shows the effect of changing the probability function bias value (*B*) on the S_0 and S_1 emissivity curves. Larger values of *B* have the effect of scaling the emissivity away from a perfect Lambertian blackbody [$\varepsilon(\theta) = 1.0$].

The next series of emissivity plots, shown in Fig. 11.16, demonstrate the effect of altering the values of τ and Ω on the S_0 and S_1 emissivity curves. A complex index of refraction value of 1.5–.5*i* was chosen for these plots. Larger values of τ and Ω will relax the shadowing and obscuration function, such that they do not attenuate the reflections as significantly. Smaller values of τ and Ω produce a stronger shadowing and obscuration function, in that reflections are attenuated for rough surfaces at large incident and reflected zenith angles.

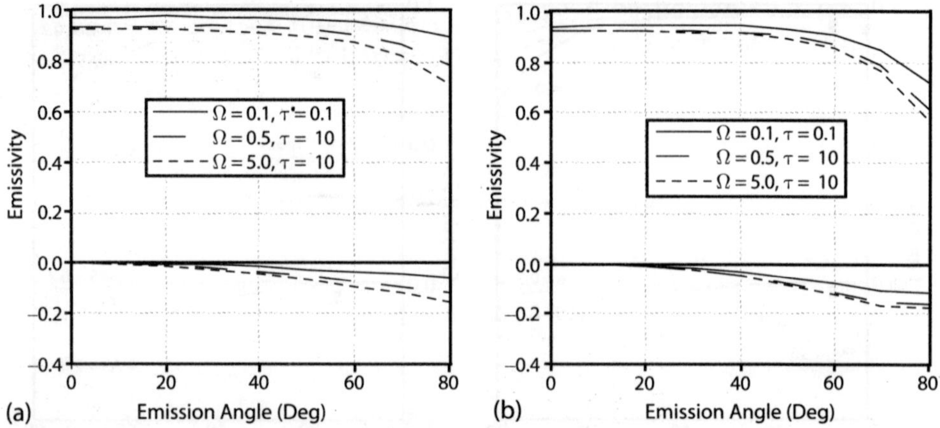

Figure 11.16 Plots showing the effect of changing the shadowing function parameters for (a) a moderately rough surface and (b) a smooth surface.

The strongest shadowing and obscuration function was configured by the smallest values of τ and Ω, chosen to be 0.1 and 0.1 radians, respectively. A moderate-strength shadowing and obscuration function was configured by setting τ and Ω to 0.5 and 1.0 radians. The mildest form of the shadowing and obscuration function was generated by setting τ and Ω to 5.0 and 10.0 radians. The plots in Fig. 11.16 show that a stronger shadowing and obscuration function has the effects of (1) increasing the emissivity for all emission angles and (2) reducing the emissivity drop-off at large emission angles. As expected, the smoother surface (right side of figure) is slightly less effected by changing the shadowing and obscuration function parameters than is the rougher surface (left side of figure).

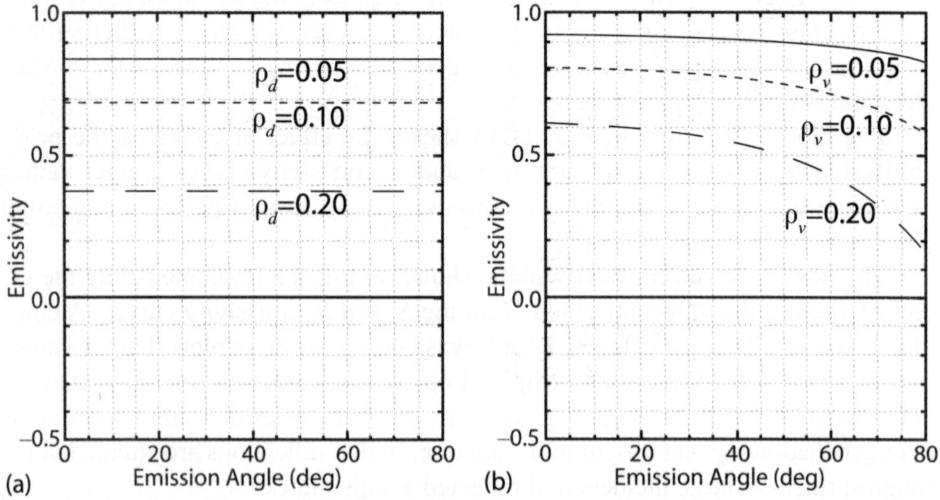

Figure 11.17 Plots showing S_0 emissivity dependence on diffuse and volume scattering.

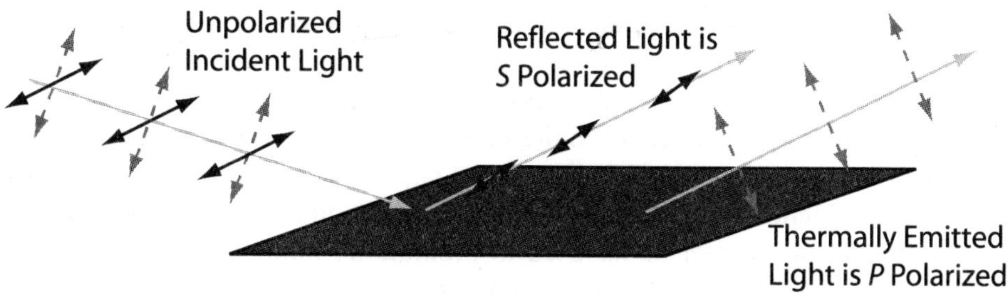

11.18 Illustration of how the reflected component (predominantly *S* polarized) and the emitted component (predominantly *P* polarized) compete to determine the amount of overall polarization.

Finally, a series of plots was generated to demonstrate the effect of altering the pBRDF diffuse scattering (ρ_d) and volume scattering (ρ_v) terms. For these examples, the bias value (B) of the probability distribution function was set to $1e^{-6}$, effectively turning off the specular reflection portion of the pBRDF.

The plot on the left of Fig. 11.17 shows the effect of changing the value of ρ_d on S_0 emissivity. This term is essentially a Lambertian reflectance term, therefore no angle dependence is present in the emissivity values, as expected. Larger values of ρ_d result in smaller values of emissivity.

The plot on the right of Fig. 11.17 demonstrates the effect of altering the value of ρ_v on emissivity. Increasing the value of ρ_v has the effect of reducing the emissivity, just as was demonstrated for the ρ_d term. However, the ρ_v term has an emission angle dependence that the ρ_d term does not; dependence produces a gradual falloff in emissivity for larger emission angles. This falloff in emissivity is similar to the falloff produced by the Fresnel term; however, it has no effect on the S_1, S_2, or S_3 terms of the emissivity Stokes vector.

The emissivity model was found to be somewhat over-parameterized, in that the same emissivity curve can be produced utilizing various combinations of complex index of refraction and surface slope distribution function *bias* parameters. The values of the S_1 component of the emissivity model are driven primarily by a combination of (1) the bias and complex index of refraction and (2) the surface slope variance parameter σ. Due to the azimuthal symmetry assumed for surface roughness, the S_2 parameter of thermal emissivity is always zero by definition. In all cases, we find the polarization of the modeled surfaces to always be negative (*P* polarized) in the S_1 component and strongest at grazing angles. This general property of the polarimetric state of emitted radiance is in contrast to reflected light, which is generally positive in the Stokes S_1 component (*S* polarized). Therefore, surfaces that have strong polarized reflection and emission properties may appear to have no polarization signature when the level of radiance reflected from the surface is comparable to the level of radiance thermally emitted from the surface (see Fig. 11.18). This situation can be more intuitively expressed in terms of temperature. If the emissivity of the target and background are high and the temperatures are approximately equal, then the polarized component of the emitted radiance and the polarized component of the reflected radiance are roughly equal and cross-polarized, producing a randomly polarized signal. Tyo et al. (2007) discuss how these effects can reduce polarimetric signatures in the LWIR. Shaw (2007) points out that, in addition to the simple competition between reflected and emitted polarization due to the temperature of target and background, atmospheric effects also influence the background radiance terms and final image contrast.

At the end of Chapter 6, we tried to promote an intuitive sense of the polarimetric behavior of materials based on how various parameters impacted the pBRDF. To do the same for objects in the thermal infrared, we need to begin by recognizing that there is a reflective component that will behave in essentially the same way as discussed in Chapter 6 for objects in the reflective region of the spectrum. However, because the sun emits negligible amounts of energy at longer wavelengths, the largest contributor to reflected radiance is usually adjacent objects, whose relative impact will depend on their temperature relative to the target temperature (i.e., Is the reflective component significant relative to the emitted component? (see Fig. 11.18)). Also recognize that in the thermal infrared, the wavelengths are approximately an order of magnitude larger than in the visible, so surfaces will tend to exhibit more specular behavior.

Keeping the reflective behavior in mind, we will focus on the emissive behavior of materials, which is usually the largest source of radiance in the thermal infrared and often a large contributor to the polarimetric behavior. We begin with illustrations depicting a simplified model of the angular emissivity as shown in Fig. 11.19(a). The model shows how the emissivity varies with view angles relative to the nadir. It assumes that the emissivity is made up of two parts. The first part is due to direct surface emisson and multiple scattered emission (i.e., energy emitted by the target and then multiply scattered by the target). The radiance due to these processes should be roughly the same in all directions, though somewhat reduced at grazing angles due to self obscuration. There is also energy from just beneath the surface that is emitted in all directions. The energy that is not immediately absorbed can reach the surface where it will be either transmitted (and refracted) or internally reflected, as illustrated in Fig. 11.19(a). At normal incidence, most of the energy is transmitted. As the incidence angle increases away from normal, the amount of energy transmitted decreases (Fresnel reflection and transmission equations apply) until we reach the point where total internal reflection occurs and no energy is transmitted. The result of this is a lobe of emitted energy due to transmission from just below the surface. The two sources are combined to yield the total emissivity as a function of view angle from the normal as seen in the polar plots in Fig. 11.17(a). Note that these plots are azimuthally symmetrical for isotropic surfaces. Note also that the net effect of these two processes is to produce angular emissivities that decrease monotonically as the view angle increases (see Figs. 11.15 through 11.17). However, for many materials the angular falloff may be quite small over the first 30–50 deg from nadir. The fine detail describing the shape and relative magnitude of the two components of the emissivity model will be a function of the surface roughness profile and the complex index of refraction

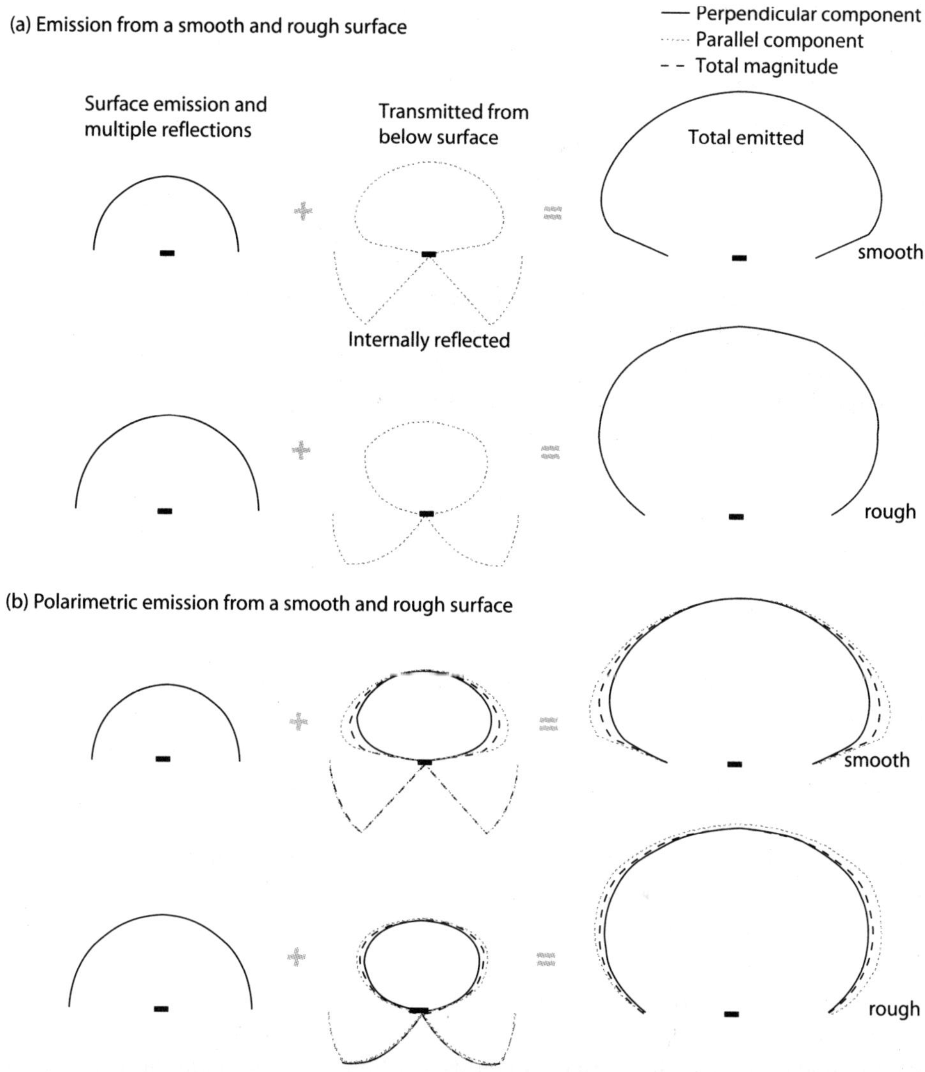

Figure 11.19 Illustration showing how emissivity varies with view angle. Note that these surfaces are azimuthally symmetrical for an isotropic surface and that external sources would bi-directionally reflect, as illustrated in Figs. 6.11 and 6.12.

of the target. In general, for rougher surfaces the multiple scattered component dominates, while the contribution from the transmitted component increases for smoother surfaces.

To understand how the polarization of the emitted energy varies with view angles, we need to look at the polarized behavior of the two components illustrated in Fig. 11.19(a). This is done in Fig. 11.19(b) where we have, as in Fig. 6.14, doubled the contribution from the parallel (||) and perpendicular ($\perp$) components such that the average value should correspond to the total emittance shown in Fig. 11.19(a). To begin, we see that the surface emission is random, and the random orientation of facets will tend to cause the multiple scattered radiation to also be approximately random such that the parallel and perpendicular components are approximately equal. Note that once again symmetry dictates that there will be equal contributions at angles on either side of vertical, so we do not expect to see any contribution that would result in deviation of the S_2 Stokes parameters from zero.

Unlike the surface term, the transmitted term is governed by the Fresnel equations and will result in polarized terms, as illustrated in Fig. 11.19(b). Here we see that the perpendicularly polarized radiation is preferentially reflected at the interface and the parallel component preferentially transmitted. The net result is that the transmitted lobe has a greater contribution of parallel polarized radiation. Note that the transmission at nadir is the same for both polarizations, and at angles well away from nadir is zero for both polarizations. This results in no polarization contrast when viewing perpendicular to the target (i.e., at nadir for horizontal targets) and at extreme grazing angles. The two components of this conceptual emissivity model combine to yield the final angular emissivity as shown in Fig. 11.19(b). Note that the total emissivity would be the average of the two curves as seen in Fig. 11.19(a), and that the DoP due to only the emissive component would be equal to the difference over the sum of the final curves in the illustration.

This conceptual model indicates that the DoP should increase from zero as the view angle increases away from the normal to the surface, and should go through a maximum near grazing and then decrease rapidly to zero at grazing. It also implies that the polarization defined relative to the surface normal should always appear in the S_1 component and always be negative (i.e., parallel dominant over perpendicular). Finally, recall that we need to combine the emissive contribution of surface leaving radiance with the reflected component (which will tend to have a positive S_1 term) to generate the net radiance and polarization that will be observed (see Fig. 11.18).

This chapter introduced a thermal pBRDF model built on the reflective pBRDF models introduced in Chapter 6. To take advantage of these models, we need to make measurements that can calibrate them (i.e., estimate the value of the free parameters) for various materials. In the next chapter we will present a simple method to take measurements to calibrate these models and then show how these thermal pBRDF models can be utilized in synthetic scene generation models to study end-to-end polarization phenomenology.

References

Cremer, F., de Jong, W., & Schutte, K. (2002). "Infrared polarization measurements and modeling applied to surface-laid antipersonnel landmines." *Optical Engineering*, Vol. 41, No. 5, pp. 1021–1032.

Forssell, G. (2001). "Surface landmine and trip-wire detection using calibrated polarization measurements in the LWIR and SWIR." *Proceedings SPIE*, Vol. 4491, pp. 41–51.

Gartley, M.G., Brown, S.D., Goodenough, A.D., Sanders, N.J., & Schott, J.R. (2007). "Polarimetric scene modeling in the thermal infrared." *Proceedings SPIE*, Vol. 6682, 66820C.

Gartley, M.G. (2007). "Polarimetric Modeling of Remotely Sensed Scenes in the Thermal Infrared." Doctoral dissertation, Rochester Institute of Technology, Rochester.

Gurton, K. & Dahmani, R. (2005). "Effect of surface roughness and complex indices of refraction on polarized thermal emission." *Applied Optics*. Vol. 44, No. 26, pp. 5361–5367.

Jordan, D.L. & Lewis, G. (1994). "Measurements of the effect of surface roughness on the polarization state of thermally emitted radiation." *Optical Letters*, Vol. 19, No. 10, pp. 692–694.

Jordan, D.L., Lewis, G.D., & Jakeman, E. (1996). "Emission polarization of roughened glass and aluminum surfaces." *Applied Optics*, Vol. 35, No. 19, pp. 3583–3590.

Maxwell, J.R., Beard, J., Weiner, S., Ladd, D., & Ladd, S. (1973). "Bidirectional reflectance model validation and utilization." *Technical Report AFAL-TR-73-303*, Environmental Research Institute of Michigan (ERIM).

Pesses, M., Tan, J., Hash, R., & Swartz, R. (2002). "Simulation of LWIR polarimetric observations of space objects." *IEEE Computer Society Proceedings of the 31st Applied Imagery Pattern Recognition Workshop*, pp. 164–170.

Priest, R.G., & Germer, T.A. (2002). "Polarimetric BRDF in the microfacet model: theory and measurements." *Proceedings of the 2000 Meeting of the Military Sensing Symposia Specialty Group on Passive Sensors*, Vol. 1, pp. 169–181.

Shaw, J.A. (2007). "A survey of infrared polarization in the outdoors." *Proceedings SPIE*, Vol. 6660, 666006.

Torrance, K.E., & Sparrow, E.M. (1967). "Theory for off-specular reflection from roughened surfaces." *Journal of the Optical Society of America A*, Vol. 57, No. 9, pp. 1105–1114.

Tyo, J.S., Goldstein, D.L., Chenault, D.B., & Shaw, J.A. (2006). "Review of passive imaging polarimetry for remote sensing applications." *Applied Optics*, Vol. 45, No. 22, pp. 5453–5469.

Tyo, J.S., Boger, J.K., Ratliff, B.M., Bowers, D.L., Black, W.T., & Fetrow, M.P. (2007). "The effects of thermal equilibrium and thermal contrast in polarimetric images in the LWIR." *Optics Express*, Vol. 15, pp. 15161–15167.

Michael G. Gartley
John R. Schott

Chapter 12
LWIR pBRDF Measurements and Modeling

This chapter builds on the thermal infrared principles introduced in Chapter 11 and parallels the simple measurements and synthetic scene modeling approach for reflective imaging polarimetry presented in Chapter 10. In Chapter 11, we introduced thermal infrared pBRDF models and the parameters they depend on. In this chapter we will look at one simple method using field measurements to calibrate pBRDF models. This method was selected based on the author's familiarity with it, for consistency with the pBRDF models presented in Chapter 11, and for its use in the scene simulation modeling presented in Sec. 12.2.

12.1 Measurement of Polarized Emissivity and pBRDF Estimation

This section describes a simple field procedure for measuring pBRDF values and ways to use these measurements to calibrate pBRDF models. The approach draws on Gartley et al. (2007) and Gartley (2007).

12.1.1 Measurement approach

Before making polarized emissivity measurements and generating infrared Stokes image sets, it makes good sense to first understand the key radiometric terms involved in the radiance reaching the front of an IR polarimeter. A system design must be developed that pays careful attention to the environmental conditions as well as to hardware constraints. The images collected and the algorithms utilized to extract thermal emissivity from them will utilize the radiometric terms and the key design points presented in this section.

Consider a generic infrared camera equipped with a linear polarizer having rotation capability. Let the rotation angle of the polarizer be designated by an orientation angle α. Let us also assume that the target-to-camera path transmission loss is negligible.

Five radiometric terms (see Fig. 12.1) contribute to the total radiance reaching an infrared sensor through an infrared *wire grid polarizer* (WGP):

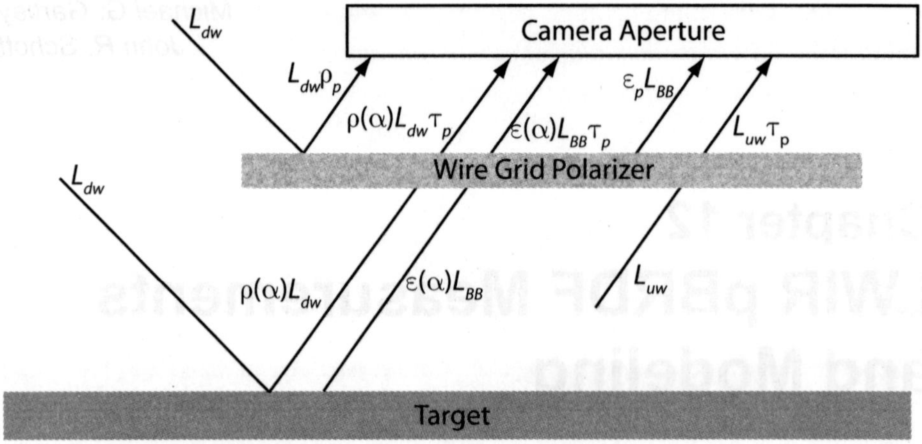

Figure 12.1 Illustration of relevant radiometric terms.

1. Downwelled radiance reflected from the target: $\rho(\alpha)L_{dw}\tau_p$
2. Thermally emitted radiance from the target: $\varepsilon(\alpha)L_{BB}\tau_p$
3. Upwelled radiance from the path between the target and polarizer: $L_{uw}\tau_p$
4. Downwelled radiance reflected from the polarizer surface: $\rho_p L_{dw}$
5. Thermally emitted radiance from the polarizer surface: $\varepsilon_p L_{BB}$,

where L_{dw} represents the downwelled radiance, L_{uw} the upwelled radiance, ρ_p the reflectivity of the polarizer for randomly polarized light, ε_p the emissivity of the polarizer, τ_p the transmission of the polarizer for randomly polarized light, L_{BB} the radiance coming from a blackbody at ambient temperature, $\varepsilon(\alpha)$ the target emissivity, and $\rho(\alpha)$ the target reflectivity.

Therefore, the total radiance incident on the camera aperture is

$$L(\alpha) = \tau_p(\rho(\alpha)L_{dw} + L_{uw} + \varepsilon(\alpha)L_{BB}(T)) + \varepsilon_p L_{BB}(T) + \rho_p L_{dw}, \quad (12.1)$$

where the variable T is the ambient air temperature.

For this experimental setup, we assume that the upwelled radiance (over 1 to 2 m) between the sample and the camera is insignificant such that $L_{uw} = 0$. Thus, Eq. (12.1) simplifies to

$$L(\alpha) = \tau_p[\rho(\alpha)L_{dw} + \varepsilon(\alpha)L_{BB}(T)] + \varepsilon_p L_{BB}(T) + \rho_p L_{dw}. \quad (12.2)$$

Drawing on Young et al. (1965), we can make the assumption that the emissivity of the wire grid polarizer is negligible ($\varepsilon_p L_{BB} = 0$). Then we can solve for the target emissivity ($\varepsilon(\alpha)$) as a function of WGP orientation angle (α):

$$\varepsilon(\alpha) = \frac{L(\alpha) - \tau_p L_{dw} - \rho_p L_{dw}}{\tau_p(L_{BB}(T) - L_{dw})}. \quad (12.3)$$

Recall that if the emissivity of the wire grid polarizer is approximately zero, we can write the Kirchoff's law relation for the polarizer as

$$\tau_p + \rho_p = 1, \tag{12.4}$$

allowing us to further reduce Eq. (12.3) to

$$\varepsilon(\alpha) = \frac{L(\alpha) - L_{dw}}{\tau_p (L_{BB}(T) - L_{dw})}. \tag{12.5}$$

Ideally, we could utilize the internal calibration of the LWIR camera and derive the blackbody radiance term (L_{BB}) from the camera metadata. The camera metadata often provides a relationship between digital count values and scene temperature, assuming each material has an emissivity of 1.0. Knowing the band-pass of the camera and the measured temperature allows us to derive an effective blackbody radiance value. However, repeated attempts demonstrated the internal calibration of the camera was not repeatable and accurate, requiring a user-based calibration method to compensate for calibration variation due to instrument temperature variation (see Fig. 12.7 and related discussion).

In order to derive the downwelled sky dome radiance term (L_{dw}), we can include a 100% longwave IR reflector in the scene. A readily available reflector in this wavelength region is aluminum foil. We include a diffuse IR reflector and a specular IR reflector in each target scene. This feature allows us to choose an IR reflector that is closest to the surface roughness of the sample target of interest.

Plugging values of $\rho = 1$ and $\varepsilon = 0$ into Eq. (12.1) gives us the radiance L_{100} we expect to see at the camera aperture from the direction of the approximately unit IR reflector as

$$L_{100}(T) = \tau_p L_{dw} + \varepsilon_p L_{BB}(T) + \rho_p L_{dw}. \tag{12.6}$$

We can again utilize Eq. (12.4) to further reduce this expression to

$$L_{100}(T) = L_{dw}. \tag{12.7}$$

The next step is to solve for the target emissivity ($\varepsilon(\alpha)$) utilizing our knowledge of L_{dw} in Eq. (12.5) to yield

$$\varepsilon(\alpha) = \frac{L(\alpha, T) - L_{100}}{\tau_p (L_{BB}(T) - L_{100})}. \tag{12.8}$$

The only unknown on the right hand side of Eq. (12.8) is the radiance due to the temperature of the target, which is easily computed from the Planck equation if the temperature is known. The temperature can either be measured with contact thermistors or assumed to be approximately equal to the air temperature under stable nighttime conditions.

Since we are primarily interested in measuring infrared emissivity, not reflectivity, we need to define the critical system design constraints. Thermal radi-

Figure 12.2 EZTherm LWIR camera and IR wire grid polarizer.

ance incident onto the target sample surfaces must be kept much lower than the thermally emitted radiance. Inspection of Eq. (12.8) demonstrates that once the downwelled radiance level approaches the thermally emitted radiance level, the fraction is numerically unstable and noisy. The system requirements are:

- The system must operate under nighttime conditions to avoid solar heating of target surfaces, and under conditions where exposed surfaces are approximately at air temperature.
- The system must operate under ambient thermal conditions, requiring no sample heating or cooling.
- Ideally, the camera would operate under ambient thermal conditions, requiring no cooling of the focal plane. This allows for rapid deployment of the imaging system to a wide variety of locations not equipped with a cryogenic coolant.
- The atmospheric conditions must be thermally stable. An acceptable rate of change in air temperature is $<1\,^{\circ}\mathrm{C}$ over 30 min. Not only do we not want the sample temperatures to change during a measurement cycle, we also want the rate of change to be slow enough that the sample temperatures track well with the ambient air temperature in order to ensure consistency between multiple samples within a scene.
- A polarizer that has high transmission and high contrast ratio in the long-wave region of the spectrum.
- An experimental setup capable of measuring emission zenith angles ranging from 0 to 80 deg.
- To meet the camera design constraints, the EZTherm long-wave infrared camera (Fig. 12.2) was chosen for imaging. The focal plane array of this camera is an uncooled barium-strontium-titinate (BST) material. Contrary to common CCD operation where charge is collected and proportional to scene intensity, the BST material produces a measurable resistance change as a function of temperature gradient. The focal plane has a temperature sweet spot where it is most sensitive, requiring active focal plane temperature control. The pixel pitch is 50-μm square and the array is capable of

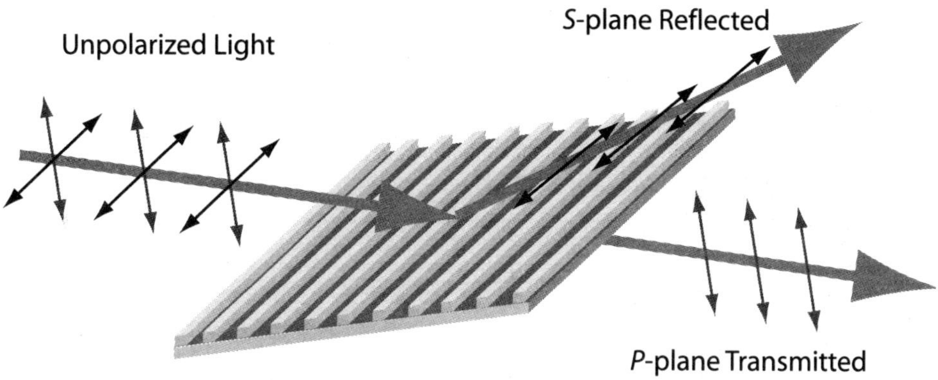

Figure 12.3 Illustration showing how a wire grid polarizer reflects one polarization state and transmits another.

12-bit digitization. The camera is capable of measuring blackbody temperatures between −20 and 500° C.

The effective focal length of the optics is 35 mm, while the primary aperture size is 29 mm, resulting in an f/1.2 imager. The camera has a specified noise equivalent delta temperature (NEDT) of 0.080K. The manufacturer designs the camera to operate between −10 and +40°C ambient air temperature.

The image data is accompanied by useful metadata such as air temperature, internal camera temperature, capture time, and date. In addition, the camera is battery operated and housed in a camcorder case, allowing data collection almost anywhere.

The polarizer chosen was a wire grid polarizer manufactured by Molectron (Fig. 12.2). The polarizer has a 75-mm diameter clear aperture. The wire grid is a fine micropatterned mesh of aluminum wires on a ZnSe substrate. An important property of wire grid polarizers, whether in the visible or infrared region of the spectrum, is that they both transmit and reflect light (see Fig. 12.3). More specifically, EM radiation that oscillates parallel to the patterned lines of the wire grid is reflected, while light that oscillates perpendicular to the grid pattern is transmitted. Wire grid polarizers are often superior to other types of polarizers due to their high contrast ratio and high transmission factors. The spectral transmission of the polarizer for incident radiance having its electric field vector perpendicular to the direction of the wire grid lines is shown in Fig. 12.4. A perfect polarizer would nominally have a transmission value of 1 for this plot, indicating that it transmits all of the light of the preferred polarization state. The contrast ratio, defined as the amount of light transmitted with the appropriate polarization state compared to the amount of light transmitted with the orthogonal polarization state, is reported by the manufacturer to be better than 400:1. Thus, the transmission of the polarizer to randomly polarized flux (τ_p) is approximately one-half of the value shown in Fig. 12.4.

Simply putting the IR polarizer in front of the uncooled LWIR camera not only reduces the scene radiance incident on the camera aperture, it also reflects

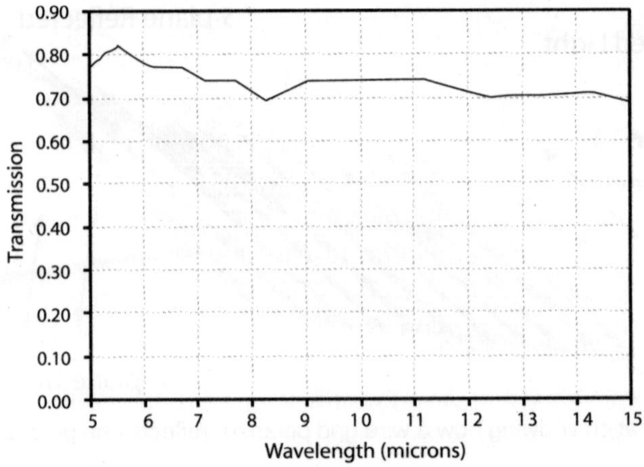

Figure 12.4 Spectral transmission of WGP for incident radiance with electric field vector perpendicular to the wire grid lines.

the thermally emitted radiance from the inside of the camera assembly. The first problem this causes is a nonuniform ghost image of the inside of the camera superimposed onto the scene image. In addition, the shot noise induced by the ghost image drastically increases the NEDT of the resulting image.

The solution is to tip the polarizer at an angle relative to the camera aperture. The polarizer can be tipped to an angle that ensures that the radiance reflected from its surface comes from a uniform and cold source. For this experimental setup, we choose to tip the polarizer such that it reflects the nighttime, cloud-free sky. An attractive alternative is to use a cooled reflectance chamber, but the overall aim here is to keep the system as simple as possible to permit wide-scale use of the approach. Nominally, the camera and polarizer are oriented as shown in Fig. 12.5 for best noise performance.

Since we have fixed the camera to have an approximate look angle of 45 deg to the ground, the sample platform must be adjustable to allow measurement of emissivity for zenith angles between 0 and 80 deg. This can be accomplished by assembling a sample stage that is approximately 0.6×0.6 m in size attached to a camera tripod with tip/tilt/rotate capability. The sample stage is made of lightweight particle board and fastened by machine screws to the camera tripod. Accurate tip angle measurements are made possible by utilizing a digital protractor. Figure 12.5 shows the relative orientation of the imaging system and the sample platform. The digital protractor measures the angle δ, which is related to the emission zenith angle to the camera by

$$\theta_{emission} = 45\,\text{deg} - \delta. \tag{12.9}$$

Orienting the sample platform at an angle of +45 deg results in a sample zenith of 0 deg toward the camera. Orienting the sample platform at an angle of 0 deg relative to the normal to the ground plane results in a measurement zenith

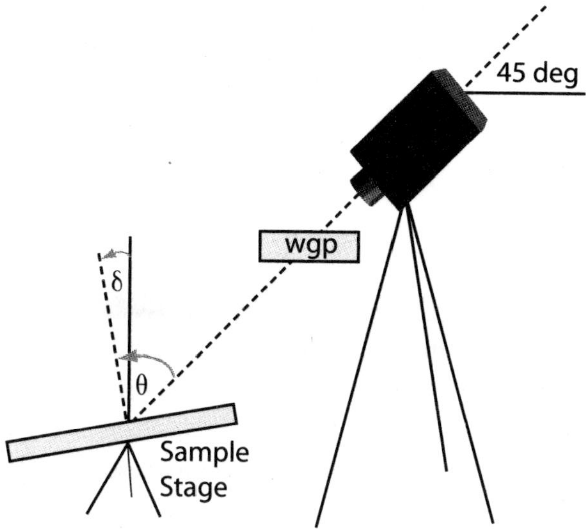

Figure 12.5 Illustration showing the relative alignment of the IR camera assembly and sample measurement stage.

angle of 45 deg. To obtain an extra degree of freedom, the camera tripod may be rotated about its primary axis to allow azimuthal rotation of sample surfaces.

12.1.2 Image data collection

Two types of image collections can be acquired with this system. The first type of collection is done in order to experimentally determine the polarized emissivity of target and background materials, herein referred to as an emissivity collection. The second is simply to generate Stokes vector images. Emissivity collections require masking of the imaging system and operator with a wall of aluminum foil. The ground surrounding the target sample stage is also covered with aluminum foil. The intent of the aluminum foil in both cases is to limit infrared radiance from the camera, the operator, and the ground from reflecting off the target materials. The emissivity measurement technique works best when the amount of thermal radiance incident on the target surfaces is much less than the amount of thermally emitted radiance. To accomplish this, the imaging measurements are always done at night under a starlit sky. In addition, the emissivity collection scenarios require embedding a glossy (pressed flat) aluminum foil target and a diffuse aluminum foil target on the sample stage to facilitate accurate measurement of downwelled radiance. For smooth target surfaces such as glossy paints and glass, the flat aluminum target is utilized to determine downwelled radiance. For rough target surfaces such as flat (diffuse) paints and soil, the diffuse aluminum foil target is utilized to estimate the level of downwelled radiance.

The concept for this approach is to have the reflecting foil target approximate the shape of the reflectance distribution function of the target surface in order to more accurately determine how much radiance is indeed reflected from the target

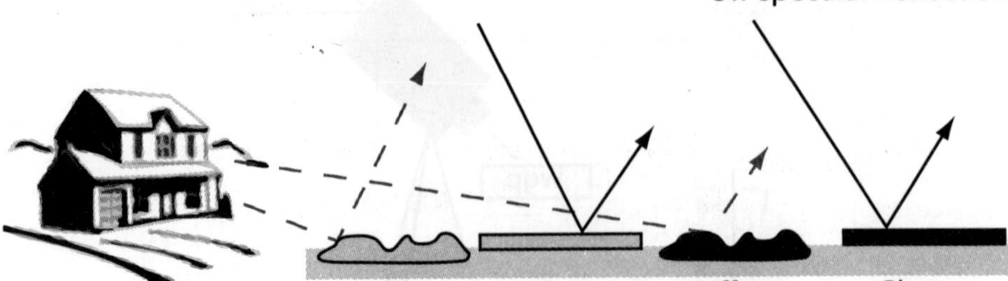

Figure 12.6 Illustration showing the importance of including a diffuse and a glossy calibration target.

surface. For example, consider a scene with a majority of the hemisphere above the sample stage consisting of the sky dome, except for a single house far off at a grazing angle (see Fig. 12.6). When the camera is viewing close to nadir, a glossy target will not reflect the house but a diffuse target will partially reflect the house. It is important that the reflecting foil target samples the hemisphere above the targets for incident radiance in a fashion similar to the way the target samples that same hemisphere. Although many varying degrees of roughness could be included to refine this concept, including simple types of reflecting targets is often sufficient if the reflected downwelled radiance is small compared to the emissive term.

Figure 12.7 illustrates the image processing flow to convert raw image data to a radiance image suitable for further analysis. The raw signal out of the camera is bias subtracted and converted to nominal temperature using the internal camera calibration. The nominal temperatures are then mapped to apparent blackbody temperatures using a calibration transfer function developed by the sensor imaging a cavity radiator over a range of known temperatures. Depending on the uniformity of the camera, this may be done with a single function or a pixel-by-pixel transform.

Next, the calibrated temperature image is converted to a calibrated aperture-reaching radiance image. The functional relationship between the calibrated temperature and aperture-reaching radiance image is determined by fitting a third-order polynomial to the value of the Planck function for temperatures between 220 and 320K in 1-deg increments, i.e.,

$$L(T) = \int \frac{2hc^2}{\lambda^5} \frac{1}{e^{hc/\lambda kT} - 1} d\lambda, \tag{12.10}$$

where the limits of integration are the sensor bandwidth.

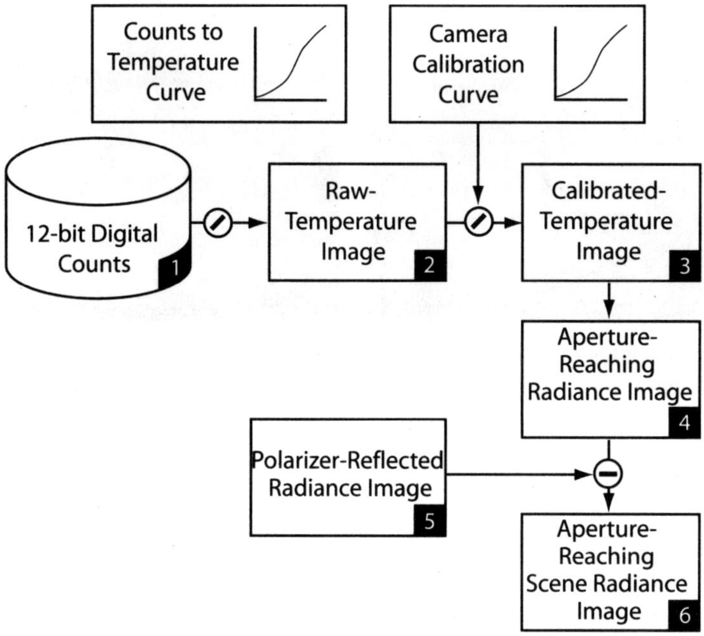

Figure 12.7 Processing flow for experimentally acquired image data.

The third-order polynomial that was a best fit between radiance and temperature was found to be

$$L(T) = 0.010225614 - 1.012849 \cdot 10^{-4} T + 2.382483 \cdot 10^{-7} T^2 + 1.552269 \cdot 10^{-10} T^3. \quad (12.11)$$

The variance between the polynomial form and rigorous integration was found to be negligible. An example of a calibrated aperture-reaching radiance image is shown on the left hand side of Fig. 12.8.

Next, the calibrated aperture-reaching radiance image is converted to an aperture-reaching scene-leaving radiance image by removing the effects of the wire grid polarizer reflections. For each collection scenario, a flat aluminum foil target is placed in front of the wire grid polarizer such that it reflects the downwelled skydome radiance. The illustration in Fig. 12.9 shows this configuration. An example of a WGP calibration image is shown on the right hand side of Fig. 12.8. For the WGP calibration image, the governing equation is

$$L_{WGP} = \rho_p L_{dw} + \tau_p L_{dw} = L_{dw}. \quad (12.12)$$

In order to remove only the polarizer-reflected radiance, the WGP calibration image is scaled by $(1-\tau_p)$, which is the same as ρ_p (derived from Fig. 12.4). In addition to removing polarizer-reflected radiance, this processing step also serves as a flat-fielding step. The image presented in Fig. 12.10 is an example of a scene-leaving aperture-reaching (SLAR) radiance image.

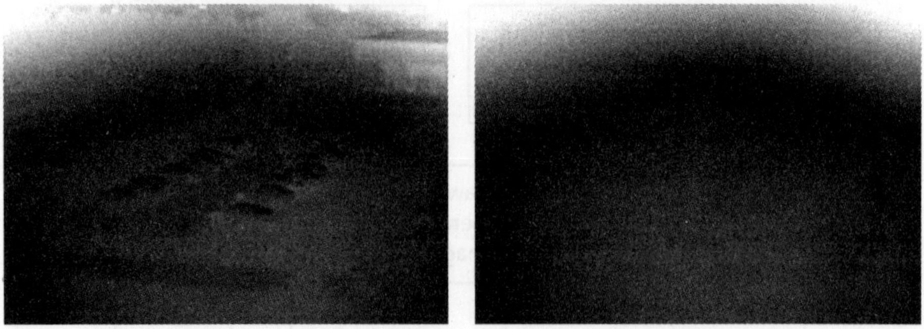

Figure 12.8 Examples of a calibrated aperture reaching radiance image (left) and a WGP calibration image (right).

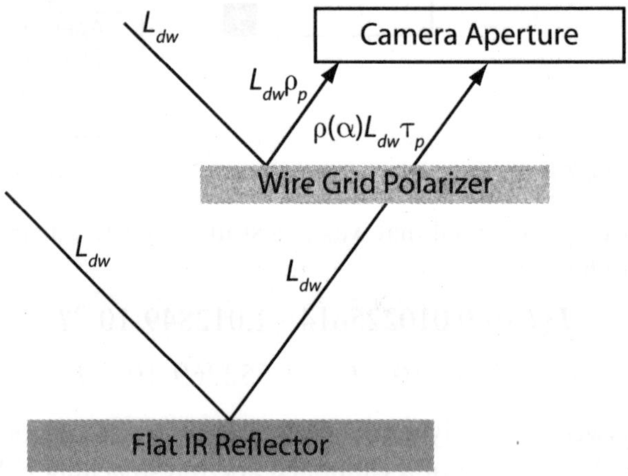

Figure 12.9 Illustration of radiance-reaching camera for WGP calibration image acquisition.

Figure 12.10 Example of surface-leaving aperture-reaching radiance image with polarizer at 0-deg orientation.

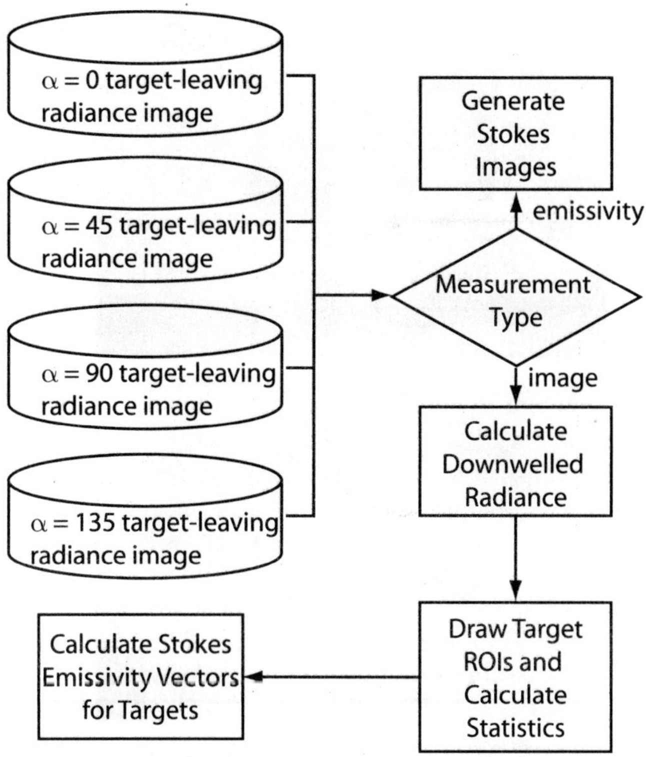

Figure 12.11 Processing paths for Stokes-generated imagery and emissivity measurements.

Once the aperture-reaching scene-leaving radiance image is produced, two distinct data processing paths may be followed. The flowchart in Fig. 12.11 shows these two paths, one to generate Stokes images of a scene and one to generate polarized emissivity values from a specific experimental setup.

For image data that is intended to be processed into Stokes images, the four image bands are simply combined as shown in Eqs. (12.13) through (12.15) to form S_0, S_1, and S_2 images. Recall that there is no S_3 image data due to the lack of a circular polarizer in the experimental setup.

$$S_0 = \frac{1}{2}[L_{SLAR}(0) + L_{SLAR}(45) + L_{SLAR}(90) + L_{SLAR}(135)]. \tag{12.13}$$

$$S_1 = L_{SLAR}(0) - L_{SLAR}(90). \tag{12.14}$$

$$S_2 = L_{SLAR}(45) - L_{SLAR}(135). \tag{12.15}$$

Recall also that when the polarizer is oriented at 0 and 90 deg, the camera system is measuring the horizontal and vertical polarization states, respectively, of the scene-leaving radiance. Although the S_0 images may be generated as a combination of the 0- and 90-deg or 45- and 135-deg radiance images, we have chosen to add all four images and then divide by two in order to reduce the NEDT

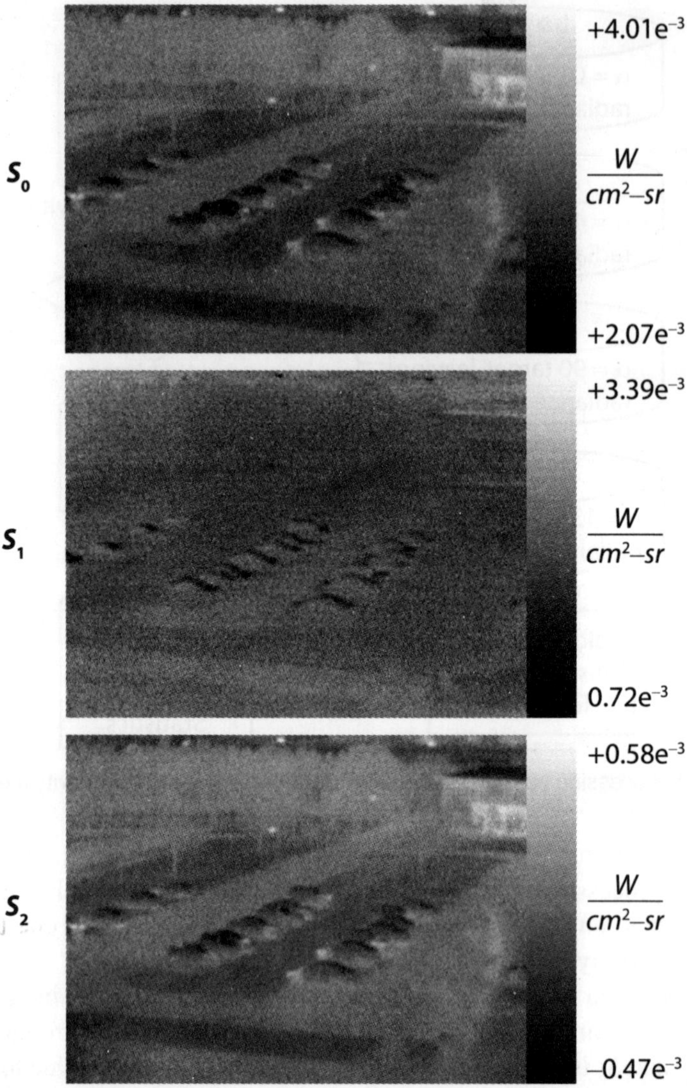

Figure 12.12 Image examples of processed Stokes radiance bands S_0, S_1, and S_2.

of the resulting S_0 image. Figure 12.12 shows an example of the Stokes S_0, S_1, and S_2 images produced following this path.

12.1.3 Emissivity model parameter fitting

In this section, we present a simple manual procedure for fitting the pBRDF measurements described in Sec. 12.1.2 to the pBRDF emissivity model introduced in Chapter 11. Note that a multiparameter fit could be employed to minimize the difference between observed and modeled values. However, we have chosen to use a simple manual procedure to illustrate the approach. The manual procedure can be utilized to fit the experimentally measured Stokes S_0 and S_1 emissivity to the

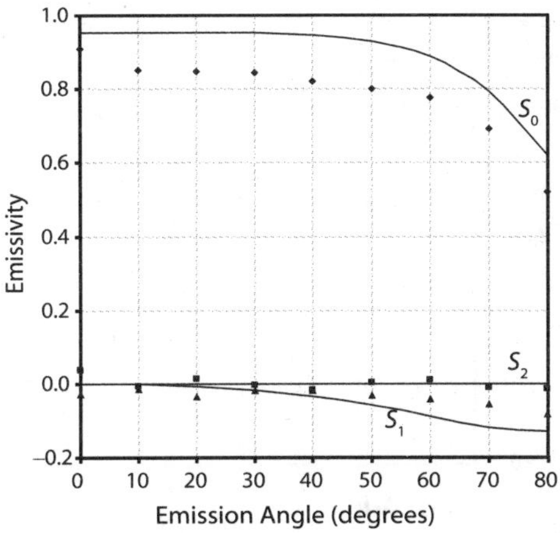

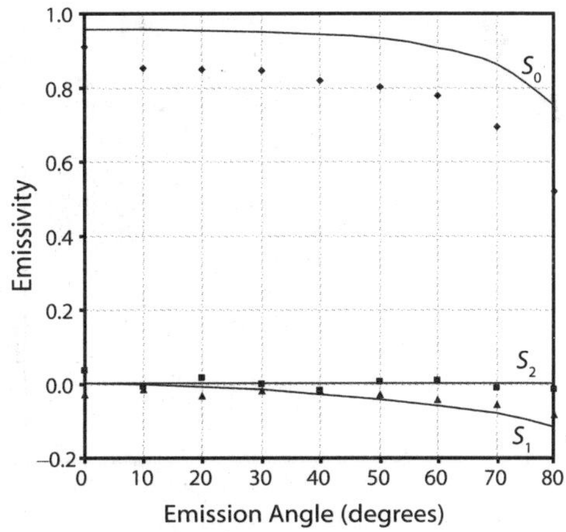

Figure 12.13 Plot of Stokes emissivity before (left) and after (right) Step 1 of fitting process. The points represent measurements and the curves represent modeled data for a pine board. Step 1 of the fitting process consists of choosing the σ parameter such that the general shape of the S_1 curve follows experimental data.

polarized emissivity model described in Chapter 11. The key model parameters driving the fit were determined to be the complex index of refraction, the diffuse reflectivity, the probability distribution function variability (σ), and the bias parameters. The following steps were followed for each material.

Parameter Fitting Step 1

As a starting point for each material, the σ, bias, and n and k values for a comparable NEF database material were chosen. A visual assessment of the initial fit between model-predicted and measured S_0 and S_1 emissivity was made. The plot on the left in Fig. 12.13 shows an example of the results for a pine board at this point.

Based on this assessment, the σ value of the emissivity model probability distribution function was varied such that the general shape of the modeled S_1 curve followed the general shape of the measured S_1 curve. The plot on the right in Fig. 12.13 shows an example of the results for a pine board after this step.

Parameter Fitting Step 2

Once a σ value was chosen, the bias value associated with the emissivity model probability distribution function was varied to bring the best visual fit of both the shape and magnitude of the S_1 curve (in that the bias value directly scales the amount of modeled specular reflections and therefore the magnitude of the S_1 curve). The plot on the left in Fig. 12.14 shows an example of the results for a pine board after this step.

Parameter Fitting Step 3

Once the σ and bias values were chosen such that a good visual fit exists between measured and modeled S_1 emissivity, the fit between the modeled and measured S_0 emissivity was visually examined. Starting with values of

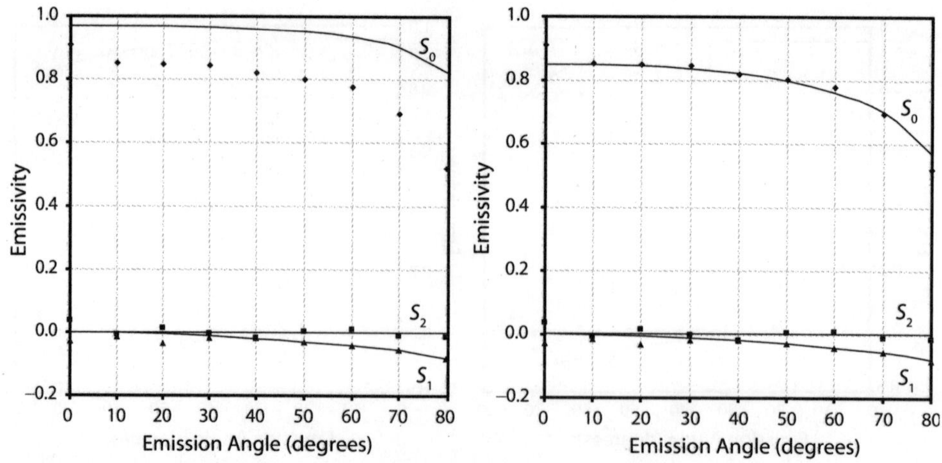

Figure 12.14 Plot of Stokes emissivity after Step 2 (left) and after Step 3 (right) of the fitting process. The points represent measurements and the curves represent modeled values for a pine board. Step 2 consists of adjusting the polarized BRDF bias parameter to get the S_1 modeled curve to match experimental data, while Step 3 consists of adjusting the ρ_V and ρ_d terms to drop the modeled S_0 emissivity down to the experimental data.

$\rho_d = 0$ and $\rho_v = 0$, the modeled S_0 emissivity was always higher than the measured value of S_0 emissivity. Therefore, the final step was to vary the values of ρ_d and ρ_v to obtain the final fit. If the gap between the measured and modeled S_0 curve was close to constant across all zenith angles, then only the value of ρ_d was increased. However, in some cases the gap between the measured and modeled S_0 curves was slowly increasing with increasing zenith angle, warranting an increase in both ρ_d and ρ_v to make up the difference. The plot on the right in Fig. 12.14 shows an example of the final modeled and measured results for a pine board.

The polarized BRDF parameters that produce the best-fit Stokes emissivity vector for emission angles between 0 and 80 deg for a sample of materials are

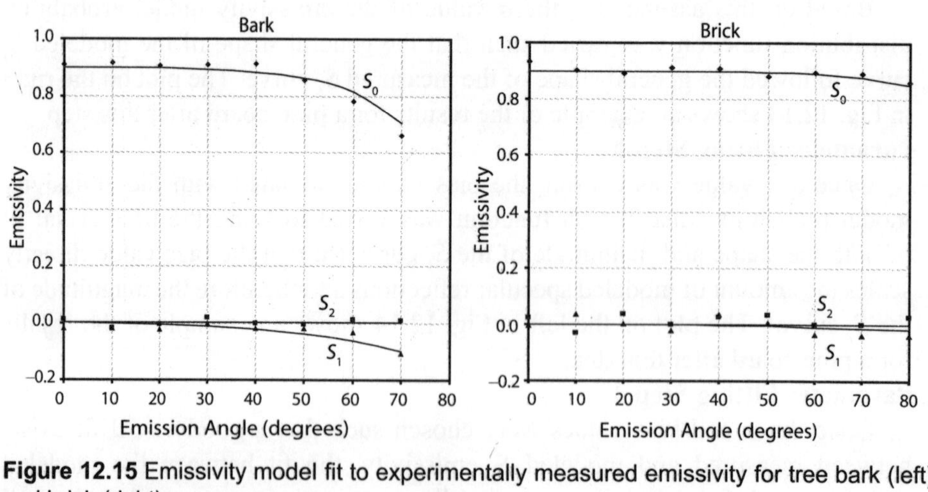

Figure 12.15 Emissivity model fit to experimentally measured emissivity for tree bark (left) and brick (right).

Table 12.1 Summary of polarized BRDF paramters that produce a polarized emissivity best-fit experimentally measured emissivity.

materials	σ	bias	n	k	ρ_D	ρ_v	DHR
bark	0.10	0.20	1.3	0.0	3.1E-02	1.0E-07	0.1007
brick	0.04	1.30	1.3	0.0	3.0E-07	2.0E-02	0.0992
cement	0.10	0.70	1.3	0.0	3.0E-07	1.0E-03	0.0503
flat black paint	0.25	1.30	1.3	0.4	1.1E-02	1.0E-07	0.0914
fresh asphalt	0.50	1.30	1.4	0.0	1.1E-05	1.0E-07	0.0286
glass	0.01	1.15	1.5	0.0	6.0E-20	2.0E-08	0.0440
glossy black paint	0.05	1.30	1.4	0.4	1.1E-05	1.0E-07	0.0699
glossy tan paint	0.02	1.15	1.5	0.4	6.0E-20	2.0E-08	0.0725
grass	0.10	0.20	1.3	0.0	6.1E-03	1.0E-07	0.0225
hood of car	0.02	1.15	1.5	0.0	6.0E-20	2.0E-08	0.0453
particle board	0.25	0.80	1.3	0.4	1.0E-03	3.0E-02	0.1538
pine wood	0.12	1.00	1.8	0.8	1.0E-11	1.0E-07	0.1487
shingle	0.12	0.50	1.8	0.8	1.0E-20	1.0E-20	0.0743
snow	0.10	0.20	1.3	0.0	4.1E-02	1.0E-07	0.1322
soil	0.10	0.05	1.3	0.0	2.5E-02	1.0E-07	0.0794
weathered asphalt	0.30	0.50	2.0	0.5	3.0E-10	2.0E-10	0.0623

listed in Table 12.1. Figures 12.15 through 12.19 show the agreement between the modeled (solid curves) and measured polarized emissivity (data points) for a sample of the materials. The asterisks correspond to measured S_0 emissivity, the triangles to measured S_1, and the squares to measured S_2 emissivity.

Note that most of the measured emissivity curves show anomalous results at an emission angle of 0 deg due to the fact that the target samples were reflecting the camera system and operator. This condition violates the assumption that the amount of background radiance reflected from the sample surfaces is minimized. Although the glossy and diffuse IR reflecting targets in the scene are meant to capture this background reflected radiance, for adequate removal of background radiance, the intensity of the radiance from the operator and camera requires a much better match in surface roughness between the reflectors and the sample surfaces. Therefore, in most cases, the emissivity values at a zenith of 0 deg were ignored during the parameter fitting process. This approach is intended to provide a simple field-capable example of a way to measure the pBRDF emissivity of materials. There are much higher fidelity means of measuring pBRDF [Fetrow et al. (2002)] that should be utilized when higher fidelity measurments are required. In the next section, we will show examples of how the pBRDF models developed here can be utilized on synthetic image generation models to help visualize the polarimetric behavior of scenes.

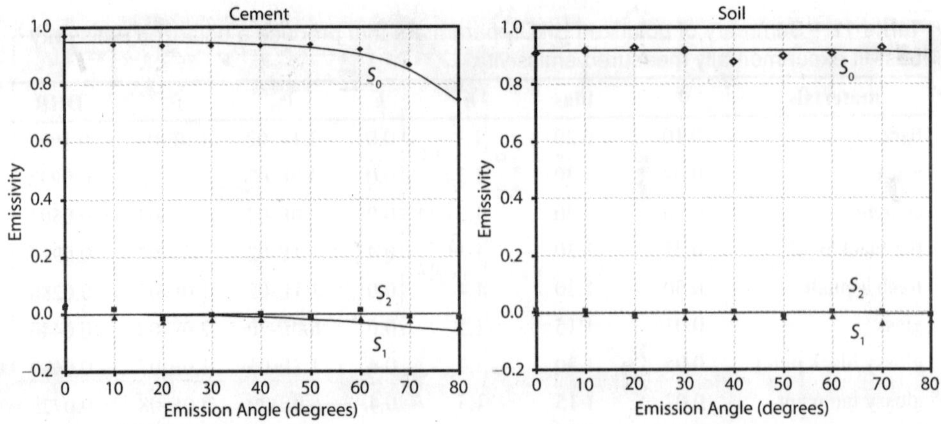

Figure 12.16 Emissivity model fit to experimentally measured emissivity for cement (left) and soil (right).

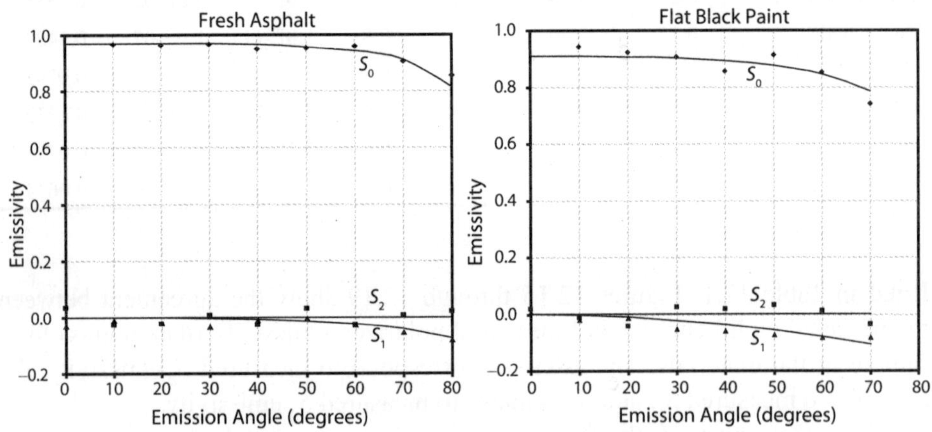

Figure 12.17 Emissivity model fit to experimentally measured emissivity for fresh asphalt (left) and flat black paint (right).

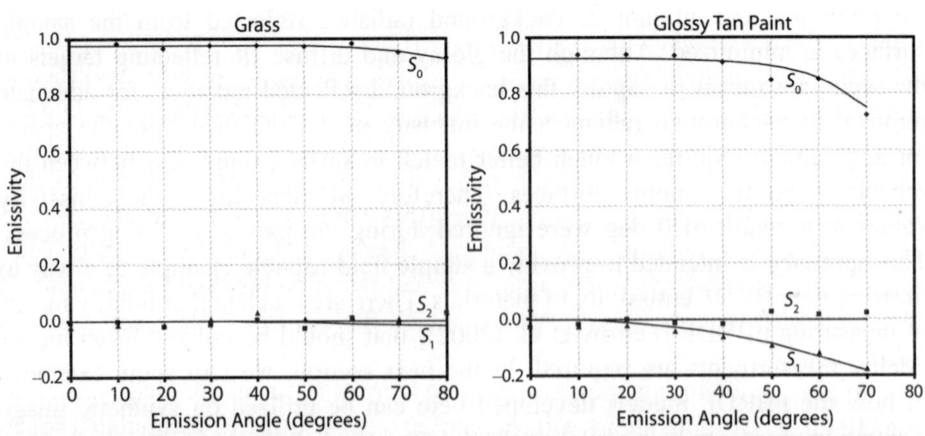

Figure 12.18 Emissivity model fit to experimentally measured emissivity for grass (left) and glossy tan paint (right).

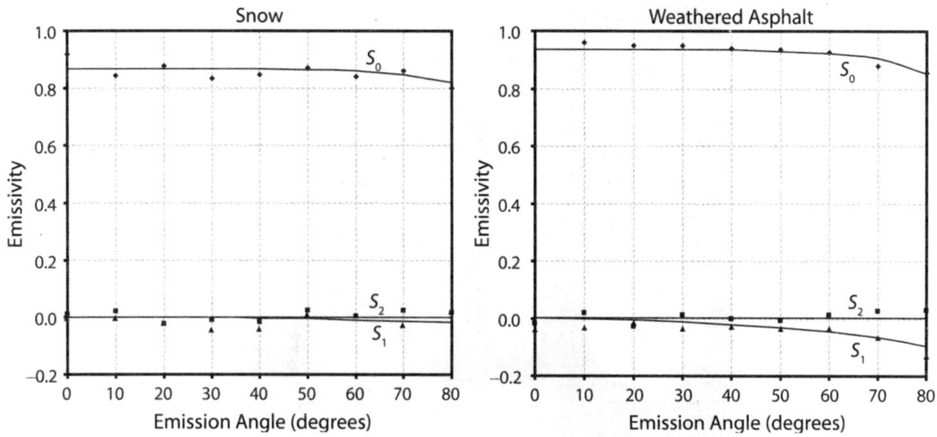

Figure 12.19 Emissivity model fit to experimentally measured emissivity for snow (left) and weathered asphalt (right).

12.2 Thermal Infrared Polarimetric Scene Simulation

As discussed throughout this text, the combination of target-background-sensor phenomenology can be quite complex. In order to understand or estimate what signatures may be observed by a polarimetric sensor, a model of all of the relevant source functions and interactions is required. Fetrow et al. (2002) describe a parametric model that simulates thermal infrared polarimetric target-background interactions and radiation propagation. Sadjadi and Chun (2004) show results using the AFRL's *Irma* scene simulation model to generate thermal infrared polarimetric image products. In this section we will use the DIRSIG model [Schott (2007)] to illustrate how the pBRDF models described in the previous section can be incorporated into the synthetic image generation process to help understand thermal polarimetric phenomenology and to predict signatures.

The DIRSIG model was introduced in Chapter 10 and has been described in numerous publications [Schott et al. (1999), Robinson et al. (2000), and Schott (2007)]. Recent enhancements have included incorporation of reflective polarization phenomenology [Meyers (2002) and Shell and Schott (2005)] and thermal polarization phenomenology [Gartley et al. (2007)]. The details of the DIRSIG model are beyond the scope of this text. For our purposes the reader should simply recognize that it incorporates CAD models for scene geometry construction, thermal models to predict target temperatures (this can be overridden if temperatures are known), pBRDF models of material behavior, and radiative transfer codes (e.g., MODTRAN) to predict illumination and radiation propagation phenomena. When coupled with models of the sensor, full Stokes vector images of synthetic scenes can be produced.

To provide an introduction to simulated thermal polarimetric images, consider Fig. 12.20. This figure shows a linear Stokes vector image of a simulated sphere used to evaluate the performance of the models during code development. The

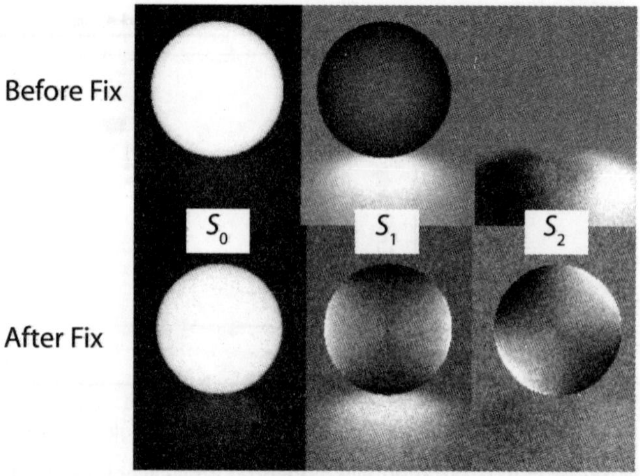

Figure 12.20 DIRSIG simulations showing the effect of a recent code change to incorporate relative orientation of each facet relative to camera coordinates.

sphere is used because its geometry incorporates nearly all surface orientation geometries into a single simple scene.

The figure shows a change made to an early version of DIRSIG to correct the orientation of linearly polarized radiance within the S_1 and S_2 bands. Previously, DIRSIG treated the orientation of linearly polarized light coming from each facet as though each facet was flat to the ground. However, one would actually expect the orientation of the linear polarization between the S_1 and S_2 bands to change as a function of the local facet normal orientation relative to the camera and global *z* (up) direction.

The simulated images in Fig. 12.20 demonstrate the polarimetric phenomenology observed before and after the above-mentioned change. This simulation shows a warm sphere sitting on a cold flat ground. Before the change is made, emissive polarization is always in the S_1 band only, regardless of the orientation of the facet relative to the camera system. After the fix is made, emissive polarization does indeed appear in either the S_1 or S_2 band, or in both, depending on the orientation of the facet relative to the camera. Note the following phenomena in the images after the correction. In the S_0 image, the warm sphere is brighter; we can see it reflected in the flat ground (the cold sky is reflected around the sphere for the rest of the ground). In the S_1 image, *P* polarization (large negative S_1) dominates the emission from the top and the bottom of the sphere. The same *P* polarization occurs from the sides of the sphere, but because we are viewing it at right angles, it appears as *S* polarization (large positive S_1) in the camera coordinate system shown in the images. Also note that in the S_1 image, the energy reflected from the ground is predominately *S* polarized because reflected energy is dominating over emitted, as we saw in the S_0 image. In the S_2 image, we see the large signal at the +45 and −135 deg orientation of the sphere and large negative values at +135 and −45 deg, as expected due to emission from the sphere.

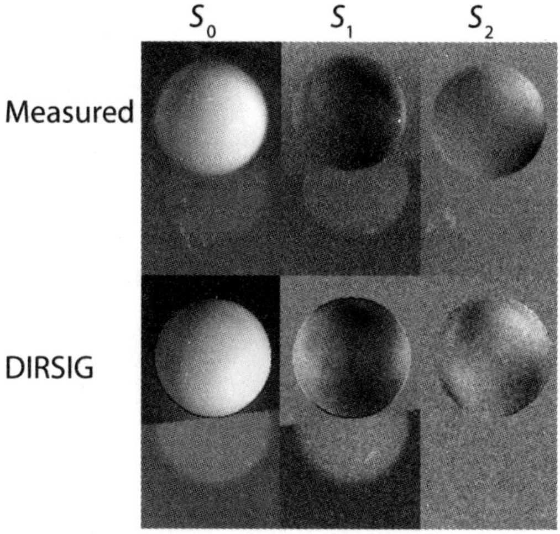

Figure 12.21 Measured and DIRSIG images showing a sphere sitting on snow with a glossy plate in front and a sun elevation of 18 deg.

In order to verify the DIRSIG model implementation of thermal pBRDF and polarimetric sensor models, experimental measurements of a flat-black painted sphere were conducted during the day (Fig. 12.21) and at night (Fig. 12.22). The simulations were configured to have target temperatures derived by the DIRSIG thermal model and thermodynamic properties similar to a paint from the DIRSIG database. Both the day and night scenes were acquired in a residential area and therefore had a significant number of objects in the background that contributed to surface reflections. The only objects considered in the simulations were two of the fences in the immediate vicinity. Surrounding homes and trees were not included in the simulated scene. The intention of the simulations was to verify the nature of the reflected and emitted scene phenomenology and angular dependence, not

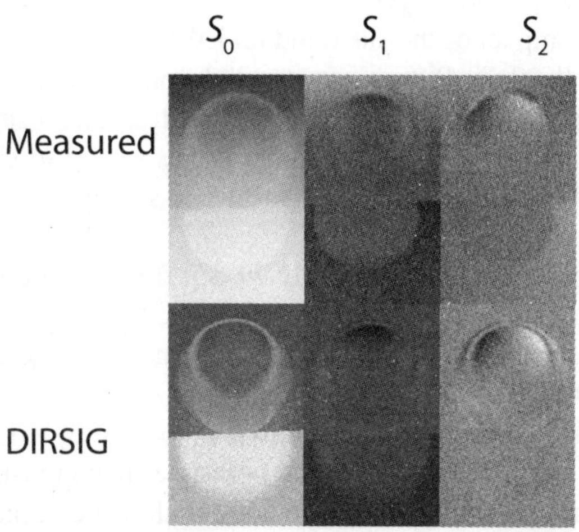

Figure 12.22 Measured and DIRSIG images showing a sphere sitting on snow with a glossy plate in front under a starry sky.

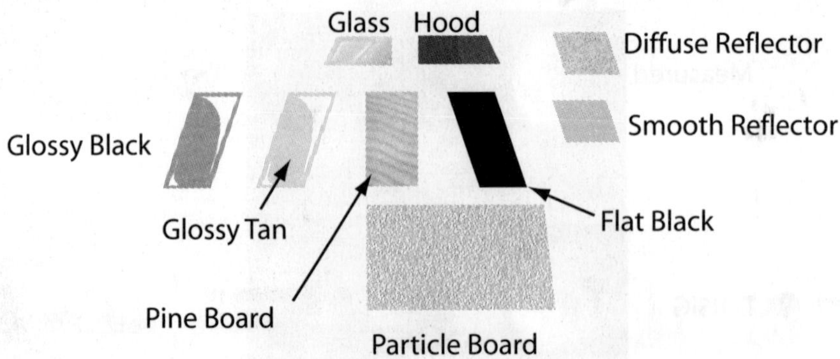

Figure 12.23 Illustration of target placement for Scene 1.

to show an exact match. Note that the phenomenology pointed out earlier in Fig. 12.20 is reproduced in Fig. 12.21 with more subtleties due to the thermal variations in the temperature of both the real and synthetic spheres.

In Fig. 12.22 the sphere (both real and synthetic) is no longer heated by the sun and the radiational cooling to the cold sky cools the top surface of the sphere as seen in the S_0 images. The very top and edges of the sphere appear warm because at grazing angles on the top and at larger angles as we move to the sides and bottom, the reflected energy comes from the warmer surround. Note how the relative dominance of emitted or reflected energy and surface orientation have varying subtle impacts on the S_1 and S_2 images and how these are properly modeled in the DIRSIG scene.

The remainder of this section describes a study [Gartley (2007)] that incorporates the pBRDF models from the previous section into DIRSIG scenes and then compares real and synthetic scenes to verify that the phenomenology was simulated properly. Once verified, these targets were used to show how synthetic data could be used to study the impact of the surround on LWIR pBRDF signatures.

A simple test scene (backyard) was constructed consisting of a series of painted target surfaces, a piece of a car hood, a piece of glass, and a smooth piece of pine wood (Figs. 12.23 and 12.24). This scenario was set up to examine the effect of background clutter on the infrared polarimetric signatures of the target materials.

The imaging zenith angle was approximately 70 deg from the ground normal, at a range of approximately 8 m. The images were acquired under a starlit sky on August 21, 2006 between 11:00 and 11:30 p.m. At the time of image acquisition, the ambient air temperature was 12.9°C.

Figure 12.25 shows the experimentally acquired S_0 (a) and S_1 (b) Stokes image bands. The S_2 Stokes image band showed no polarimetric contrast, in that all targets were flat to the ground and had a surface normal almost completely in the bottom, the plane of incidence. Note that the ultraflat black painted surface and the car hood showed the least amount of contrast in the S_1 band. Although this

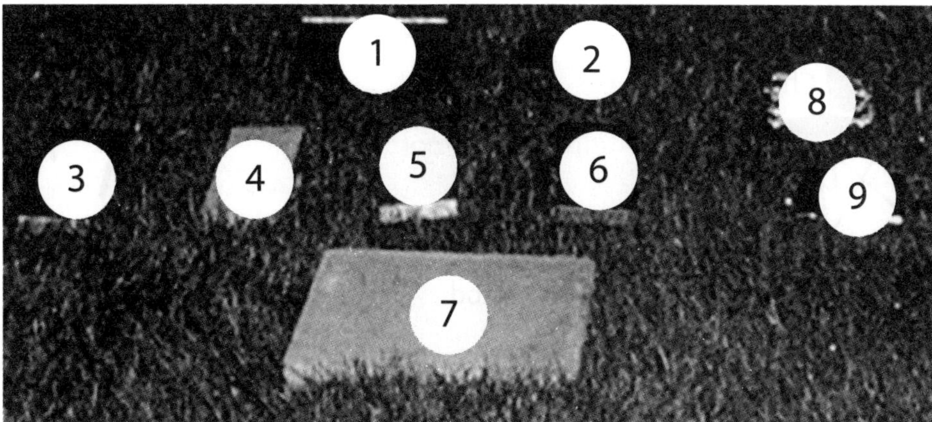

1. Glass
2. Car hood (cut-out)
3. Krylon glossy black on smooth wood
4. Glossy tan paint on smooth wood
5. Bare pine wood
6. Krylon ultraflat black on smooth wood
7. Smooth pine wood
8. Diffuse IR reflector
9. Flat IR reflector

Figure 12.24 Digital camera photo of target range.

is expected for the diffusely scattering flat black surface, the car hood was not expected to have a diminished signature. However, close examination of the car hood sample after imaging operations were complete showed a small amount of dew. This would tend to raise the emissivity, causing it to be more Lambertian.

Figure 12.25 also contains the DIRSIG-simulated version of the backyard target scene. The simulated S_0 (c) and S_1 (d) images were post-processed to contain the same level of instrument noise as the measured S_0 and S_1 bands. There is

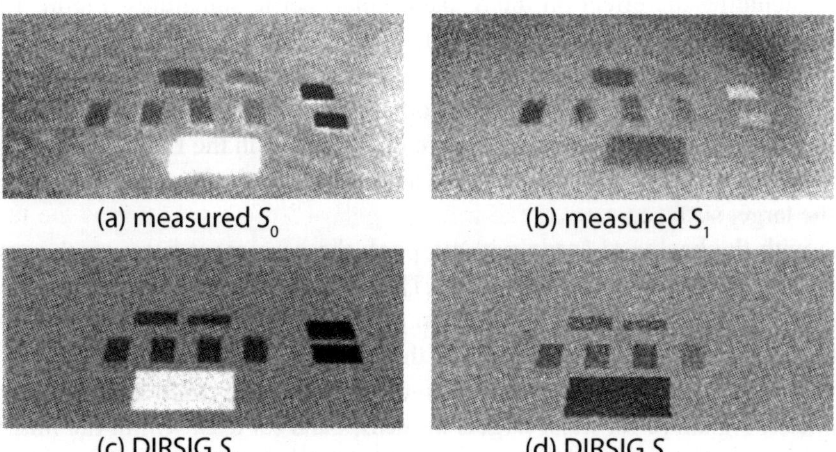

Figure 12.25 Images of target range: measured (a) S_0 and (b) S_1 and DIRSIG-rendered (c) S_0 and (d) S_1. The IR reflectors were not rendered with polarimetric properties; therefore they do not have contrast in the DIRSIG S_1 image.

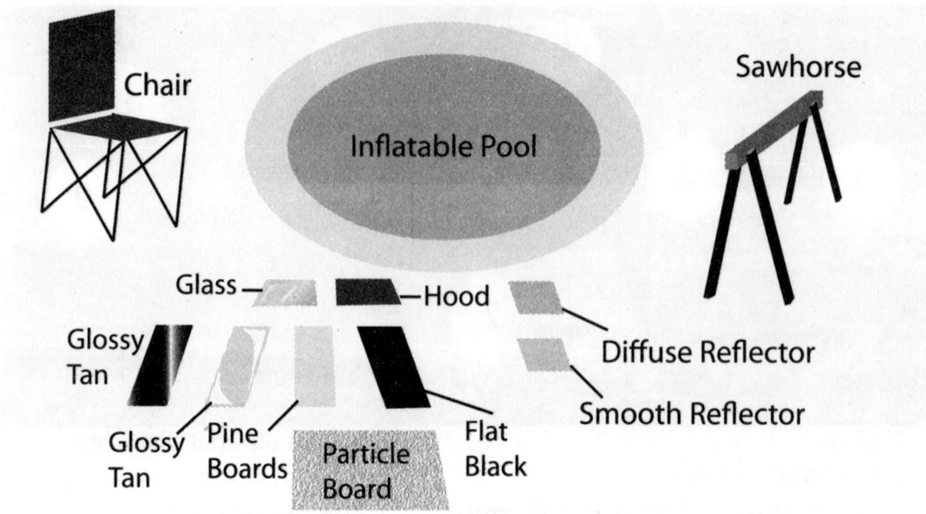

Figure 12.26 Illustration of target placement for Scene 1 with pool.

excellent agreement between the simulated and actual S_0 and S_1 bands, except in the car hood sample as noted previously. Note that the 100% diffuse and specular IR reflectors (targets 8 and 9) in the scene have polarized components in the experimentally measured images, but not in the DIRSIG-rendered images. The reflector targets were not experimentally characterized in this work; therefore, the DIRSIG simulation treats them as unpolarized.

The same backyard target range was imaged with a large plastic kiddie pool positioned behind the targets (Fig. 12.26). The intent of this scenario was to examine the effect of adding a significant infrared source in the background hemisphere, including the effect on the S_1 band polarimetric signatures. Figure 12.27 shows the measured S_0 (a) and S_1 (b) bands next to the DIRSIG-simulated S_0 (c) and S_1 (d) bands. The bright objects in the measured S_0 image are a sawhorse (right) and a folding chair (left) utilized to hold the pool on its side behind the targets. The sawhorse and folding chair were not rendered in the DIRSIG simulation due to the fact that they did not provide a significant level of background radiance from the target surfaces.

As with the backyard scene with no pool, the agreement between the actual and simulated Stokes bands is excellent. The effect of the pool is that is provides a source of radiance that is reflected from the target surfaces. This reflected radiance has a positive value in the S_1 band that is almost equal in magnitude to the negative value due to thermal emission in the S_1 band. The result is essentially no polarimetric signature for most targets in the S_1 band (at least within the limits of the image noise).

The next scene was developed to verify the DIRSIG implementation of polarized infrared scene simulation with targets possessing complex geometry. This scene involves three automobiles on an asphalt surface. Figure 12.28 shows a

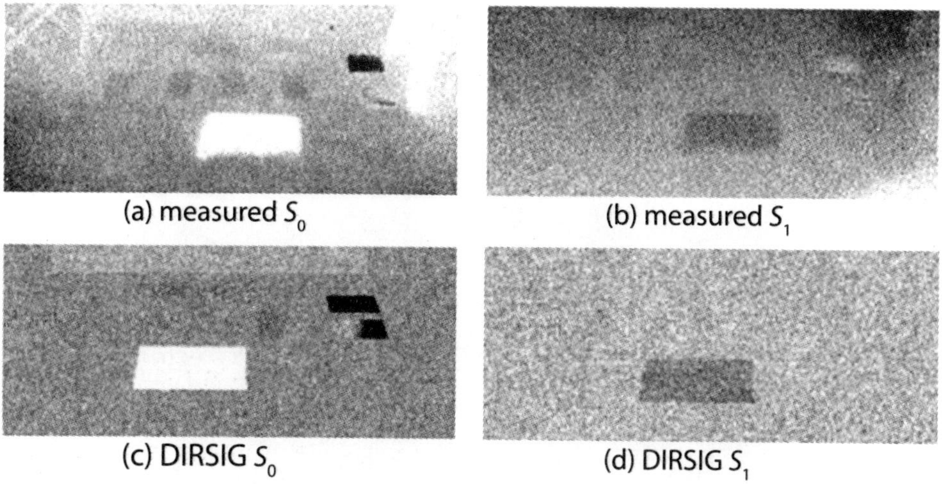

Figure 12.27 Images of target range with pool behind targets: measured (a) S_0 and (b) S_1 and DIRSIG-rendered (c) S_0 and (d) S_1.

digital camera photo of the scene containing a Volkswagon Beetle, a sedan, and a sport utility vehicle.

Figure 12.29 shows the experimentally measured S_0 (a), S_1 (b), and S_2 (c) images next to the DIRSIG-simulated S_0 (d), S_1 (e), and S_2 (f) images. Most notable within the polarized bands of the experimentally measured images are the surfaces facing the sky, such as the hoods and roofs, and the surfaces facing sideways. The surfaces facing the sky are expected to have a significant polarimetric S_1 signature due to (1) the glossy nature of the car surfaces and (2) a lack of significant reflected background radiance to dampen the negative thermally emitted S_1 signature. The surfaces facing sideways are expected to have a minimal polarimetric signature due to the balance between positive S_1 reflected background radiance

Figure 12.28 Digital camera visible image of three automobiles utilized for test scene.

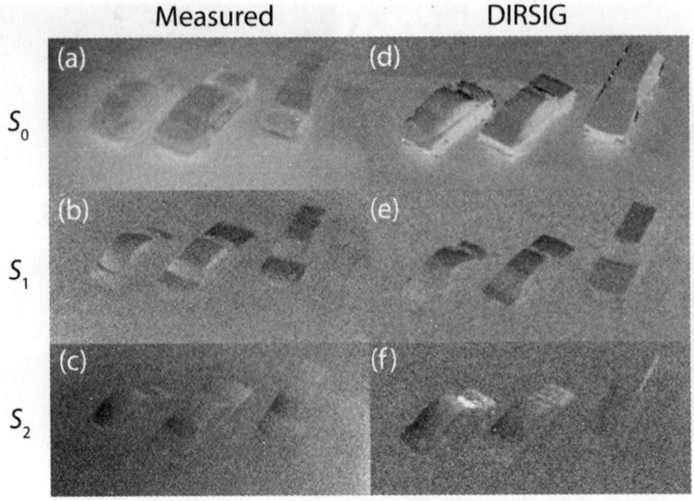

Figure 12.29 Images of automobiles: measured and DIRSIG-rendered S_0, S_1, and S_2.

and negative S_1 emitted radiance. This effect of negligible S_1 signature on the car sides is observed experimentally as expected.

The DIRSIG versions of the S_0, S_1, and S_2 Stokes bands require careful explanation. The DIRSIG S_0 band agrees roughly with the measured S_0 band. The roofs and car hood facing the sky are generally darker than the rest of the surfaces in the scene due to the minimal amount of reflected background radiance. The sides of the cars are brighter than the hoods and roofs in the DIRSIG S_0 band as expected, but the effect is more dramatic than what is seen experimentally. This may be due to incorrect modeling of the car temperatures as well as inadequate sampling of the background radiance reflected from the car sides. *No significant effort was made to match the thermodynamic properties of the modeled cars (e.g., specific heat, conductivity, etc.) to the actual vehicles.*

The DIRSIG S_1 and S_2 bands correlate very well with the measured S_1 and S_2 bands. Specifically, the roofs and hoods of the cars show up as dark regions in both simulated and measured S_1 images. There is also a slight brightening of the SUV windshield going from right to left, due to the fact that the surface angle rolls away from the imager in this direction. In fact, this rolling away of the S_1 signature on the SUV windshield shows up as a light-to-dark transition (from right to left) in both the measured and simulated S_2 images.

In addition, the S_1 and S_2 signatures of the car sides show excellent agreement between measured and simulated imagery. The polarized signature from the cars' sides is actually within the noise of the camera due to the balance between thermally emitted radiance and reflected radiance. Note that the artifacts in the DIRSIG scene at extreme grazing angles are due to artifacts in the sampling function at angles close to 90 deg that had not been fixed when these images were produced.

Figure 12.30 Digital visible camera photo of manmade targets placed in the open, away from trees.

The final scene constructed for verification of the DIRSIG implementation of polarized infrared scene simulation has manmade targets placed in a complex natural background. Specifically, 2 ft $\times$ 2 ft painted panels, a car hood, a window, and a laminate floor plank were placed in the courtyard outside of the Center for Imaging Science building at the Rochester Institute of Technology campus. The courtyard consists of asphalt walkways, grassy areas, and multiple kinds of trees.

Two versions of this scene were examined. The first version has the targets placed in the grass with no trees immediately overhead or behind them. The second version has the targets placed with minimal line-of-sight obscuration, but a significant level of tree cover overhead, immediately behind, and on the sides of the targets. The intent of both of these scenarios was to keep the target geometry simple, but the background geometry complex and significant.

Figures 12.30 and 12.31 show the targets placed in front of the grove of trees. Figure 12.32 shows the DIRSIG (a) and measured (b) versions of the S_0 band for this first version of the scene. Figure 12.33 shows the DIRSIG (a) and measured (b) S_1 band for this version of the scene. By design, there is good agreement between the measured and DIRSIG S_0 bands because the thermodynamic properties of each scene material were adjusted to obtain this agreement. In the measured S_1 band, six out of seven of the targets are visible. The one target that is not detected is the window (which may have been due to dew accumulation on the window surface inhibiting the polarization signature). In fact, inspection of the targets after the imaging operation was complete showed dew on the painted panels—this most likely contributed to a reduction in the strength of the panel S_1 signatures relative to the DIRSIG S_1 signatures. All seven targets are detectable above the

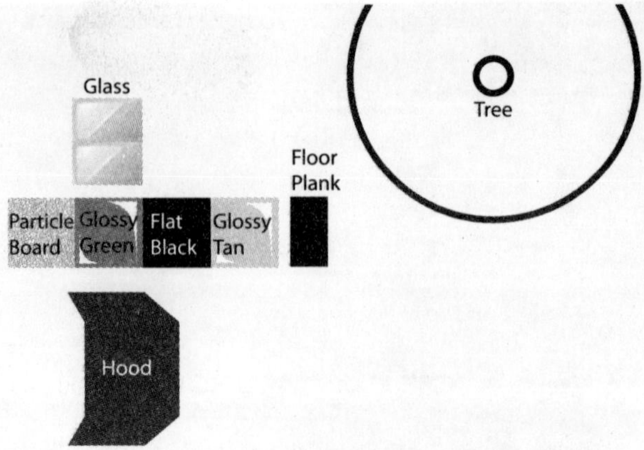

Figure 12.31 Illustration of target placement for Scene 2 with targets out in the open.

noise level in the DIRSIG-simulated S_1 band. The measured S_2 band shows no polarimetric contrast within the noise level and is therefore not presented.

Note that the measured S_1 image has a system artifact that appears to show a large dark and light region on the very right hand side of the image. This is not due to actual polarimetric contrast in the scene, but rather to the polarizer being slightly too small for the camera aperture.

Figure 12.34 shows a digital camera photo of the seven targets placed within the grove of trees with the target array shown in Fig. 12.35. Figure 12.36 shows the DIRSIG (a) and measured (b) S_0 bands, while Fig. 12.37 shows the DIRSIG (a) and measured (b) S_1 bands. As with the previous version of the scene, there is excellent agreement between the S_0 bands by design. In the measured S_1 band, only the car hood and the flat green painted panel are detected (2/7 targets). In the DIRSIG S_1 band, the car hood, the flat green panel, the flat black panel, and the window are detected (4/7 targets).

Although the agreement between measured and DIRSIG-simulated S_1 bands is not exact, it is obvious that DIRSIG adequately integrates the effect of reflected

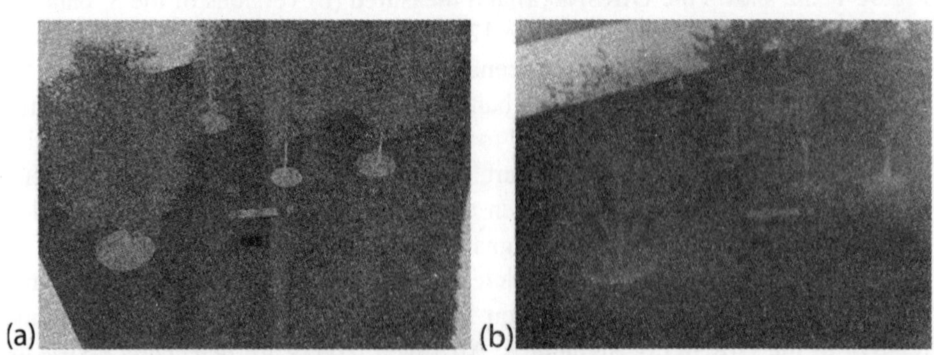

Figure 12.32 S_0 images of targets in open: (a) DIRSIG rendered and (b) measured.

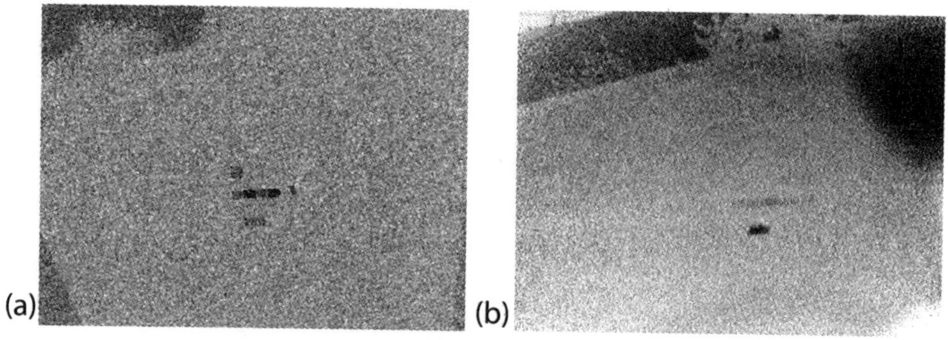

Figure 12.33 S_1 images of targets in open: (a) DIRSIG rendered and (b) measured.

Figure 12.34 Digital camera photo of manmade targets placed within a grove of trees.

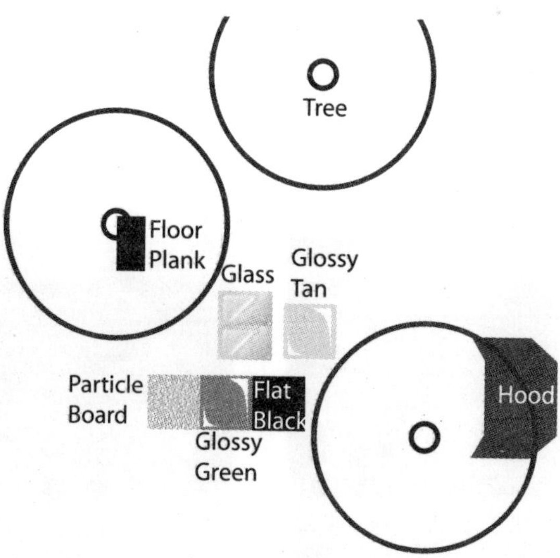

Figure 12.35 Illustration of target placement for Scene 2 with targets embedded in a cluster of trees.

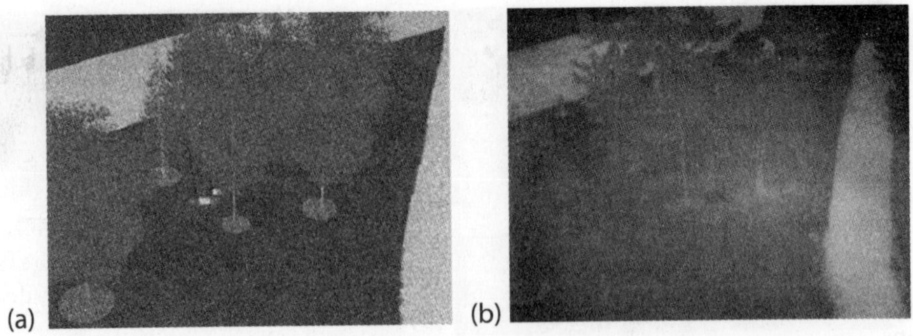

Figure 12.36 S_0 images of targets embedded in trees: (a) DIRSIG rendered and (b) measured.

background radiance, diminishing polarimetric signatures. It should also be noted that the DIRSIG scene was constructed with tree sizes and types that only approximately represented the trees that existed in the measured scene. However, differences between actual and simulated tree geometry and radiometric properties could have significant impacts on the amount of background radiance reflected from the manmade target surfaces, which would affect the detectability in the S_1 band.

It is anticipated that a more accurate correlation between the DIRSIG images and measured images would be found if the DIRSIG scene was configured closer to ground truth. For this demonstration, the significant level of effort required to ground truth and configure the scene in DIRSIG was not justified.

Note that the measured S_1 image once again has a system artifact that appears to show a large dark region on the very right hand side of the image. As previously mentioned, this is not due to actual polarimetric contrast in the scene, but to the polarizer being slightly too small for the camera aperture.

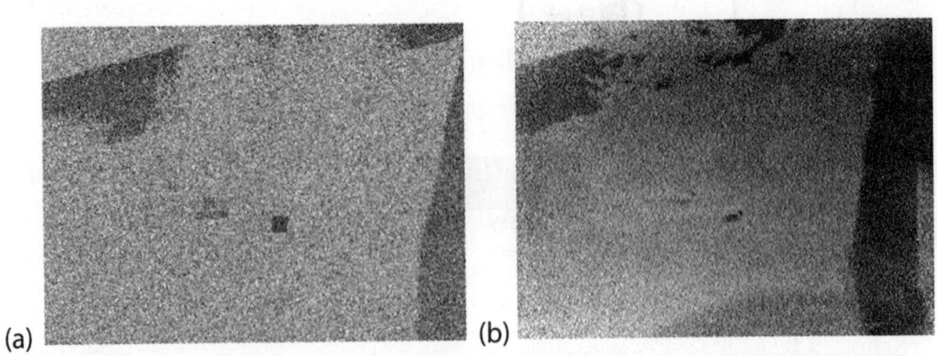

Figure 12.37 S_1 images of targets embedded in trees: (a) DIRSIG rendered and (b) measured.

12.3 Closing Thoughts

In closing this chapter and the book, a few final thoughts are in order. First, let me remind the reader that this text was intended to provide an introduction to this topic and that the current literature is rapidly expanding in scope, depth, and clarity. Second, as I expressed in the Preface, unlike other topics on which I regularly write as an expert, I am myself still very much a student of polarimetric phenomenology. As one student to another, I encourage you to question carefully as you study this field (including this text) and apply basic physical principles to analyze for yourself each topic, scene, or application. Don't let one demonstration or example sway you one way or another, but delve into the "how and why" and the potential to produce predictable, repeatable results.

References

Fetrow, M.P., Wellems, D., Sposato, S.H., Bishop, K.P., Caudill, T.R., Davis, M.L., & Simrell, E.R. (2002). "Results of a new polarization simulation." *Proceedings SPIE*, Vol. 4481, pp. 149–162.

Gartley, M.G. (2007). "Polarimetric Modeling of Remotely Sensed Scenes in the Thermal Infrared." Doctoral dissertation, Rochester Institute of Technology, Rochester.

Gartley, M.G., Brown, S.D., Goodenough, A.D., Sanders, N.J., & Schott, J.R. (2007). "Polarimetric scene modeling in the thermal infrared." *Proceedings SPIE*, Vol. 6682, 66820C.

Meyers, J.P. (2002). "Modeling Polarimetric Imaging Using DIRSIG." Doctoral dissertation, Rochester Institute of Technology, Rochester.

NEF9.4. (2004). Nonconventional Exploitation Factors (NEF) Modeling. *Tech. Rep. v9.5.*

Robinson, G.D., Gross, H.N., & Schott, J.R. (2000). "Evaluation of two applications of spectral mixing models to image fusion." *Remote Sensing of Environment*, Vol. 71, No. 3, pp. 272–281.

Sadjadi, F.A. & Chun, C.S.L. (2004). "Remote sensing using passive infrared Stokes parameters." *Optical Engineering*, Vol. 43 No. 10, pp. 2283–2291.

Schott, J.R., Brown, S.D., Raqueño, R.V., Gross, H.N., & Robinson, G. (1999). "An advanced synthetic image generation model and its application to multi/hyperspectral algorithm development." *Canadian Journal of Remote Sensing*, Vol. 25, No. 2, pp. 99–111.

Schott, J.R. (2007). *Remote Sensing: The Image Chain Approach*. 2nd Ed., Oxford University Press, New York.

Shell J.R. & Schott, J.R. (2005). "A polarized clutter measurement technique based on the governing equation for polarimetric remote sensing in the visible to near infrared." *Proceedings SPIE*, Vol. 5811, p. 34–45.

Young, J., Graham, H., & Peterson, E. (1965). "Wire grid infrared polarizer." *Applied Optics*, Vol. 4, No. 8, pp. 1023–1026.

Index

Dr. John R. Schott is the Frederick and Anna B. Wiedman Professor of Imaging Science at the Rochester Institute of Technology. Dr. Schott founded and for decades oversaw the evolution of the remote sensing program at RIT into one of the premier programs in the Unites States for quantitative remote sensing. He has published hundreds of papers on remote sensing, supervised a wide range of research projects for both the civil and defense/intelligence communities, and served on various corporate and government scientific advisory boards. In recent years, Dr. Schott conducted a number of studies of polarimetric remote sensing phenomenology. These studies focused on the incorporation of polarimetric phenomenology into synthetic scene simulation models. To demonstrate and test the improved modeling capabilities, Dr. Schott has worked with his students to develop practical methods to measure the polarimetric bidirectional reflectance distribution function of materials in the field. These measurement and modeling studies span a spectral range from the visible to the long-wave infrared.